cinematography
theory and practice

imagemaking for
cinematographers,
directors &
videographers

cinematography
theory and practice

*imagemaking for
cinematographers,
directors &
videographers*

blain brown

**Focal
Press**

An Imprint of Elsevier

Amsterdam Boston London New York Oxford Paris
San Diego San Francisco Singapore Sydney Tokyo

Library of Congress Cataloging-in-Publication Data
Brown, Blain
    Cinematography: imagemaking for cinematographers, directors and videographers/
Blain Brown.
    p.cm.
    Includes bibliographical references and index.
ISBN-13: 978–0–240–80500–9   ISBN-10: 0–240–80500–3 (alk. paper)
    1. Cinematography. I. Title.
    TR850 .B7598 2002
778.5-de21
                            2002019924

ISBN-13: 978–0–240–80500–9
ISBN-10: 0–240–80500–3

British Library Cataloguing-in-Publication Data
A catalogue record for this book is available from the British Library.

The publisher offers special discounts on bulk orders of this book.
For information, please contact:

Manager of Special Sales
Elsevier
200 Wheeler Road
Burlington, MA 01803
Tel: 781-221-2212
Fax: 781-221-1615

For information on all Focal Press publications available, contact our World Wide Web home page at: http://www.focalpress.com

10   9   8   7

Printed in China

contents

Introduction:
writing with motion

The term cinematography is from the Greek roots meaning "writing with motion." At the heart of it, filmmaking is shooting — but cinematography is more than the mere act of photography. It is the process of taking ideas, actions, emotional subtext, tone and all other forms of non-verbal communication and *rendering them in visual terms.* As is discussed in the first chapter, cinematic technique is the entire range of methods and techniques that we use to add layers of meaning and subtext to the "content" of the film — the dialog and action.

The tools of cinematic technique are used by both the director and DP, either working together or in doing their individual jobs. As mentioned, cinematography is far more than just "photographing" what is in front of the camera — the tools, the techniques and the variations are wide ranging in scope; this is at the heart of the symbiosis of the DP and the director.

THE DP AND THE DIRECTOR
To a great extent the knowledge base of the cinematographer overlaps with the knowledge base of the director. The cinematographer must have a solid familiarity with the terms and concepts of directing, and the more a director knows about cinematography the more he or she will be able to utilize these tools and especially be better equipped to fully utilize the knowledge and talent of a good DP. Any successful director will tell you that one of the real secrets of directing is being able to recognize and maximize what every member of the team can contribute.

The DP has some duties that are entirely technical, and the director has responsibilities with the script and the actors, but in between those two extremes they are both involved with the same basic task: *storytelling with the camera* — this is what makes the creative collaboration between them so important. In that regard, one of the main purposes of this book is to discuss "what directors need to know about using the camera" and "what cinematographers need to know about the process of directing," with the goal of improving communication between them and fostering a more common language for their combined efforts.

The primary purpose of this book is to introduce cinematography/ filmmaking as we practice it on a professional level, whether it be on film, video, digital, High Def or any other imaging format. Storytelling is storytelling and shooting is shooting, no matter what medium you work in. Except for two specific sections which relate to motion picture emulsions and the laboratory, the information here is universal to any form of shooting — film, video or digital.

The first chapter, *Filmspace*, is a basic introduction to the essential concepts of visual storytelling. It is absolutely essential to understand that a cinematographer or videographer can not be just a "technician" who sets up "good shots." Directors vary in how much input they want from a DP in selecting and setting up shots; but the DP must understand the methods of visual storytelling in either case.

A good deal of the information in the chapters on *Filmspace* and *Cinematic Continuity* relates directly to narrative filmmaking, but most of it is still of use in all types of shooting: commercials, music videos, industrials, documentaries, even animation.

Cinema is a language and within it are the specific vocabularies and sub-languages of the lens, composition, visual design, lighting, image control, continuity, movement and point-of-view. Learning these languages and vocabularies is a never-ending and a fascinating life-long study. As with any language, you can use it to compose clear and informative prose or to create visual poetry.

While wielding these tools to fully utilize the language of cinema, there are, of course, continuous and unyielding technical requirements; it is up the DP to ensure that these requirements are met and that nothing gets "screwed up." Those requirements are covered here as well, as not only are they an integral part of the job, but many seemingly mechanical requirements can also be used as forms of visual expression as well. This is why it is important for the director to have at least a passing knowledge of these technical issues. Another reason is that many less experienced directors will get themselves into trouble by asking for something that, for purely practical reasons, is not a good idea in terms of time, budget, equipment or crew resources.

This is not to suggest that a director should ever demand less than the best or settle for less than their vision — the point is that by knowing more about what is involved on the technical side, the director can make better choices and can work with their DP to think of solutions that are better suited to the situation and often are even more visually expressive than the technique originally conceived.

I DON'T NEED NO STINKING RULES
It is an old and well-worn saying that you should "know the rules before you break them." This is never more true than in filmmaking. Nearly every working film professional can tell stories of first-time directors who declared that, "I know that's the way it's usually done, but I'm going to do something different." Sometimes (rarely) the results are brilliant, even visionary. More often, they are disastrous. The problem is that, unlike nearly every other art form, in film, "doing it over" is extremely expensive and sometimes impossible.

All of the basic rules of filmmaking exist for good reasons: they are the result of 100 years of practical experience and experimentation. Can you break the rules: absolutely! Great filmmakers do it all the time. Once you not only know the rules but *understand why they exist*, it is possible to use a violation of them as a powerful tool.

THE SCOPE OF THIS BOOK
What does the cinematographer need to know about filmmaking in order to do the job properly? Almost everything.

The knowledge base encompasses lenses, exposure, composition, continuity, editorial needs, lighting, grip, color, the language of the camera, even the basic elements of story structure. The job is storytelling with the camera, and the more you know about the elements of that art the better you will be able to assist the director in accomplishing those goals. The DP need not command all these techniques at the level of detail of the editor, the writer or the key grip, but there must be a firm understanding of the basics and more importantly the *possibilities* — the tools and their potential to serve the storytelling and the vision of the director.

This is especially true as the task of directing is more and more accessible to writers, actors and others who may not have as broad a background in physical production and the visual side of storytelling. In this situation, being a DP who has a thorough command of the entire scope of filmmaking but is able and willing to work as a collaborator without trying to impose their own vision in place of the director's is a strong asset. By the same token, to have a reputation as a director who can utilize the talents of their creative team and get the best from everybody is also a goal to aim for.

I started out 5 years ago just to write a simple book containing the basic factual information required to be a working cinematographer. Nothing fancy, not even getting into issues of style and aesthetics. This is the third book in that effort now; it just won't fit into a single volume. The first book covered the theory and practice of lighting, one of the DP's most important jobs. There is a great deal to know even if you are shooting entirely with available light in a cinema verité style. The second book, *Filmmaker's Pocket Reference,* includes the technical facts and figures essential to the job.

Now, in this volume, we cover the storytelling issues, continuity, and providing what the editor needs as well optics, special effects, exposure, composition, filters, color control and all the other aspects of cinematography that go into the job — all of them approached from the point of view of their value as storytelling tools. The craft of lighting is included here, but for a much more in-depth and thorough discussion of lighting, see the first book, *Motion Picture and Video Lighting.* It is also important to note that if you are dedicated to the idea of using the medium of cinema to its fullest extent and employing every tool of the art form to serve your story, then lighting for video or High Def is not essentially different from lighting for film.

WHAT IT MEANS TO BE A PROFESSIONAL

To be a true professional you need to know all this "stuff." Even if you specialize in one particular type of shooting, or subscribe to a minimalist aesthetic, you ignore other types of information at your own peril. At any rate, the term "director of photography" refers to someone who can pretty much handle any type of job that comes their way. Someone who applies this term to themselves should never show up on a set not knowing how to handle the job and never just "pretending" to know.

Also, there are certain courtesies, ethics and standards of behavior inherent in the job, and these seem to be fairly universal from country to country; however, like standards of behavior everywhere they always seem to decline as time marches on. Professionalism encompasses these standards as well. For example, occasionally you will see first-time directors who are reluctant to hire a DP who has a great deal more experience than them — they are afraid that the more experienced DP might ridicule their use of terminology, intimidate or embarrass them in front of the crew or even try to impose their own vision on the project. Sadly, this does occasionally happen. Most often these rare unfortunate incidents are the result of the arrogance of people who suffer from the classic "a little knowledge is a dangerous thing" syndrome. Someone who truly aspires to being thought of as a professional must take time to learn and understand the standards of etiquette, ethics and behavior in addition to learning the practical aspects of the craft.

Being a professional cinematographer is not a job to be taken lightly: a great deal of money, time, effort and personal vision are at stake even on the smallest low-budget projects. If you know your stuff and have the attitude and personality to be a real team player, it can be one of the best jobs in the world. When things are really cooking on a set and all the hundreds of diverse elements are coming together to get it right, the joy of creation is at a level that is hardly matched in any other profession.

TERMINOLOGY: VIDEO AND FILM

As mentioned above, the word cinematography means "writing with motion." No reference is made to what you are writing on — be it film, videotape, digital media or whatever. However, since the term cinematographer is still associated in many people's minds with silver-based emulsion, I also use the term videographer where appropriate or the more general term "director of photography." Nor do I engage in the endless argument over which format is "better" — film, video, High Def 24P and digital video are different tools for different jobs. Whenever there is more to the decision than just money, the director of photography should be involved in the choice of format and has the responsibility to be a reliable consultant to the director and the producer concerning which one is most appropriate for a particular project.

Also, despite its long and venerable history, the term "cameraman" is no longer appropriate. I use director of photography, cameraperson or alternate gender references instead. The same applies to other positions as well, as the jobs of director, editor, gaffer, electrician and even grip have become increasingly open to women and people from all cultures and backgrounds.

A NOTE ON THE ILLUSTRATIONS

Many of the illustrations here are from the films of great directors such as Stanley Kubrick, Orson Welles and Akira Kurosawa. This may seem to be an endorsement of a formalist and highly stylized type of filmmaking or one in which every shot needs to be a precious little gem — perfectly lit and exquisitely well composed. While I do admire these great filmmakers, the primary reason so many of the illustrations are drawn from their films is more instructional: not only do they serve as excellent examples of framing, composition, use of lens, blocking and color, but more importantly you know that nothing in the frame is an accident — it is easier to follow the choices that they made in order to serve their story.

Making every frame a Rembrandt can be a very satisfying artistic challenge, but there are a nearly infinite number of possible visual styles; each one is valid for its own reasons — the opportunity to explore many different styles and filmmaking aesthetics is one of the main things that makes this job so interesting.

Film is a dream — but whose?
Bruce Kawin

filmspace

1.1. (previous page) *The Lady From Shanghai* (Columbia Pictures, 1948).

1.2. (top) Scene from an early silent film (*Quo Vadis*, 1909) — literally a filmed play on a stage set.

1.3. (above) One of the earliest pieces of film publicly exhibited — a train arrives. Shot by the Lumiere brothers.

CINEMATIC TECHNIQUE

When the motion picture camera was invented in the late nineteenth century, the first efforts were straightforward presentations of simple events: a man sneezing, workers leaving the factory, a train pulling into the station. When the filmmakers turned to dramatic presentations, they conceived of them as "filmed plays" — they positioned the camera as if it were a member of the audience seated in the auditorium. In this type of film, you can never get away from the feeling you are looking at the scene from this detached, impersonal point of view.

It is an easy analogy to say that this proscenium approach to shooting is much like filming a play (Figures 1.2 and 1.3), but there are important differences: when viewing a play you are still seeing three-dimensional objects, albeit at a distance and more importantly, the actors (aside from mimes) speak. Fairly early on, filmmakers began to realize that the flatness of the screen and its other limitations demanded more. Their first response was to break the action up into shots and sequences of shots; this is sometimes called separation. As soon as the idea of shots is introduced it is clear that a logical and expressive arrangement of the shots and sequences is essential. Shots are "fragments of reality." It is the filmmaker who decides which fragments and in what order the audience will see the overall reality. It is the filmmaker who decides that this piece and that piece are what the audience sees and in what order they see them.

It is not unlike the old parable of the three blind men touching an elephant to understand what it is like. Since each one touches a different part of the elephant, each one has a completely different idea of what the whole animal is like. Filmmaking is a little like the idea of someone guiding the three men: first this part, ignore that part, then touch this part, and so on. In this way, all three blind men will have the same idea of what the whole elephant is like. But it will be the idea that the guide wants them to have, and it won't necessarily be the "true" picture of what an elephant is really like.

More importantly he can change that point of view as he wishes: given the same elephant, dozens of different points of view are possible. This is the essence of cinema. The set with the props and actors on it is a three-dimensional reality. It is what it is. By choosing what pieces of this reality the audience sees and arranging them in a certain order, the filmmaker introduces a point of view. Imagine if the filmmaker has a little viewer made of cardboard. It sort of like a truncated, four sided pyramid (Figure 1.5) which is reminiscent of the "perspectival apparatus" used by artists as shown in this scene from Peter Greenaway's *The Draughtsman's Contract* (Figure 1.4).

The audience will always see what is at the small end of the box.

1.4. The "perspectival apparatus" from Peter Greenaway's *The Draughtsman's Contract* (BFI/ United Artists Classics, 1982) — the fundamental idea of selecting a viewpoint and defining a frame.

(In actuality the view that is projected onto the rectangle at the small end of the box is recorded on film or videotape or digital medium or whatever, but let's forget about the technical stuff for now, enough of that later.) For now let's just think of it as an eyeball that moves around with the box, and the eye may be open or closed while the box is being moved around — it's our choice. We tell the eye when to open and when to close: we "edit" its perception of the scene.

A SIMPLE SCENE

Now let's take a little scene: a tree, a broad horizon with a sunset, a man and a woman (Figure 1.6). If we just take the viewer and put it over here, we are making one choice. Aside from that we have no other influence over what the audience sees (in this example).

And that's how most people would respond if you asked them, "What do you see" Most would say, "a man, a woman and a tree." Only if you asked them, "What time is it?" would they probably then say, "Around sunset." If you moved the viewer so the horizon was in another place and the sunset not visible they probably wouldn't even be able to say what time it is.

But that's important — even by making that one choice of where on the perimeter we put the viewer, we are already influencing what the audience perceives. Take it one step further, put the viewer so that the man is hidden by the tree; suddenly it's a very different scene: where before it might have been perhaps a picnic, it's now a woman out in the woods alone with a dog. Is she lonely? Is she in danger? We don't have much information yet and it could be a lot of things, but certainly our perception of what may be happening will be different than before. What we have done is change the framing. Framing is the first element of composition (Figure 1.7 and 1.10). Framing involves two choices:

- Picking a position from which to view the scene.
- Isolating some part of it to look at.

Let's think about that second part. We want to choose not just the angle from which the scene is viewed, but whether they see all of it or just a part of it. Human vision, including peripheral vision, covers roughly 180°; let's use that as our definition of "all of it." How do we change how much and what part of the scene they will see? Well, we take out our matte knife and make a new viewer. We either make a big wide one or a long narrow one.

The little end doesn't change shape or size. (The shape and size of the little end is our aspect ratio. An almost square one is Academy and a shorter but wider one is Cinemascope but we'll talk about aspect ratios in another place.) The big wide one is a like a wide-angle lens (Figure 1.8) and the long narrow one is like a long focal length lens (Figure 1.9). Without moving, we affect whether the audience sees a lot of the scene or just a piece of it. As the viewer becomes longer and narrower, it becomes more important how much we aim it left or right — now we are really isolating certain parts of the scene.

If we take the long viewer and point it at the sun, then the first thing they see is just a sunset. Right away this sets a certain mood and conveys important information: not just what time it is, but that we are in a place where you can see a beautiful sunset, which almost certainly is a good place; after all, it has a great view. If the next thing we see is a shot of the couple kissing, right away, we know it's a beautiful day and this couple is enjoying it and are probably in love. But what if the next shot isolates the man and we now see he is wearing bandages over his eyes: oh, what a sad irony: it's a beautiful sunset, but his eyes are damaged. Is he permanently blinded? Is the woman his lover or his nurse? Not only do we get new information, we get new emotions, and perhaps most importantly: we ask new questions. This is crucial — it is part of what makes a narrative film

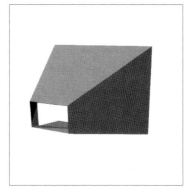

1.5. (top) A basic viewing device.

1.6. (middle) Our basic scene.

1.7. (bottom) Selecting a place from which to view the scene and how much of it we see establishes the "proscenium" in the perception of the audience.

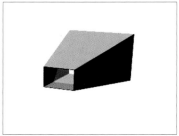

1.8. (top) A wide angle viewing device.

1.9. (bottom) A narrow viewer.

1.10. (right) The viewer within a frame from *The Draughtsman's Contract*.

different from a documentary: so much of what we do with film technique involves not just conveying selected information but also imposing subtext and emotional content on it.

QUESTIONS AND EXPECTATIONS
Cinematic technique is very much about setting up questions and expectations in the audience's mind. Why is he blind? Is she responsible for his accident? Was it deliberate? Or is she the nurse who fell in love with him? Is this love story going to turn out wonderfully or with terrible sadness? All from two shots — if they are done right.

It is manipulating the shots and their sequence in a way that sets up these questions and expectations that distinguishes simply "shooting" from cinema. It is not a small difference, it is a vast chasm; it is the difference between video on the evening news and an Alfred Hitchcock movie. Setting up questions in the audience's mind is what keeps them involved in the story. This is true of any literary form, whether it be the novel, a theatrical play or a short story. If the audience isn't always subconsciously asking the question, "I wonder what will happen next?" well, you've lost 'em.

Altering The Viewer's Perception
If that question isn't always present there are two words to describe it: boring and predictable. But the other element is even more important. By setting up certain expectations in the audience's mind, you can then manipulate those questions and expectations. Let's take our scene. *Without moving our viewer* but only using the wider one, the medium one or the long narrow one, we can arrange shots in the following sequence:

- Long shot: a miraculous sunset. What a beautiful day.
- Wide shot: of two people looking at the sunset; an idyllic landscape; a dog sleeps peacefully nearby.
- Close on: the man's face. He is wearing bandages that indicate a terrible, possibly blinding injury to his eyes.
- Close on: the woman kisses him lovingly and lays her head on his shoulder.

So far: wow, what a great gal but who is she? She loves him despite his terrible affliction. A real love story, even if a very sad one. A question and an expectation.

- Close on: her hand reaches into her pocket and pulls out a very deadly looking knife. We follow as she raises it toward his head.
- Close on: her face as she stares at him. Her eyes are grim, her face tense. Our expectation has been completely turned on its head. But now we have another expectation: homicide. Why is she doing it? Another question.

- She uses the knife to cut his bandages. He looks at the sunset and he can see. He kisses her.

Quite a little story: happiness, sadness, love, suspense, fear and loathing, then finally complete joy and again love. All in seven shots. Throw in a shot of a dog and you've got a helluva picture. This kind of turning expectations on their head is often used in its most obvious form in horror films:

- Close on: a girl looks around nervously, fearfully.
- Close on: a hand grabs her shoulder.
- Close on: she screams in terror!
- Wide shot: both of them. It's her boyfriend.

What makes this different than if we had just done it as one static wide shot? What technique of cinema have we used here? Suppose we had done it all as just one wide shot? Even though she is looking around and it's dark, the whole time we see this big friendly looking guy standing behind her, smiling. Sure he grabs her shoulder and she's startled, but clearly it's non-dangerous and innocent.

1.11. The basic scene can be viewed from a nearly infinite variety of points of view and lens lengths; these are just a few examples.

So what if she looks a little nervous, what could she be concerned about that's any worse than maybe she thinks she saw a rat? It's a completely different scene: no questions, no expectations and certainly no reversal of expectations. Now we're ready for the next technique. The next step is crucial, as is an analogy for the next significant innovation in film technique.

Let's take our collection of viewers and walk around anywhere we want in the scene. Not only can we isolate pieces and show them in any order we want; we can now see each isolated piece from a different angle. We can also move higher or lower (Figure 1.11).

We can start with a close view of something and move to another close view. We can start with a close view and move back to see a wider view. We can tilt the viewer so that what the audience sees is off-kilter or disorienting. The possibilities are limitless.

There are two more important elements to add before we move on. We have to add something to our viewer analogy. It is no longer a cardboard box — now it's real optics. This means that as the box gets longer and narrower, the perception of depth gets shallower — things seem compressed, closer together (we'll talk about why in the chapter on *Optics*). Not only does the perception compression of space get greater, but even if two things are fairly close together (one behind the other) one of them is in focus and the other isn't. As we shall see, focus is an important storytelling tool.

As the box gets wider and shorter, the opposite happens: the perception of the depth of the view expands. Two things, one behind the other, even if they are close together in reality, will now seem to be separated by a great distance, but both of them will still be in focus. Let's take these little cardboard viewers as our analogy and review what we can do with them.

- Change the position from which we see the scene.
- Isolate certain parts of the scene.
- Move from one isolated part to another.
- Move the view higher or lower.
- Change the perception of depth.

FILMSPACE

Let's give it a name — this method of separating the three-dimensional reality into pieces and showing them to the audience in an arranged order. Let's call it filmspace.

Filmspace is a different way of viewing a real scene. In fact it is a whole collection of ways of viewing a real three-dimensional scene. And don't forget that we can tell the little eye to close while we change to a different viewer or move it to a different place. This means that we can take any of those different views and put them in any order we want. Filmspace, then, is a means of using visual manipulation to take real space and real objects and look at them, perceive them and feel about them in many different ways — ways that we can command.

We have control, but control can also be a dangerous thing. Here's the issue. It is possible to shoot these views in a way that only confuses, annoys and frustrates the audience. And this is where we reach the confluence and overlap of what the director does, what the cinematographer does and what the editor does.

The cinematographer has a primary responsibility, which is to get all the shots the director needs; all the pieces that are needed to tell the story. There is another requirement: they have to provide what the editor needs as well. (For purposes of this discussion we will assume that the director is not involved in the editorial process, which is sometimes the case in projects such as series television.)

If how we make a film work is a language, then the types of shots are our vocabulary— there has to be a grammar of how these pieces of the language fit together. There are a number of rules of grammar that shots have to follow in order to be usable by the editor. It is possible to get any number of really great shots; good lighting, good camerawork, terrific acting, etc. that the editor simply has to throw away because she simply can't use them.

SPATIAL ORIENTATION IN PROSCENIUM SHOOTING
As we discussed, in the early days of cinema, dramatic films were conceived as recorded theater: everything was viewed as if it were happening on a proscenium stage. In the theater, the audience sits in front and can clearly discern the right/left and front/back of the stage. That spatial orientation remains fixed the entire time (Figure 1.12).

The camera merely took the place of the audience and never moved in relation to the scene before it. If the front door of the house was on the right side, it never moved; it was always on the right. If the train tracks were going left to head west, they never moved; there was no possibility of deviation from the set scheme of directions as long as the camera doesn't move.

The filmspace was simply the three-dimensional world projected on the two-dimensional proscenium frame (just as in theater), but this frame was static, definitively bounded and perceptually flat. A great deal of the progress in film technique has been the movement away from this simplistic methodology. Indeed, a year-by-year study of the progression of camera movement, cutting and pacing would constitute a major part of the story of the history of filmmaking, as would an analysis of the progress from flat, bland, featureless lighting to almost "anything goes."

SUBJECTIVE AND OBJECTIVE POV
Recall the three forms of literary voice: first person, second person and third person. In first person storytelling, a character in the story is describing the events. He can only describe things that he himself sees. First person speaks as "I."

Second person speaks as "you"; third person speaks about "they." Third person is completely objective, and first person is completely subjective. Second person is somewhere in between. There is no clear-cut line of delineation between subjective and objective — only gradations (Figures 1.13 and 1.14). We have previously talked about giving the scene a "point of view." Each camera angle has a point of view as well, and there are several variations to that meaning. The term point of view, or POV, is used in a number of different ways in filmmaking. Our two people are talking; the camera stands off to one side of them. The camera is essentially part of the scene since it sees the people but it is not involved in the scene in any way. It is a neutral observer. It is completely objective — third person.

This is like the omniscient narrator in a novel or story. An omniscient narrator or POV is a voice that tells the story but is not a character in the story and can "see" everything that is going on. The voice can tell us what each and every character is doing at any time. What is a completely subjective shot? It is when the camera takes the place of one of the characters. In the case of our two people talking, if the other character is talking, she would look directly into the lens as if she were looking into the eyes of the man.

In actual practice this is almost never done in narrative filmmaking, although it is used on very rare occasions. Probably the most famous example is the noir film *The Lady In the Lake*. (Figures 1.15 and 1.16) In this case the story is seen in an entirely first person, purely subjective fashion as if the camera is the detective.

When other characters speak to the detective they look directly into the lens. As a result we can never see the detective because "we" (the camera) are the detective. The only time we see him is when he looks into a mirror. A fascinating and very successful modern variation of this is a film titled *84 Charlie Mopic*, a Vietnam war film. (The title refers to the Army designation for a combat motion picture cameraman.) The premise is that a cameraman along with a journalist/interviewer are sent along with a long-range reconnaissance team to record everything they do. Throughout the entire film everything we see is only what is photographed by Mopic's camera. It's a terrific conceit and is executed beautifully. Here we see Mopic only one time in the entire film. At the very end they are under fire and are being evacuated by helicopter. Mopic is just about to get into the chopper and he is shot. He tosses the camera into the chopper and it lands on the floor facing him. It records his death as the chopper takes off without him.

Other forms of POV are things like "doggie cam." If there is a dog in the scene and the camera is placed low to the ground and moves along in a fashion resembling how a dog moves, we are seeing the scene from a dog's point of view. This is often used in werewolf films, for example. Another example is often used in thrillers or horror films. The "victim" is doing some action and we see him as a stalker might. The camera is handheld and moves with a human motion: not too steady and always following the action as if staring.

A characterizing of this is that when the "victim" looks over suddenly, the camera will quickly "hide" behind a curtain or doorway. It is a standard operating procedure in film that true POV shots are almost always done handheld.

1.12. Cinema as a "filmed play," such as this frame from *The Great Train Robbery* (Edwin S. Porter, 1903) means that the left/right relationships never change for the audience. Once we get away from this simplistic type of filming, methods are needed to maintain the directional continuity in the mind of the viewer.

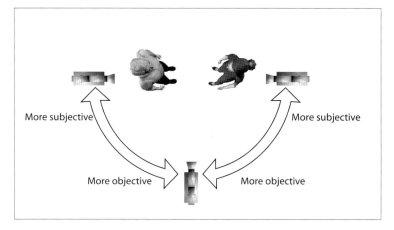

1.13. In general, the closer the camera gets to the performer's perspective, the more subjective the shot becomes.

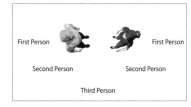

First Person
Second Person
First Person
Second Person
Third Person

1.14. Subjective and objective camera angles are analogous to the literary concepts of first person, second person and third person. These are generalities — there are no hard and fast boundaries.

The difference is that it is never carried all the way through. For example, if the "victim" were to see the stalker and walk over to confront him, logically he would look directly into the camera. There are two problems with this. First it would break the illusion of the film. The audience would be made jarringly aware that they are watching the movie. In the theater it would be called "breaking the fourth wall." This is when an actor in the play talks directly to the audience. To take it to its most extreme and ridiculous logical end, if the man were to ask the stalker a question and he agreed, we would have to nod the camera up and down. This is played as a joke even when we do it in home movies.

The second problem is that it would then be impossible to ever show the "stalker" in the scene. If he is looking directly into the lens, then the camera is "him." There is then no possibility of doing another shot which includes him. As a result, even if the shot is theoretically a subjective POV, it is almost never carried through to the looking-in-the-lens conclusion.

The most frequently used type of character POV is "the look." An example of this is when we see someone looks up and then the next shot is a view of an airplane. The important part of this type of POV is the setup: that is when we see the person looking. The next thing we see will be assumed to be what she is looking at. But for this to work, the "look" must be set up properly. If she looks down and then the next shot is an airplane, it will make no sense — the audience will perceive this as something completely unrelated; worse they will be momentarily confused and distracted.

In their book *Film Art — An Introduction*, David Bordwell and Kristin Thomson call this the "Kuleshov effect." This is named for Lev Kuleshov, one of the early experimenters in Russian formalist filmmaking in the 1920s. He performed an experiment in which is used the same shot of a famous Russian actor with a neutral look intercut (at various times) with shots of nature, some soup, a baby and a dead woman. When quizzed about what the actor was expressing, the audience said he was either showing tranquility, hunger, joy or great sorrow.

This illustrates the storytelling power of simply putting two shots together. When we show someone tilt his head up and his eyes turn toward something off-screen, then cut to a clock tower or an airplane, the audience will always make the connection that our character is looking at that tower or plane.

This demonstrates not only the usefulness of subjective POVs for storytelling and emotional subtext, but also hints at the importance of the off-screen space as part of our narrative. It also reminds us that we are almost never doing shots which will be used in isolation: ultimately shots are used in combination with other shots.

1.15 and **1.16**. *The Lady In The Lake* (MGM, 1947) is one of the very rare examples of truly subjective point of view sustained throughout the entire film.

THE BUILDING BLOCKS OF SCENES

There are a number of types of shots which are basic building blocks of film grammar. They are:

- Wide Shot (or long shot)
- Full Shot
- Medium
- Head and Shoulders
- Big Head
- Cowboy
- Tight Two
- Dirty Single
- Clean Single

Except for the first two, most of these shots apply to the human form, but the terminology carries over to any subject. As they appear in the script they are called stage directions. Let's look at them individually. As with many film terms, the definitions are somewhat loose and different people have slight variations in how they apply them; particularly as you travel from city to city or work in another country; they are just general guidelines. It is only when you are lining it up through the lens that the exact frame can be decided on and all the factors that go into a shot can be fully assessed.

As they appear in the script, stage directions are completely non-binding. The screenwriter really has no say over what shots will be used, but they are helpful in visualizing the story as you read the script. Some shots are specific to the story, such as "Close on — the ticking bomb," but ultimately it is up to the director to determine which shots will be done. These shots are the basic vocabulary we deal with. These basic elements and how they are combined in editorial continuity are the grammar of cinema.

WIDE SHOT

The wide shot is any frame which encompasses the entire scene. This makes it all relative to the subject. If the script reads "Wide shot — the English Countryside" we are clearly talking about a big panoramic scene done with a short focal length lens taking in all the eye can see (Figure 1.17). On the other hand, if the description is "Wide shot — Leo's room" this is clearly a much smaller shot but it still encompasses all or most of the room.

ESTABLISHING SHOTS

The establishing shot is usually a wide shot. It is the opening shot of a scene which tells us where we are (Figure 1.18). A typical one

1.17. (below) A classic wide shot used here as both an establishing shot and a transitional shot for the next scene. *Days Of Heaven* (Paramount Pictures, 1978).

1.18. (left) Throughout *Barry Lyndon* (Warner Bros., 1975), Kubrick uses perfectly composed formal framing to reflect the static social structure of the time, as in this establishing shot.

might be "Establishing shot — Helen's office." This might consist of a wide shot of an office building, thus when we cut to a shot of Helen at her desk, we know where we are: in her office building. We've seen that it is a big, modern building, very upscale and expensive and that it is located in midtown Manhattan and the bustling activity of streets indicate it's another hectic workday in New York. The establishing shot has given us a great deal of information.

LAYING OUT THE SCENE

A phrase that is often used is that we have to "establish the geography." In other words we have to give the audience some idea of where they are, what kind of place it is, where objects and people are in relation to each other. (This is different from establishing the place — both are discussed in more technical detail in the chapter *Cinematic Continuity*).

Establishing the geography is most important within the scene — it is very helpful to the audience to know the "lay of the land" within a scene, it helps them orient themselves and prevents confusion which might divert their attention from the story. There are times when you want to keep the layout a mystery, of course. As we will see throughout the discussion of film grammar and editing, one of the primary purposes is to not confuse the audience. There will be times of course where you will want to confuse or trick them, but in general, if you don't give them information and they have to spend time trying to figure something out, however subconsciously, you have taken their minds away from the characters and the story. Kurosawa is a master of this type of establishing, as in these shots from *Seven Samurai* (Figures 1.19 and 1.20).

An establishing shot, such as our office building example, might also include a tilt up to an upper floor. This indicates to the audience that we are not just seeing an office building, but that we are going inside. A further variation is to end with a zoom in to a particular window, a more obvious cue as to where we are headed.

Shots of this type are sometimes considered old-fashioned and prosaic, but they can still be effective. Even though they do give us a good deal of information, they are still a complete stop in the dramatic action. Many filmmakers consider it more effective if the establishing shot can be combined with a piece of the story. One example: say we are looking down that same bustling street and our character Helen comes into view, rushing frantically and holding a big stack of documents; we pan or dolly with her as she rushes into the lobby and runs to catch a departing elevator. The same information has been conveyed, but we have told a piece of the story as well. Something is up with Helen; all those documents are obviously something important that has put her under a great deal of stress.

Of course, in the story, Helen may already be in her office. One of the classic solutions has been to combine a bit of foreground action with the establishing shot. For example, we start with a medium shot of a sidewalk newsstand. An anonymous man buys a paper and we can read the headline "Financial Scandal Disclosed," and we then tilt to the building. What we have done here is keep the audience in the story and combined it with showing the building and the context.

In a sense it is a bit of distraction such as a stage magician might use, but in another sense it does convey some useful information. Certainly it's a lot better than just cutting to Helen and have her do some hackneyed "on the nose" dialog such as, "Oh my god, what am I going to do about the big financial scandal?" Of course, there is one more level you can add: the guy who buys the newspaper is not an anonymous man, he turns out to be the reporter who is going to uncover the real story. These are just examples, of course, but the

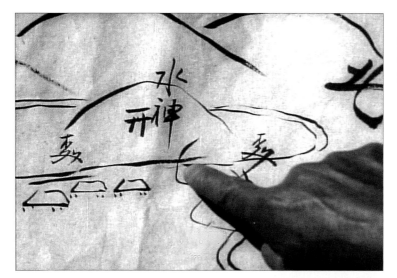

1.19 and **1.20**. Ever the master of making the abstract concrete, Kurosawa cuts directly from the map of the village to a shot of the samurai walking in the location indicated (*Seven Samurai*. Toho/Columbia Pictures, 1954).

point is to convey the location information in combination with a piece of the story or something that conveys a visual idea, a sound track inflection or anything that increases our understanding of the place, the mood, or anything that is useful to you as the storyteller.

FULL SHOT

Refers to a shot which includes all of the subject, whether it be an entire building or a person. For example, a "full shot" of a car includes all of the car. A shot which only includes the door and the driver would be more of a medium shot.

MEDIUM SHOT

The medium shot, like the wide shot, is relative to the subject. Obviously, it is closer than a wide shot. Typical medium shots might be people at a table in a restaurant, or someone buying a soda, shown from the waist up. By being closer in to the action than we were in the wide, we can now see people's expressions, details of how they are dressed, etc. We thus become more involved in what they are saying and doing, without focusing on one specific character or any particular detail.

In other contexts, a medium shot might be even smaller, such as a man reading at his desk. We see him and can read the expression

1.21, **1.22** and **1.23**. An elegantly executed triple reveal from *High Noon* (Republic Pictures/United Artists, 1952). In one shot, the bad guys ride into town; as the horse rears up we see the sign that reads "Marshal" the bad guys ride on and then from behind we see the sign that reads "Justice of the Peace," and the camera pulls back to show the marshal in the process of getting "hitched." This shot also clearly tells us where we are (in town outside the marshal's office) and starts to establish the geography of the place. It also establishes the main characters and conflicts.

1.24. The basic shots as defined by the body. The terms apply in the same fashion to most subjects.

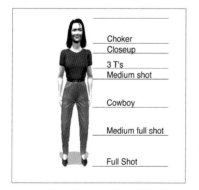

on his face, but we also see some of his context and his surroundings. If his secretary comes in with a phone message we can see her, though probably not from head to toe. If we are positioned so that we see the office door behind him, we can then see the door open and her entrance. That way she doesn't just pop into frame, magically appearing out of nowhere. This is definitely something to be avoided, as it is jarring and distracting. Wherever possible, we should see the character's entrance, although this can be accomplished in a wide variety of ways; it doesn't always have to be a static shot of the door which then opens.

Such a shot might be boring and, subliminally, the audience might for a moment be wondering why we are looking at this door. There are hundreds of ways to make this a smoother part of the flow and give it meaning. One simple example: the businessman speaks into his intercom and says "David, would you bring me the Anderson contracts?" This idea is somewhat an extension of the establishing the geography concept. We might consider it "establishing the geography of the character." We just don't want to have the audience spend time trying to figure out who's who and where did they come from and why (except when that is the intended effect). An especially well done case of this is shown in Figures 1.21, 1.22 and 1.23.

There are, of course, many exceptions to this rule. The simplest and most obvious: the babysitter has heard a noise in the basement and is going to investigate; the house is dark and she approaches the basement door with great fear and trepidation.

Suddenly, out of nowhere, a hand clamps onto her shoulder! It usually turns out to be her best friend of course, but the point is that by having someone appear suddenly out of nowhere we have created a moment of shock and surprise. We assume it is the serial killer in the basement. If it were, it would be a true moment of shock and surprise. In this case, it turns out to be a shock with an ironic twist. We have led the audience toward expecting disaster and it turns out to be something completely different. As with all shot descriptions, the medium shot might not include characters at all, it might just be a scene or objects, but the concept is still the same.

TWO SHOT

The two shot is any frame which includes two characters. The interaction between two characters in a scene is one of the most fundamental pieces of storytelling; thus the two shot is one you will use frequently. The two characters don't have to be arranged symmetrically in the frame, they might be facing each other, both facing forward, both facing away from the camera, etc., but the methods you use for dealing with this type of scene will be the same in any case.

CHARACTER SHOTS

There are a number of terms for different shots of a single character. Full shot indicates we see the character from head to toe (Figure 1.24). A "cowboy" is from the top of head to mid-thigh, presumably named because it is important to see the six-guns on his belt. In Europe, the term *plán americain* or *plano americano* refers to a shot framed from mid-leg up, basically a cowboy shot. Beyond this we are into the realm of close-ups.

CLOSE-UPS

Close-ups are one of the most important shots in the vocabulary. There are a number of variations: A medium close-up would generally be considered as something like from top of head to waist or something in that area (Figures 1.25 and 1.26).

1.25. A classic medium shot from *Shanghai Express* (Paramount, 1932). Note also how the lighting is very specific for this shot and for her pose. If her head were not just the right position, the lighting would not achieve such an elegant and powerful effect.

A close-up (CU) would generally be from the top of the head to somewhere just below the shirt pockets. If the shot is cut just above the shirt pocket area, it is often called a "head and shoulders." A "choker" would be from top of head down to just below the chin. A tight close-up would be slightly less: losing some of the forehead and perhaps some of the chin, framing the eyes, nose and mouth. An extreme close-up or ECU might include the eyes only. Just as often, an ECU is an object: perhaps just a ring lying on a desktop, a watch, etc. Any CU, medium or full shot that includes only a single character is called a single. A system that is sometimes used is based on "Ts." Terminology of close-ups includes:

- Medium: waist up.
- 3-Ts: from the breasts up
- Choker: from the throat up. Also known as 2 Ts (teeth and throat).
- Big Head CU or "tight CU": from just under the chin and giving a bit of "haircut." That is cutting off just a little bit of the head.
- ECU: Varies, but usually just mouth and eyes.

A close-up is also known as a single. If we are shooting someone's CU and don't include any piece of the other actor's this is called a "clean" single. If we do include a little bit of the actor in front of him, it's called a "dirty" single.

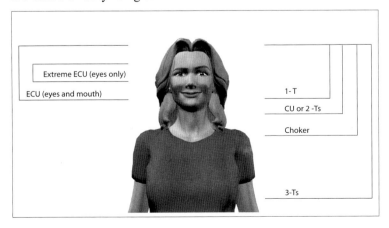

Extreme ECU (eyes only)

ECU (eyes and mouth)

1-T

CU or 2-Ts

Choker

3-Ts

1.26. The basic closeups.

1.27. An over-the-shoulder; one of the most fundamental shots in the camera vocabulary.

OTS

A variation of the close-up is the over-the-shoulder or OTS (Figure 1.27), looking over the shoulder of one actor to a medium or CU of the other. The over-the-shoulder is a variant of a connecting shot. It ties the two characters together and helps put us in the position of the person being addressed. As it is very engaging and involving in this way, the OTS is a major part of the vocabulary of narrative filmmaking. Even when we are in close shot of the person talking, the OTS keeps the other actor in the scene.

CUTAWAY

A cutaway is any shot of some person or thing in the scene other than the main characters we are covering but that is still related to the scene. An example would be a cutaway to the clock on the wall or to the cat sleeping on the floor. Cutaways may emphasize some action in the scene, provide additional information or be something that the character looks at or points to.

An important use of cutaways is as safeties for the editor. If the editor is somehow having trouble cutting the scene, a cutaway to something else can be used to solve the problem. A good rule of thumb is if there is any uncertainty about the coverage of a scene: always shoot some sort of cutaways — safety first!

REACTION SHOT

A specific type of cutaway is the reaction shot. Something happens or a character says something and we cut to another person in another part of the room reacting to what happened or what was said. This is different from coverage within the master. A reaction shot is a good way to get a safety cutaway for the editor. The more a cutaway is directly related to the scene, the better it will cut into the flow. Sometimes the term just refers to the other side of the dialog.

Some reaction shots do involve the main characters in the scene. Say we have a medium shot side view of the detective looking out the window with binoculars, then we cut to a shot of what he sees through the binoculars — the gang boss he has under surveillance. If we want to come around to the front and see his eyes widen at what he sees, then we say we want to grab his reaction shot.

This kind of close-up of his facial expression demands to be shot from front on and with him facing the direction he was looking through the binoculars. Anything else just won't work as well. In this particular case, it would probably call for cheating him back from the window because otherwise there is probably no place to put the camera unless we have a fire escape or a crane. It is unlikely to be worth it to move the entire camera rig and crew out onto the fire escape or onto a crane for just one shot. If it is part of a series of shots needed from that vantage point, that's a different matter, of course.

Except in rare cases, just having the actor step back from the window three feet to fit the camera in makes for a completely unnoticeable cheat. On the other hand, a shot that includes the glass in the foreground can be useful — it is not unusual to fly in a set piece of a matching window just for this effect. It's quick, cheap and effective; it's just up to the DP to create a matching lighting ambiance to sell it.

INSERT

An insert is an isolated, self-contained piece of a larger scene. Example: she is reading a book. We could just shoot the book over her shoulder, but it is usually hard to read from that distance. Inserts tend to fit into a few general categories:

- Practical inserts. The clock on the wall, as in Figure 1.28, is a practical insert, as is the headlines on the newspaper or

1.28. (below) An example of a practical insert from *High Noon*.

1.29. (bottom) An "atmosphere" cutaway — it conveys little or no information specific to the story but it reinforces and adds to the mood and tone of the scene and possibly also the rhythm of the cutting. This one is from *Nine and 1/2 Weeks* (MGM/Warner Brothers, 1986);

the name of the file being pulled from the drawer. These are mostly informational.

- Emphasis inserts. The tires skid to a halt. The coffee cup jolts as he pounds the table. The windows rattle in the wind. Emphasis inserts are usually closely connected to the main action but not absolutely essential to it, for example, a very old person coming toward us in a walker. An insert of the tired old feet in slippers shuffling along the concrete adds to our empathy for his plight and our understanding of how difficult it is for him to move.
- Atmosphere inserts. These are little touches, grace notes, if you will, that contribute to the mood or tone of a scene. These are particularly well used in moody films like *Angel Heart* or *Nine and 1/2 Weeks* (Figure 1.29): cutaways to fans slowly revolving in the wind, or a black cat looks into the lens. They can be used for pure mood or as ironic counterpoint.

Atmosphere inserts may have almost no connection to the scene other than mood, tone or a sort of generalized symbolism. They are generally reserved for more stylized filmmaking. They should be used with caution; such shots can easily be arch, heavy-handed and obvious, and then they are what are sometimes called "film student" shots.

CONNECTING SHOTS
Any time the scene includes people or objects that cannot be framed in the same shot at some point in the scene, a connecting shot is called for. This applies especially to point-of-view shots where the character looks at something, then in a separate shot, we see what she is looking at; but it also applies to any scene where two or more people are in the same general space, whether they are aware of each other or not.

In our surveillance example, of course, it is no trick at all to use shots of the detective, his POV through the binoculars and close-ups of the gang boss being observed and cut them together in a way that makes eminently clear the physical relationships and who is watching whom. There is always a danger, however, that it will seem a bit cheap and easy and the fact that it is an editing trick will somehow undermine the scene.

Connecting shots just make a scene feel more complete and whole (Figures 1.30 and 1.31). The fragmentation of doing it all with POVs and reaction shots is after all a cheat which calls upon movie magic to piece together the whole scene. It works, but is not as involving or emotionally satisfying to the audience, especially if overused. A connecting shot is a way to tie everything together in a way that clarifies and emphasizes the physical, which are usually story relationships as well — clearly, one of the prime objectives of good directing and good shooting is to have the physical elements reflect, reinforce and comment on the narrative elements.

In our example we could shoot from over the shoulder of the detective using a long lens so we see the window of the person under surveillance. As long as this view has a matching window close to the window we see in the POV shots of the detective, it works as a connecting shot. Better still if we see the character under surveillance or at the very least, a stand-in double.

WINDOW MATCHING AND THE FINE ART OF CHEATING
The technique of window matching and door matching deserves a mention in this context. Although they are largely a technical consideration, they are crucial to these film techniques and also are an excellent illustration of how the "movie magic" comes together, so we will discuss them here rather than in the chapter on *Cinematic*

1.30. A connecting shot from *Killer's Kiss* (MGM/US, 1955), Kubrick's first film.

1.31. A helicopter shot from *Perfect Duo* (Vidmark, 1993). Both establish the geography and, more importantly, the relationship between two important story elements.

Continuity. They are indicative of a larger issue of cheating, something that is done all the time in film. It is important to know how it is done and it is absolutely crucial that a professional cinematographer, videographer or director know when you can cheat and just how much you can get away with.

Knowing how far you can go comes from understanding the editorial process and also having a feel for how things photograph as opposed to how they look in real life. The fact that this knowledge must come from two very different areas of film production illustrates how important it is that there be a cross-over in knowledge and in communication from director to cameraman to editor and even the art department. Only by having a solid understanding of the other parts of the process are you able to do your job properly, no matter which of these people you might happen to be on any particular project.

To a large extent, both for the cameraperson and the director, how far you can go in cheating is something you just need to learn by experience. The more you do it, the more adept you become. It's a subtle art but one that is absolutely necessary to learn. As mentioned above, the window we see over the shoulder of the detective does not have to be the same actual window in which we see the actor playing the character under surveillance. Indeed, for logistical or scheduling reasons, it often is not the same window. To take an extremely simple example: our detective is on the roof of a ten-story building. Perhaps he's on the roof because there is a great view of the city skyline behind him — the reason doesn't matter.

If he is on the roof, it only makes sense for him to be doing surveillance on someone on an upper floor of the building across the street; he wouldn't be able to see into a window that is on the second floor, for example. (These are the kinds of things you have to think about in scouting locations.)

Once we have all the shots of the detective and the appropriate connecting shots showing the window it comes time for the closer shots showing what the gang boss is doing inside the room. The easy way, of course, would be to throw on a much longer lens and have the actor appear in that same room. There may be problems, however. Perhaps that room is not available as a location or, more likely, shooting all of that scene with a very long lens just isn't appropriate. In any case, it is often desirable to get closer to the window. In most cases shooting just outside a window on the 10th floor is just not practical, no matter what your budget. Even if there is a fire escape, that is actually a little too close. It is difficult to get far enough back to still show a piece of the window.

"GET A PIECE OF IT"

This concept of "showing a piece of it" is something that comes up all the time in setting up shots, especially cheating shots. In a way, it is related to the idea of connecting shots. Say we are framing someone at a poker table, then we go in for a tighter shot of the poker player. Frequently the director will say, "I still want to see a piece of the table." It may be just so we can maintain some of the crucial poker chips in the frame or just to preserve the ambiance of sitting at the table, but either way, it is a way of showing the character in a way that is still connected to the reference of his surroundings.

Given the possibility of shooting everything as separations (pieces of the overall scene) there is always a danger of going too far; these types of connecting shots or showing a "piece" of something are a way of keeping everything still tied together and in reference to one another. Often when the table has been cheated away (in order to get the camera in) the director will ask the camera operator (who has the advantage of seeing directly through the lens), "Will I miss it?"

meaning will the cheat be obvious; will the audience perceive that the table is not there.

It's all about keeping the audience in the scene in a way that they don't get lost or confused. The more they are oriented and grounded in the filmspace of the scene, the easier it is for them to go with the narrative or emotional flow of it. There are times, of course, where you will deliberately want to disorient or confuse the audience, but these situations must be carefully chosen.

Back to our window example: the simple solution to all of this is to put the actor in a similar room on the first or second floor, then the camera can go on a tripod, dolly, crane or scaffolding. Precision isn't crucial; as in the shots from the roof it is unlikely that the audience will have learned much about the room itself. They will have a clear knowledge of the window, though, so it is important that the window itself be very similar. How similar depends on how good a view of it they got and for how long.

Window matching works from both sides. If we see a medium shot of the gang boss as framed by a six foot high double hung casement window, we cannot cheat his interior scenes and have him looking out a Modernist floor to ceiling glass window — the cheat would not work. It has to be a reasonably similar type of window with a view that roughly matches. We can't have seen him clearly from the window of the building directly across the street and then have him look out a window that has a great view of the desert.

All of these same principles apply to door matching as well. It is quite common to shoot the exterior of someone going in a door and then shoot the interiors somewhere else. In fact, if the interiors are on a sound stage, it is almost always the case. Here again, it must be roughly the same kind of door and not be a jarringly different color. There is one additional factor: if the door we saw him entering in the exterior shot is a right-hand door, then the matching interior door should also be a right-hand door and vice-versa. It is always possible to frame the shot so that we don't see outside or the art department can rig a few plants and a backdrop; these are not usually big problems as long as the door (and of course, the weather) are a good match.

PICK-UP

A pick up can be any type of shot, master or coverage, when you are starting it at any place other than at the top. For example, perhaps you have shot a master of the businesswoman entering the office, sitting at the desk and answering the phone. For whatever reason you need another take of the dialog on the phone. If it is not necessary to get the entrance again, you can "pick it up" from when she answers the phone. To do this, you have to be sure that you don't need the whole entrance, the sitting and the answering of the phone as a continuous take. You can pick it up only if your are sure you have coverage to cut to along the way. Usually a "PU" is added to the scene number on the slate.

THE MASTER SCENE METHOD

All working professionals know the basic techniques and rules of the master scene method, but some just follow them by rote without understanding the underlying theory and reasons for why we do the things we do. The master scene method is used in probably 95% of narrative films shot today. The techniques evolved during the silent era and were largely in place by the early 20s.

The fundamentals of the master scene technique are not complicated although there are many refinements, techniques and cheats which can get a bit tricky. Some can be real brain teasers and, when it's hour 16 of a rough shooting day, can have the director and DP drawing little diagrams to confirm their thinking.

1.32. A master shot from *Ronin* (MGM/UA, 1998). Once the master has established the basic layout of the scene and the physical relationships of the characters, the editor can easily cut to medium shots, closeups, reactions and so on without confusing the audience.

What we want in the end are all the different types of shots that give the editor everything she needs to cut the scene together without problems and have the freedom to cut creatively, alter the pacing, the emphasis and even the point of view of the scene. On the other hand, we want to make sure there are no mismatches of continuity, no gaps that the editor can't fill and of course, to keep the producer happy, not shoot grossly more film than is really necessary.

Say we're looking for the basic shots we need for the scene; we want a wide shot of them entering the room, some close-ups of the characters talking, the woman adjusting a clock and so on. We could just go ahead and shoot each shot as it comes along; shooting in order or out of order and then say "there, we've got the scene." Only later the editor might discover that an important piece is missing, or when the woman goes to adjust the clock, the man is standing behind her instead of in front of her, etc.

In other words, if you take it one shot at a time, no matter how carefully you've thought it out ahead, there is always room for error. Even with a shot list (which is always recommended) and story board there is still a danger of leaving something out or shooting it in a way that will not work. The master scene technique is a methodical way of ensuring that you get all the shots needed efficiently and with many safeguards against continuity errors and other editorial problems.

INVISIBLE TECHNIQUE
The master scene method and coverage are "invisible" techniques. Properly done, the audience is rarely aware of them. They can convey information, tell the story and add inflections of tone and mood without distracting the audience. The basic method can be summed up in a few words: we shoot the master and then go in for coverage. First, some terminology.

Master
A master is the entire scene including all the key elements, usually done as one continuous take. Some scenes need to be broken down into two or more "mini-masters," especially if there is movement (Figure 1.32).

Coverage
Coverage consists of all the mediums, close-ups, over-the-shoulders, inserts and cutaways needed to successfully edit the scene. The master is basically the whole scene in one shot (not necessarily a static shot). It should include all of the key characters and all of the essential elements and certainly it should contain all of the dialog of the scene. However, it does not have to be so wide that it includes the clock, for example. When it comes to that we will either pan with her or let her exit frame.

The master often resembles the old proscenium style of shooting, and essentially it is, but that's OK, because it will eventually only be used as a small part of the final edited product. Still, you want to set up as interesting a master as you can. Sometimes a scene is shot only as a master. This is sometimes called an "in one." This may be a stylistic choice (Jim Jarmusch's first film *Strangers in Paradise* is shot entirely this way) or, as a simple matter of economy or speed (if the sun is going down or the location permit is about to run out). Although there are slight differences, it is related to plán scene, which is discussed below. One important thing is that the master should have a beginning and an ending. By this we mean the editor should have some way of finding a logical place to fluidly cut into the scene and a similar way to end it.

The Cutting Point

Editors are always looking for a "cutting point." This is some place where the edit is motivated, logical and flows smoothly. Don't make the mistake of thinking that this is just "the editor's problem." Not all cutting points can be preplanned, but you should be aware of them as you shoot; more on cutting points in *Cinematic Continuity*.

Beginning The Scene

Let's take an example of two people seated on a sofa, talking. You can just cut in to a scene in *medias res* (the Greek term for just starting in the middle of the action). In other words, you can open the scene with them already sitting at the table and they just begin the dialog. In practice, it is often perfectly OK to start a scene this way but it is not always the best way; it gives the editor almost no freedom in how to begin or end the scene and if used all the time, would be very boring.

TRANSITIONS

It is often best to transition in and out of a scene. In any case where the elapsed time between scenes is other than more or less around the same time, it may be important to plan a shot which explains the transition of time. Sometimes passage of time will be obvious. If one scene ends during midday and the next scene starts in the dead of night, there will be no confusion: we are at a different point in time.

Standard time transitional devices include a sunset or sunrise, the exterior of the building day or night or similar shots. Some older devices are now simply considered too "quaint" to use: pages flying off the calendar, a time-lapse shot of the spinning hands on the clock, etc. Panning over to a clock or off the clock onto the action are still often employed effectively as are larger transitions such as a dissolve from the trees in summer to the bare limbs of winter. A cut from shot to shot where an extended time change occurs without transitional device is called an elliptical cut. Elliptical means that something is missing, as in the punctuation mark ellipsis: three periods (...) or when someone speaks elliptically.

ELLIPTICAL CUTS

The opposite of this expansion of time is the acceleration of time. This is largely editorial but it may be reinforced with shooting techniques such as high-speed slow motion shooting, time-lapse photography or very frenetic, high energy shots.

REAL TIME CONTINUITY

The third case would seem to be the easiest but is actually the most difficult and rarest of all: real time shooting over extended sequences or the entire film. There are only a few examples of real time continuity being maintained for an entire film. Probably the best known is Hitchcock's film *Rope*. The film is staged as one continuous take, with only a few camera cuts or breaks in action from beginning to end. (It is a myth that there are no cuts at all, but there are not many.)

In reality, since a standard roll of film lasts only eleven minutes, there are cuts but Hitchcock cleverly disguises them. For example, in one case the camera tracks past a column which fills the screen. It appears to be a smooth dolly past the obstruction but Hitchcock hides a camera cut. (This type of invisible cut is discussed in the chapter *Cinematic Continuity* as it applies to editorial continuity and logistics.) In actual fact, staging an entire film as one continuous action was a miracle of logistics, camera/actor choreography and stagecraft. It involved wild walls which could fly in and out silently just off camera.

1.33, **1.34** and **1.35**. A match cut from *Ronin*. From the character's face, it cuts to a black screen which, as it is closed, is revealed to be the cover of a Pelican case. As the cover is lowered further, the next scene is established. Although this type of cut can be used anywhere, it is of particular importance here because the cut is to the *same location* at a *later time.* The opening and closing of the case serves as a time transition: we know it is a later time because there was no open case in the previous shot. Without this transition a cut to the same men standing elsewhere in the same shop might have been jarring and distracting: why have they suddenly jumped to another spot in the room? (The completely black frame is omitted here.)

Another example of near real time continuity is the consummate western *High Noon*. Although the film plays out as a standard drama, if you look closely you will notice that the films occupies almost real time. This is a master stroke in that the name of the film is "High Noon" and the entire drama centers on a confluence of events moving inexorably toward a single moment in time. Real time, is, of course, one of the Aristotelian unities. The spare, simple cinematography by Floyd Crosby beautifully reinforces this dramatic flow. The no-frills imagery, the powerful black-and-white photography and the straightforward staging all tie into this inexorable forward movement.

OTHER TRANSITION SHOTS

An example of a transition shot might be to start with a close-up of the telephone, then pull back to reveal the master. This is a commonly used technique. What you start on is your opening frame, and it can be anything in the scene that is interesting, but it is best if it is something that is relevant to the story. It is even better if the opening frame tells a little story in itself.

In our case, perhaps they are anxiously waiting for a life or death phone call and our opening frame of the telephone reveals that the telephone has been unplugged in a way that they wouldn't see. Then, when we pan over to see them anxiously waiting, an important and suspenseful piece of the story has been added — something that we know, but they don't.

EMPTY FRAME

Another way of transitioning into a scene is to start with an empty frame and have them enter. This may not be the most exciting way to start a scene, but it is always safe. The beauty of this is that it gives the editor a choice. Giving the editor options should always be a goal. Otherwise the scene will always just be what it is; there is no chance in editing to make it better or use it in a way that better serves the story or to alter the pacing and flow of the scene.

More importantly, it gives the editor a chance to fix problems. This is a key point; beyond that, keep in mind that the editor may not just be trying to fix a problem with this scene, she may be trying to solve something with the scene that comes before or after it. One of the things that changes most often in editing is the order of the scenes. Let's say that in the script the scene that comes before this is one involving a car chase. In that case, it's no problem that we start with an opening frame of them already sitting in the room, talking. But what if, for story reasons, the scene that comes immediately before this one involves the same characters in a different location and the scene ends with them just sitting there. There is no way you can cut from that scene to this one without it seeming jarring.

Entering and Exiting Frame

This is why it is important, whenever possible, to let the characters both enter frame and exit frame, or to provide some other sort of transitional device. Remember, the editor can always start the scene after they have sat down, so all you are doing is shooting a few extra feet of film or tape — well worth it for the safety factor it gains.

This is true of all shots where the character is moving. It is always safest to start with a clean frame and end with the character exiting frame. The alternative is to pan on and pan off at the end. This idea carries through to many other situations as well. If someone is coming in a door, never start with the door already partially open, always start rolling and wait a beat or two before calling action. The same applies to someone running into frame or a train crossing frame or a telephone ringing — any form of action.

The term beat is difficult to define, but in this context it usually means roughly a second. There can also be emotional beats, dialog beats and so on. Basically it means a self-contained moment — one of a series. Sometimes, there is a change in position during the scene or some other factor makes a full, all the way through the scene master undesirable. In this case, it may be useful to shoot a mini-master, which gets you the parts you want. Now we have a "buy" take on the master and we are ready to move on.

THINKING ABOUT THE COVERAGE

It is important to remember that in most cases, the scene will rarely be used only as a master, and for the most part only the beginning and the end of the scene will be used in the wide master. One mistake often made by fledgling directors is to do take after take of the master just because an actor flubs a single line in the middle, or because the director liked the beginning of the take but not the ending; this is often just a waste of film. The beauty of this technique is that the editor can go use other shots in the middle of the scene and then come back to the master in an entirely different take. Since the master scene technique in essence "goof proofs" against continuity errors, the ability to use pieces of different masters is assured.

There are exceptions to this, however, for example, if there is a dramatic change in weather conditions from one master to the other. In another case, say the director has a last minute inspiration and tells the actor, "No, don't slug him so he falls down, just threaten him with your fist." In this case we have two very different masters. Shooting the coverage for each one would be very different. In one case the second actor is lying on the ground and in the second case he is still standing. In that case, the director has to make an on the spot decision about which master is the buy take. It is possible, and sometimes even necessary, but "we'll shoot both versions" is not a phrase producers or assistant directors like to hear.

BOOKENDING

One method which is sometimes used on low budget production is called "bookending." It can save a tremendous amount of film and considerable time but has certain inherent risks and limitations. In bookending, you shoot only the beginning and ending of the scene in a master. If, and only if, you know you are going to use the master just for the beginning and ending, you jump over the bulk of the scene and get it in coverage. While it is quite common to use only the first and last part of the master, deciding to bookend a scene is still not a decision to take lightly.

In practice, an editor rarely goes back to the master in the heart of coverage and much of the footage of wide masters goes to waste. There are, however, times when an editor will go back to the master as an editorial choice and perhaps more frequently as a problem fixer — to save a scene which is for some reason uncuttable otherwise. Certainly, the editor will go back to a master when some action takes place that is somehow larger than the realm of the coverage, for example, two people sitting at a restaurant table. Once they have been seated and the waiter has left, most of the scene will play out in coverage. However, if someone else enters the restaurant, the waiter comes back or there is a fight at the next table, the scene will almost certainly go back to the master or some type of wider shot.

There is an old film saying that a day of shooting is often *Gone with the Wind* in the morning and *Cops* at the end of the day, meaning that it is possible even for experienced filmmakers to lavish a great deal of time and attention on relatively simple shots at the beginning of the day which later robs of them of time they desperately need for the last scene of the day. This is just one of many reasons that a really good assistant director is such an essential part of any film

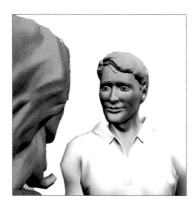

1.36 and **1.37**. Answering shots from the same coverage. Because the lens, the focus distance, lens height and angle are the same, the head sizes remain the same and the physical relationships are constant and the scene cuts back and forth.

team. Pacing the day so that each scene is allotted an appropriate amount of time is crucial to avoiding this and not having to rush the later scenes.

COVERAGE
Coverage is the general term meaning all of the medium shots, close-ups, over-the-shoulders and other shots that are cut into the master to make a complete scene. We can think of the master as a frame-work into which we lay the infill of the coverage cutaways and inserts.

ANSWERING SHOTS
When shooting a dialog scene with two or more people, the over-the-shoulders and close-ups will always come in sets: an OTS and CUs for each person in the shot. The OTS or CU for the second person filmed is called an answering shot. There is one rule above all others when it comes to answering shots: they must match the shot they are answering. They must match in every way: lens focal length, distance from subject to camera, lens height and horizontal angle. This is a very important rule. If the shots don't match very closely they will look very awkward when cut together. (Figures 1.36 and 1.37)

> The golden rule of coverage: answering shots should match in focal length, focus distance, lens height and horizontal angle.

There are some exceptions to this rule. First, if the two actors are of different heights, you should adjust so that the camera is over their shoulder, that is, higher for the taller actor and lower for the shorter actor. Alternatively you can cheat it by putting the shorter actor up on an apple box. But you don't want to go too far with a cheat like this or the audience will perceive that all of a sudden the actor has grown.

The second exception is when one actor is a very big person with a large head and the second is a person with a small head. This is another area where many first-time directors go wrong by believing that the rules are carved in stone and must never be violated. What really matters is not so much that the camera be the exact same distance away from each subject, what counts is that the image sizes and perspective are roughly the same. You may want to leave a slight difference because they audience does know that the actors are of different sizes. It is important to remember that the rules are only guidelines; in the end judgment and experience must be the final arbiters and they can only be based on an understanding of why the rules are the way are.

SHOOTING ORDER
Ordinarily, the master is shot first, which is really the heart of the whole method. Once the director is satisfied that he has a "buy" take, the AD announces that "we're going in for coverage." It is always best to start with the widest shots and move in step-by-step. This works best for lighting and grip but it is also easier to match the action in close-ups as it was established in the wider shots. In this regard, the master "sets" the scene; once something is done in the master it is part of the continuity. Once you have a buy take of the master, that is the template for all later action, dialog and coverage.

In the case of this scene we'll probably want to go the two-shot next. The two-shot is a frame which just includes the two charac-ters. In the case of three characters, it's a three-shot. A two-shot from the side with the two characters facing each other is called a 50-50. Next comes the over-the-shoulders. A true over-the-shoulder includes something of the foreground actor, sometimes just a little piece and sometimes most of the head and shoulder. Moving in so that none of the foreground actor is visible is called a clean single. It's a close-up and still from the subjective angle.

After that comes close-ups. As mentioned above, sometimes you can just go to a longer lens and stay in the same position — this is called "punching in." More often, it is necessary to move in and have the foreground actor move aside to make room for the camera. It is always desirable to have the actor doing the dialog be able to have the foreground actor feed him the lines.

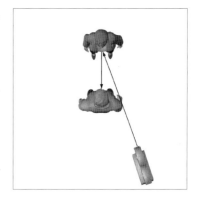

EYELINE

This presents one problem: now the eyeline will be wrong because the off-screen actor can't physically be in the right position. The eyeline is the actor's direction of look in relation to the lens axis. The eyeline in the over-the-shoulder was very close to the lens because the actor speaking was looking into the eyes of the foreground actor and their head was very near the lens (Figure 1.41).

It's a matter of angles. Even though the foreground actor's head is still very close to the lens because we are closer, the angular difference will be greater. When moving from a wider shot to a tight CU, the actual eyeline is rarely the correct eyeline: it won't look right on film. There is a geometrical reason for this as shown in Figures 1.38, 1.39 and 1.40.

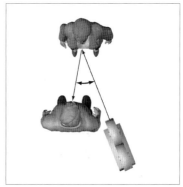

In practice, the correct line is often very close to the lens, so close in fact that a mark is sometimes placed inside the matte box. It is always a good a idea to make a mark where the actor's eyeline should be when it is not in the other actor's eyes. This prevents his eyes from wandering or not being consistent from take to take. This is a cheat, of course. In the end it often up to the camera operator who has the best view through the viewfinder to give the final word on whether the eyeline looks correct or not. It's a judgment call and demands experience to get it right.

Eyeline may also refer to the direction of the actor's look in a POV shot or a reaction shot. Since we are often filming the actor entirely separately from the actual thing she is looking at or reacting to, it is crucial for the director and DP to work out the imaginary geography of the scene and give the actor a reference so that the eyeline will be correct.

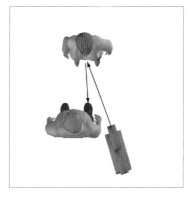

As above, it is important to give the actor a mark of some kind for her to fix her gaze on. It is also important that no crew member or actor not involved in the scene stand too close to an actor's eyeline. If someone does, there is a danger that the actor will catch the eye of the crewmember, and it will cause them to take an incorrect eyeline.

1.38, **1.39** and **1.40**. As the camera moves in for tighter coverage, the lens must be closer to the eyeline axis. If it doesn't, the geometry will force the eyeline on screen to seem to be moving farther off-axis.

TURNAROUND

Obviously you would never do the over-the-shoulder on one actor, then move the camera to do the OTS on the other actor, then go back to the first for the close-up and so on. This would be very inefficient and time consuming. So naturally you do all the coverage on one side then move the camera and reset the lighting. This is called the turnaround. The turnaround is where we get all the answering shots.

After window and door matching, the turnaround is the other major area where cheating is employed, in cases where some physical obstacle precludes a good camera position for the turnaround, or perhaps the sun is at a bad angle or maybe it's a complex lighting setup and there simply isn't time to break it down and re-light for the answering shot. If the backgrounds were neutral or largely in darkness, this final step would not have been necessary. This is important because often the purpose of cheating the turnaround is to avoid a major re-light. Moving everything over a couple of feet would involve some re-lighting — not much, but perhaps more than you can afford, time-wise — see Figure 1.42.

1.41. (a, b and c) Top: eyeline too far from the lens. Middle: correct eyeline. Bottom: eyeline on wrong side of lens.

PREPLANNING COVERAGE

Which brings us to another key point which is easily overlooked: whenever you are setting up a master, take a moment to think about the coverage that will come later. Make sure that there is some way to position the camera for proper answering shots. It is very easy to get yourself backed into a corner or up against an obstruction that makes it difficult or impossible to position the camera for a proper answering shot.

Remember that ideally, an answering shot should be the same focal length, focus distance and angle as the shot it is paired with. In a pinch, if you can't get quite far back enough (or close enough) you can cheat a bit with a different focal length to end up with the same image size, which is by far the most important parameter. The first choice, however, is to always match everything.

The second possibility is to cheat the actors out a bit. For over-the-shoulders and close-ups, it is usually only necessary to have them move a few feet. They will be in a slightly different position in the room, but normally this will not be noticeable. Like many issues of continuity, it is a question of judgment and experience as to how much you can cheat. An example is shown in Figure 1.42.

PLÁN SCENE

The master scene method is not, however, the only way to shoot a scene. Another approach is called plán scene. A French film term, plán scene is played out as a choreographed single shot. This is in essence shooting the whole scene as a master, but calling it a master implies that there is going to be coverage, whereas plán scene anticipates none. This form of shooting was normal in Hollywood films up till the 60s and is still used quite a bit in television. In both cases it is not unusual to have the camera just pan back and forth as characters cross the room. Both of these situations are much more accepting of the proscenium style of viewing the scene

This scene from Kubrick's *Paths of Glory* employs plán scene as a device to illuminate character (Figure 1.42). Here, in the grand chateau that serves as the general's headquarters, the camera follows as the generals move in curving, deviating paths. As one general seduces the other into following an unwise and unethical course of action, he "dances" him around the room. Because the camera moves do not exactly echo their movements, we get a much greater sense of the devious, slippery nature of their movements. This is in strong contrast to the movements of Kirk Douglas (the straight arrow hero of the film). Whenever we see him, he moves in straight lines: purposeful and direct — clearly an honest man.

TOUCH OF EVIL

Another example of plán scene is the opening scene of *Touch of Evil*. In this Orson Welles tour-de-force, we are introduced to most of the main characters, the story is set-up, backstory is introduced, most of the important exposition of the story is accomplished effortlessly, a great deal of the landscape used in the rest of the story is established, there is a mini-suspense story and finally a dramatic car explosion. All of this done is one long gracefully choreographed and elegantly performed tracking, craning, panning and tilting shot.

The Shot

The picture's most remarkable photographic feat is its opening scene, an unbroken 3 1/4-minute rolling crane shot. The action covers several blocks of downtown Venice, California (dressed to look like a rundown Mexican border town) from an amazing array of angles, including close-ups, low tracking shots, very long shots and bird's-eye views (Figures 1.43 thru 1.46).

The sequence begins with a close-up of a time bomb in a man's hands as the clock is being set. The camera swings up as the culprit looks down the street to see if anyone is coming, pulls back as the man runs to the right, and follows his shadow along a building wall to a convertible parked behind the building. This anonymous man puts the bomb in the trunk of the convertible and runs away as a man and a woman emerge from the back door of a nightclub and climb into the vehicle.

Pulling away from camera, the car circles behind the building as the camera moves to a high angle to show it pulling out on the far side and turning right onto the street. The camera then races past and ahead of the car, craning down to eye level and panning back as the car moves toward the lens. Newlyweds Vargas (Charlton Heston) and his wife (Janet Leigh) cross the street in front of the car, and the camera moves close to follow them as they walk ahead of the auto.

1.42. Plán scene and camera movement combine to help tell the story by giving us clues about the devious, slippery nature of these French generals in *Paths of Glory* (United Artists, 1959).

The camera again moves ahead, to the American side of the checkpoint. The guard and the driver chat with Vargas, congratulating him for nabbing a local crime boss while the female passenger complains that she hears a ticking sound. After the auto passes them, the camera moves in close and picks up the conversation between Vargas and his new bride, "Do you realize I haven't kissed you in over an hour?" As they draw close, a terrific explosion occurs off-screen left. Only then is there a cut, to the Vargas' view of the exploding convertible. We can be sure there were big smiles and lots of backslapping after they had a "buy" take on that one.

This brings us to the question: what is the *cinematic* purpose of this elaborate and difficult shot? The answer is surprisingly simple: for the entire three and a half minutes, during all the introductions, the discussion, the business and incidental dialog — there is a bomb ticking! Notice that in the first frame (Figure 1.43) the timer of the bomb in set in tight close-up. The entire sequence is paid off by the first cut away from the shot as the car explodes nearby (Figure 1.46). By not cutting away, by not employing any elliptical cuts or transitions, not even a simple close-up to introduce a character — the scene never lets us go.

1.43, **1.44**, **1.45** and **1.46**. (below) Individual frames from the opening sequence of *Touch of Evil* (Universal Pictures, 1958).

There is no subconscious escape hatch for the viewer, no possibility of trickery, not unlike the magician saying "nothing up my sleeve." We know that bomb is ticking and we clearly saw that the timer was set for just a few minutes. Thus Welles employs the long take (or plán scene method) as a technique of building and maintaining dramatic tension in the most direct and engaging way: all the while serving all of the various other story purposes we have mentioned.

HITCHCOCK'S RULE
The scene also contains an excellent example of what we will call "Hitchcock's Rule," so called because it was Alfred Hitchcock who first delineated it in his discussions with Francois Truffaut in the book *Hitchcock/Truffaut*. The rule is:

> The size of an object in the frame should equal its importance in the story at that moment.

Here, as Quinlan takes out the gun, the entire tone of the scene changes (Figure 1.47). Grandi has thought he was a co-conspirator with Quinlan; it is at this moment that he realizes he is to be the victim. The low wide angle with the camera placed just beside Quinlan emphasizes the gun, but shows the victim in the same shot.

Welles had used the same method in an earlier film, *The Lady From Shanghai*, where he is the victim rather than the aggressor (Figure 1.48). In that scene, the gun is also crucial. He is to fire the gun to draw attention and get himself arrested for a murder that did not occur. He seems to realize he is the victim of a cruel plot, but he fires the gun anyway.

1.47. (above) An example of Hitchcock's rule in *Touch of Evil*.

1.48. (right) *The Lady From Shanghai*.

Most of the picture consists of hard-lit night scenes with jagged, opaque shadows and, toward the end, a few Dutch tilts. Day exteriors were done without fill lights. A few auto interiors were filmed on the process stage, but most were done on location with the camera mounted on the car.

TRIPLE TAKE OR OVERLAPPING METHOD

Although the master scene method is by far the most common type of shooting in narrative filmmaking, it is not the only way. The simplest type of shooting is what is called the triple take or overlapping method.

Let's hypothesize a basic scene: a woman walks in the door, sits at her desk, answers the phone, then leaves.

If you do it with the overlapping method, nothing is repeated (aside from blown takes). First you set up and photograph her coming in the door, making sure that you take the action further than you actually need for that shot. For example following her to the desk and sitting down even though you know you don't need the last part of the shot.

You then set up and shoot her coming toward the desk, sitting down and answering the phone. You overlap again, starting the shot before where you really need it to begin and ending it after where you think you need it to stop. This overlapping is essential, it ensures that the editor will be able to make smooth cuts that flow together naturally, without "jump cuts" where there is a gap in the action.

You continue this overlapping until the scene is done. It is a simple, straightforward methods that gives you the scene you need with minimum complications and maximum efficiency. Obviously, there is little room for artistic treatment and subtlety. It is most often used in industrials, in-house productions and documentaries. This method is often used in industrial films where you are shooting something that can't be repeated.

Let's take an industrial example: a grinding machine is shaping a large metal part. It's the real part, it's very expensive, they're only making one and the factory is on a tight schedule. Clearly there is no chance of shooting a whole master all the way to the end, then starting over again to get coverage. The only factor that can be controlled is that the machine can be stopped and started.

Shooting would then go like this: you set up for a wide shot showing the factory and interior, then you go for another wide shot showing the featured machine, hopefully including some of the previous wide shot to clearly establish where the machine is and that we are still in the same scene.

You hold on this wide shot as the metal blank is fitted into the machine, then you ask them to stop.

They hold everything while you go in for a medium shot showing the machine and the men working on it. It's always good to get some shots of smiling workers — they love it and so does the company PR department. (It will also make the rest of your day go easier — everybody loves to be a star and they will be far more likely to co-operate with you even if it means a disruption in their workday). This shot continues as they fit it in place and prepare it.

You again ask for a halt and set up a tighter shot just showing hands making the final preparations. If you're lucky maybe you can continue this shot as you tilt down to a hand switching the machine on. Again a halt. It is very possible that the workers may be getting a little annoyed by now — another reason to be sure you've already done a few shots that their family will be proud of.

And so on like this. You may need to stop the machine to set up certain tricky close-ups or go back to a wider shot, but if the process takes ten or twenty minutes you can also let it run while you make smaller camera position, lighting or lens changes.

Finally you'll ask them to stop while you go back to a high wide shot for the finishing and removal of the finished piece. And there you have it. You have complete coverage and all the angles you want on a process that can't be rehearsed or repeated.

If you're shooting something like this that can't be stopped it's a free for all. Just hope you've got a hot shot camera assistant and on-the-ball grip and gaffer with you who aren't the kind to melt under pressure: it gets pretty hectic and tense in these situations, there's a lot at stake and it's critical not to panic. The adrenaline level runs high on these kinds of shoots but when you nail it's usually high-fives all around.

MONTAGE

Another method is montage or compile cutting. Montage consists of a series of shots which may not be related to each other in terms of screen direction, continuity, subject, character, lighting or anything else but they do share a common thematic element (the railroad moves forward), mood (the city sleeps as torrential rain falls) or poetic semi-narrative: nature awakens as spring approaches.

Montage is generally only useful for short sequences in narrative storytelling. It can be useful informational work such as documentaries or industrials but most often just for short sequences to establish a mood or give an overall impression of a process or situation.

The early Russian filmmakers were much enamoured of montage: they believed that the sequence and length of the shots were as important as the content, it fit in well with their social theory that all aspects of life can be reduced to mechanical rules. Their definition of montage was somewhat more complex than is discussed here.

This view of shots as mechanical pieces in themselves still applies in experimental or "pure art" films and clearly the editing and pacing of a film is one of it's most critical cinematic aspects — something which adds additional layers of meaning and effect to the content of a scene, but in narrative film, pure montage has limited uses outside of "scene setting," "mood building" or "passage of time" sequences.

The mechanistic approach to filmmaking which places the highest value of duration and sequence of shots is explored in Peter Green-away's great short film *Vertical Features Remake* which simultane-ously lampoons the genre and is at the same time one of the finest examples of it.

CONCLUSION: A MIXTURE OF TECHNIQUES
Of course none of these definitions of shooting techniques are set in stone, there are always variations, permutations and combinations of all of these techniques. Most well-made films use more than one shooting technique, depending on the requirements of the scene, the location, etc.

In the end, it is up to the director and the cinematographer to work together to find the appropriate methods staging each shot and shoot-ing each scene.

visual language

MORE THAN JUST A PICTURE

Let's think of the frame as more than just a "picture" — it is information. Clearly some parts of the information are more important than others and we want this information to be perceived by the viewer in a certain order — we want the information organized in a particular way. Composition is how this is accomplished. Through composition we are telling the audience where to look, what to look at and in what order to look at it. The frame is fundamentally two dimensional design. 2-D design is about guiding the eye and directing the attention of the viewer in an organized manner that conveys the meaning that you wish to impart. It is how the artist imposes a point of view on the material that may be different from how others see it.

If all we did was simply photograph what is there in exactly the same way everyone else sees it, the job could be done by a robot camera; there would be no need for the cinematographer, videographer or editor. An image should convey meaning, mode, tone, atmosphere and subtext on its own — without regard to voice-over, dialog, audio or other explanation. This was in its purest essence in silent film, but the principle still applies: the images must stand on their own.

Good composition reinforces the way in which the mind organizes information. In some cases it may deliberately run counter to how the eye/brain combination works in order to add a new layer of meaning or ironic comment. Composition selects and emphasizes elements such as size, shape, order, dominance, hierarchy, pattern, resonance and discordance in ways which give meaning to the things being photographed that goes beyond the simple: "here they are." We will start with the very basic rules of visual organization then move on to more sophisticated concepts of 2-D and 3-D design and visual language. The principles of design and visual communication are a vast subject; here we will just touch on the basics in order to lay the foundation for discussion.

2.1. (previous page) Caravaggio's *The Calling of St. Matthew (1600)*. See a disscussion of this painting also in the chapter on *Lighting As Storytelling*. (Reproduction courtesy of San Luigi dei Francesi, Rome.)

2.2. In its own way, this frame from the finale of *The Big Combo* (Allied Artist, 1955) is as much of a unified visual composition as is the Caravaggio. It is not only graphically strong, but the many visual elements all work together to reinforce and add subtext to the story content of the scene.

2.3. (above) Balance plays a key role in visual tension.

2.4. (left) An unbalanced frame from *The Third Man* (London Film Prod., 1949). It both creates visual tension appropriate to the tone of the scene and also draws the viewer's mind to what is off-screen.

DESIGN PRINCIPLES

Certain basic principles pertain to all types of visual design, whether in film, photography, painting or drawing. These principles work interactively in various combinations to add depth, movement and visual force to the elements of the frame.

UNITY

Unity is the principle that the visual organization be a "whole," self-contained and complete. This is true even if it is a deliberately chaotic or unorganized "informal" composition. In Figure 2.1, Caravaggio's powerful composition uses elements of line, color, positive/negative space, chiaroscuro and other visual elements to tell a visual story that is powerful and subtle at the same time. In Figure 2.2, this climactic final shot from *The Big Combo* uses simple, graphic frame-within-a-frame composition to tell the story visually: having defeated the bad guy in a shoot out, the hero and heroine emerge from the darkness into the light — both are completely unified designs.

BALANCE

Visual balance is an important part of composition. Every element in a visual composition has a visual weight. These may be organized into a balanced or unbalanced composition. The visual weight of

2.5. (below) Visual rhythm.

2.6. (left) Rhythm with an ironic twist in this shot from Stanley Kubrick's *Killer's Kiss* (MGM/UA, 1955).

2.7. Many elements of visual design work together to make this extremely powerful shot from *The Conformist* (Marianne Production/ Paramount Pictures, 1970).

an object is primarily determined by its size but is also affected by its position in the frame, its color and the subject matter itself. A number of factors can be used to create a balanced or unbalanced visual field.

VISUAL TENSION
The interplay of balanced and unbalanced elements and their placement in the frame can create visual tension, which is important in any composition which seeks to avoid boring complacency (Figure 2.4). Visual tension plays a role even in composition which is balanced and formal, such as Figure 2.3.

RHYTHM
Rhythm of repetitive or similar elements can create patterns of organization. Rhythm plays a key role in the visual field, sometimes in a very subtle way as in Figures 2.5 and 2.6 and 2.7.

PROPORTION
Classical Greek philosophy expressed the idea that mathematics was the controlling force of the universe and that it was expressed in visual forces in the Golden Mean. The Golden Mean is just one way of looking at proportion and size relationships in general.

CONTRAST
We know a thing by its opposite. Contrast is a function of the light/ dark value, the color and texture of the objects in the frame and the lighting. It is an important visual component in defining depth, spatial relationships and of course carries considerable emotional and storytelling weight as well.

TEXTURE
Based on our associations with physical objects and cultural factors, texture gives perceptual clues. If we can perceive a great deal of texture, we know that an object must be relatively close, as the farther away something is, the less we can perceive its texture. Texture is a function of the objects themselves, but usually requires lighting to bring it out as in Figure 2.8.

DIRECTIONALITY

One of the most fundamental of visual principles is directionality. With a few exceptions, everything has some element of directionality. This directionality is a key element of its visual weight, which determines how it will act in a visual field and how it will affect other elements. Anything that is not symmetrical is directional.

2.8. (top) In this shot from *The Conformist*, texture and contrast are emphasized and reinforced by lighting.

2.9. (above) Lighting, perspective, choice of lens and camera position combine to give this Gregg Toland shot tremendous depth.

2.10. Overlap in a composition from the noir film classic *The Big Combo*.

THE THREE-DIMENSIONAL FIELD

In any form of photography, we are taking a three-dimensional world and projecting it onto a two dimensional frame. A very big part of our jobs in directing and shooting is this essential idea of creating a three dimension world out of two-dimensional images. It calls into play a vast array of techniques and methods, not all of them purely design oriented, as we shall see later. There are, of course, times when we wish to flatten the perception of space and make the frame more two-dimension; in that case the same principles apply, they are just used in a different fashion.

DEPTH

Except where a perception of flat space is the goal, we are often trying to create a perception of depth within what is actually a flat two-dimensional space. There are a number of ways to create the illusion of depth in a two dimensional field: figure 2.9 shows great depth in a visual field.

- Overlap
- Size change
- Vertical location
- Horizontal location
- Linear perspective
- Foreshortening
- Chiaroscuro
- Atmospheric perspective

OVERLAP

Overlap clearly establishes front/back relationships; something "in front of" another thing is clearly closer to the observer; as in this frame from the noir classic *The Big Combo* (Figure 2.10).

RELATIVE SIZE

Although the eye can be fooled, the relative size of an object is an important visual clue to depth, as in Figure 2.11. Relative size is the key component of many optical illusions and a key compositional element in manipulating the viewer's unconscious perception of the subject. It is, of course, the main element of Hitchcock's rule as discussed in the chapter *Filmspace*.

2.11. (top) Relative size is key in this shot from *High Noon*, but clearly linear perspective and overlap also play a role.

2.12. (above) Kubrick uses linear perspective to convey a sense of the rigid military and social structure in *Paths of Glory* (United Artists, 1957).

2.13. Chiaroscuro is what makes this shot from *The Black Stallion* mysterious and engaging. (United Artists, 1979.)

2.14. Chiaroscuro usually involves a high contrast ratio.

2.15. Foreshortening is especially noticeable with the human form.

VERTICAL LOCATION
Gravity is a factor is visual organization; the relative vertical position of objects is a depth cue. This is particularly important in the art of Asia, which has not traditionally relied on linear perspective as it is practiced in Western art. See the chapter on *Lens Language* for an example of how Akira Kurosawa translates this concept in his use of lenses.

LEFT/RIGHT
Largely a result of cultural conditioning, the eye tends to scan from left to right. This has an ordering effect on the visual weight of elements in the field. It is also critical to how the eye scans a frame and thus the order of perception and movement in the composition.

LINEAR PERSPECTIVE
Linear perspective as we know it today was an invention of the Renaissance. The architect and artist Leon Battista Alberti (1406-1472) first formulated the rules of constructing perspective drawings, elaborating on earlier observations by Brunelleschi. He also formulated the theory that beauty is harmony. For us in film and video photography, it is not necessary to know the formal rules of perspective (except in some cases in visual effects work and shooting for front or rear projection) but it is important to recognize its importance in visual organization. Kubrick uses it to reinforce the rigid, formal nature of French society and military in Figure 2.12, a frame from *Paths of Glory*.

FORESHORTENING
Foreshortening is a phenomenon of the optics of the eye (Figure 2.15). Since things that are closer to the eye appear larger than those farther away, when part of an object is much closer than the rest of it, the visual distortion gives us clues as to depth and size.

CHIAROSCURO
Italian for light (chiara) and shadow (scouro, same Latin root as obscure), chiaroscuro, or gradations of light and dark (Figure 2.14), establishes depth perception and creates visual focus. Since dealing with lighting is one of our major tasks, this is an important consider-

ation in our work. Figure 2.13 is a shot from *The Black Stallion.* See also Figure 2.1 — Caravaggio, is of course, one of the great masters of chiaroscuro.

ATMOSPHERIC PERSPECTIVE

Atmospheric perspective (sometimes called aerial perspective) is something of a special case as it is an entirely "real world" phenomenon. Objects that are a great distance away will have less detail, less saturated colors and generally be less defined than those that are closer. Most of this is a result of the image being filtered through more atmosphere and haze. Haze filters out some of the long (warmer) wavelengths, leaving more of the shorter, bluer wavelengths. Its most immediate application in film and video is often seen when shooting with backdrops or translights (very large transparencies used as backgrounds). Often they will have too much detail, which gives away the fact that they are close to us and not real. The solution is to fly a large net between the back of the set and the translight. This decreases detail and creates the perception of haze. See Figure 2.16.

FORCES OF VISUAL ORGANIZATION

All of these basic elements can then be deployed in various combinations to create a hierarchy of perception: they can create an organization of the visual field which makes the composition coherent and guides the eye and the brain as it puts the information together. These include:

THE LINE

The line, either explicit or implied, is a constant in visual design. It is powerful in effect and multifaceted in its use. Just a few simple lines can organize a two-dimensional space in a way that is comprehensible by the eye/brain (Figure 2.17) The types of line are many, but there are a few that deserve special mention for their importance in visual organization.

2.16. Atmospheric perspective is an important element of this shot from *City of Last Children* (Studio Canal+, 1995) not only for the sense of sadness and isolation but also because it is a set built in a studio. Without the sense of atmospheric perspective added by the smoke and backlight, it is doubtful the illusion would hold up so well.

2.17. (below) The brain organizes these simple lines into something meaningful.

2.18. (bottom) The sinuous S; a specialized type of line that has a long history in visual art.

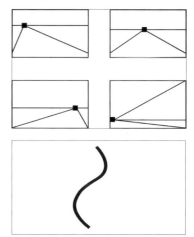

2.19. (top) Line as form and movement in this frame from *Seven Samurai*.

2.20. (above) The classic sinuous S in this shot from *The Black Stallion*.

THE SINUOUS LINE

The sinuous line, which is sometimes referred to as the "reverse S," is a constantly recurring theme in visual art (Figure 2.18) and has been since it was used extensively as a compositional principle by the Classical Greek artists; it has a distinctive harmony and balance all its own, as seen in these examples from *The Black Stallion* and *Seven Samurai* (Figures 2.19 and 2.21).

COMPOSITIONAL TRIANGLES

As with the sinuous curve, triangles are a powerful compositional tool. Once you start looking for them, you will see compositional triangles everywhere — they are a fundamental tool of visual organization. Figure 2.22 is a frame from *The Big Sleep*, an outstanding

2.21. (left) The sinuous S and its use in Kurosawa's *Seven Samurai*. As we will discuss in *Lens Language,* the use of a long lens is also an element in bringing out this pure line element of the composition.

2.22. (left below) Compositional triangles in the film noir classic *The Big Sleep*. (Warner Bros., 1946.)

example of the noir genre. The compositional triangles keep the frame active even through a fairly long expositional scene.

HORIZONTALS, VERTICALS AND DIAGONALS

The basic lines are always a factor in almost any type of composi-tions. Nearly infinite in variety, they always come back to the basics: horizontal, vertical and diagonal. Lines may be explicit, as in these shots from *Seven Samurai* (Figure 2.19 and 2.23) or implied in the arrangement of objects and spaces.

THE HORIZON LINE AND VANISHING POINT

Our innate understanding of perspective lends a special association to lines which are perceived as horizon lines, lines of perspective and vanishing point. Figure 2.16 shows how ingrained the horizon line is in our perception: three simple lines on white space are enough to suggest it.

THE POWER OF THE EDGE: THE FRAME

As we visually identify an object or group of objects in a frame, we are also subconsciously aware of the frame itself. The four edges of the frame have a visual force all their own. Objects that are close to the frame are visually associated with it and viewed in relation to it

2.23. (above) Vertical and diagonal lines in *Seven Samurai*.

2.24. (right) Verticals and horizontals in this shot from *JFK* (Warner Bros., 1991) are especially strong given the wide screen aspect ratio. Notice also how the unbalanced frame and negative space on the right side are especailly important to the composition. Imagine if they had framed only the "important elements" on the left. It would not be nearly as strong a composition and would not work nearly so well for wide screen.

2.25. (right, below) Diagonal lines are crucial to this shot from *The Conformist*.

more than if they are farther away. The frame's field of forces exerts visual weight on the objects within the frame and any grouping of elements in the frame are affected by it, even more so as the objects or groups of objects are very close to or even overlapping the edge. The frame also plays an important role in making us aware of those spaces off-frame: left/right, up/down and even the space behind the camera — all part of the filmspace of the entire composition and crucial to making the visual experience more three-dimensional.

OPEN AND CLOSED FRAME
This is particularly true in the case of an open or closed frame. An open frame is one in which one or more of the elements either pushes the edge or actually crosses the edge (Figure 2.26). A closed frame is one in which the elements are comfortably contained within the frame (Figure 2.27). Although we look at the frames here as still photographs, most frames of a motion picture are dynamic.

2.26. (top) An open frame composition from *Seven Samurai*.

2.27. (above) Closed frame composition: *Dr. Strangelove* (Columbia/Tristar, 1961).

2.28. (right) Negative space and unbalanced composition in *The Black Stallion*.

2.29. (top) Formal composition from *Days of Heaven* (Paramount Pictures, 1978).

2.30. (above) Frame within a frame: *Killer's Kiss*.

2.31. The rule of thirds.

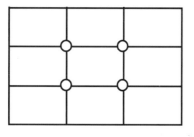

FRAME WITHIN A FRAME
Sometimes the composition demands a frame that is different from the aspect ratio of the film. In this case, filmmakers often resort to a "frame within a frame" as in this example from *Killer's Kiss* (Figure 2.30). Frame within a frame is an especially important tool when working in a wide format such 2.35:1 or High Def — 1.77:1.

BALANCED AND UNBALANCED FRAME
We touched on balance before; now let's look at it in the context of the frame. Any composition may be balanced or unbalanced. This can be further broken down in to balanced/formal, balanced/informal, unbalanced/formal and unbalanced/informal. This shot from *Dr. Strangelove* (Figure 2.27) is both a closed frame and also a formal/balanced composition. Using formal geometry to comment on social structure is a constant in Kubrick's work; see also examples from *Barry Lyndon*, *Killer's Kiss* and *Paths of Glory* in this and other chapters. See also Figures 2.29 and 2.30.

POSITIVE AND NEGATIVE SPACE
The visual weight of objects or lines of force can create positive space, but their absence can create negative space, as in this frame from *The Black Stallion* (Figure 2.28). The elements that are "not there" and thus unseen have a visual weight as well. In the frame from *The Third Man* (Figure 2.4) the off screen look suggests that unseen and unknown elements are at play in the story — which is, of course, about a mysterious and unknowable city.

MOVEMENT IN THE VISUAL FIELD
All of these forces work in combination, of course — in ways that interact to create a sense of movement in the visual field. There are also cultural factors which influence our understanding of space. One of many is that in Western culture we read from left to right and from top to bottom. This influences how the eye moves in the frame. All of these factors combine to create a movement from front to back in a clockwise fashion and top to bottom, also usually clockwise (Figure 2.32). This movement in the frame is important not only for the composition but also plays an important role in what order the viewer perceives and assimilates the subjects in the frame. This influences their perception of content.

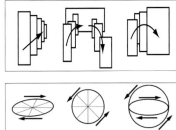

2.32 and **2.33**. (top and above) A number of forces combine to create movement in the visual field.

2.34. (left) Strong movement in the frame reinforces character relationships and subtext in this shot from *Seven Samurai*.

FILM AND VIDEO COMPOSITION

The film and video frame have some of their own broad rules of composition that have become generally accepted rules of thumb — as with all such guidelines, the exceptions are nearly as numerous as the application. In general, all of the visual forces we have discussed so far apply to composition in film and video. There are also a few special cases specific to composition of the moving image which deserve mention.

Often we work instinctively on the set and "fiddling around till it looks good on the monitor" has become a dangerous bad habit. It is perfectly possible to work this way, but being able to think out and preplan a composition in advance is time saving and can be indispensable if the camera had to be pre-rigged in a position before the action.

THE RULE OF THIRDS

The rule of thirds starts by dividing the frame into thirds (Figure 2.31). Again, a ratio of one third to two thirds approximates the Golden Mean. The rule of thirds proposes that a useful approximate starting point for any compositional grouping is to place major points of interest in the scene on any of the four intersections of the interior lines.

MISCELLANEOUS RULES OF COMPOSITION

If ever there were rules made to be broken, they are the rules of composition, but it is important to understand them before deviating or using them in a contrary style.

Don't cut off their feet — generally, a frame should end somewhere around the knees or include the feet. Cutting them off at the ankles will look awkward; likewise, don't cut off their hands at the wrist — this is especially disturbing. Naturally, a character's hand will often dart in and out of the frame as the actor moves and gestures, but for a long static shot, they should be clearly in or out.

Watch out for TV Safe — as video is currently broadcast, there is considerable variation in the size of the picture on the home screen. For this reason, most ground glass markings include both the entire video frame (TV broadcast) and a marking that is 10% less, called TV Safe. All important compositional elements should be kept inside TV Safe.

Heads of people standing in the background — when framing for our important foreground subjects, whether or not to include the heads of background people is a judgment call. If they are prominent enough, it is best to include them compositionally. If there is enough emphasis on the foreground subjects and the background people are strictly incidental or perhaps largely out of focus, it is OK to cut them off wherever is necessary.

If the situation does call for not showing their heads, you will probably want to avoid cutting through their heads at nose level. For example, in a scene where two people are dining, if the waiter approaches and asks them a question, you clearly have to show all of the waiter. If the waiter is not a speaking role and he is merely pouring some water, it would be acceptable just to show him from the shoulders down, as the action with his arm and hands is what is relevant to the scene.

BASIC COMPOSITION RULES FOR PEOPLE

HEADROOM

Certain principles apply particularly to photographing people, particularly in a medium shot or close-up. First is headroom — the amount of space above the head. Too much headroom makes the figure seem to be lost in the frame. Headroom is also wasted compositionally as it is often just sky or empty wall — it adds no information to the shot and may draw the eye away from the central subject. The convention is to leave the least amount of headroom that doesn't make the head seem to be crammed against the top of the frame. As the close-up gets bigger, it becomes permissible to leave even less headroom. Once the shot becomes a choker, you can even give the character a "haircut," and bring the top of the frame down to the forehead. The idea is simply that the forehead and hair convey less information than the lower part of the face and neck. A head shot cut off above the eyebrows seems perfectly normal. A shot that shows the top of the head but cuts off the chin and mouth would seem very odd — unless it's a shampoo commercial.

NOSEROOM

Next is noseroom, also called "looking room." If a character is turned to the side, it's as if the gaze has a certain visual weight. As a result, we never position the head in the exact middle of the frame. Generally, the more the head is turned to the side, the more noseroom is allowed. Think of it this way: the "look" has visual weight, which must be balanced.

lens language

THE LENS AND THE FRAME

As we use the term in this book, cinematic technique means the methods and practices we use to add additional layers of meaning, nuance and emotional context to shots and scenes in addition to their objective content. The lens is one of the prime tools in achieving these means. Together with selecting the frame, it is also the area of cinematography in which the director is most heavily involved.

As we discussed in *Filmspace*, setting the frame is a series of choices which decide what the viewer will see and not see. The first of these decision is where to place the camera in relation to the scene. After that, there are choices concerning the field of vision and movement, all of which work together to influence how the audience will perceive the shot: both in outright content and in emotional undercurrent and subtext to the action and the dialog.

STATIC FRAME

A static frame is a proscenium. The action of the scene is presented as a stage show: we are a third person observer. There is a proscenium wall between us and the action. This is especially true if everything else about the frame is also normal, i.e., level, normal lens, no movement, etc. This does not mean, however, that a static frame is not without value. It can be a useful tool which carries its own baggage and implications of POV and world view.

In Stanley Kubrick's film *Barry Lyndon*, the fixed, well composed, balanced frames reflect the static, hierarchical society of the time (Figure 3.2). Everyone has his place, every social interaction is governed by well defined and universally known rules. The actors move within this frame without being able to alter it. It is a reflection of the world they live in and while it strongly implies a sense of order and tranquility, it also carries an overpowering lack of mobility: both social and physical.

This is similar to Jim Jarmusch's use of the fixed frame in *Stranger Than Paradise*. The world is static: the characters try to find their place in it. Each scene is played out completely within this fixed frame: without movement, cuts or changes in perspective. This use of the frame conveys a wealth of information independent of the script or the actions of the characters. It adds layers of meaning.

In both the examples, the distancing nature of the frame is used for its own purpose, in the Brechtian sense. The filmmakers are deliberately putting the audience in the position of the impersonal observer. This can either lend an observational, judgmental tone or much like objects in the foreground of the frame, make the audience work

3.1. (previous page) Choice of lens, lens height and placement in relation to the subject are all critical to the visual power and the introduction of a character in this shot from *Touch of Evil*.

3.2. (right) The well composed, balanced frame; the completely static camera position and the centered "head on" viewpoint all add up to reinforce the story content of a rigid social structure and a highly formalized social milieu in which the story of *Barry Lyndon* takes place.

harder to put themselves into the scene, or a combination of both. As with almost all cinematic techniques they can be used "in reverse" to achieve a completely different effect than normal.

FOREGROUND/MIDGROUND/BACKGROUND

As we discussed in *Filmspace*, one of the key elements of film is that we are projecting 3-dimensional space onto a 2-dimensional plane. Except in rare cases where we want this flatness, it is the job of the filmmakers to re-invent the depth that existed in the original scene or manipulate it in a way that serves the purpose of the scene.

In the book *Hitchcock/Truffaut*, Hitchcock makes the point that a basic rule of camera position and staging is that the importance of an object in the story should equal its size in frame. We see that principal employed in this shot from *The Lady From Shanghai* (Figure 3.4). The gun is what is important in the scene, so Welles uses a low camera angle, a wide lens and positioning to feature the gun prominently in the frame.

LENS PERSPECTIVE

WIDE LENSES AND EXPANSION OF SPACE

As we discussed in the previous chapter, the fundamental aspect of the frame is that it constitutes a selection of what the audience is going to see. Some things are included and some are excluded. The first decision is always where the camera goes in relation to the subject. But this is only half of the job. Once the camera position is set there is still a decision to be made as to how much of that view is to be included. This is the job of lens selection.

Normal human vision, including peripheral, extends to around 180°. Foveal vision, which is more able to perceive detail, is around 40°. In 35mm film, the 50mm is generally considered the normal lens, equivalent to a 25mm in 16mm film. In fact, something around a 40mm is closer to typical vision. In video, the normal lens varies depending on the size of the video receptor. The focal length of a lens is significant in another way in addition to its field of view. Again, remember that all optics (including the human eye) work by projecting the three-dimensional world onto a two-dimensional plane. Lenses in the normal range (35mm to 50mm for 35mm film) portray the depth relationships of objects in a way fairly close to human vision. Technically, a normal lens is considered to be one where the focal length equals the diagonal of the aperture.

With a wider than normal lens, depth perception is exaggerated: object appear to be farther apart (front to back) than they are in reality. This exaggerated sense of depth has psychological implications. The perception of movement towards or away from the lens is heightened; space is expanded and distant objects become much smaller. All this can give the viewer a greater sense of presence. A greater feeling of being *in* the scene — which is often a goal of the filmmaker. As the lens gets even wider, there is distortion of objects, particularly those near the lens. This is the fundamental reason why a lens longer than 100mm is considered necessary for a portrait or head shot. It's a simple matter of perspective. If you are shooting a close-up and you want to fill the frame, the longer the lens, the closer the camera will have to be. As the camera gets closer, the percentage difference in distance from the nose to the eyes increases dramatically (Table 3.1).

For example: if the tip of the nose is 30cm from the lens, then the eyes may be at 33cm, a 10% difference. With a wide lens, this is enough to cause a mismatch in size: the nose is exaggerated in size compared to the face at the plane of the eyes. With a longer than

Table 3.1. Field of view of some typical lenses. This is based on a 35mm Academy format.

18mm	76°
25mm	51°
32mm	39°
50mm	25°
85mm	14°
135mm	9°
300mm	4°
600mm	2°

3.3. (above) Extreme wide-angle optics are frequently thought of as "comedy" lenses due to the distortion and the breaking of the "fourth wall" which they often imply. (*City of Lost Children*.)

3.4. (right) The very wide lens creates a palpable space between the characters in this climactic scene in *The Lady From Shanghai*; he is heading out toward the light and she is in complete silhouette; all of which precisely underpin the exact story point at this moment in the film.

normal lens, the camera will be much farther back to achieve the same image size. In this case, the tip of the nose might be at 300cm, with the eyes at 303cm. This is a percentage difference of only 1%: the nose would appear normal in relation to the rest of the face. The same fundamental principle applies to the perception of all objects with very wide lenses (Figure 3.3).

Another aspect of wide lenses is that at a given distance and f/stop, they have greater depth-of-field. Not to get too technical here (enough of that in the chapter on *Optics*), but suffice it to say that the depth-of-field of a lens is inversely proportional to the square of its focal length. This is discussed in detail in the chapter on *Optics*, but its perceptual ramifications are very much a part of the psychology of the lens. This greater depth-of-field allows more of the scene to be in focus. This was used to great effect by master cinematographers of the 30s and 40s such as Gregg Toland, who used it to develop an entire look called deep focus, such as in the shot from *The Long Voyage Home* (Figure 2.9 in *Lens Language*). In this film and in *Wuthering Heights* (William Wyler, 1939), Toland perfected deep focus as a visual system.

DEEP FOCUS
The high point of deep focus as a storytelling tool is *Citizen Kane* (Orson Welles, 1941). According to David Cook in *A History of Narrative Film,* "Welles planned to construct the film as a series of long

3.5. A deep focus shot from *Citizen Kane*. (RKO Radio Pictures, 1941. Now owned by Turner Classic Movies). Three levels of the story are shown in the same frame.

takes, or sequence shots, scrupulously composed in depth to eliminate the necessity for narrative cutting within major dramatic scenes. To accomplish this, Toland developed for Welles a method of deep focus photography capable of achieving an unprecedented depth-of-field" (Figure 3.5).

This deep focus also facilitates composition in depth to an unprecedented degree. Throughout the film we see action in the background which compliments and amplifies what we are seeing in the background. For example, early in the film we see Mrs. Kane in the foreground, signing the agreement for Mr. Thatcher to be the young Charles Foster Kane's guardian. Throughout the scene, we see the young man through a window, playing outside with his sled even as his future is being decided (Figure 3.5).

Welles also uses the distortion of wide angle lenses for psychological effect. Frequently in the film we see Kane looming like a giant in the foreground, dwarfing other characters in the scene — a metaphor for his powerful, overbearing personality. Later, Welles uses the exaggerated distances of wide lenses to separate Kane from other characters in the scene, thus emphasizing his alienation and self-absorption.

COMPRESSION OF SPACE

At the other end of the spectrum are very long lenses. They have effects that are opposite of wide lenses: they compress space, have less depth-of-field and de-emphasize movement away from and towards the camera (Figures 3.6, 3.7 and 3.8).

This compression of space can be used for many perceptual purposes: claustrophobic tightness of space, making distance objects seem closer and heightening the intensity of action and movement. Their ability to decrease apparent distance has many uses both in composition but also in creating the psychological space.

The effect of having objects seem closer together than they really are is often used for the very practical purpose of making stunts and fight scenes appear more dramatic and dangerous than they really are. With careful camera placement and a long lens, a speeding bus can seem to miss a child on a bicycle by inches, when in fact, there is a comfortably safe distance between them.

The limited depth-of-field can be used to isolate a character in space. Even though foreground and background objects may seem closer, if they are drastically out of focus, the sense of separation is the same. This can result in a very detached, third person point of view for the shot. This detachment is reinforced by the fact that the compression of space makes more tangible the feeling that the real world is being projected onto a flat space. We perceive it more as a two-dimensional representation.

Movement toward us with a long lens is not as dynamic and therefore is abstracted. It is more of a presentation of the *idea* of movement than perceived as actual movement of the subject. This is especially effective with shots of the actors running directly towards the

3.6. (below, left) Perspective and space as affected by a very long focal length lens.

3.7. (below, middle) A normal perspective.

3.8. (below, right) Perspective and space as rendered by a very wide angle lens.

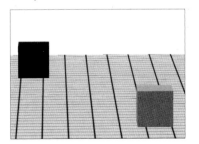
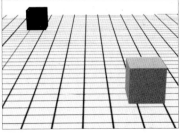
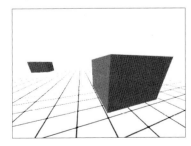

3.9. Very long lens perspective makes this shot and the action of the characters more abstracted — it is reduced to the simple idea of leaving. (*Rain Man*. United Artists, 1988).

camera; as they run toward us, there is very little change in their image size. We would normally think of this as decreasing the sense of movement, but in a way, it has the opposite effect. The same is true of slow-motion. Although shooting at a high frame rate actually slows the movement down, our perceptual conditioning tells us that the people or objects are actually moving very fast — so fast that only high speed shooting can capture them on film. Thus shooting something in slow motion and with a long lens has the ultimate effect of making the moving seem faster and more exaggerated than it really is — the brain interprets it in a way that contradicts the visual evidence (Figure 3.11).

This is an excellent example of cultural conditioning as a factor in film perception. If you showed a long lens, slow motion shot of someone running to a person who had never seen film or video before, they might not understand at all that the person is running fast. More likely they would perceive the person as almost "frozen in time," through some sort of magic.

MANIPULATING PERSPECTIVE

There are many tricks that can be used to alter the audience's perception of space. In *The Lady From Shanghai*, Welles uses a subtle and very clever trick to add subtext to the scene. In the film, Welles plays an ordinary seaman who is seduced into an affair and a murder plot by Susan Hayward. There are double and triple crosses and the Welles character is in way over his head. This scene is a meeting between him and the beautiful woman who is at the bottom of all the schemes and machinations. She asks him to meet her in an out-of-the-way public place: the aquarium. On the face of it this seems like a perfect place for them to meet without being seen by her husband or otherwise attracting attention. In fact she has a darker purpose (Figures 3.12 and 3.13).

The staging also seems perfectly straightforward. They meet and then talk while they stroll in front of the glass windows of the aquarium. Welles uses several subtle tricks to make this happy, innocent place mysterious and foreboding. First, the motivated light from the aquarium backlights them, dramatically in a classic film noir fashion. As the Welles character begins to realize the danger of the situation he is in, they move to a spot where they arc completely silhouette. When he goes in for coverage, Welles doesn't chicken out. Most directors would ask the DP to add a little light on their faces for the close-ups, but Welles actually goes darker and the close-ups are totally silhouette. The motivated lighting is also a water effect so the ripples play naturally across their faces.

The third trick is even more clever. In the wide shots, we see the fish in the aquarium: ordinary exhibition fish and turtles of one or

3.10. (below) Linear perspective and converging lines as affected by focal length.

3.11. (bottom) A very long lens shot isolates action from a crowd shot. (*Nine and 1/2 Weeks*).

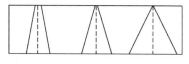

3.12. (left, top) This wide master from *The Lady From Shanghai* shows a normal perspective.

3.13. In the close-ups, Welles uses projections of the fish at ten times their normal size to introduce menace and a feeling of strangeness to the otherwise pleasant setting of the aquarium. The huge fish and the rippling motivated lighting from the water all work together to suggest that the character is "in over his head."

two feet in length. In the close-ups, however, Welles had film of the fish back-projected at a greatly enlarged size. As a result, the fish are now gigantic. Although just barely seen behind their heads, the effect is powerful, mysterious and a little frightening. In combination with the silhouette and the rippling water effects the subtext is clear: the character is in over his depth, his head is under water and he may not survive. It is a masterful stroke that is completely unnoticed by the vast majority of the audience. Like all the best technique, it does its job seamlessly and invisibly.

Kurosawa uses very long lenses in a way that is stylistically distinctive. See Figures 3.14, 3.19 and 3.20 for examples of how he uses lenses to achieve certain compositional perspectives and character relationships. Another example of lens use is the punch-in, shown in Figures 3.17 and 3.18).

SELECTIVE FOCUS

The characteristic of relative lack of depth-of-field can be used for selective focus shots. As discussed above, shallow depth-of-field can isolate the subject. The essential point is the focus as a storytelling tool. This is a drawbacks of 16mm film and High Def — they have far more depth-of-field than 35mm film, thus making it more

3.14. Kurosawa consistently uses very long lenses to form compositions and character relationships that would not be apparent with normal or wide lenses. He also employs a small f/stop for deep focus — very unusual with lenses this long. To achieve this, his cameramen had to use enormous quantities of light, even on day exteriors such as this shot from *Seven Samurai*.

3.15. This wide shot comes at the end of a chase scene in *Nine and 1/2 Weeks*; out on the town, the characters have been chased by a gang of violent thugs.

3.16. At the moment they realize they have lost their attacker, a severe lens change punches into the scene. It is a high energy cut which gets us closer so that we are experiencing the scene along with the characters rather than as an abstract, at-a-distance chase scene. We are drawn into their excitement and identify with their exhuberance. The sudden loss of depth-of-field isolates them in the landscape and gives our attenttion nowhere else to go. The punch-in changes the visual texture to match the mood and provides a perfect "button" to end the scene.

difficult to use focus as in this way. Digital video makes it almost impossible, as nearly everything is in focus, no matter what. Selective focus to concentrate attention on the character is shown in Figures 3.15 and 3.16.

Some people will say "pull back and use a longer lens" or "shoot wide open." Unfortunately these two are not always options, especially on a cramped location. Focus can also be shifted during the shot, thus leading the eye and the attention of the viewer. The term for the classic use of this is "rack focus," in which the focus is on an object in the foreground, for example, and then, on cue, the camera assistant radically changes the focus so that the focus shifts dramatically to another subject either in front of or behind the original subject. Occasionally a director will ask for a dramatic rack focus when the situation does not lend itself to the technique; especially when there is not enough of a focus change to make the effect noticeable. In this case it may just look like sloppy focus pulling.

Also with tracking shots that are very tight and close (as in table top shooting), we can watch as objects come into view, then slowly come into focus then go soft again. Selective focus and out-of-focus can also be highly subjective visual metaphors for the influence of

3.17. (near right) A medium shot from *The Third Man*.

3.18. (far right) A classic punch-in; very little changes except that we get closer and more intimate with the character. The term punch-in usually refers to switching to a longer lens, but some directors will use the term to mean moving the camera straight forward on the lens axis.

drugs or madness, as well. The bottom line is that focus is an important storytelling tool.

Another issue in selective focus is when two or more players are in the same shot but at different distances. If you don't have much t/stop, it may be necessary for the focus-puller to chose one or the other to be in focus. This is up to the DP or director to decide and they should consult before the shot — and don't forget to let the focus puller know.

A few basic rules of thumb:

- Focus goes to the person speaking. It is permissible to rack back and forth if they both do dialog.
- Focus goes to the person facing the camera or most prominent in the frame.
- Focus goes to the person experiencing the most dramatic or emotional moment. This may countermand the principal of focusing on the person speaking.
- If there is doubt or if the actors don't hit their marks, most camera assistants put the focus on the actor who has the lower number on the call sheet.

This may sound frivolous but it's not. Call sheets list the actors in numbered order of their characters. The lead is actor #1, etc. If you are playing it on the fly, the safe bet is to go with the actor with the lower number on the call sheet.

If they are close enough the AC may split the focus between them or very subtly rack back and forth. Major focus racks need to be discussed in advance and rehearsed. This is true of all camera moves that are motivated by dialog or action. If the AC and the operator haven't seen what the actors are going to do, it is difficult to anticipate the move just enough to time it correctly. Rehearsal is a time saver, as it usually reduces the number of blown takes.

It is interesting to note that older books on cinematography barely mention focus at all. There is a reason for this. Until the '60s, it was the established orthodoxy that pretty much everything important in the frame should be in focus. The idea of deliberately having key elements in the frame that are deliberately out of focus really didn't fully take hold until it was popularized by fashion photographers in the '80s.

3.19. (above) Japanese and Chinese traditional art do not employ linear perspective; instead they rely on above/below relationships to convey depth. (Private collection of the author.)

3.20. (left) Kurosawa almost exclusively employs very long lenses and slightly elevated points of view to render a similar type of compressed spaced. In this shot from *Seven Samurai*, we clearly see the influence of composition and perspective from Japanese prints.

3.21. (below) A normal lens keeps the background in focus; it can be distracting.

3.22. (bottom) A very long lens throws the background out of focus and the viewer's entire attention is drawn to the character.

IMAGE CONTROL

FILTRATION

Modern lenses are remarkably sharp. For the most part this is what we want. In some cases, however, we are looking for a softer image. The most frequent reason is beauty. A softer image, especially of a woman's face, will generally be prettier. A soft image may also be more romantic, dreamlike or, in a subjective shot, may translate to a state of mind less in touch with reality. A softer image can be achieved in a number of ways. Some of these are discussed in the chapter on *Image Control*; here we deal with altering the image quality with the lens and shutter only.

SOFT LENSES

Some shooters use older lenses for an image that is subtly soft in a way that is difficult to achieve with filters. Soft lenses can give a slightly greater apparent depth-of-field. This is because the fall-off from critical sharpness is somewhat masked by the softness.

Besides not being made with the latest, computer aided optical design and manufacturing, older lenses also have less sophisticated optical coatings. The coating on lenses is there primarily to prevent internal flares and reflections, which slightly degrade and soften the image. This can be seen clearly if the sun or other strong light source directly hits the lens — the internal flares and reflections are very apparent in an old lens as compared to a modern one. In a few cases, filmmakers have either used old lenses or even had the special coatings chemically stripped off of lenses to create this effect.

FLARE/GLARE

A direct, specular beam of light that hits the lens will create a flare that creates veiling glare, which appears as a sort of milky whiteness over the whole image. This is why so much attention is paid to the matte box or lens shade and why the grips are often asked to set lensers — flags that keep direct light sources from hitting the lens. There are execptions, such as in Figure 3.23.

FRAME RATE

The speed at which the film runs through the camera also has a great effect on our perception of the shot. Since film is almost always projected or transferred to video at 24 fps, running the camera at a higher speed will slow the action down and running at a lower than normal frame rate will speed the action up.

3.23. The way in which deliberate glare in the lens affects image quality is often used to put the audience in the position of someone caught in the headlights or to give the psychological feeling of someone who's vision is partially obscured — impressionistic, even surreal (*The Big Combo*).

High speed filming generally produces an image with a dreamlike, otherworldly effect. Low speed filming, which speeds the action up, is most often used for a comedy effect. The slowing effect of off-speed filming can result in a very subtle emphasis of a particular moment when the frame rate is from 26 to 28fps. Higher speeds can even further underscore and dramatize a particular moment. Scorsese used this very effectively in some of the fight scenes in *Raging Bull*; at times the camera was running at as much as 120fps, definitely high speed photography. It has always been possible to change the frame rate during a shot but now many cameras can automatically compensate exposure with the aperture or shutter, thus making "ramping" during the shot far easier. Ramping has become a popular and useful technique.

Higher frame rates are frequently used in commercials, especially in shots of water soaked vegetables dropping to the table or beer cans opening. These frame rates are generally at least 120fps or higher. 120fps can be achieved with standard cameras such as the Arri III or 435 or the Panavision Panastar II. Anything over 120fps calls for a special high-speed camera. Photo-Sonics manufactures a number of high speed cameras as does NAC. These are discussed in detail in the chapter *Technical Issues*.

3.24. (top) A very long lens on a panning shot makes the background and foreground swoosh by in an impressionistic blur.

3.25. (above) A combination of shutter speed, very wide lens and dutch tilt give this shot extra punch.

SLOW SPEED BLUR

There is a special case of off-speed filming which produces a very dramatic, blurring effect which is often used in commercials and occasionally in narrative films. The effect is achieved by running the camera slower than usual, most often at either 12 fps (frames per second) or 6 fps and then transferring to video at the same rate. The effect is blurring but the action runs at normal speed. It looks very much like it is slowed down, but it isn't (Figures 3.24, 3.25 and 3.25). The reason it works is that when the camera is run at a very low speed, the shutter is open for a much longer than normal time. Anyone with experience in still photography knows that 1/60th of a second is about the slowest you can shoot any moving subject without noticeable blurring. Shooting at six FPS makes each frame approximately 1/12th of a second.

At 24 frames per second and a typical 180° shutter, the film camera is exposing each frame for 1/50th of a second. The reason that it is acceptable to shoot at such a low speed is that, due to the persistence of vision, the frames perceptually overlap slightly and mask the

3.26. Slow speed blur is a combination of shutter angle and telecine.

3.27. This shot from *Three Kings* employs a combination high frame rate and wide shutter angle.

unsharpness. With very rapidly moving objects, the blur is apparent, but this generally reinforces the feeling of speed and energy. Blur which renders a single frame as nearly unrecognizable by itself reminds us that we are not taking still photos. As a still photograph this would not stand up itself, but as part of the scene, it is even more effective that a perfectly lit, well composed detailed photograph.

SHUTTER ANGLE

Another factor in the sharpness of an image is the shutter angle. Most film cameras run with a shutter of approximately 180°. This means that the film is being exposed for half the time and for the other half, the image is being projected into the viewing system for the operator to see. Many cameras have variable shutters. The widest standard shutter is 210°, which is not appreciably different from 180°. Closing the shutter down more and more has an effect on the image. The more closed the shutter, the shorter the exposure and therefore the sharper the image. A shutter of 90°, for example, will be a much cleaner, sharper image of any moving object. Beyond 90° there will be another effect in addition to sharpness. Since the shutter is now closed significantly longer than it is open, the subject has longer to move between exposures. This will result in a "strobe" effect with a stuttering motion effect. This was used extensively in *Saving Private Ryan, Three Kings* and other films as well as many music videos (Figure 3.27).

Changes in shutter angle can also be used in conjunction with strobe lighting such as Unilux. As in still photography, strobe lighting has the effect of "freezing" action. Details of lighting with strobes are discussed in the chapter on *Technical issues*. The ability of strobe lighting to sharpen and delineate moving images is often used in product shots of beverage cans opening or shower shots for shampoo commercials. As discussed later, pure strobe lighting can usually be too sharp. In a shower shot, for example, using strobe only makes the drops of water look like sharp needles. To moderate this effect, the strobe lighting is usually combined with a continuous source such as tungsten lighting.

TIME LAPSE

An extreme example of slow motion is time lapse photography. In time lapse, there is a significant amount of time between each exposure. As a result, the action will be speeded up considerably. Clouds will slide across the sky, day can turn to night in a few seconds or a rose can bloom in less than a minute. Time lapse is usually achieved with an intervalometer. See *Technical Issues* for information on doing the calculations to determine frame rate and duration.

LENS HEIGHT

Variations in lens height can also be an effective tool for adding subtext to a shot. As a general rule, dialog and most ordinary "people" shots are done at the eye level of the actors involved. Some filmmakers attempt to avoid using many straight on eye level shots as they consider them boring. Variations from eye level have filmspace implications, psychological undertones and are useful as a strictly compositional device.

Variations from eye level are not to be done casually, especially with dialog or reaction shots. Keep in mind that deviations from eye level are asking the viewer to participate in the scene in a mode that is very different from normal, so be sure that there is a good reason for it and that it is contributing in a way that helps the scene. This does not apply to establishing shots, in which the viewer is well accustomed to seeing the scene from above.

High Angle

When the camera is above eye height, we seem to dominate the subject. The subject is reduced in stature and perhaps in importance. Its importance is not, however, diminished if the high angle reveals it to be a massive, extensive structure, for example. This reminds us that high angles looking down on the subject reveal overall layout and scope in the case of landscape, streets or buildings. This is useful if the intent is an establishing or "expository" shot where it is important for the audience to know something about the layout.

The opposite is true for a low angle. When a character is approaching a complex or landscape as seen from a low angle, little is revealed beyond what the character might see himself — we share the character's surprise or sense of mystery. The two can be used in combination for setting up a shock or suspense effect: if the shots associated with the character are from a low angle, we share his foreboding and apprehension at not knowing.

If these are then combined with high angle shots which reveal what the character does not know, we are aware of whatever surprise or ambush or revelation awaits him: this is the true nature of suspense. As Hitchcock so brilliantly observed — there can be no real suspense unless the audience knows what is going to happen. His famous example is the bomb under the table.

If two characters sit at a table and suddenly a bomb goes off — we have a moment of surprise that is quickly over, a cheap shock at best. If the audience knows that the bomb is under the table and is aware that the timer is clicking steadily towards exploding, then there is true suspense which engages and involves the audience in a way that simple shock never can. If the audience is on the edge of their seats knowing that the time on the clock is growing shorter, then the fact that the two characters seated at the table are nattering on amiably about the weather is both maddening and engaging. The audience is drawn into the scene, frustrated by their inability to warn the people to run for their lives.

The high angle is, of course, impersonal by its very nature. As with subjective and objective camera views on the lateral plane, we can see camera angles that diverge from eye level as increasingly objective, more third person in terms of our literary analogy. This applies especially to higher angles. A very high angle is called a "God's eye view," suggesting its omniscient, removed point-of-view: distant, separate from the scene, a world view, philosophical and contemplative. We see all parts of the scene, all interacting forces equally without particularly identifying with any of them. See the example from *Fargo* in Figure 3.28.

3.28. If this shot was not done from a very high angle, it would not be so graphically strong and abstract, which are the qualities which reinforce the scene values of isolation and ominous portent. (*Fargo*, Grammercy Pictures/MGM, 1996.)

lens language

57

3.29. This very low angle from *Citizen Kane* is the scene the morning after Kane has suffered the devastation of losing the election as his affair with the singer was revealed. The low angle reinforces the feeling that the world is out of whack, nothing is normal, all is lost. The usual eye-level angles would convey none of this.

Low Angle

The same is not quite as true for low angles. Although any time we get away from human eye level we are decreasing our subjective identification with the characters, low angles can become more subjective in other ways. Clearly a very low angle can be a dog's eye view: especially if it is cut in right after a shot of the dog and then the very low angle moves somewhat erratically and in the manner of a dog. (Figures 3.30 through 3.32).

This was used very effectively in the film *Wolf*, when the character turns into a werewolf. There is a special rig, called "Doggy-cam" specifically designed for these types of shots. The relative subjectiveness of a shot relates to things for which we have a height reference: a very low lens height can be a pig's view, an eye level POV can be a stalker POV and perhaps a 7 or 8 foot lens height could be a giants or a robots POV, but beyond that we do not have a subject reference and it is no longer subjective, it is perceived by the audience as an objective view and nothing more. With low angles, the subject tends to dominate us. If the subject is a character, that actor will seem more powerful and dominant. Welles used low angles extensively in *Citizen Kane* to suggest the power and overbearing personality of the central character (Figure 3.29). Any time the actor being viewed is meant to be menacing or frightening to the character we are associating the POV with, a low angle is usually appropriate. Certainly if it is any sort of villain or monster, an eye level shot will diminish the sense of danger.

3.30 (below) and **3.31**. (bottom) In *Touch of Evil*, Welles uses this smash cut from a very low angle to a very high angle to convey disjointed frenzy juxtaposed with quiet conspiracy.

TILT

In most shooting we strive for the camera to be perfectly level. It is the job of the camera assistant and the dolly grip to recheck every time the camera is moved and ensure that it is still "on the bubble." This refers to the bulls-eye or transverse bubble levels that are standard on all camera mounts, heads and dollies.

This is crucial because human perception is much more sensitive to off-level verticals than to off-level horizontals. If the camera is even a little off, walls, doorways, telephone poles, any vertical feature will be immediately seen as out of plumb. There are instances, however, where we want the visual tension of this off-level condition to work for us to create anxiety, paranoia, subjugation or mystery. The term for this is "dutch tilt" or "dutch angle."

This is used extremely well in the mystery/suspense film *The Third*

3.32. Kubrick is a master of choosing the right angle and lens to tell the story powerfully. In this shot, the lens height and angle make a clear statement about the state of mind of the character (*Dr. Strangelove: or How I Learned to Stop Worrying and Love the Bomb*. Columbia Pictures, 1964).

Man, where at least half the shots are done with the camera off level. Orson Welles also uses it very effectively in *The Lady From Shanghai*. In this example, he is trapped in the carnival crazy house at the end of the film. He is also still under the influence of the pills he took as part of his escape from the courthouse. In this shot, the camera is tilted radically right as he enters in the distance. Then, as he crosses frame and goes through a door to a second room, the camera, instead of tracking, tilts to the opposite angle and ends with a hard left tilt (Figures 3.34 and 3.35).

This of course is entirely in keeping with the surrealistic atmosphere of the crazy house and of his deranged, drugged state of mind, but it has another advantage as well. Tracking shots which move past walls are not at all unusual. In this type of shot we track along with the character who walks through a door into the next room. The camera passes through the wall and what we see is usually a black vertical line which represents the edge of the wall which we are magically transversing.

REVEAL

As we have mentioned, what the audience does not see can be as important as what the audience does see. Camera positions and perspectives may be chosen which deliberately obscure some key object or character until the filmmaker chooses to show it. This type of move is called a reveal. Reveals not only uncover new information, they can also be an important part of adding layers of depth to the frame. A simple example: let's go back to Helen on the way to her office. The purpose of the scene is to reveal that Helen is somehow trapped in a financial scandal. We discussed how the establishing shots can be used to not only show where we are and orient us within Helen's world but can also impart valuable information that then does not have to be spelled out in "on the nose" expository dialog.

We know we have a newsstand in front of her building and that the financial scandal is on the front page. Let's say Helen stops on her way to the office and picks up a newspaper. As she opens it, the headline fills the frame. The information is shown to the audience in a fairly unself-conscious way. The newspaper is then lowered. We expect to see Helen. Instead we see over her shoulder. Just past her is the reporter who broke the story. It is thus revealed and introduced into the scene in a very natural and seamless way. This is a reveal with the use of props. Reveals are more often accomplished with a camera move.

3.33. Carol Reed uses dutch tilt very effectively throughout *The Third Man*.

lens language

59

3.34 and **3.35**. In the "crazy house" sequence from *The Lady From Shanghai*, Welles uses a tilt from dutch right (near right) to dutch left (far right) in the same shot. It serves as a transition from one room to another and introduces an element of off-balance drunkeness that is even stronger than a simple dutch shot.

CAMERA MOVEMENT

Camera movement associated with first or second person POV is very involving and engaging. We are drawn in because we constantly strive to reorient and "place" ourselves in the scene. As movement is disorienting our brain is engaged in to try to keep us oriented — to "keep up" with the movement and figure out where we are and what is going on — it becomes interactive. Movement can of course be very third person as well: if nothing about the shot such as camera placement suggests a subjective reference, then the movement is objective and is merely showing us different subjects or is taking us from one subject to the next. It should always be a goal that the journey from opening frame to ending frame be visually interesting and engaging all along the way. If it becomes so prosaic as to be nothing more than traveling from one frame to another, you are better off with a cut.

In terms of pacing, very rapid and erratic camera movements suggest energy or restlessness or chaos, especially in conjunction with rapid cutting. Truffaut and others of the early sixties broke away from the received wisdom that all camera movement must be stable, smooth and flowing. They reveled in the randomness and immediacy of the slightly shaky, handheld camera — different from the Steadicam look. Welles used handheld for certain scenes in *Touch of Evil* — one of the early examples in American film.

The introduction of smaller cameras in film as well as in video has prompted many directors today to use free-flowing, loose handheld as their constant technique. Remember that just because you *can* doesn't mean that you *should* — certainly not all the time. Loose hand-held has specific meaning and effect in the vocabulary of cinematic and should not be abused just because it *seems* like a faster and less stressful way to shoot. Don't make the mistake of substituting it for carefully thinking about the visual effect and cinematic meaning of your framing, lens choice and camera choreography.

3.36. Truffaut used hand-held camera for specific story effect in *Jules and Jim* (Les Films du Carrosse/Janus Films, 1961).

camera dynamics

4.1. (previous page) Billy Bitzer, D.W. Griffith's constant collaborator, in a very early moving camera rig.

4.2. (above) An early dolly shot, this one on the film *Sunrise* (F.W. Murnau — Fox Film Corp, 1927), famous for its extraordinary floating, extended camera moves.

Along with sequential editing, the ability to move the camera is the most fundamental aspect which distinguishes film and video from photography, painting and other visual arts. As we have seen, moving the camera is much more than just going from one frame to another. The movement itself, the style, the trajectory, the pacing and the timing in relation to the action all contribute to the mood and feel of the shot: they add a subtext and an emotional content independent of the subject.

We talked about the cinematic uses of camera moves in *Lens Language*; here we can cover the techniques and technology of moving the camera. The most basic use of the camera is where you put it. Camera placement is a key decision in storytelling. More than just "where it looks good," it determines what the audience sees and from what perspective they see it. As discussed in the chapter on *Filmspace*, what the audience does not see can be as important as what they do see.

Since Griffith freed the camera from its stationary singular point of view, moving the camera has become an ever increasing part of the visual art of filmmaking. In this section we will look at the dynamics of camera movement and also take a look at some representative ways in which this is accomplished. The dolly as a means of moving the camera dates from the early part of the 20th century. The crane came into its own in the 1920s (See Figure 4.3 for a modern version). Shots from moving vehicles were accomplished in the earliest of silents, as we see from this photo of the D.W. Griffith's great cameraman and collaborator Billy Bitzer (Figure 4.1). After the introduction of the crane, little changed with the means of camera movement until the invention of the Steadicam by Garrett Brown. It was first used on the films *Bound For Glory* and Kubrick's *The Shining*.

MOTIVATION AND INVISIBLE TECHNIQUE

In narrative filmmaking, a key concept of camera movement is that it must be motivated. The movement should not just be for the sake of moving the camera; doing so usually means that the director is suffering from a lack of storytelling skills. Motivation can come in two ways. First, the action itself may motivate a move. For example, if the character gets up from a chair and crosses to the window, it is perfectly logical for the camera to move with her. Not necessary, but clearly one way to do it.

Both the start and the end of a dolly move or pan should be motivated. The motivation at the end may be as simple as the fact that we have arrived at the new frame, but clearly it must be a new frame, one with new information composed in a meaningful way, not just be "where the camera ended up." A big part of this is that the camera should "settle" at the end of any move. It needs to "alight" at the new frame and be there for a beat before the cut point.

Particularly with the start and end of camera moves that are motivated by subject movement, there needs to be a sensitivity to the timing of the subject and also a delicate touch as to speed. You seldom want the dolly to just "take off" at full speed then grind to a sudden halt. Most of the time, you want the dolly grip to "feather" in and out of the move.

The camera movement itself may have a purpose. For example, a move may reveal new information or a new view of the scene. The camera may move to meet someone or pull back to show a wider shot. Unmotivated camera moves or zooms are distracting; they pull the audience out of the moment and make them conscious that they are watching a fiction; they do however have their uses, particularly in very stylized filmmaking.

There are many ways to find a motivation for a camera move and they can be used to enhance the scene and add a layer of meaning beyond the shots themselves. They can also add a sense of energy, joy, menace, sadness or any other emotional overlay. Camera movement is much like the pacing of music. A crane move can "soar" as the music goes upbeat or the camera can dance with the energy of the moment, such as when Rocky reaches the top of the museum steps and the Steadicam spins around and around him. Motivating and timing a camera move is a part of the goal of invisible technique. Just as in with cutting and coverage in the master scene method, the goal is for the "tricks" to be unnoticed and not distract from the story telling.

BASIC TECHNIQUE

There is an endless variety of ways to move the camera and it would be impossible to catalog every one here. It is useful to look at a few basic categories of types of moves to provide a general vocabulary of camera dynamics. The most fundamental of camera moves, the pan and tilt can be accomplished in almost any mode, including handheld. The exception is when a camera is locked off on either a non-movable mount (as it might be for an explosion or big stunt) or where it is on a movable head, but the movements are locked down and there is no operator. Many types of effect shots require the camera to be locked down so that not even the slightest movement of the camera is possible.

Beyond the simple pan and tilt or zoom, most moves involve an actual change of camera position in the shot. Other than handheld, these kinds of moves involve specific technologies and also the support of other team members: the grip department. Grips are the experts when it comes to mounting the camera in any way other

4.3. A Chapman Lenny Arm rigged on a camera car for some moving shots in Greenwich Village. (Photo courtesy of Mark Weingartner.)

camera dynamics

than right on a tripod or a dolly and they are the people who provide the rigging, the stabilization and actual operation when it comes to performing the move.

A good grip crew makes it look easy, but there is considerable knowledge and finesse involved in laying smooth dolly track on a rough surface (Figure 4.4) or rigging the camera on the front of a roller coaster. All the details of rigging are beyond the scope of this chapter but we will touch on some of the major issues.

TYPES OF MOVES

PAN
Short for panoramic, pan applies to left or right horizontal movement of the camera where the camera position does not change. Pans are fairly easy to operate with a decent camera head. There is one operational limitation that must be dealt with. If the camera is panned too quickly, there will be a strobing effect which will be very disturbing.

As a general rule of thumb, with a shutter opening of 180° and a frame rate of 24 or 25fps, it should take at least 5 seconds for an object to move from one side of the frame to the other. Any faster and there is a danger of strobing. Higher frame rates call for slower panning speeds. There are tables which enumerate exact panning speeds but they require using a protractor and stopwatch and are not really practical on the set.

TILT UP OR DOWN
The tilt is up or down movement without changing camera position. Technically, it is not correct to say "pan up," but as a practical matter everybody says it. The tilt, being a vertical move, is used much less frequently than the pan. For better or worse, we live most of our lives on a generally horizontal plane and that is the way most action plays out in narrative, documentary and informational filmmaking. As we will see below, the use of the crane, the Steadicam and aerial mounts is to a large extent used to break out of the confined horizontal plane and make the scenes more truly three-dimensional.

Standard filmmaking is confined, to a large degree, by where we can put the camera. Certainly the ability of the Steadicam to move with action up and down stairs and slopes has opened up a new variety of moves which help with this three-dimensional effort and keep us "with" the characters as they move through space. Given the technology now available and the ingenuity of our grips and camera assistants, there is hardly anywhere a camera can't go.

MOVE IN / MOVE OUT
Move the dolly toward or away from the action. Common terminology is push in or pull out. For example, to the dolly grip: "When he sits down, you push in." A good dolly grip will have a feel for the exact moment to start the move. This is different from a punch-in (see below). Moving into the scene or out of it are ways of combining the wide shot of a scene with a specific tighter shot. It is a way of selecting the view for the audience in a way that is more dramatic than just cutting from wide shot to closer shot. It has the effect of focusing the viewer's attention even more effectively than just doing a wide establishing and then cutting to the scene; by moving in toward the scene, the camera is saying "of all the things on this street, this is the part that is important for you to look at."

Of course, there are infinite uses of the simple move in/move out. We may pull back as the character moves out of the scene or as another character enters; the move is often just a pragmatic way of allowing more room for additional elements of the scene or to tie in something else to the immediate action we have been watching. Conversely, when someone leaves a scene, a subtle push-in can take up the slack in the framing.

ZOOM
An optical change of focal length. Moves the point of view in or out without moving the camera. Zooms are not popular in feature film making, but almost all video work is done with zooms. When a zoom is used it is important that the zoom be motivated. Also, it is best to hide a zoom. Hiding a zoom is an art. The zoom may be combined with a dolly move or with a move by the actors so that it becomes unnoticeable. An unmotivated zoom is distracting and usually looks unprofessional.

DIFFERENCE BETWEEN A ZOOM AND A DOLLY SHOT
Say you want to go from a wide or medium to a close-up during the shot. On the face of it, there would seem to be no real difference between moving the dolly in or zooming in. In actual effect, they are quite different, for several reasons.

First, a zoom changes the perspective from a wide angle with deep focus and inclusion of the background to a long lens shot with compressed background and very little of the background. It also changes the depth of field, so that the background or foreground might go from sharp focus to soft. These might be the effects you want, but often they are not. Second, the dolly move is dynamic in a way that a zoom cannot be. With a zoom your basic point of view stays the same because the camera does not move; with a dolly the camera moves in relation to the subject. Even if the subject stays center frame, the background moves behind the subject. This adds a sense of motion and also the shot ends with an entirely different background than it opened with. This is not to say that a zoom is never desirable, just that it is important to understand the difference and what each type of move can do for your scene.

A very dramatic effect can be produced with a combination of zoom and a dolly. In this technique you zoom out as you dolly in. This keeps the image size relatively the same, but there is a dramatic change of perspective and background. This was used very effectively in *Jaws*, when Roy Scheider as the sheriff is sitting on the beach and first hears someone call "shark." It was also used effectively in *Goodfellas* in the scene where Ray Liotta is having lunch

4.4. A very simple pipe dolly rig for this Imax shot in China. Pipe dolly rigs are especially useful for situations like this where a rental dolly is unavailable and it is impractical to fly one in. Many people carry the wheels and hardware with them and build the dolly and track with locally available materials. (Photo courtesy of Mark Weingartner).

4.5. An ordinary track-with move. Camera move matches the direction of the subject.

4.6. Countermove.

4.7. Dolly across the line of movement. This one has to be used with caution. If the entire shot is not used, the screen direction will be flipped without explanation. See the chapter *Cinematic Continuity* for further discussion of this issue.

with Robert De Niro in the diner. At the moment Liotta realizes he is being set up for killing by his old friend, the combination move effectively underscores the feeling of disorientation, of having the rug pulled out from under him.

PUNCH-IN

Different from a push in, which involves actually moving the camera, a punch-in means that the camera stays where it is, but a longer focal length prime is put on or the lens is zoomed in for a tighter shot. The most common use of a punch-in is for coverage on a dialog scene, usually when going from an over-the-shoulder to a clean single. Since moving the camera forward from an over-the-shoulder may involve repositioning the off-camera actor and other logistics, it is often easier to just go to a longer lens. There is some slight change in perspective but for this type of close-up it is often not noticeable as long as the head size remains constant.

MOVING SHOTS

TRACKING

The simplest and most clearly motivated of camera moves is to track along with a character or vehicle in the same direction (Figure 4.5). For the most part, the movement is alongside and parallel. It is certainly possible to stay ahead of and looking back at the subject or to follow along behind, but these kinds of shots are not nearly as dynamic as tracking alongside, which gives greater emphasis to the moving background and the sweep of the motion.

Technically any dolly move is a tracking shot, but this general terminology is not much used anymore. Now, the term tracking shot usually means moving along with the subject. One variation of the tracking shot is when the camera moves in the same overall direction as the subject, but not exactly parallel to it.

The most dynamic of this type of shot is when the camera comes around to meet someone, as in Figures 4.8, 4.9 and 4.10. The purpose here is not to present an exhaustive catalog of every type of moving shot, the point is that in a shot like this, moving the camera changes the shot. Here it progresses dynamically from a wide shot to a close-up. When both camera and subject are heading toward the same goal, the move can be quite powerful and dramatic.

COUNTERMOVE

If the camera always moves only with the subject, matching its direction and speed, it can get a little boring. In this case, the camera is "tied to" the subject and completely dependent on it. For the camera to sometimes move independently of the subject can add a counterpoint and an additional element to the scene. Certainly it can be dynamic and energetic; it adds a counterpoint of movement which deepens the scene (Figure 4.6). Whenever the camera moves in the opposite direction the background appears to move at twice the rate it would move if the camera was tracking along in the same direction as the subject. A variation is to move across the line of travel, as in Figure 4.7. A variation of the countermove is where the dolly moves in the opposite direction and the subjects cross the axis of motion as in Figure 4.12.

REVEAL

A simple dolly or crane move can be used for an effective reveal. A subject fills the frame, then with a move, something else is revealed. This type of shot is most effective where the second frame reveals new content which amplifies the meaning of the first shot or ironically comments on it.

CIRCLES

When ordering a dolly and track it is quite common to also order at least a couple of pieces of circle track. Circular track generally comes in two types: 45° and 90°. These designate whether it takes four pieces or eight pieces to make a complete circle, which defines the radius of the track. A very specific use of circle track is to dolly completely or halfway around the subject; this type of move is easily abused and can be very self-conscious if not motivated by something in the scene. Some companies specify track by radius.

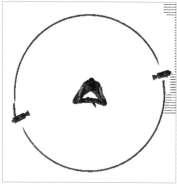

One important note on setting up a circle track scene: as it is quite common to use circle track to move very slowly around the subject in a tight shot, focus pulling can get quite complex. The best way to simplify a circle move is to set up the shot so that the subject is positioned at dead center of the radius of the track. This will make life much easier for the focus puller and help ensure that numerous takes will not be necessary to get one that stays sharp (Figure 4.11).

CRANE MOVES

The most useful aspect of a crane is its ability to achieve large vertical moves within the shot. While a crane may be used only to get the camera up high, the most basic variety of crane shot is to start with a high angle view of the overall scene as an establishing shot and then move down and in to isolate a piece of the geography: most often our main characters who then proceed with the action or dialog. This is most often used to open the scene by combining the establishing shot with the closer-in master of the specific action.

The opposite move, starting tight on the scene and then pulling back to reveal the wide shots, is an effective way to end a scene as well and is often used as the dramatic last shot of an entire film — a slow disclosure. Depending on the content of the scene and the entire film, it can have a powerful emotional content. If, for example, the tight shot is of the young man bleeding to death on the pavement, pulling back to a wide shot of the deserted street, with no help in sight can have a tragic, hopeless feel. Such shots make a very specific statement and should not be used casually. The ability of the crane to "swoop" dramatically and flowingly can be used for exhilarating and energetic effect; more than any other type of camera move, it can really "dance" with the characters or the action.

Another aspect of the crane that is important to keep in mind is that most cranes are capable of going below the level of their mounting surface. This can be used to get you down into a ditch or other place where setting a tripod or dolly would be impractical. Of course, such use can always be enhanced by building a platform for the crane. This has the effect of raising the top end of the move. Since you are now also using the below the surface capability, you can employ the full range of motion of the crane for the most dynamic shot.

4.8, 4.9 and **4.10**. (top, left to right) A "going to meet them" move. This is a very dynamic shot as the subject distance changes. This can be used to start with a wide tracking shot and end up with a tight close-up or vice-versa.

4.11. (above) The secret of a circle dolly move is to get the subject as close to the center of the circle as possible. This minimizes focus shifts during the move and makes it easier on the AC.

4.12. (below) A complex and very dynamic move: the shot tracks, pans and subject distance and direction change all at the same time.

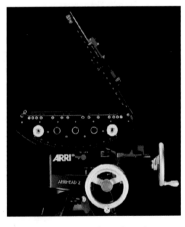

4.13. (top) A leveling head — an essential part of almost all camera mounting systems.

4.14. (middle) A fluid head (Photo courtesy of OConnor.)

4.15. (above) A geared head. Long a staple in classic studio production, it is essential not only for the ability to execute perfectly smooth and repeatable moves but also for the ability to hold very heavy cameras. (Photo courtesy of Arri Group.)

ROLLING SHOT

The term rolling shot is used wherever the camera is mounted on a vehicle, either on the picture vehicle or a camera car which travels along with the picture vehicle. The "picture" vehicle is the one being photographed.

CAMERA MOUNTING

HANDHELD

Handheld is any time the operator takes the camera in hand, usually held on the shoulder, but it can be held low to the ground, placed on the knees or any other combination. For many years, handheld was the primary means of making the camera mobile in cases where a dolly was not available or not practical (on stairs, for example). Now, with so many other ways to keep the camera mobile, handheld is most often used for artistic purposes.

Handheld has a sense of immediacy and energy that cannot be duplicated by other means. *Saving Private Ryan*, for instance, was shot 90% handheld, even though obviously the budget was there to mount the camera in any conceivable way. It suggests a documentary approach and thus subtly implies that "you are there," and "this is really happening." Handheld can convey a sense of honesty, immediacy and simplicity that makes it popular in many commercials.

CAMERA HEAD

The camera cannot be mounted directly on a tripod or dolly. If it was, there would be no way to move the camera. On dollies, cranes and car mounts, there is also an intermediate step: the leveling head (Figure 4.13). This is the base the camera head sits on which allows for leveling of the camera. In the case of a tripod, leveling is accomplished by lengthening or shortening one of the legs to get the camera level. Camera heads make smooth, stable and repeatable moves possible. Heads fall into four categories:

FLUID HEAD

These use oil and internal dampers and springs to make extremely smooth left/right and up/down moves possible (Figure 4.14). The amount of resistance is adjustable. Most camera operators want the head to have a good amount of resistance working against them. This makes smoother moves possible; a free floating head is very difficult to control.

GEARED HEAD

These heads are operated with wheels which the operator can move very smoothly and precisely repeat moves (Figure 4.15). The geared head has a long and venerable history in studio production. The geared head is useful not only for the ability to execute smooth and repeatable moves but also because it can handle very heavy cameras.

REMOTE HEAD

Geared heads can also be fitted with motors to be operated remotely or by a computer for motion control (mo-co). Remotely controlled heads are used for a variety of purposes and have made possible the use of cranes which extend much farther and higher than would be possible if the arm had to be designed to carry the weight of an operator and camera assistant. Remote heads can also perform moves which would not be possible if the operator had his eye to the viewfinder: 360° rolls, for example, or moves which rotate more than 180° vertically.

FRICTION HEAD
The most primitive form of camera head, they use adjustable friction to help the operator control the move. Friction heads are rarely used nowadays.

UNDERSLUNG HEADS
These are fluid heads but the camera is not mounted on top. It is suspended on a cradle below the pivot point. Underslung heads can rotate vertically far past where an ordinary fluid head can go and thus are good for shots which need to go straight up or down or even further. Some underslung heads, such as the one shown here (Figure 11.8) are true nodal point heads, which will be discussed in *Technical Issues*.

THE TRIPOD
The tripod is the oldest and most basic type of camera mount but still sees constant use on all types of film and video sets. Being smaller, lighter and more portable than just about any other type of mount, its versatility makes up for its shortcomings. It can be quickly repositioned and can be made to fit into very tight, odd places. Its main advantage is that it can be transported just about anywhere.

HIGH-HAT
The high-hat is strictly the mounting surface for the camera head; it has no leveling or movement capability at all. It is used when the camera needs to go very low, almost to the surface. It is also used when the camera needs to be mounted in a remote place, such as on top of a ladder. The high-hat is usually bolted to a piece of plywood which can be screwed, bolted or strapped in to all sorts of places.

4.16. (top) A tilt plate — used when the camera angle needed is greater than what can be achieved with the camera head in use.

4.17. (bottom) A compact and highly maneuverable crab dolly — the Chapman Peewee. (Photo courtesy of Chapman/Leonard Studio Equipment.)

ROCKER PLATE
The drawback of a high-hat is that the camera head (fluid or geared) still has to go on top of it. As a result, the lens height is still at least 18" or more above the surface. If this just isn't low enough, the first choice is usually to prop it on a sand bag. The pliable nature of the sand bag allows the camera to be positioned for level and tilt. Any moves, however, are pretty much handheld. If more control is desired, a rocker plate can be used. This is a simple device which allows the camera to be tilted up and down. Smooth side to side pans are not possible.

TILT PLATE
Sometimes, a shot calls for a greater range of up and down tilt than a typical camera head can provide. In this case, a tilt plate can be mounted on top of the camera head (Figure 4.16). It is usually geared and can be tilted to the desired angle. The gearing (if there is any) is generally not smooth enough to be used in a shot.

THE CRAB DOLLY
The crab dolly is by far the most often used method of mounting and moving the camera. A crab dolly in the hands of a good dolly grip is capable of a surprising range and fluidity of movement. Figure 4.17 is a typical dolly widely used in production today.

DOLLY TERMINOLOGY
Dolly In/Out
Move the dolly toward or away from the subject (Figure 4.19). When a dolly is on the floor and you want to move forward, there are two choices. "Move in" can either mean move forward on the axis of the lens or on the axis in which the crabbed wheels are aiming. These are "in on the lens" or "in on the wheels."

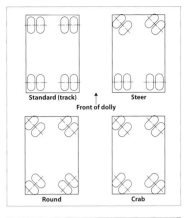

Standard (track)   Steer

Front of dolly

Round   Crab

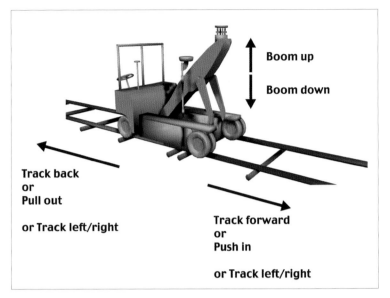

Boom up

Boom down

Track back
or
Pull out

or Track left/right

Track forward
or
Push in

or Track left/right

4.18. (top left) Dolly wheel positions for various types of moves.

4.19. (top right) Dolly and boom terminology.

4.20. (above) A fluid head that quickly converts to a dutch head. (Photo courtesy of Cartoni S.p.A.)

Dolly Left/Right
Move the dolly left or right. If the dolly is on tracks, it is left or right in relation to the axis of the track. If the dolly is on the floor, then it is left or right in relation to the subject (Figure 4.19).

Boom Up/Down
Nearly all dollies have a boom: a hydraulic arm capable of moving vertically in a smooth enough motion to be used in a shot without shakes or jarring. Some boom terms include: top floor (ladies lingerie) and bottom floor (bargain basement).

Crab Left/Right
Most dollies have wheels that can crab (Figure 4.18), that is, both front and rear wheels can be turned in the same direction, allowing the dolly to move laterally at any angle. Crab function is absolutely essential if the dolly is to be used directly on the floor and not on track. For most normal operations, the rear wheels are in crab mode and are the "smart wheels." The front wheels are locked in and function as the "dumb" wheels. For a true crab move, all four wheels are switched to crab mode. There is another variation of crabbing which can be done only with certain dollies. This is roundy-round, where the wheels can be set so that the dolly revolves in a full 360° circle on its own center. To do this, the front and rear wheels are crabbed in opposite directions. This can be done with some Fischer dollies as well as the Panther and the Elemack (Figure 4.18).

DANCE FLOOR
Stable, shake free dolly moves can only be accomplished on smooth floors. If there is no room for track to be laid or if the director is looking for dolly moves that can't be accommodated by straight or curved track, a dance floor can be built which allows the camera to move anywhere. A dance floor is built with good quality 3/4" plywood (usually birch) topped with a layer of smooth masonite. The joints are then carefully taped. This forms an excellent surface for smooth moves. A good dolly grip can crab and roll anywhere, and combination moves can be quite complex. The only drawback is that you have to avoid showing the floor. Smooth floors or dance floor becomes especially critical if anything other than a wide lens is up on the camera. Once you get to a normal lens or longer, every little bump in the floor or the dolly track is going to show on screen.

DUTCH HEAD

Dutch angle is when the camera is tilted off horizontal. The variations are dutch left and dutch right. As with many obscure terms in film, there is much speculation as to the origin. In fact, it goes back to 17th century England, when a Dutch royal, William of Orange, was placed on the throne of Britain. There was much resentment and all things considered "not quite right" were called "dutch." Hence: dutch doors, dutch dates and dutch auctions. Specially built dutch heads are also available which convert back and forth between dutch and normal operation very quickly (Figure 4.20).

EXTENSION PLATE

When the camera is mounted on the dolly, it may be necessary to extend it to the left, right or forward of where the dolly can go (Figure 4.21), for example if you need to place the dolly at the center of a bed. This can be done with an extension plate which mounts on the dolly, then the camera head is mounted at the end.

LOW MODE

Sometimes the camera needs to be lower than the boom can go. In this case, there are two possibilities. Some dollies can have their camera mounting arm reconfigured so that it is only a few inches above the floor. If this is not available or is not enough, a Z-bar can be used to get the camera all the way to the floor (Figure 4.23). The Z-bar is basically an extension arm that extends out then down.

FRONT PORCH

Some dollies have a small extension which fits on the front of the dolly; this is also known as a cowcatcher. This can be used to hold the battery or as a place for the operator or the camera assistant to stand during a move (Figure 4.22).

SIDE BOARDS

Sideboards fit on either side of the dolly as a place for the operator to stand. They are removable for transportation and for when the dolly has to fit through tight spaces.

SEAT EXTENSION

Allows the seat to be more mobile and lets the operator get into better position for some camera moves.

RISERS

6", 9", 12" or 18" extensions can place the camera higher than the boom travels. The longest extensions can get the camera very high but at the cost of somewhat reducing stability.

STEERING BAR OR PUSH BAR

Allows the dolly grip to push/pull the dolly and also to steer the dolly in standard mode (where only the rear wheels pivot) or in crab mode, where both sets of wheels pivot.

CRANES

Cranes are capable of much greater vertical and horizontal movement than a dolly. There are two types: jib arms have no seat for the cameraperson and are usually operated by someone standing on the floor or perhaps an apple box. True cranes generally have seats for the operator and a camera assistant. Large cranes can generally get the camera, operator and assistant up to a lens height of around 27' or more above the base. We say above the base because often a crane will be mounted on a platform, vehicle or other crane for additional height. A typical crane is shown in Figure 4.29.

4.21. (top) An extension plate. (Photo courtesy of Matthews Studio Equipment, Inc.)

4.22. (middle) Side boards and front porch. (Photo courtesy of J.L. Fisher, Inc.)

4.23. (bottom) A drop down plate, sometimes called a Z-bar. Used to get the camera very low but still maneuverable. (Photo courtesy of J.L. Fisher, Inc.)

4.24. The Chapman Titan II, a truck mounted crane. The truck can run on battery power for sync-sound shots. (Photo courtesy of Chapman/ Leonard Studio Equipment, Inc.)

Both cranes and jib arms have one fundamental characteristic that may become a problem. Because they are all mounted on a pivot point, the arm always has some degree of arc as it moves up, down or laterally. With dolly arms this degree of arc is usually negligible for all except exacting macro or very tight work that calls for critical focus or a very precise frame size.

With cranes the arc can be quite large, but as the crane can also move in or out, the arc can often be adjusted for with a compensating move of the crane arm or by also moving the dolly the crane is mounted on slightly.

CRANE/JIB ARM

A crane is any camera support where the arm can rotate freely as well as boom up and down (Figure 4.24). For nearly all cranes, there is a pivot point and behind this point are counterweights. This is different from a dolly, where the boom arm is fixed and operated by hydraulics. A jib arm generally means a smaller crane arm. Most jib arms do not have a seat for the operator and camera assistant; the camera is operated from the floor or perhaps on a small ladder or an apple box (Figure 4.28).

The counterweights extending behind the pivot point have two important consequences. First, it is important to take this backswing into account when planning or setting up a crane move. If there isn't sufficient room at best your moves will be limited and at worst something will be broken. The second is a safety issue and it is one that cannot be emphasized enough. Cranes can be extremely dangerous.

When you are on a crane, the key grip or crane grip is in charge. Nobody gets on or off the crane without permission of the crane grip. The reason for this is that your weight and the camera weight are precisely counterbalanced by the weights on the back end. If you were to suddenly get off the crane without warning, the camera end would go flying up in the air and very likely cause damage or injury. With anyone getting on or off, or with any changes in equipment, the crane grip and the back-end grip communicate loudly and clearly so that every step is coordinated. If you are the camera operator, show courtesy to the grips. It can be a big job for them to get you on and off. Don't do it frivolously.

Two other safety issues when working on a crane: #1. Wear your safety belt. Always. #2. Be extremely careful around any electrical wires. After helicopters and camera cars, cranes around high voltage wires are the leading cause of serious injury and death in the motion picture industry. Take it seriously. The best bet is to tell your crane grip what you want and then just let him or her be in charge. This leaves your attention free to focus on the shot itself.

CRANE OPERATION

Crane operation should always be a three man job; anything less is absolutely not safe. (This does not apply to jib arms which don't have seats for the operator and AC.) The key grip usually operates the front part of the arm and guides the move; another grip pushes and pulls the chassis and a third grip is at the rear of the crane with weights.

This grip helps the key swing the arm and serves as a "damper" to cushion the end of the move, so that the inertia of the crane doesn't let it overshoot the mark. A good crane crew executing complex moves is a joy to watch. They make it look easy, but it calls for muscle power, coordination, careful choreography and nearly ballet-like precision.

The Arc

Another issue with cranes is that, because they pivot on a central point, any crane arm (or any dolly arm) moves in an arc, not along a straight vertical line. In most cases this is not a problem. It only becomes an issue with very tight shots with limited depth of focus. Very few rigs allow you to compensate for the arc. The Stinger jib (Figure 4.32) is one of them. The camera support slides back and forth on rails; Panther makes a similar rig.

Chassis Left/Right Or In/Out

The chassis is a dolly or specially built platform that supports the crane. Most small and medium size jib arms or cranes mount either on a dolly or a braced rolling platform similar to a dolly. The chassis may roll on a smooth floor or may be mounted on dolly track for more repeatable movements.

Crane Up/Down

These terms are the same as boom up/boom down but apply to cranes. Operationally, a crane is more difficult than a dolly. One of the main reasons is that the crane is floating freely, unlike a dolly which has specific limits and specific marks. It is relatively easy for the dolly grip to make marks on the boom arm for the high and low stop points, as well as marks on the dolly track for precise start and end points. This is not possible on a crane.

One thing that most crane grips will do is attach a rope to the camera platform and braid it with knots. These knots make it easier to grasp and pull the crane but they also help with marking. Since the rope hangs down right under the camera, it is possible to make marks on the floor to indicate camera position and colored tape on the rope can indicate lens height. The best crane grips can hit these marks again and again with great precision.

NON-BOOMING PLATFORMS

If all that is needed is height, especially for height greater than can be accomplished with the available crane, the camera might be mounted on a construction crane such as a Condor, which is frequently used as a mounting for lights. These types of cranes can get the camera where you need it but they usually aren't capable of booming up or down without visible shake.

CAMERA ON A LADDER

The simplest and cheapest method of getting the camera higher than normal is to put it on a ladder as in Figure 4.25. This is done by having the grips clamp and strap a high-hat on top of the ladder. A second ladder should stand alongside to provide a place for the focus-puller. Both these ladders should be well stabilized with sand bags and a grip should always stand by for safety.

REMOTE HEADS

Remote control heads have revolutionized crane shots. Since it is now possible to design cranes that do not need to support the weight of the operator and camera assistant, cranes can be longer, higher, lighter, more portable and faster to set up.

TECHNOCRANE

All cranes move up/down and left/right. The Technocrane adds one more axis of movement. The arm can be extended or retracted smoothly during the move. Like many remote heads, it can also be revolved so that the camera spins horizontally. The in/out movement can be used to compensate for the arc problem.

4.25. Camera on a ladder, one of the quickest ways to get a camera up high. It is usually done with a high hat clamped and strapped to the top rung. (Photo courtesy of Mark Weingartner.)

4.26. A crane on top of a crane. Not only does it get the camera higher and farther out, it also makes possible some very fluid compound moves. (Photo courtesy of Mark Weingartner.)

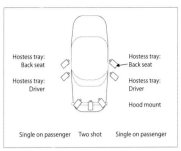

4.27. (top) Standard camera positions for car mount rigs.

4.28. (above) A fully tricked out car rig with multiple mounting positions.

CRANES ON TOP OF CRANES
Some cranes can be stacked on top of large cranes such as the Titan for additional height and mobility as in Figure 4.26. Obviously, a top notch grip team is critical for this type of work, as safety is crucial. This type of rig can accomplish some highly complex compound moves. Walkie-talkies with headsets are important as coordination between the grips on both cranes is essential.

PEDESTALS
One type of camera mount is capable of vertical movement without arcing: the pedestal. Pedestals are the norm for television studios but are rarely, if ever used in film or video field production.

CAR SHOTS
Car shots have always been a big part of film production. In the old studio days they were usually done on sets with rear projection of moving streets visible through the rear or side windows. Special partial cars called bucks had the entire front of the car removed for ease of shooting.

Rear or front projection of exterior scenes is rarely used these days, partly because the technology of shooting on live locations has been perfected as well as film or digital replacement of the background. Car shots are accomplished with car mounts. There are two basic types: hood mounts allow one or more cameras to be placed on the hood area for shooting through the windshield.

Hostess trays (named for the trays that used to be standard at drive-in hamburger joints) allow the camera to be positioned on the side, usually shooting through the driver's window and the passenger's window.

CAMERA POSITIONS FOR CAR SHOTS
The standard positions for car shots are shown in Figure 4.27. Those at the side widows are accomplished with a hostess tray (Figure 4.28). The ones on the front are done with a hood mount. These two components are the standard parts of a car rig kit, but be sure to specify both if you need them.

VEHICLE TO VEHICLE SHOOTING
Camera cars are specialized trucks with very smooth suspension and numerous mounting positions for multiple cameras (Figure 4.29). Camera cars are used in two basic modes. For close-ups of the actors, the picture car is usually towed by the camera car or mounted on a low-boy trailer which is towed. The reason that it needs to be a low trailer is so that the perspective relationship of the car to the road will seem natural. If the car is too high it will look odd. Towing has two advantages. First, the position of the picture car doesn't change radically and unpredictably in relation to the cameras, which can be a problem for the camera operators and the focus pullers. Second, it is much safer since the actor doesn't have to perform and try to drive at the same time.

A simpler technology for towing shots is the wheel mount tow. This is a small two wheel trailer which supports only the front wheels of the car. As the picture car is still at ground level, there are few problems with perspective. This can be an advantage if, for example, the car has to stop and someone approaches the window. This could all be done in one shot, where it would be difficult if the car is mounted on a full trailer. One safety consideration for front wheel tows: the tires are usually held onto the tow carriage with straps. If the actor tries to "steer" too much, it is possible for these straps to come loose. If the actor does have to drive, there should definitely be a follow

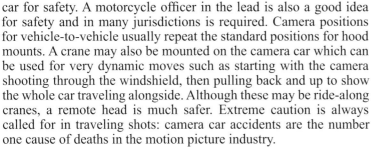

car for safety. A motorcycle officer in the lead is also a good idea for safety and in many jurisdictions is required. Camera positions for vehicle-to-vehicle usually repeat the standard positions for hood mounts. A crane may also be mounted on the camera car which can be used for very dynamic moves such as starting with the camera shooting through the windshield, then pulling back and up to show the whole car traveling alongside. Although these may be ride-along cranes, a remote head is much safer. Extreme caution is always called for in traveling shots: camera car accidents are the number one cause of deaths in the motion picture industry.

AERIAL SHOTS

Aerial shots were also attempted very early in film history. As soon as helicopters were available after the Korean war, they were pressed into service for aerial shots. Vibration has always been a problem with aerial shots as with the pressure of the windstream. Both make it difficult to get a good stable shot and control the camera acceptably. The Tyler mounts for helicopters isolate the camera from vibration and steady it so it can be operated smoothly.

Today, most aerial shots are accomplished with "hot head" type mounts, with the camera mounted to the exterior of the aircraft and the operator inside using remote controls but in tight budget or impromptu situations it is still sometimes necessary for the camera operator to lean outside and balance on the pontoon — hopefully with the proper safety rig. In such cases, don't forget to secure the camera as well as any filters, matte box or other items that might come loose in the slipstream. You may want to tape your shirt sleeves and pants legs as well; their flapping in the extreme wind conditions can get in the way of smooth operation.

There are many candidates for the best helicopter shot of all time, but a leading contender is the opening shot of *Working Girl* which starts with a tight CU of the face of the Statue of Liberty, then in a sweeping move circles around the head, peels off to a wide shot of New York Harbor, then gracefully moves in to a tight shot of the Staten Island ferry, then in a hidden cut goes inside the ferry to find the main character. It is a virtuoso piece of camera operation and helicopter flying and one can only wonder how many takes were necessary to come around and catch the ferry in exactly the right spot to complete the move.

4.29. (left) A towed vehicle shot set up for *Three Kings* (Warner Bros., 1999).

4.30. (top) A Chapman Lenny Arm Plus has a reach of up to 34'. (Photo courtesy of Chapman/Leonard Studio Equipment, Inc.)

4.31. (middle) The Cable Cam in use on the film *Gone In 60 Seconds* (Touchstone Pictures, 2000).

4.32. (bottom) The Chapman Stinger arm, one of the only rigs that can boom up and down without an arc. (Photo courtesy of Chapman/ Leonard Studio Equipment, Inc.)

4.33. (top) A mini-helicopter by Flying Cam. (Photo courtesy of Flying Cam, Inc.)

4.34. A low mode prism. (Photo courtesy of Century Precision Optics).

MINI-HELICOPTERS

A recent development in aerial shots is the use of remotely controlled mini-helicopters which are adapted with camera mounts (Figure 4.33). Generally only very lightweight cameras such as a modified Arri IIc or motorized Eyemo can be flown on these helicopters. Smaller video cameras can also be used. New rigs give the camera as much mobility as might be found on a full aerial mount — including 360° roll.

CABLE-CAM

Invented by Garrett Brown, who also conceived the Steadicam, the Cable-Cam (Figure 4.31) can perform some truly amazing shots in places that a helicopter might not be usable, such as over a stadium crowd. The Cable-Cam can carry an operator or use a remote head. The unit comes with its own crew and generally requires at least a day of setup.

OTHER TYPES OF CAMERA MOUNTS

RICKSHAW, WHEELCHAIR & GARFIELD

Camera mounts can be put on anything that moves as we see in some of these photographs. The poor man's dolly, often used by film students, is a wheelchair. With its large radius wheels and the operator hand-holding, it can provide some remarkable smooth dolly shots. The Garfield is a mount which goes on a wheelchair to allow for mounting of a Steadicam.

STEADICAM

The Steadicam revolutionized camera movement (Figure 14.1). It can smoothly move the camera in places where a dolly would be impractical or difficult such as stairs, rough ground, slopes and sand. A skilled operator can pull off amazing shots that can almost be an additional character in the scene. In standard mode, the film or video camera is mounted on top of the central post and the operators video monitor and batteries ride on the sled at the bottom of the rig. The only limitation is that since the post extends down from the camera, that is the lower limit of travel for the camera. To go any lower than this, the entire rig must be switched to low-mode.

LOW MODE PRISM

Getting the camera low to the ground can sometimes be difficult. Even if the camera is taken off the dolly or tripod, it is still mounted on the geared or fluid head. This means that the lens is still at least a foot or more off the ground. The head still has to be mounted on something; generally the lowest thing available is a sandbag.

To get even lower, a prism may be necessary. This is a prism that fits in front of the lens and optically lowers the lens so that the shot appears to be flat on the ground (Figure 4.34). Great care must be taken to keep lens flare off the prism and to keep the optical surface absolutely clean. The only way to get lower is to dig a hole or build one in the set as was done on *Citizen Kane*. The set was constructed on risers so that it is off the floor. Sections of the set floor can then be removed to get a below the floor camera position. Building portions or all of the set on risers is not as difficult or as expensive as one might imagine.

CRASH CAMS

For explosions, car wrecks, train crashes and other dangerous stunts, cameras must sometimes be placed where there is great danger of them being destroyed (Figure 4.36). In this case, crash cams are used. These are usually Eyemos that have been fitted with crystal-

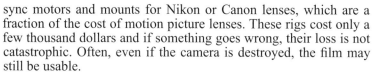

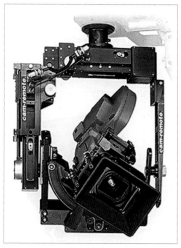

sync motors and mounts for Nikon or Canon lenses, which are a fraction of the cost of motion picture lenses. These rigs cost only a few thousand dollars and if something goes wrong, their loss is not catastrophic. Often, even if the camera is destroyed, the film may still be usable.

SPLASH BOXES

In cases where the camera doesn't have to be actually submerged but will be very near the water or even slightly under the surface, a splash box can be used. These combine a clear optical port with a waterproof box or plastic bag which protects the camera without encasing it in a full underwater casing which can be clumsy and time consuming to use.

UNDERWATER HOUSINGS

For actual underwater work, a fully waterproof housing is necessary. These are specially constructed rigs which have exterior controls for the on/off switch and focus. Underwater housings are also available for light meters.

MOTION CONTROL

(The following is courtesy of Mark Roberts Motion Control.)
What is motion control? Some filming special effects techniques need highly accurate control of the motion of the film camera, so that the same move can be repeated many times, with each camera pass being identical to previous passes (Figure 4.38).

Where the movement of the camera is controlled by hand, it is virtually impossible to get an exact duplication of a previous pass. Traditionally, this problem has been solved by holding the camera in a fixed position (known as "locking off" the camera), and then layering the resultant takes to produce the composite image. But to look really natural, and to produce some stunning visual effects, the camera can be made to move during the pass.

This requires what is essentially a "robot" that controls every aspect of the camera throughout each take, and completcly controls the motion of the camera in space. As the term "robot" sounds a little forbidding and not very creative, these highly technical pieces of machinery have come to be called "motion control rigs." Because these rigs are controlled by computer, the exact position of the camera in 3D space is always known, no matter how rapidly the camera is being moved.

4.35. (left) Imax cameras rigged for a helicopter shot. (Photo courtesy of Mark Weingartner.)

4.36. (top) A crash cam and armored box; in this case an Eyemo is used. (Photo courtesy of Keslow Camera.)

4.37. (middle) A multi-axis remote control head. (Photo courtesy of Chapman/Leonard Studio Equipment, Inc.)

4.38. The MILO motion control rig. (Photo courtesy of Mark Roberts Motion Control.)

The best motion control rigs are "frame accurate." This means that on multiple passes, at any given film frame on a camera pass, the camera will be in an identical position to that of previous passes, regardless of the physical speed of movement of the camera. This means that matching up passes in the post-production phase to produce the composite image becomes very fast and painless, and consequently cheaper.

Aside from the obvious benefits of multiple camera passes, this also provides a major advantage when combining live action with computer generated images (CGI) for the following reasons. In order to have digitally created images appear to interact photo-realistically with the real world, they have to meet three basic criteria. Firstly, the digital image has to be in perspective with the background. Secondly, the digital image has to have the same lighting and color balance as the background. Thirdly, the digital image has its own three-dimensional shape which always has to be oriented to the viewpoint provided by the film camera.

A motion control rig also has other major benefits when filming. For example, the director always knows exactly what the camera is going to do once the move has been set up, so he can devote all of his attention to the action and not the camera. It has also been remarked that because a camera move can be set up so simply and rapidly, it can even make single-pass live action shooting easier.

And with the latest pre-visualisation software, the director can even plan the camera move or moves beforehand, and know that the rig will be able to physically perform the move before he even gets into a studio. So, what then is motion control? It is an essential production tool in the toolbox of filming techniques, which allows that extra depth of reality in many special effects shots. (© Mark Roberts Motion Control Ltd.)

cinematic continuity

SHOOTING FOR EDITING

Filming is ultimately shooting for editorial. The primary purpose of the shoot is not merely to get some "great shots": in the end it must serve the purpose of the film by giving the editor and the director what they need to actually piece together completed scenes and sequences which add up to a finished product that makes sense and accomplishes its purpose. There are four primary categories of continuity.

CONTINUITY OF CONTENT

Continuity of content applies to anything visible in the scene: wardrobe, hairstyle, props, the actors, cars in the background, the time set on the clock. As discussed in the chapter on *Set Operations*, it is the script supervisor in conjunction with the various department heads who must ensure that all of these items match from shot to shot.

These kinds of problems extend from the very obvious: she was wearing a red hat in the master, now it is a green hat in the close-up, to the very subtle — he was smoking a cigar that was almost finished when he entered and now he has a cigar that is just started. While the script supervisor, on-set wardrobe and prop master are the first line of defense in these matters it is still up to the director and camera person to always be watchful for problems.

As with almost anything in film there is a certain amount of cheating that is possible; the audience can be very accepting of minor glitches. Absolutely perfect continuity is never possible and there is a large gray area. It is sometimes said that, with creative cheating, you can get away with anything but errors in wardrobe continuity.

CONTINUITY OF MOVEMENT

Anything that is moving in a shot must have a movement in the next shot which is a seamless continuation of what was begun. Whether it be opening a door, picking up a book or parking a car, the movement must have no "gaps" from one shot to the next. This is where it is so critical to be aware of how the shots might be cut together later.

To play it safe in shooting any type of movement and be sure that the editor is not constricted in choices, it is important to overlap all movement. Even if the script calls for the scene to cut away before she fully opens the door, for example, it is best to go ahead and let the camera roll for a few seconds until the action is complete. Never start a shot exactly at the beginning of a movement — back up a bit a roll into it, then let it run out at the end.

One prime example of this is the "rock in." Say you shot a master of a character walking up to the bank teller. He is there and already has his checkbook out and is talking to the teller in the master. You then set up for a close-up of the character over-the-shoulder of the bank teller. You may know for certain that the edit will pick up with the character already in place, but the safe way to do it is to have the character do the final step or two of walking up as shot in the close-up OTS position.

There are times, however, when focus or position is critical. It is difficult to guarantee that the actor will hit the mark with the precision necessary to get the shot in focus. In this case a "rock in" is the way to go. The technique is simple: instead of actually taking a full step back, the actor keeps one foot firmly planted and steps back with the other, then when action is called he can hit his mark again with great precision. The most important aspect of continuity of movement is to screen direction, which is discussed in more detail later in this chapter.

5.1 (previous page) A continuity sequence from *High Noon*. As discussed later in this chapter, when the geography is very clear and well established, it is possible to be a bit looser about some of the rules of continuity and in fact the editor does so a few times in this scene.

CONTINUITY OF POSITION

Continuity of position is most often problematic with props. Props that are used in the scene are going to be moved in almost every take. Everyone must watch that they start and end in the same place, otherwise it will be an editor's nightmare. This is often the dividing line between a thoroughly professional performer and a beginner: it is up to the actor to use the props and place them exactly the same in every take. If, for some reason, there is a mismatch in placement of a prop between the master and a element of coverage, it is up to the director to either reshoot one or the other or to do some sort of repair coverage that will allow the editor to solve the problem.

This can be done in a variety of ways. One simple example: if the actor put the glass down on the left side of the table in the master, but it is one the right side in the medium, one solution is to do a shot where the actor slides it across the table. This solves the problem, but there is one drawback: the editor has to use that shot. This may end up creating more problems than it solves.

CONTINUITY OF TIME

This does not refer to the problem of resetting the clock so that it always reads the same time (that is prop continuity and comes under continuity of content — see Figure 5.2), rather it has to do with the flow of time within a scene. For example, if Dave North is walking away from Sam South in the wide shot, then you cut to a close-up of Sam South, by the time you cut back to Dave North, his action must be logical timewise. That is, if the close-up of Sam South was for three seconds, when cutting back to the wide shot, Dave North can't have walked fifty feet away. Clearly he can't have walked that far in three seconds and the effect will be jarring. This applies mostly within a scene which is being played out realistically. There are many exceptions, as discussed below in the section on manipulation of time.

Internally within the scene, certain conventions help maintain pacing and flow, particularly in cases where a character moves within a scene. The action or background at the beginning of the move may be important as they may be important at the end of the scene (indeed, they must be, otherwise why are they being shot?) The middle part of the move, however, is often not important information. If the character has to cross a wide room or walk up a flight of stairs, it may be helpful to skip over some of that move.

To just skip it would be, of course, a jump cut and a serious error in continuity but there are several work-arounds. The simplest is to let the character exit frame then enter frame in the next shot. This is a simple form of an elliptical cut (see below) and a good deal of movement time can be left out without disturbing smooth continuity. This is a culturally conditioned film convention that audiences worldwide have come to accept. To preserve movement continuity and screen direction, if the actor exits the left side of frame she must enter the next frame on the right side.

In his book *The Technique of Film and Video Editing*, Ken Dancyger points out another device used by Kurosawa in *Seven Samurai* and by Kubrick in *Paths of Glory* and, of course, in many other films: a tight close-up of the character that tracks or pans as the character moves. As long as the direction, action and speed match that of the wide shot, the movement of the character can either be longer or shorter than the real time move would take. If the character changes direction in the shot, then that change of direction must be preserved when cutting back to a wider shot.

5.2. Occasionally continuity of time can be reinforced by cutting to the clock, but this cannot be the primary means of keeping the audience aware of "when" they are.

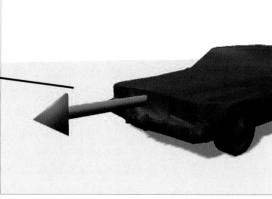

5.3. (above) The movement of the car establishes the line. The woman at top will see the car moving to her left (**5.4**, above right); the woman at the bottom will see the car moving to her right (**5.5**, right).

5.6. (below) If both of the women are viewing the car from the same side of its movement of direction, then they will both see it moving in the same direction, as in **5.7.** (below right). This is the basic principle of "the Line" and screen direction.

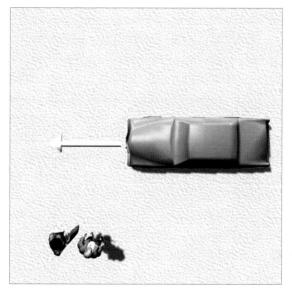

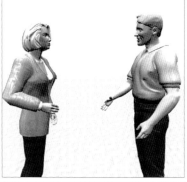

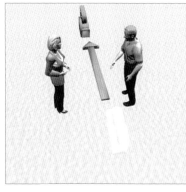

5.8. (above, far left) Two people relating to each other in some way creates a "line" — indicated here by the dashed line. With the camera on one side of them (shown here at the bottom of the picture, the woman will be on the left and the man will be on the right, as in **5.9** (above, middle).

5.10. If the camera is shifted to the other side of the line (lower far left) their positions are reversed; the man is now on the left and the woman is on the right, as shown in **5.11** (lower left). These two shots could not be cut together without creating a jarring effect.

5.12. (above, right) Where the camera can go without creating this jump in directional relationships is defined by a 180" semi-circle on one or the other side of the line. The camera can go anywhere in that 180° arc and directional continuity is maintained. This semi-circle sweep will be used throughout this chapter as a symbol for camera positions that maintain continuity. It is a symbol only — the camera can go closer or farther away, higher or lower as long as it stays on the same side of the line.

THE PRIME DIRECTIVE

Most of these techniques and rules are based on one principle — to not create confusion in the mind of the audience and thus distract them from the story or annoy and frustrate them. Let's take a fundamental example (Figures 5.3 through 5.7). Two women are standing on opposite sides of the street. Woman "A" sees the car going right. Woman "B" sees the car going left. If we move them to the *same* side of the street, they will both see the car going in the same direction in relation to their own sense of orientation (left/right). Thus their perception of the car will be the same. The movement of the car establishes direction, but there is another aspect: where the women are viewing the movement from is also important. In combination, these two establish the spatial orientation of the scene.

THE LINE

Anybody standing on the same side of that line will see things from the same orientation. "A" will always be on the left and "B" will always be on the right. Anybody standing on the other side of the line will see the opposite: "B" on the left and "A" on the right. It doesn't matter where on the other side, the result is the same.

This is what we call screen direction. Let's take this simple two shot (figures 5.8 through 5.11). From our first camera position (Figure 5.9), the woman Lucy is on the left and the man Ralph is on the right. Then, in Figure 5.10, the camera position is shifted to the other side of the line. In Figure 5.11, the audience will see, for no reason they can understand, Ralph is on the left side facing right and Lucy is on the right side facing left. It will confuse the audience, they won't be able to readily understand and assimilate the information. While their brains try to sort it out, their attention will be drawn away from the story. Not only will they be distracted from what the characters are saying and doing, if it happens often enough, it will annoy and frustrate them. What is it that delineates where we can put the camera to maintain continuity and where we can't?

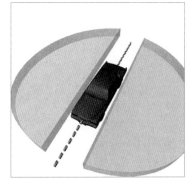

THE ACTION LINE

There is an imaginary axis between these two characters. In our first example of the car, the movement direction of the car establishes what we call the *line*. In all of these diagrams, it is represented by the large dashed line. The line is referred to by several terms; some people call it the *action axis* or the *action line*. If we stay on one side of it for all our shots — everything cuts together perfectly as in Figures 5.8 through 5.10. If we cross over to the other side — the characters will jump to opposite sides of the screen. Safe locations for the camera are symbolized by the 180° half circle — Figure 5.12. This semi-circle sweep will be used throughout this chapter to represent the camera locations which will result in consistent directional continuity. It is a symbol only; in practice the camera can go nearer or farther, higher and lower in relation to the subjects.

THESE ARE THE RULES — BUT WHY?

The basic rules of "not crossing the line" are known to all working filmmakers, but many do not stop to consider the fundamental theory and perceptual issues that underlie this principle. It is important to understand it at a deeper level if you are to be able to solve the trickier issues that do not conveniently fall into one of the basic categories of this system. More importantly, it is only when we understand the whole theoretical system that we can truly understand when it is permissible to break the rules.

First, we have to consider directionality. What do we mean by that? What is something that's not directional? Not much really. A featureless cylinder or a globe painted all the same color are non-directional, but just about everything else is. A sofa is directional; so is a car. A woman looking at a building is directional. More importantly, her *look* is directional.

Movement is also directional. Say we took that featureless globe and rolled down the sidewalk. Its line of movement is the line. If we see it from one side of the line, its going to our left and if we see it from the other side of the line it is going right. A man picking up a book is directional. The imaginary line exists between any two objects that have some sort of relationship. Even between a book and a telephone sitting on a table.

WHAT ESTABLISHES THE LINE?

Is the line always there? No, the line only exists once it has been created by something in the scene in conjunction with the position of the camera. As we saw in the example of the two women and the car, your first camera set-up in the series of shots establishes the line but it works in conjunction with elements of the scene itself. Several things can establish the line for a particular scene. They are:

- A look
- Movement
- A specific action
- Exiting frame
- Physical geography (e.g., a courtroom).

Examples are shown at left in Figures 5.13 through 5.16. Another way of thinking of it is called the *180° rule*. Once the camera is placed on one side of the line, you can move around anywhere in that 180° space and the shots will cut together (Figure 5.12).

SCREEN DIRECTION

Screen direction serves two important purposes: it gives the audience clues about the story and it helps keep the audience from getting confused about where someone is or what they are doing.

5.13. (top) A look establishes line.

5.14. (2nd from top) Directional movement establishes line.

5.15. (3rd from top) A specific action establishes line.

5.16. (above, bottom) Exiting frame establishes the line for next shot.

5.17. (left) The line established by clear and easily understood geography. The action line is practically visible itself in this shot from *High Noon*. Interestingly, the filmmakers actually purposely violate the line a few times in this scene, but since the geography is so strong these violations do not create a continuity problem.

DIRECTIONAL CONVENTIONS

The classic example of this is in low budget cowboy movies of the fifties. In these films it was always well established that one direction on screen was "towards town" and the opposite direction was "away from town" (Figures 5.18 and 5.19). Once we knew that we could tell if the good guys (white hats) or the bad guys (black hats) were heading toward town or away. Any deviation from this would have been very confusing. This type of editing was employed by D.W. Griffith, most notably in his epic *Birth of a Nation* (1915) where he used cross-cutting (cutting from one advancing army going one way to the other advancing army going the other way) to establish tension and drama. Typically as they get closer and the moment of confrontation nears, the cuts become quicker.

Another convention applies to trains, planes and automobiles. If someone is leaving the east and going to the west the plane or vehicle should be traveling left in the frame and vice versa. This is derived from the fact that nearly all maps have north at the top, thus west is left and east is right.

DELIBERATELY BREAKING THE RULES

One of the aims of editing is to *not* confuse the audience. If a character is walking towards the left of the screen in one shot and without explanation in the next shot he is walking toward the right, the audience will (even if only subconsciously) wonder why he changed. Their attention will be momentarily drawn away from the story as they try to sort it out.

This is the basic principle of all continuity in film shooting and editing. For example: she was just wearing a red dress outside the restaurant but once she stepped through the door she is wearing a blue dress. Is this a different day? A dream sequence? What hap-

5.18. (far left) In this sequence from *High Noon*, leaving town is clearly established as going left. It is consistent throughout all the shots.

5.19. (left) When the marshall decides he must stand and fight, we clearly see him turn the carriage around and head back the other way. When we next see the carriage moving toward the right, we know without any confusion that they are going back toward town.

5.20. (above) Early films, such as the *Great Train Robbery*, which treated cinema as a "filmed play" maintained a static frame and constant, unchanging left/right relationships as viewed by the audience. Since the camera rarely moves, it never changes the directional relationships of the actors or the set.

5.21 (below) An example of a true reverse from *Seven Samurai*. The camera jumps cleanly and completely to the other side of the line. (**5.22**, bottom).

5.23. (below right) A very high shot, such as this one from *The Lady From Shanghai*, is another example of a neutral shot. From this frame you can cut to any angle and any camera position in the scene without creating a continuity clash.

pened? Of course a filmmaker can use this as a storytelling device. Perhaps most famously is the breakfast sequence in *Citizen Kane*. In three seamlessly cut together shots we see Charles Foster Kane and his wife at the same dining table in the same room. Nothing changes except their appearance and attitude toward each other.

We only know that time is progressing because they are wearing different clothes and makeup in each shot. Through this simple device the deterioration of their marriage is told with great efficiency. Most famously, in the payoff shot she is reading a newspaper put out by a rival publisher: we know the marriage is doomed. Similar devices can indicate we've gone into a fantasy sequence or flashback. They can be quite subtle (a small change in makeup or hair) or dramatic: the little match girl on the street is suddenly in a gorgeous ball gown.

MAINTAINING SCREEN DIRECTION

In the early days of cinema, dramatic films were conceived as recorded theater: everything was viewed as if it were happening on a proscenium stage. The audience sat in front and could clearly discern the right and left sides of the stage. The camera merely took the place of the theater audience and never moved in relation to the scene before it (Figure 5.20). Similarly, if the front door of the house was on the right side, it never moved either. The filmspace was purely the three-dimensional world on the stage projected on the 2-D proscenium frame, but this frame was static, definitively bounded and perceptually flat. This underlines a key concept of continuity and screen direction; as filmspace has become increasing complex, fluid and fast paced, it has become more of a challenge to keep from completely confusing and frustrating the audience.

EXCEPTIONS TO THE RULE

There are several important exceptions to the rule of the line.

- If we see things change position *in the shot*, then we understand that things have changed position. If a car is moving right in the shot, and then we see it turn around so that it's going left, then there's no problem (Figures 5.18 and 5.19).
- When the camera position moves *during* the shot.
- If you cut away to something completely different, when you cut back, you can change the line.
- In the case of something that is moving, you can cut to a neutral axis shot, then go back to either side of the line.

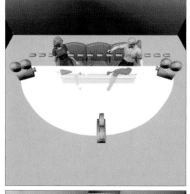

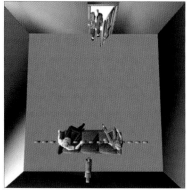

5.24. (top, left) In this scene of a couple sitting on a couch, the action line is clearly established. We can do any shots we want as long as we stay on the correct side of the line.

5.25. (top, right) A new character enters and we would like to include him in a shot which shows all three. Doing so puts the camera definitely on the wrong side of the line — **5.26** (lower left).

5.27. (lower right) Even though it is technically an error, the shot works fine because it is done boldly and the sofa helps the viewers orient themselves.

5.28. (below) Cutting to a neutral shot such as a car coming directly toward you can help transition from one side of the line to the other.

5.29. The area which can be considered a truly neutral angle is usually quite small — represented here by the small semi-circle sweeps.

A neutral shot is one where the movement is either directly towards or away from the camera (Figures 5.28 and 5.29). In essence, the line itself has moved. Some people tend to think of the line as very rigid and static, that once the line is established it can never move the whole rest of the time you are shooting the scene, but actually it is fluid and can change throughout the scene, as we will see later.

There is another exception, although it must be applied with caution. Remember, the whole point of the rule is to not confuse the audience. That is it's only reason for being; it is not a carved in stone dictum that exists independently. That means that if we can cross the line without confusing the audience, then we're still OK.

Example — a courtroom. Its layout is very clear and visually strong. At the front of the room is the bench, a large identifiable object with the judge sitting on it. On one side is the jury, then facing the judge are the counsel tables. Not only is it strong and identifiable, it's very familiar. In a situation like this you have a great deal of leeway in crossing the line without creating confusion. Still, it is not something to be taken lightly. Another example would be two rock climbers ascending a cliff. You can jump to the other side and no one is going to not understand what happened — there will be no problem. For an example see Figure 5.17.

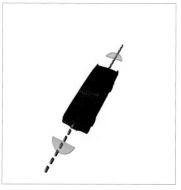

REVERSE
Another case of crossing the line is when you deliberately go to the other side for a reason. Say two people are seated on a sofa and we do extensive coverage of them from in front of the sofa, the most logical place to shoot from (Figures 5.21 and 5.22; also 5.24 through 5.27). Clearly the line has been well established. But now there is another important action. A new character has to enter through the door and have a conversation with the two people on the sofa.

It always better to show a character entering the room rather than just having them enter frame when we don't know where they came

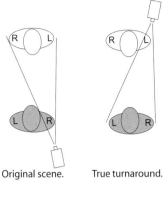

Original scene.　　　True turnaround.

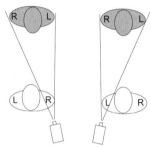

Just spinning the actors puts the camera over the wrong shoulder.

A corrrect cheat must get the camera over the proper shoulder.

5.30. Cheating a turnaround requires careful thought — it is not a matter of simply switching the actors. To make it work you have to move the camera over so that it ends up shooting over the correct shoulder of the near subject.

5.31. Cheating the turnaround sometimes includes cheating the background or set dressing. Preplanning all the coverage for a scene can often help avoid this.

from. The simple solution would be to just turn the camera around and see him enter the door. There are a few problems with this. First of all, it doesn't connect the new character to our two people.

Second, we wouldn't really know where the door is and that he is entering the same room. Since they have not seen the door before, for all the audience knows, we have gone to a completely new scene and this man is entering another room somewhere. Finally, we don't have a chance to see their reaction to him coming in; for example, do they stand up quickly when he comes in, as if they are frightened by him? What we would really like to do is put the camera in the back of the room behind the sofa, so we see them in the foreground and see him entering. This establishes everything: it's the same room, the door was behind us all the time, we see their reaction, and so on. But that would be crossing the line so we can't do it, right?

Yes it is crossing the line, but yes, you can do it. It's called a reverse or a reverse angle. But you can't just do it willy-nilly. You can't do it on a close-up; that would be just crossing the line. The important thing is that we still see the two people in the foreground, but we see the new character and the door in the background. There is motivation for being on the other side; there is an understandable reason. We may be in a new orientation, but it is comprehensible.

Another factor in a successful reverse is the boldness of it. Just crossing the line slightly would probably not work. It is when you definitely and unquestionably are on the other side of the line that a reverse is understandable. The audience does have to do some mental reorientation, but given the proper clues they can do so without disruption.

TURNAROUND

Obviously you would never do the over-the-shoulder on one actor, then move the camera to do the OTS on the other actor, then go back to the first for the close-up and so on. This would be very inefficient and time consuming. So naturally you do all the coverage on one side then move the camera and reset the lighting. This is called the turnaround. The group of OTSs and close-ups which match the ones done on the first actor are called the answering shots. Every shot you do in the first set-up should have an answering shot. After

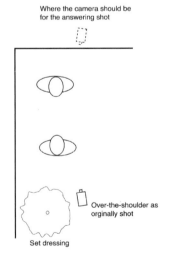

Where the camera should be for the answering shot

Set dressing

Over-the-shoulder as orginally shot

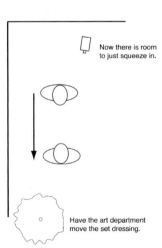

Now there is room to just squeeze in.

Have the art department move the set dressing.

window and door matching, the turnaround is the other major area where cheating is employed. In cases where some physical obstacle precludes a good camera position for the turnaround, or perhaps the sun is at a bad angle or maybe it's a complex lighting setup and there simply isn't time to break it down and re-light for the answering shot.

CHEATING THE TURNAROUND

In any of these cases, it is possible to leave the camera and lights where they are and just move the actors. This is a last ditch measure and is only used in cases where the background for one part of the coverage is not usable or there is an emergency in terms of the schedule, if for example, the sun is going down. The theory is that once we are in tight shots on the coverage, we really don't see much of the background.

It is not correct, however, to just have them switch places. In our sample scene, we are over the shoulder of Jennifer, looking at Dave. In the OTS of Dave, we are seeing over Jennifer's right shoulder. If we did a real turnaround, we would be over Dave's left shoulder. (Figure 5.30). In this illustration we see two cases: in #1 we rotate the camera 180°. This is a real turnaround. In case #2 we just spin the actors and leave the camera where it is. You can see the problem: the camera is over the wrong shoulder.

In cheating a turnaround, you have to either move the camera a couple of feet or better, just slide the foreground actor over so you are over the correct shoulder. (Fortunately, moving the foreground actor seldom involves any substantial relighting.) The key to a successful cheat is that the background either be neutral or similar for both actors as established in any previous wide shots. If there are recognizable objects in the background, it may be helpful to shift a bit.

PREPLANNING COVERAGE

Which brings us to another key point which is easily overlooked: whenever you are setting up a master, take a moment to think about the coverage. Make sure that there is some way to position the camera for proper answering shots. Particularly if one character's coverage is more dramatic or more crucial to the story than the other, it is very easy to get yourself backed into a corner or up against an obstruction that makes it difficult or impossible to position the camera for a proper answering shot (Figure 5.31).

Remember that ideally, an answering shot should be the same focal length, focus distance and angle as the shot it is paired with. In a pinch, if you can't get quite far enough back (or close enough) you can cheat a bit with a different focal length to end up with the same

5.32 (above, far left). A walk-and-talk is not as simple as it seems. There are actually two action lines here.

5.33. (above, middle) Their direction of walking is one, but the look between the two of them is the stronger of the two. It is easier to cross the line of their direction of travel without disturbing the continuity **(5.34)** (above, right).

5.35. The 20% rule and the 30° rule are pretty much the same thing.

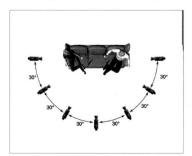

5.36 and **5.37** (above) In this door shot from *Touch of Evil*, the character switches direction.

5.38 and **5.39** (above right and far right) Maintaining the same direction while going through a door is often desirable, but by no means required.

5.40. (below) Covering curved walk.

5.41. (bottom) Some positions which seem to be on the wrong side of the line (A-1 and E) are OK because they are actually neutral angles which can pan into either screen direction.

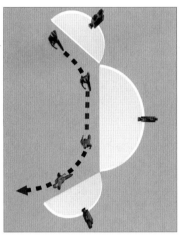

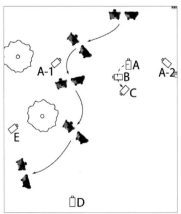

image size, which is by far the most important parameter. The perspective and depth of field may be slightly different, but, depending on the background, this may not be noticeable. The second possibility is to cheat the actors out a bit. This is especially workable if we haven't seen too much of the background behind #1. For over-the-shoulders and close-ups, it is usually only necessary to have them move a few feet. They will be in a slightly different position in the room, but normally this will not be noticeable.

CUTTABILITY
So that's the 180° rule and we can shoot anywhere in the 180° circle, right? Well, not quite. First let's define what makes shots *cuttable*. when we put a sequence together it is important that when one shot follows another, it does so smoothly, not jarringly.

Example — our two people are on the sofa. We are doing a shot from the side that includes both of them and the arms of the sofa. Then we move in just a bit and get a similar shot of the two of them but without the sofa arms. How would it look if we cut these two together? The effect would be jarring. Suddenly the image size changes just slightly, as if the camera accidentally got kicked or maybe the film broke and some frames are missing. It would look awful. For two shots to be cuttable, there needs to be a more substantial change. If instead of moving in just slightly, for example, we moved in a lot so that the shot is just a close-up shot of one of the characters. Then the two shots would be cuttable.

THE 20% RULE
How do we know how much we have to change to make two similar shots cuttable? It's called the 20% rule. In general, a shot must change by at least 20% to be cuttable. That can be a 20% change in angle, in lens size or camera position. It's a rough guideline, of course; no need to get out the calculator (Figure 5.35).

A particular example of this is the 30° rule — it's not a different rule, just a specific application of the 20% rule (Figure 5.35). Let's go back to our 180° circle. Without changing the lens, or moving closer or farther away, as long as we move 30° to the left or right along that circle, we're OK. With lens changes, it is more subjective. Depending on other factors in the shot, moving up or down one lens, say from a 50mm to a 35mm, may or may not be enough. Frequently, it is necessary to change two lens sizes: say from a 50mm to a 25mm. In the end it usually comes down to a judgment call.

OTHER ISSUES IN CONTINUITY
MOVING SHOTS
Two types of shots predominate in moving shots: the driving shot and walk-and-talk. The same rules apply to both. At first glance we would think that the direction of the car or the walk is the major axis, but in fact it is only a secondary axis. The major axis for screen direction is between the two people as in Figures 5.32 through 5.34.

5.42. Before you shoot a character turning a corner, you have to think about where the line will be. The positions indicated by the "X" here would inexplicably have the character walking toward the right instead of to the left. In cases of this general type, if you shoot a neutral angle you can technically go to another screen direction, but it still may not be a good idea. As with all issues of continuity and matching, judgment and experience are preferable to blindly adhering to cut and dried rules.

Since our attention is on the principles in the foreground, the movement of the background becomes a minor issue as we don't notice that the direction flips back and forth. (Figures 5.43 and 5.44). When we are outside and the car itself is the principle object, this is no longer true, then screen direction of the car matters.

GOING THROUGH A DOOR
There are two schools of thought on door entrances and exits. Some will say that if a character goes through a door going to the right (in an exterior shot), they have to emerge on the other side also going right (in the interior shot). Others maintain that once someone goes through a door it is a "new deal" and anything goes. Again it is a subjective call. If there is a very clear connection between the two, and the directionality is very strong, then it is a good idea to maintain directional continuity between the two. If there is a great deal of difference between the interior and exterior and there is a greater change in angle, camera position, or lens size between the two, it is possible to go to the other side when the character emerges on the other side of the door, as in this example from *Touch of Evil* (Figures 5.36 and 5.37).

5.43 and **5.44**. Car shots are an example of camera positions which seem to violate continuity but are perfectly acceptable. The screen direction of the actors changes completely but since the car so clearly establishes where they are, there is no problem.

5.45. (below right) Standard camera positions for car mounts.

5.46. (below left) A neutral angle tail-away shot from *Touch of Evil*.

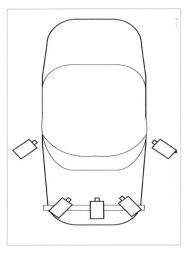

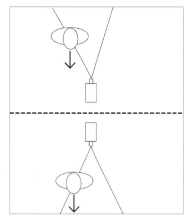

5.47. (above) When a character exits the frame, this establishes a direction which must be observed when the character re-enters. Think of it as if you were panning the camera.

5.48 and **5.49**. (right and far right) To be a truly neutral angle, the object or character must exit the top or bottom of the frame.

COVERING A CURVING WALK
A shot where a character or group walks in curves can be tricky, but as long as you remember the fundamentals, it can be easy to figure out as in Figures 5.40 and 5.41.

TURNING A CORNER
Turning a corner is subject to the same rules as covering a curved walk. If the camera cuts when the character disappears around the corner of a building, when we pick him up on the other side, the screen direction should be maintained (Figure 5.42).

ENTERING AND EXITING FRAME
As we noted before, exiting frame establishes screen direction. Once a character exits either frame left or right, they should enter the next from the opposite side (Figure 5.47). You can think of it as an imaginary pan. As the character exits frame, you mentally pan with her — this positions you correctly for the next shot of entering frame. As with all continuity sequences if something else comes in between the exit and the entrance, anything goes.

NEUTRAL AXIS TO EXIT FRAME
If the moving vehicle or character exits on a completely neutral axis, then you are free to go anywhere you want on the next cut. For something to exit on a truly neutral axis, however, it has to exit either above or below the frame (Figure 5.48 and 5.49).

5.50. (below left) A two shot with a prop between them.

5.51 and **5.52**. (below middle and right) Unless you cheat the prop in coverage it will tend to "pop" back and forth in the frame as you cut to each closeup. It is better to remove it entirely or cheat it so that it stays relatively consistent.

THREE SHOTS
Screen direction is basically the same in three shots, but one thing to watch out for is overlapping the person in the center. If you break it up as a pair of two shots, the person in the center will appear in both shots and there will be unavoidable continuity problems. The center character will "pop" as you cut from shot to shot (Figures 5.53 through 5.55).

KEEP THE NOSE OUT

For the same reason it is important to avoid getting a part of the foreground person in the shot when doing a clean single over the shoulder of the second character. When two characters are fairly close to each other in the master, it is often difficult to completely frame the second person out, especially if they move around a lot. Often their nose, or a hand or some small piece of them will creep into the single.

This is not only compositionally annoying but will cause continuity problems. It will often be necessary to shift the off screen character back a bit so they don't creep in. You don't want to do it so much that you "miss" his presence in the coverage. If there is a large shift, be sure to set a new eyeline for the on-screen character so that their head doesn't shift too much from the master. It may be necessary for the actor to look at a mark rather than at the other actor, which is something to avoid as it does make it difficult for the performer.

PROP CONTINUITY IN COVERAGE

The principle of overlapping applies to foreground props as well as three shots. In this example (Figures 5.50 through 5.52), there is a candlestick on the table between them. If it is left in its position from the master, it will seem to jump back and forth as you cut from medium shot on one actor to medium on the other. Your choices are to cheat it out of the mediums altogether (the safest) or cheating it back and forth for each medium — riskier, but it may make the mediums a better match to the master.

THREE SHOTS WITH DOMINANT CHARACTER

Three shots where one character is separate or dominates in some way call for a slightly different treatment (Figures 5.56 and 5.57). If we open with 5.56 as the master, coverage is then dictated by what we can think of as two screen direction lines — a major and a minor. The major axis (between the bartender and the man) applies to the whole scene, as in Figure 5.57. The minor axis applies to over-the-shoulders between the bartender and the woman.

5.53. (above left) A three shot with a dominant character in the middle.

5.54 and **5.55**. (above middle and right) If coverage is not clean singles, then you need to be sure that hand and head continuity match for the character that appears on both sides of the coverage. In this example we see that he is gesturing with different hands. This will drive your editor crazy.

 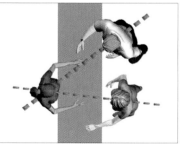

5.56. and **5.57**. (far left and left) If group shots have no other dominant direction such as the bar in these shots, coverage can be pretty much anywhere, however it is often better to pick one side or the other and stick to it. In this example the bar establishes a major action line (heavy dashed line) and the physical relationship between the two women establishes a minor action line.

5.58 (top left) This master from *Ronin* establishes the main group and their places around the table.

5.59. (top middle) The next cut reveals the person separate from the group in a way which shows her relationship to them — it orients us to the overall arrangement.

5.60. (top right) This cut to a three shot maintains the screen direction established in the master (5.57). This is a good example of how seeing a piece of the table helps keep us grounded in the scene. If it wasn't there we would definitely miss it.

5.61. (above left) This over-the-shoulder of the girl is on the opposite side of the line from **5.60**; it is outside the group. However, since the previous sequence of shots has clearly established all the relationships there is no problem.

5.62. (above middle) This single on the man in the suit also benefits from seeing a piece of the table. If it was necessary to move the table to get the shot, the set dressers will often have something smaller that can stand in for it.

5.63. (above right) This shot is from the POV of the man in the suit but we don't see any of him in the foreground. In this case we are said to be "inside" him — not inside his body, but inside his field of vision.

EYE SWEEPS

When an off-screen character walks behind the camera, the on-screen character may follow with her eyes. Many inexperience directors are reluctant to do this as they think it won't work. It's perfectly OK as long as the eye sweep is slightly above or below the lens. As always, it is important that the actor not look directly into the lens, even for just a moment. The most important thing about eye sweeps is that they match the direction and speed of the crossing character. This means that the on-screen actor will move their head in the opposite direction of the movement of the crossing, since we are essentially crossing the line in a reverse. If you are shooting the eye sweep first, it may be desirable to shoot a few different speeds as when the crossing is shot later, the speed may not match.

GROUP SHOTS

Scenes with more than three characters generally require a good deal of coverage. If there is a dominant direction to the arrangement of the group, that will most likely dictate a screen direction line based on where you shoot the master from. In practice it may be possible to shoot from almost anywhere as long as you get the proper answering shots and coverage, however, it may be better to pick an arbitrary line and stick to it — this will reduce confusion in the audience's perceptions. If there is a dominant character standing apart from the group, this will often establish the line. These frames from a group scene in *Ronin* illustrates some of these principles. (Figures 5.58 through 5.63) Notice in particular the slight difference between 5.59 and 5.63. Both are shots down the middle of the axis; 5.63, however is an over-the-shoulder past the man in the suit while 5.59 does not include him. It is more of his POV. In this case we are said to be "inside" the character, that is, we are near him and his POV but no part of him is included in the shot.

CHASE SCENES

Chase scenes can be problematic for screen direction. As a general rule of thumb you want to maintain an overall direction within the scene but there is considerable room for variation. When the chase itself changes direction, your screen direction may change as well. For car chases especially, some directors prefer to mix it up more, with opposing shots of the same car from different directions and angles cut together dramatically to slightly disorient the audience and emphasize the kinetic nature of the chase. This is in keeping with Eisenstein's theory of the "collision" of shots.

CONVERGING ACTION
Converging action or parallel cutting was first made famous by D.W. Griffith in *Birth of a Nation* (although he had used it before in smaller films). The idea is that as two opposing forces are moving toward each other, the visual tension and pacing should intensify. Naturally, they must be moving in opposite directions.

CUTAWAY EYELINE CONTINUITY
Since cutaways are not part of the main scene but are physically related to it, directional continuity must be maintained between the location of the scene and the cutaway element. This is especially important for cutaways that involve a look from the additional character, which they often do (Figures 5.64 and 5.65). Since you are moving away from the main scene and it is usually for a quick pick-up shot, often you will be up against limitations of the set, your lighting or other problems which will make it necessary for you to cheat the additional character a bit. In this case, it is important to be careful about the eyelines. Since often it is the look that is important, eyeline direction is critical.

LOOK ESTABLISHES NEW LINE
In a related issue, let's focus on the couple at the table. In our scene of a couple in a restaurant, the conversation between the couple has it's own line. When she turns to look at the gangster, that establishes a new line which must be respected in all shots which involve the couple at the table and the gangster (Figures 5.67 through 5.69). It does not replace the line established by the couple's conversation, which must still be used for any coverage at their table.

EYELINES IN OVER-THE-SHOULDER COVERAGE
When shooting over-the-shoulder coverage, the camera height will generally be at eye level for the characters. If the two performers are of unequal height, some modification is usually necessary. In this case, the camera height will approximately match that of the character over whose shoulder you are shooting.

5.64. (above left) This master establishes the background group and that the man with the mustache is looking to the left of camera.

5.65. (above) In the cutaway to the background group, the directional relationships are maintained and most importantly the man with the mustache is still looking to camera left — there can be no question but that he is looking toward the foreground group.

5.66. (below) For a standing figure in a scene with a seated character, there are several choices — a straight over-the-shoulder from the standing character might be too extreme.

5.67. (bottom left) Two people at a table establishes a strong action line.

5.68. (bottom middle) If one of them looks off-screen to something else, this establishes a new line beween the two, as in **5.69** (bottom right).

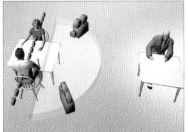

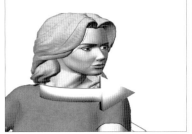

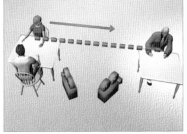

5.70. As the action moves, so does the line. The camera position marked with an "X" would reverse the two characters. In rapid action scenes, however, this type of continuity break is not unusual; some directors do it deliberately to increase the sense of frantic confusion.

5.71. (below) The opening frame of a very long slow deliberate zoom out from *Barry Lyndon*.

5.72. (bottom) The last frame from that same zoom. Kubrick uses this type of slow disclosure thematically throughout the film, always ending in a perfectly balanced formal composition, often based on a painting of the period. The slow zoom out works on many levels, both visually and storywise.

EYELINES FOR A SEATED CHARACTER

The same principle applies when one or more of the characters is seated or on the floor, but with an important exception. Since shooting over the shoulder of the standing character might be an extreme angle, it also works to keep the camera at the eye-level of the seated performer which makes it sort of a "past the hips shot."

In situations like this, for the clean singles, when there is a difference in height or level of the characters in coverage, the eyelines may also need some adjustment. This does not apply to over-the-shoulders, as we can see the off-screen performer's head and thus we know the actual eye-level. In this case the eyeline of the seated characters should be slightly above the lens and the eyeline of the standing character should be slightly below the lens (Figure 5.66). Be careful not to overdo this. As with all eyelines and cheats, the final judgment should be made while looking through the lens. How it looks and how it will work in editing always trumps a rote rule.

OTS AND INSERTS

Inserts generally are not critical in terms of screen direction except in a general way. One instance where they are important is reading inserts. This type of insert is quite common as the master scene or even an over the shoulder is usually not tight enough to allow the audience to actually read what the character is looking at. In these cases, it is important to conform to the eyeline and screen direction of the character reading the material, even if they are not holding it in their hand.

MOVING ACTION

Once you thoroughly understand the underlying principles and the cognitive reasons for the these rules, it is easier to see when there are exceptions and flexibility. It is important to remember that "the line" is not some physical thing that has an independent existence on the set. The line is only in relation to where you have first established the scene by the camera placement of the first shot that appears on screen (Figure 5.70). Also, the line moves, as we saw in the example of the couple and the gangster in the restaurant. Most importantly, in a scene with moving action, such as a fight scene, the line will be shifting constantly.

In highly frenetic fight scenes photographed with lots of angles and cuts to be edited in a rapid fire sequence, the director and editor might want to ignore the line altogether to add a sense of action and disorientation to the scene. In general, however, it is good to observe screen direction rules — especially if the two people fighting are not physically distinct in look or wardrobe. Otherwise the audience might end up rooting for the wrong guy.

INTRODUCTIONS

When you are bringing the viewer into a scene, you can think of it much the same as bringing a stranger into a party. Some of the concepts have been mentioned before, but now let's consider them in the context of narrative continuity. There are four basic introductions that need to be made: Place, Time, Geography and the Main Characters.

Many aspects of introductions and transitions are functions of the script, but they must be actualized by the director and the cinematographer on the set. Some are improvised at the time of shooting as they may be based on some prop or aspect of the set or location that has not been apparent before, such as a perfect full moon just above the scene.

THE PLACE

We need to let the audience know where they are. Establishing shots and variations are discussed in the chapter on *Filmspace*. There is an important exception to this called slow disclosure. In this technique, instead of opening with a wide shot, the scene begins with a tight shot of a character or another scene element. Only as the scene progresses does the camera pull back to reveal where we are and what is going on. This is a variation of the basic reveal where the camera starts on something that either moves or the camera moves past it to show some other scene element.

Not only a master formalist but also a great visualist, Stanley Kubrick uses slow disclosure masterfully in *Barry Lyndon* (Figures 5.71 and 5.72). Throughout the film, one of the key formal devices is the very long, very slow zoom back. He starts with a telling detail of the scene and then very deliberately pulls back to reveal more and more. As with so many other aspects of the film (its perfectly composed fixed frames based on paintings of the period, the emphasis on formal geometry and the slow pacing of action and editing) this slow pull back underlines the rigid formalism of society and culture at that time as well as the fatalistic inevitability of Lyndon's decline.

THE TIME

Beyond *where* we are, the viewer must know *when* we are. Internally within the scene, this is either a function of a transition shot or other types of temporal clues. In these two frames from *Ronin* (Figures 5.73 and 5.74) the director needed to find a way to establish that fifteen or twenty minutes had passed. This can be much more difficult that conveying that days have past or that it was summer and now it's winter — which can be accomplished by a simple exterior shot of the green trees which dissolves to a shot of the same tree barren of leaves and a layer of new fallen snow on the ground. Here he has done something very subtle. In the first shot we see the bellboys starting to put decorations on a tree in the hotel lobby. In the second shot, as the camera pans to follow the character's exit, we see that the decorations have been completed. For the vast majority of the audience, this is no doubt completely subconscious, but it does help to convey the passage of time.

THE GEOGRAPHY

This was discussed previously, but it deserves mention here as there are several aspects to establishing the geography which relate to actual shooting on the set. Establishing the place usually just serves the purpose of showing us where the scene will take place. This is just called the establishing shot. Establishing the geography is a bit different than just letting the viewer know where the action takes place. Where an establishing shot is generally an exterior view of the building, establishing the geography relates to the scene itself, particularly, but not exclusively, the interiors. It is not enough that the audience knows the general location of the scene, it is also important that they have a general comprehension of the layout of the place — the overall geography. This prevents confusion as characters move around or as the camera cuts to other viewpoints or other action within the scene.

THE MAIN CHARACTERS

Introducing the characters is of course mostly a function of the script and the actors but a general principle is to introduce key characters in some way that visually underlines some aspect of their importance, their nature and their story function. Also, making this

5.73. Devices to convey a short passage of time are often more difficult than demonstrating a long passage of time between cuts. In *Ronin*, the director uses the fact that the Christmas tree is being decorated in one shot (below).

5.74. (bottom) In the next shot, the tree is fully decorated. Very subtle but the audience will subconsciously register that some short amount of time has passed bewteen the two shots.

5.75. A dramatic and suspenseful introduction of the main antagonist in *High Noon*. The director delays showing his face until the most dramatic story moment.

introduction visually interesting helps the audience remember the character: a form of visual punctuation.

For the entire first half of *High Noon*, we have been waiting for the arrival of the bad guy on the noon train. He has been discussed, feared, even run away from. Finally we meet him (Figure 5.75). Zinnemann handles his introduction cleverly. As he first gets off the train, we do not see his face. Then for an entire sequence of shots, we see him being greeted, strapping on his guns — still we do not see his face. Finally, his former lover is getting onto the train; she is leaving town only because he has come back. She turns to look at him and it is only then that we first see his face as his eyes lock with hers. It is a dramatic and distinctive way to introduce him.

OTHER EDITORIAL ISSUES IN SHOOTING

EDITORIAL FODDER

In the course of shooting the scene, it is important to not be so focused on the essential action and storytelling that there is no thought of the small shots that will help the editor put the scene together in a way that is seamless, logical and also suits the tone, pacing and mood of the sequence. These include cutaways, inserts, and little character type shots that may not be directly related to the scene but contribute to the overall ambiance. Some directors keep a running list of "things to get," but the safer strategy is to let the script supervisor keep this list.

JUMP CUTS

Disruptions of continuity can result in a jump cut. Although clearly an error in methodology, jump cuts can be used as editorial technique. Truffaut and others of the nouvelle vague in France in the early sixties were among the first to employ jump cuts effectively. According to Ken Dancyger, in his discussion of *The 400 Blows*: "How did the stylistic equivalent of the personal story translate into editing choices? The moving camera was used to avoid editing. In addition, the jump cut was used to challenge continuity editing and that it implied. The jump cut itself is nothing more than the joining of two noncontinuous shots. Whether the two shots recognized a change in direction, focus on an unexpected action, or simply don't show the action in one shot that prepares the viewer for the content of the next shot, the result of the jump cut is to focus on discontinuity. Not only does the jump cut remind viewers that they are watching a film, it is also jarring. This result can be used to suggest instability or lack of importance.... The jump cut asks viewers to tolerate the admission that we are watching a film or to temporarily suspend belief in the film." (Ken Dancyger, *The Technique of Film and Video Editing*).

THE SIX TYPES OF CUTS

Some aspects of editing are beyond the scope of what we deal with in day-to-day production on the set, but directors, cinematographers and videographers must know most of the major concepts of editorial cutting in order to avoid mistakes and to provide the editor with the material she needs to not only cut the film together seamlessly, but also to control pacing and flow, delineate overall structure and give the scenes and the whole piece unity and cohesion. There are six basic types of cuts, some of which have been touched on above. They are:

- The content cut
- The action cut
- The POV cut
- The match cut
- The conceptual cut
- The zero cut

THE CONTENT CUT

The content cut applies to whenever we cut to a new shot within a scene only to add new information or carry the story forward. In its simplest form, content cutting is used in the coverage of a conversation. We cut from the master, to the over-the-shoulder, to the close-up. Nothing changes in these shots except the content. We were seeing both of them, now we see one of them, etc. The content cut is just a part of the overall forward progression of the narrative. As with all cuts, it must obey the basic rules of the line and the 20% rule in order to be cuttable.

THE ACTION CUT

The action cut, sometimes called a continuity cut or a movement cut, is employed whenever action is started in one shot and finished in the next. For example: in the first shot we see him opening the door, in the next shot we see him emerging from the other side of the door. Or: she reaches across the table, then cut to her hand picking up the cup of coffee. Shooting for the action cut must be done properly if it is to work in editing.

First of all, you should always overlap the action. In this example, it would be a mistake to have her reach for the cup of coffee then call "cut" as soon as her arm extends, then proceed to a close-up of her arm coming in to pick up the shot. There is a grave danger that there will be a piece missing which will result in a jump cut. In this case, if her arm extends only to the edge of the table in the first shot but when we see it in the next shot it is all the way to the middle of the table that missing part will be very noticeable.

Shooting the overlap also gives the editor the choice of exactly when to time the cut. This is important not only for pacing but for continuity as well. Seldom will there be an absolute exact match between her arm movement in the wide shot and in the close shot. If the editor has some freedom to time the cut, small problems in movement can be smoothed over. In this small example, the overlapping action is fairly small. In the case of entering and exiting doors, getting in and out of vehicles, etc., fairly substantial overlaps should be shot. This is especially true if there is important action or

5.76 and **5.77**. (right and far right) The characters look followed by a cut to the clock shot from an angle consistent with where their eyes would be. Likewise, their head angle and eyeline must match where the clock is on the wall (*High Noon*).

dialog going on during the move. In that case, the editor needs to have the ability to adjust for performance and narrative flow as well as simple continuity.

In shooting close shots which continue the action in a larger shot, it is also important to match the speed of the action. In the case of picking up coffee, the actor may have been in the middle of a big speech as she reached for the coffee and thus did it slowly and deliberately. If a good deal of time has passed between shooting the wide shot and picking up an insert of the hand picking up the coffee, it is possible that she will not be doing the dialog and all she is doing is sticking her hand in the frame to grab the cup. In this case, it is very easy for her to forget the pacing of the original shot and think of this as something independent. The urge is to just stick your hand in and grab it.

Cutting On Action

While shooting for an action cut it is important to always be aware of the possibilities of the cut point. It is always best to cut "on the action." If someone is seated at a desk and rises to go to the door, you want to shoot while he is rising from the chair. If the phone rings, you want to cut to the next shot while he is reaching for the phone, and so on. Cutting on action makes for a smoother cut and a more invisible one. The audience is a bit distracted by the action and less likely to notice the cut. It also makes continuity and flow much easier. Take the example of answering the phone. Let's assume that in the medium shot, the phone rings, he picks it up and starts talking. Then we cut to a close-up of him talking. In this case, it is critical that his head be in exactly the same position, that he is holding the phone in exactly the same way and his facial expression be an exact match. If any of these fails, it will be bad continuity and will be distracting. Cutting as he reaches for the phone avoids these problems.

THE POV CUT

The POV cut is sometimes called "the look." It is one of the most fundamental building blocks of continuity and is especially valuable in cheating shots and establishing physical relationships. A POV cut occurs anytime a look off-screen in the first shot motivates a view of something in the next shot (Figures 5.76 and 5.77). The simplest case:

Shot #1: A character looks off screen and up.

Shot #2: A view of a clock tower.

There will be no question in the mind of the viewer that we are seeing the tower as he would see it; that is from his point-of-view. In order to do this, the POV shot must satisfy certain conditions.

- Direction of look. If it is to a shot of the clock tower, clearly, he has to look up. Further, he must look up at approximately the right angle. If his gaze only rises about 10°, for example, and the clock tower is ten stories high, it won't work. Similarly, if we have seen in a wide shot that the clock tower is on his right side, then his look must go to the right as well.

- Angle of the POV. The shot of the clock tower must bear some logical relationship to where the viewer is. If we have seen that he is standing on the plaza right under the tower, then we cannot cut in a shot of it as seen from a hundred yards away as seen over the trees.

The POV cut is a classic means of cheating locations. For example, our story is based on him seeing a murder in the building opposite him but unfortunately, the building opposite our location is unavailable for use. In this case, the POV cut from him looking out the window to a POV of his view through the window of the building across the street will sell the concept that he can see the murder.

As discussed in the chapter on *Filmspace*, it is easy to over-rely on the POV cut to the extent that it makes the scenes artificial and empty. It is always best to get a connecting shot that ties it all together if at all possible (Figure 1.30).

THE MATCH CUT

The match cut is most often used as a transitional device between scenes. An example from a western: the telegrapher sends the message that the governor has not granted a pardon; the hanging will go on as scheduled. From the telegrapher, we go to a shot of the telegraph pole (probably with an audio cut of the clicking of the telegraph). Then from the shot of the telegraph pole we cut to a shot of the gallows: a vertical pole approximately the same size, shape and in the same position as the telegraph pole. One image exactly replaces the other on screen.

One of the most effective uses of a match cut is in *Apocalypse Now*, where Coppola cuts from the spinning blades of the ceiling fan in the Saigon hotel room to the spinning blades of a helicopter deep in the combat zone. Great care must be taken in shooting both sides of a match cut. It is not enough that the objects be similar in shape: the screen size (as determined by focal length) and the position in the frame must also match. One method is to have a video tape of the previously shot scene and play it back on the director's video monitor. For precision work, a monitor with an A/B switch allows the image to be quickly switched back and forth from the freeze frame of the video tape to the live picture from the video tap. As an additional guide, a grease pencil or china marker can be used to outline the object on the monitor.

THE CONCEPTUAL CUT

We previously discussed the editorial cut that spans tens of thousands of years used to transition from pre-historic times to the era of space travel in Kubrick's *2001: A Space Odyssey*. This is a match cut because the direction, movement, shape and screen size of the bone almost exactly matches that of the spacecraft. It is also a conceptual cut, however, in that Kubrick is using the bone as a metaphor for man's very first use of a tool. The spacecraft then is the ultimate result of the first use of tools—a tool that can carry humans into space. These types of cuts are always spelled out in the script. What is relevant for the cinematographer and the director working on the set is that these shots must be pre-visualized, planned and executed with an eye towards their final purpose.

There are other types of conceptual cuts which are not match cuts. For example, in a war film, the general might say, "We'll bomb 'em back to the stone age," and slam his fist down on the table. This cuts immediately to a shot of a bomb. The cut is carried over by the action, by the idea and by the sound edit. Audio often plays a role in conceptual cuts.

5.78, **5.79** and **5.80**. This shot from *Ronin* appears to be one continuous pan but in fact when a passing pedestrian wipes the frame, there is a cut which enables the filmmaker to use two entirely different locations as the beginning and end of the same shot.

THE ZERO CUT

The zero cut is a type of match cut that rarely gets mentioned in discussions of shooting and editing. It is often used in action scenes. Near the beginning of *The Last Boy Scout*, there is an action scene in which the character is thrown over an embankment. We see him hit the ground in a medium shot, then roll out of the way of an oncoming car. It is very high energy and it is almost impossible to see that what seems like one continuous shot is actually two shots cut together. At the moment he hits the ground, there is a cut to another shot from the same angle, same lens and same image size which continues the action.

Technically, this is something you are not supposed to do. Here, it is not intended as an editorial cut at all, it is used to stitch together two shots to make one. It was to put together two pieces of a dangerous stunt so that we see the actor fall over the embankment and then think we see him just missed by a speeding car, when, in fact we are seeing a stunt man in the second shot. The same device is used several times in that particular scene.

A similar technique is used by John Frankenheimer in *Ronin* (Figures 5.78 through 5.80). In this case, the camera tracks with a man as he walks down a street in Austria. An extra wipes the frame (blocking it entirely for a frame or two) and the character walks on. Nothing especially remarkable about the shot. The trick is that it is actually two shots that were done thousands of miles and weeks apart. The first part of the shot was done on location in Europe and the second part of the shot is on a studio lot in Los Angeles. This gives the director the opportunity to use the strong points of two locations combined into one continuous shot.

This technique is the same as is used by Hitchcock in his "one shot" film *Rope* — they are what made it possible for him to shoot the entire film so it appears to be one long continuous take, even though a roll of film in the camera lasts only 11 minutes. Although *Rope* gives the impression of one long take, it is a myth that there are no cuts at all; in fact there are a few, most of them at reel changes.

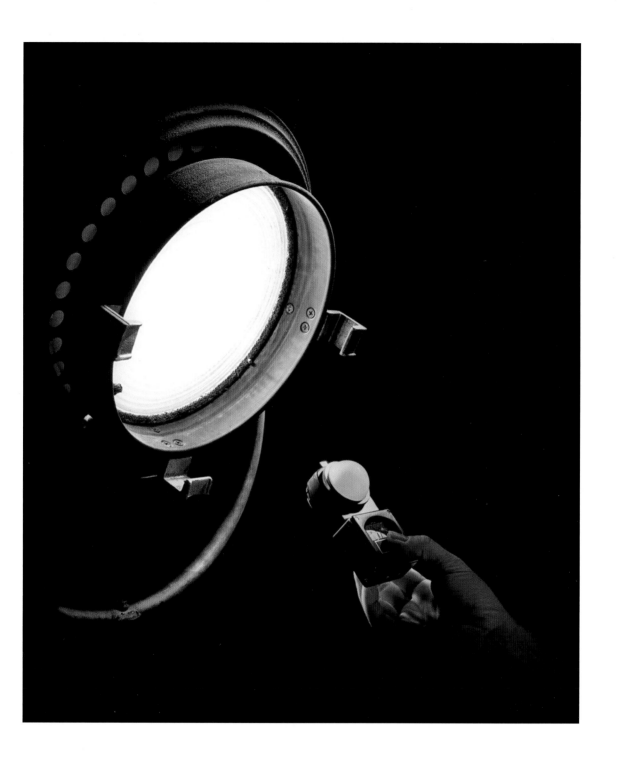

exposure

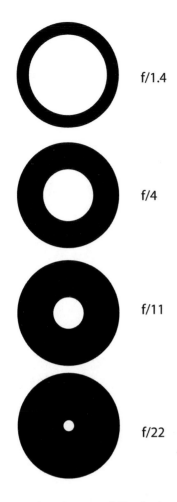

f/1.4

f/4

f/11

f/22

6.1. (previous page) The basics of exposure: a source and a light meter. (Photo by author.)

6.2. (above) The aperture at various f/stops.

LIGHT AS ENERGY

Energy from the Sun comes to the Earth in visible and invisible portions of the electromagnetic spectrum. Human eyes are sensitive to a small portion of that spectrum that includes the visible colors from the longest visible wavelengths of light (Red) to the shortest wavelengths (Blue).

Intensity of light is measured in foot-candles (in the United States) or in lux (in most other countries). A foot-candle (fc) equals about 10.08 lux (or, for a rough conversion, multiply foot-candles by 10 to get lux). A foot-candle is the light from a standard candle at a distance of one foot. One lux is the illumination produced by one standard candle from a distance of 1 meter. When a film is exposed for 1 second to a standard candle 1 meter distance, it receives 1 lux-sec of exposure. What's a standard candle? It's like the standard horse in horse-power. To provide some points of reference:

- Sunlight on an average day ranges from 32,000 to 100,000 lux (3,175 to 10,000 fc)
- Typical TV studios are lit at about 1,000 lux (99 fc)
- A bright office has about 400 lux of illumination (40 fc)
- Moonlight represents about 1 lux (a tenth of a foot-candle)

The f/stop is covered in more detail in the chapter on *Optics*, but for our discussion here it is important to know how it fits into the exposure system. F/stop and lighting calculations apply equally to both film and all forms of video as does much of the information in this chapter.

F/STOP

Most lenses have a means of controlling the amount of light they pass through to the film or video receptor; this is called the aperture. The f/stop is the mathematical relationship of overall size of the lens to the size of the aperture.

"Stop" is a short term for f/stop. A stop is a unit of light measurement. An increase in the amount of light by one stop means there is twice as much light. A decrease of one stop means there is half as much light. A lens with an f/stop of 1.0 would theoretically pass all of the light reaching through to the focal plane. The f/stop is the ratio of the focal length of a lens to the diameter of the entrance pupil as shown in Figure 6.2. This works out to each stop being greater than the previous by the square root of 2.

F/stop is derived from the simple formula:

$$f = F/D$$

f/stop = focal length/diameter of lens opening

If the brightest point in the scene has 128 times more luminance than the darkest point (seven stops), then we say it has a seven stop scene brightness ratio.

EXPOSURE, ISO AND LIGHTING RELATIONSHIPS

The units we deal with in exposure are:

- F/stops
- ASA, ISO or EI (different names for the same thing)
- Foot-candles or lux
- Output of sources as affected by distance
- Reflectance of objects

It turns out that all of these can be arranged in analogous ways. They all follow the same basic mathematical pattern. The data in these tables was compiled by Wade Ramsey. Remember that f/stop numbers are fractions, the relationship of the aperture diameter to the focal length of the lens. For example, f/8 really means 1/8; the diameter is 1/8 the focal length. F/11 is 1/11, which is obviously a smaller fraction than 1/8. Each time we open the aperture one whole f/stop we double the quantity of light reaching the film; each time we close it one stop, we halve the light reaching the film.

The f/stop scale (Table 6.1) is tiered to show that the same relationships that apply to whole f/numbers, such as f/8 and f/11, apply to intervals between them. So the difference between f/9 and f/13 is one whole stop, etc. Modern digital meters measure in 1/10ths of a stop. This is helpful for calculations and comparisons, but for most practical purposes, this level of accuracy is not necessary. One third of a stop is the practical limit of precision, given the vagaries of optics, lab chemistry and telecine transfer. This is not to say that accurate exposure is not important, only that the degree of precision in the overall process has limits.

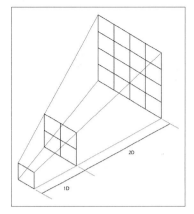

LIGHTING SOURCE DISTANCE
The f/stop scale applies to the inverse square law of illumination. Changes in illumination due to distance with small sources follow this scale (Table 6.2). For example, if the lamp is 11 feet from the subject, moving it to 8 feet will increase the subject illumination by 1 stop, just as opening the lens diaphragm from f/11 to f/8 would do. The inverse square law applies to point sources, strictly speaking, but spotlights follow it fairly well at the distances usually utilized.

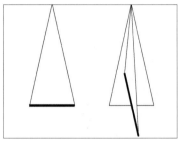

6.3. (top) The inverse square law. This is important not only to understanding exposure measurement, but to lighting as well.

6.4. (above) The cosine law: how the angle of the subject affects its exposure level.

INVERSE SQUARE LAW AND COSINE LAW
Similarly: a given output at a certain distance: say 1,000 fc at 10 feet, can be used to calculate the output at other distances by dividing by the distance squared. This is the inverse square law in application (Table 6.1).

Figure 6.3 illustrates the inverse square law graphically. A similar principle is the cosine law (Figure 6.4). As a surface is turned away from the source, less of the surface is "visible" to the source and therefore there is less exposure. Mathematically, the decrease in exposure is equal to the cosine of the angle of the surface so this is called the cosine law.

ISO SPEEDS
Since one-third stop is the minimum exposure difference detectable by the unaided eye (for most negative stocks), film sensitivity is rated in no finer increments than this. This scale is tiered to make the relationships between intervals more easily seen. Just as ISO 200 is 1 stop faster than ISO 100, so ISO 320 is 1 stop faster than ISO 160. (Table 6.3).

Although this is obvious, memorizing this scale makes it easier to see the differences between odd intervals, such as ISO 80 to ISO 32 (1-1/3 stops.) The scale may be expanded in either direction by adding or subtracting digits (the intervals below 6 are 5, 4, 3, 2.5, 2, 1.6, just as the intervals below 64 are 50, 40, 32, 25, 20, and 16.

Table 6.1. (left) Lighting source distance and exposure.

Table 6.2. (below) Light levels and exposure. "X" represents a given amount of light — each step to the left doubles the amount of light at the subject.

	LIGHTING SOURCE DISTANCE								
DISTANCE IN Ft.	64'	50'	40'	32'	25'	20'	16'	12'	10'
F/Stop	4	4.5	5	5.6	6	7	8	9	10

Light	2048x	1024x	512x	256X	128X	64x	32X	16X	8x	4X	2X	X
F/Stops	1	1.4	2	2.8	4	5.6	8	11	16	22	32	45
1/3 Stops	1.1 1.3	1.6 1.8	2.2 2.5	3.2 3.6	4.5 5	6 7	9 10	13 14	18 20	25 29	36 40	

6	12	25	50	100	200	400	800
8	16	32	64	125	250	500	1000
10	20	40	80	160	320	640	1250

Table 6.3. ISO or ASA in one-third stop increments. The same series can be interpreted as percentage of reflection or shutter speeds.

Foot-candles: The ISO scale can also be applied to foot-candles. Doubling the foot-candles doubles the exposure. The third-stop intervals give the intermediate fc values. For example, the difference between 32 fc and 160 fc is 2 1/3 stops.

Percentage of Reflection: The ISO scale from 100 on down relates to percentage of reflection. For example, ISO 100 can represent 100%, pure white. Other reflectances, such as 64% and 20%, can then be seen to be, respectively, 2/3 stop and 2-1/3 stops darker than pure white (Table 6.4).

Shutter speeds: Referring to the ISO scale, it can be seen that, for example, 1/320 sec. is 1-2/3 stops faster than 1/100 sec. This can be helpful when unusual combinations of shutter angle and frame rate produce odd effective shutter speeds.

LIGHT AND FILM

It is the energy in each photon of light that causes a chemical change to the photographic detectors that are coated on the film. The process whereby electromagnetic energy causes chemical changes to matter is known as photochemistry.

All film is coated onto a base: a transparent plastic material (celluloid) that is 4 to 7 thousandths of an inch (0.025mm) thick. Onto the base, the emulsion is adhered where the photochemistry happens. There may be 20 or more individual layers coated here that are collectively less than one-thousandth of an inch in thickness. Some of the layers coated on the transparent film do not form images. They are there to filter light, or to control the chemical reactions in the processing steps. The imaging layers contain sub-micron sized grains of silver halide crystals that act as the photon detectors.

These crystals are the heart of photographic film. These crystals undergo a photochemical reaction when they are exposed to various forms of electromagnetic radiation — light. In addition to visible light, the silver halide grains can be sensitized to infrared radiation. A halide is a chemical compound of a halogen (any of a group of five chemically related nonmetallic elements including fluorine, chlorine, bromine, iodine, and astatine) with a more electropositive element or group, in this case silver. Silver halide grains are manufactured by combining silver nitrate and halide salts (chloride, bromide, and iodide) in complex ways that result in a range of crystal sizes, shapes, and compositions.

The unmodified grains are only sensitive to the blue part of the spectrum, and thus are not very useful in camera film. Spectral sensitizers are added to the surface of the grains to make them more sensitive to blue, green and red light. (Remember, we're talking about black-and-white film here.) These molecules must attach to the grain surface and transfer the energy from a red, green, or blue

Table 6.4. The relationship of f/stops and reflectance.

F/STOPS		-1/3	-2/3	-1	-1 1/3	-1 2/3	-2	-2 2/3	-3	-3 1/3	-3 2/3	-4	-4 1/3
REFLECTANCE	100%			50%			25%			12%			6%
		80%			40%			20%			10%		
			64%			32%			16%			8%	

photon to the silver halide crystal as a photo electron. Other chemicals are added internally to the grain during its growth process, or on the surface of the grain. These chemicals affect the light sensitivity of the grain, also known as its speed — that is, how sensitive to light it is.

The speed of an emulsion is quantified by standards set by the ISO (International Standards Organization) or ASA (American Standards Association) rating. ISO is the technically the correct designation, but by tradition, most people still refer to it as ASA. The higher the ASA, the lower the light level the film is capable of responding to. For color film, manufacturers list the sensitivity of film as EI or Exposure Index. When you make film faster, the trade off is that the increased light sensitivity comes from the use of larger silver halide grains. These larger grains can result in a blotchy or "grainy" appearance to the picture. Photographic film manufacturers are constantly making improvements that result in faster films with less grain. For Kodak, a major advance was the introduction of "T" grains in the 70s. These tabular grains are roughly triangular which allowed them to be packed closer together, thus reducing apparent grain.

THE LATENT IMAGE
When the shutter is open, light affects the chemistry of the emulsion and a latent image is formed. When a photon of light is absorbed by the spectral sensitizer sitting on the surface of a silver halide grain, the energy of an electron is raised into the conduction band from the valence band, where it can be transferred to the conduction band of the silver halide grain electronic structure.

This atom of silver is unstable. However if enough photoelectrons are present at the same time in the crystal lattice, they may combine with enough positive holes to form a stable latent image site. A latent image site must contain a minimum of 2 to 4 silver atoms per grain to remain stable. A silver halide grain contains billions of silver halide molecules, and it only takes 2 to 4 atoms of uncombined silver to form the latent image site. In color film, this process happens separately for exposure to the red, green, and blue layers of the emulsion. The reason for this is simple — there is no way to sensitize a grain to "color," you can only sensitize it to a specific band of the spectrum. The image that is formed is called "latent" because it remains invisible until chemically developed.

Any photon that reaches the film, but does not form a latent image, is lost information. Most color films generally take 20 to 60 photons per grain to produce a developable latent image. This is called the "inertia point" for the film. Below the inertia point, no image is recorded at all. Video receptors are silicon based and of course different in operation, but the basic theory is quite similar.

6.5. Black-and-white negative.

CHEMICAL PROCESSING
In order for the latent image to become visible, it must be amplified and stabilized, in order to make a negative or a positive (Figure 6.5). In black-and-white film, the silver halide grains have to be sensitized to all wavelengths of visible light so the silver halide grains are coated in just one or two layers. As a result, the development process is easier to understand.

- The film is placed in developing chemistry that is actually a reducing agent. If the film were left in the solution long enough, the reducing agent would convert all the silver ions into silver metal — resulting in a uniform gray fog with no discernible image. Those grains that have latent image sites will develop more rapidly. If the film is left in the develop-

6.6. Color negative with its distinctinve orange mask.

ing chemistry for the proper amount of time, only grains with latent image information will become pure silver. The unexposed grains remain as silver halide crystals.

- The development process must be "stopped" at the right moment. This is done by rinsing the film with water, or by using a "stop" bath that brings the development process to a halt.

- After development, some of the altered halide and all of the unaltered silver halide remains in the emulsion. It must be removed or the negative will darken and deteriorate over time. The removal of this undeveloped material is accomplished with fixing agents, usually sodium thiosulfate (hypo) or ammonium thiosulfate. The process is called fixing. The trick is to fix just enough and not too much, as excessive contact with fixers can begin to remove some of the desirable silver material.

- Finally, the film is washed with water to remove all the processing chemicals. Then it is dried. The washing must be extremely thorough.

When all the steps are finished, the film has a negative image of the original scene. Other types of chemistry can result in a positive image, but this is not commonly used in motion picture applications. It is a negative in the sense that it is darkest (has the highest density of opaque silver atoms) in the area that received the most light exposure. In places that received no light, the negative is clear.

COLOR NEGATIVE
Color negative is basically three layers of black-and-white film, one on top of the other (Figures 6.6 and 6.7). The difference is that each layer is treated with a different spectral sensitizer so that it is receptive to a different band of the spectrum. These translate to roughly red, blue and green.

- With color film, the development step uses reducing chemicals, and the exposed silver halide grains develop to pure silver. Oxidized developer is produced in this reaction, and the oxidized developer reacts with chemicals called couplers in each of the image forming layers. This reaction causes the couplers to form a color, and this color varies depending on how the silver halide grains were spectrally sensitized. A different color forming coupler is used in the red, green and blue sensitive layers. The latent image in the different layers forms a different colored dye when the film is developed.

- The development process is stopped either by washing, or with a stop bath.

- The unexposed silver halide grains are removed using a fixing solution.

- The silver that was developed in the first step is removed by bleaching chemicals. (Note: it is possible to skip this step or reduce it so that some of the silver remains in the negative. This is the basis of "skip bleach" or ENR processing, which is discussed elsewhere.)

- The negative image is then washed to remove as much of the chemicals and reaction products as possible. The film strips are then dried.

Unlike a black-and-white negative, a color negative contains no silver with the exception of special processes known as "bleach bypass." These are covered in the chapter on *Image Control*.

The end result is a color negative in the sense that the more red exposure, the more cyan dye is formed. Cyan is a mix of blue and green (or white minus red). The green sensitive image layers contain magenta dye, and the blue sensitive image layers contain yellow dye.

The colors formed in the color negative film are based on the subtractive color formation system. The subtractive system uses one color (cyan, magenta or yellow) to control each primary color. The additive color system uses a combination of red, green and blue to produce a color. Video is based on an additive system. The overall orange hue is the result of masking dyes that help to correct imperfections in the color reproduction process.

ADDITIVE VS. SUBTRACTIVE COLOR
In a photograph, the colors are layered on top of each other, so a subtractive color reproduction system is used. In subtractive color, each primary is affected by its opposite on the color wheel.
- Red sensitive layers form a cyan colored dye.
- Green sensitive layers form a magenta colored dye.
- Blue sensitive layers form a yellow colored dye.

FILM'S RESPONSE TO LIGHT
There are two steps in the making of a negative, as represented by the thin slice from the negative shown in Figure 6.7.
- Exposure. The useful property of silver halide is that its state is altered when subjected to light, in direct proportion to the amount of light energy absorbed. This change is not visible, and if film is examined before and after exposure, little change can be seen.
- Development. Silver halide which has been altered by contact with light can be reduced to pure silver if placed in contact with specific chemicals referred to as developing agents. The activity of the developer and time of development will determine how much of the sensitized halide will be converted.

DENSITOMETRY
To understand film response we must look at its curve. This classical approach to densitometry (the scientific analysis of exposure) was devised by Hurter and Driffield in 1890 and so is called the H&D curve or sometimes the D log E curve. It plots the amount of exposure "E" in logarithmic units along the horizontal axis and the amount of density change in the negative "D" along the vertical axis. This is sometimes shortened to "Log E" curve (Figure 6.8).

In theory, it makes sense that we would want the film to change in density in exact proportion to change in the amount of light reflected by different parts of the scene. After all we are trying to make an image which accurately portrays the real scene, right?

Let's look at a theoretical "linear" film (Figure 6.9). For every additional unit of exposure, the density of the negative changes exactly one unit. That is, there is an exact correspondence between the amount of light in the scene and the change in the density of the

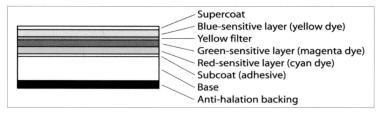

6.7. The layers of color negative film.

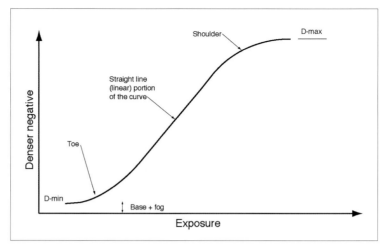

6.8. The Hurter and Driffield D Log E curve for negative density.

negative. Sounds perfect, doesn't it? The slope of the line for this film would be 45 degrees exactly.

The slope of this line is a measure of the contrastiness of the film. In a film where large changes in exposure only change the negative density a little (low contrast reproduction) the slope is very shallow. Where a film is very contrasty, the slope is very high; in other words small changes in the amount of light cause the film density to change drastically. The extreme is something called "litho" film which is used in the printing industry. Everything to litho film is either black or white — there are no shades of gray. In other words if the light is above a certain level, the image is completely white. If it is below a certain level, it is completely black. This is as contrasty as a film can get. The slope for litho film would be a vertical line.

No film acts in the perfectly linear manner of this first example (i.e., the changes in the film exactly correspond to the change in the amount of light). In Figure 6.10, the lower curve graphs a film which only changes 1/2 unit of density for each additional unit of light. This is a "low-contrast" film.

Figure 6.10 shows the difference between a high-contrast emulsion and a low-contrast one. In the high-contrast example, for each

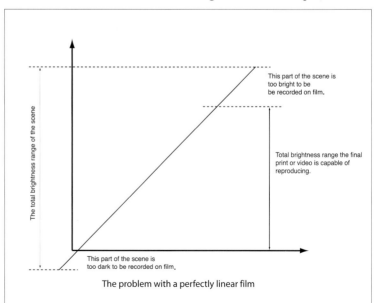

6.9. A theoretical "ideal" film — one that exactly reproduces the exposure changes of the subject in a one-to-ratio with negative density.

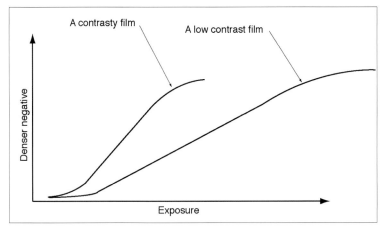

6.10. Differences between a high contrast and a low contrast film.

additional unit of exposure, it changes 2 units of negative density. Looking at the brightness range of the exposure against the brightness range of the negative density, we see that it will show more contrast in the negative than actually exists in the scene. The slope of this line is called the gamma of the film: it is a measure of its contrastiness.

Contrast refers to the separation of lightness and darkness (called "tones") in a film or print and is broadly represented by the slope of the characteristic curve. Adjectives such as flat or soft and contrasty or hard are often used to describe contrast. In general, the steeper the slope of the characteristic curve, the higher the contrast. The terms gamma and average gradient refer to numerical means for indicating the contrast of the photographic image.

Gamma is measured in several different ways as defined by scientific organizations or manufacturers. They are all basically a way of calculating the slope of the straight-line portion of the curve by more or less ignoring the shoulder and the toe portions of the curve. Gamma is the slope of the straight-line portion of the characteristic curve or the tangent of the angle (a) formed by the straight line with the horizontal. The tangent of the angle (a) is obtained by dividing the density increase by the log exposure change. Gamma does not describe contrast characteristics of the toe or the shoulder, only the straight line portion.

But there is another wrinkle. In the lowest range of exposure, as well as in the highest range, the emulsion's response changes. In the lowest range, the film does not respond at all as it "sees" the first few units of light. There is no change in photochemistry at all until it reaches the inertia point where the amount of light first begins to create a photochemical change in film or an electrical change on a video tube. After reaching the inertial point, then it begins to respond sluggishly: negative density changes only slightly for each additional unit of light. This region is the "toe" of the curve. In this area, the changes in light value are compressed (Figure 6.11.)

At the upper end of the film's sensitivity range is the "shoulder." Here also, the reproduction is compressed. The emulsion is becoming overloaded; it's response to each additional unit of light is less and less. The end result is that film does not record changes in light value in the scene in a linear and proportional way. Both the shadows and the highlights are somewhat crushed together. This is, in fact, what gives film the "film look" that video has never been able to achieve (High Def comes a lot closer than previous systems but still has trouble with the highlights). It is a way of compressing very contrasty scenes so that they "fit" onto the film.

6.11. Gray scale compression in the toe and shoulder.

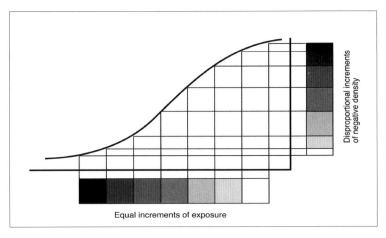

Disproportional increments of negative density

Equal increments of exposure

THE LOG E AXIS

Let's think about the log E axis (horizontal) for a moment. It is not just an abstract scale of exposure units. Remember that it represents the various luminances of the scene. All scenes are different, and thus all scenes have different luminance ratios. What we are really plotting on the horizontal axis is the range of luminances in the scene, from the darkest to the lightest.

In 1890, the German physiologist E. H. Weber discovered that changes in any physical sensation (sound, brightness, pain, heat) become less noticeable as the stimulus increases. The change in level of stimulus that will produce a noticeable difference is proportional to the overall level: if three units of light create a perception of brightness that is just noticeably brighter than two units, then the smallest perceptible increase from 20 units of light will require 30 units. To produce a scale of steps which appear to be uniform, it is necessary to multiply each step by a constant factor. In fact, the perception of brightness is logarithmic.

What is a log?

Logarithms are a simple way of expressing large changes in any numbering system. If, for example, we wanted to make a chart of something which increases by multiplying by 10: 1, 10, 100, 1000, 10,000, 100,000, we very quickly reach numbers so large as to be unwieldy. It would be extremely difficult to make a graph which could handle both ends of the range.

In log base 10, the most common system, the log of a number represents the number of times 1 must be multiplied by 10 to produce the number. 1 must be multiplied by 10 once to make 10, so the log of 10 is 1. To arrive at 100, you multiply 1 by 10 twice, so the log of 100 is 2. The log of a number is the exponent of 10: $10^2 = 100$, the log of 100 is 2. 10^4 is 10,000, so the log of 10,000 is 4 (Table 6.5). This means that we can chart very large changes in quantity with a fairly small range of numbers. Logs are used throughout lighting, photography and video.

BRIGHTNESS PERCEPTION

Our perception of brightness is logarithmic and we shall see that this has far ranging consequences in all aspects of lighting for film and video. If we chart the human perception of brightness in steps that appear smooth to the eye we can follow its logarithmic nature. It is apparent that each step up in a seemingly even scale of gray tones is, in terms of its measured reflectance, spaced logarithmically. As we shall see later, this chart is in fact fundamental to the entire process of lighting and image reproduction (Table 6.6).

Remember that these are not fixed values (the darkest point on the log E axis is not a certain number of candles-per-sq-foot for example), because we open or close the aperture of the camera to adjust how much light reaches the film and we use faster or slower film and so on. What really counts is the *ratio* between the darkest and lightest, and that is what we are plotting on the log E axis. This is called the brightness range of the film, sometimes abbreviated as BR. Each unit on the log E axis represents one stop more light.

CONTRAST

The word contrast has different meanings depending on whether you are talking about the contrast of the subject we are photographing or the negative that we will use to make the print. In general, contrast refers to the relative difference between dark and light areas of the subject or negative. Subject contrast refers to the difference between the amounts of light being reflected by the darker, or "shadow," areas of the scene and the lighter, or "highlight," areas (for example a dark door as opposed to a white wall).

Negative contrast refers to the relative difference between the more transparent areas of the negative and those that are more opaque. The negative is described in terms of density. These densities can be measured with an instrument called a densitometer, which measures how much light passes through the negative and how much is held back. The contrast of photographic subjects can vary a great deal from one picture to another. On clear, sunny days the contrast of an exterior scene can be great, while on cloudy days it can be relatively low in contrast. The contrast of a given scene depends on how light or dark the objects in the picture are when compared to each other and how much light is falling on them. Let's get back to our theoretically "ideal" film. This film would change the density of the negative exactly one unit for each one unit of change in the brightness of the subject.

Figure 6.9 shows the problem with this. No reproduction medium now known is capable of reproducing anything near the brightness range exhibited in most real world situations. Nearly all film emulsions are non-linear. This linearity fails for two reasons.

- It takes a certain amount of light energy to initiate the activation of the photosensitive elements in the emulsion (the inertia point). Thus the density rises gradually at first in this area called the toe, finally accelerating into the straight line portion of the curve.
- With increasing exposure to light, more silver halide is converted, until it has no more sensitive material to activate. At that point, increasing the exposure does not increase the ultimate density of the developed negative. This "saturation" occurs gradually and produces what is known as a shoulder.

The toe of the film is a result of the fact that film reacts slowly to small amounts of light. It is only when greater amounts of light reach the emulsion that the change becomes linear. This is the straight line portion of the film. The film base itself always has some density, however slight. On top of this there is always a slight amount of fog due to light scattering in the camera, the lens, the emulsion and also chemical fog in the processing. The cumulative effect of all of these is called base plus fog. Density measurements are usually described as x density above base plus fog. (For more on measurement of density, see the section on neutral density filters in the chapter *Filters*.)

This toe and shoulder behavior actually results in a compression of

Number	Log
1	0.0
2	0.3
4	0.6
8	0.9
10	1.0
16	1.2
32	1.5
64	1.8
100	2.0

Perception	% Reflectance
White	100%
	70%
	50%
	35%
	25%
Middle gray	17.5%
	12.5%
	9%
	6%
	4.5%
Black	3.5%

Table 6.5. (top) Some values for log base 10.

Table 6.6. (above) Reflectance and gray scale values.

the actual scene. If the contrast gradient of the film is correct and exposure is correct, this compression behavior will allow the full brightness range of the scene to be represented on the final print. In effect, it is the failure of film emulsion and video receptors to accurately represent the real world that allows us to produce photographs and video that are usable. Each film emulsion reacts to light in a special way. Some react more quickly to low light than others creating a rather abrupt initial rise in density or "short toe." Others react more gradually to increases in light and have what is called a "long toe." Films with similar sensitivities and ranges can have quite different response curves requiring dissimilar exposure and development.

Another important factor is the range of subject luminance that can be usefully recorded (Figure 6.12). Low contrast films can continue to build density over a long luminance range, whereas contrasty films saturate rather quickly and tend to "block" at either end. This is how we can match the type of film used to the type of scene being photographed. Cinematographer David Watkin used a low contrast film stock for the movie *Out Of Africa*, where he dealt with many very contrasty situations in the harsh African sun. The results were outstanding. Both Fuji and Kodak now make emulsions that are more moderate in contrast than normal film stocks.

Determining the precise film speed, coupled with precise exposure, is critical when the range of light in the scene is greater than the scale of the film. In Figure 6.13, we see three exposures of the same scene represented by the bars at the bottom of the diagram. Not enough exposure places much of the information completely off the low end of the curve, while too much exposure places it off the high end — in either case, once you are off the curve, further changes in exposure register no change in the negative; the film doesn't "see" them. The ideal exposure places all of the information where it makes some change on the negative.

If there is too much exposure, two things happen. First, even the darkest parts of the scene are in the middle range of the curve: even the darkest shadows will reproduce as middle gray tones. Graphically, overexposure appears as a shift of the subject brightness range (log E) to the right. (In effect we are making the scene values "brighter" by opening up the aperture.) Here we see that this overexposure places the scene values too much in the shoulder. Some information is lost in the flat part of the shoulder: lost because the differ-

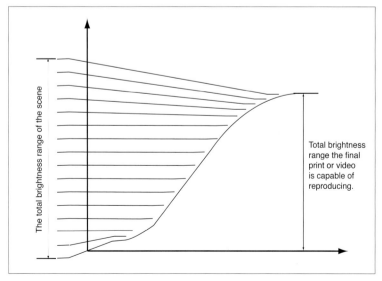

6.12. Compression of the real world brightness values so that they fit onto the film. This is what makes it possible to make usable images even from scenes with high contrast ranges. The same principle applies to video, whether analog or digital. A great deal of the progress of video as a more acceptable imaging medium has been improvements in its ability to compress the image brightness in a way that gets closer to what film can usefully manage.

The total brightness range of the scene

Total brightness range the final print or video is capable of reproducing.

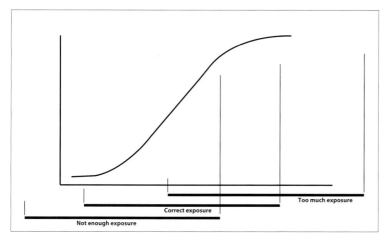

Too much exposure

Correct exposure

Not enough exposure

ences of scene brightness values result in no change in the density of the negative.

Further, because everything is shifted to the right none of the scene values fall in the toe of the curve: there will be no deep black values at all in the final print, even though they existed in the original scene. Underexposure is shown as a shift of the log E values to the left. Here every subtle nuance of the high tones will be recorded because they fall in the straight line portion of the curve. But at the dark end of the scale — trouble. The dark values of the scene are mushed together in the toe. There is little differentiation of the medium gray values, the dark gray values and the black shadows: in the final print they will all be a black hole. There will be no detail in the shadows.

"CORRECT" EXPOSURE

"Correct" exposure, then, is essentially the aperture setting that will best suit the scene brightness range (the horizontal axis: log E) to the characteristic curve of the imaging medium. What is needed is to slip the scene values comfortably in between the toe and the shoulder. A typical scene with a seven stop range of light values fits nicely on the curve if we place the exposure exactly in the middle. It is important to remember, however, that correct exposure is a purely technical thing; there are occasions where you will want to deviate from ideal exposure for pictorial or technical reasons (Figures 6.14 and 6.15). The relationship of the gamma (the angle of the straight line portion of the film) to the toe and the shoulder is what determines a film's "latitude." It can be viewed as two characteristics: the emulsion's room for error in exposure or the ability of the film to accept a certain brightness range.

HIGHER BRIGHTNESS RANGE IN THE SCENE

The problem is exacerbated if we consider a scene which has more than seven stops of brightness (seven stops is just an average, it all depends on the particular film stock). Here there is no aperture setting which will place all of the values on the useful part of the curve. If we expose for the shadows (open up the aperture): we get good rendition of the dark gray areas, but the light values are hopelessly off the scale. If we "expose for highlights" (by closing down to a smaller f/stop) we record all the variations of the light tones, but the dark values are pushed completely off the bottom edge.

How do we deal with this situation? Later we will discuss some rather abstruse solutions to the problem (flashing, Varicon, Panaflasher, etc.) but there is one solution which is really what we are all about: we change the brightness range of the scene so that it will fit the curve of the film, in other words we alter the illumination of the scene. This is done by lighting or by modifying the existing lighting. This then, is one of the most essential jobs of lighting and grip work: to render the scene in a scale of brightness values that can be accommodated by the optics and emulsion of a film camera or by the optics and electronics of video. It's why we get the big bucks. It also is critical in the choice of locations, camera angles and time of day to shoot.

Modern films have consistently improved in latitude even as they have increased in speed and reduced grain. The new high speed emulsions in particular are amazing in their ability to record subtleties even in heavily overexposed highlights and in very dark shadows. Although there has been some improvement, the ability to handle brightness ratios is still one of the most crucial differences between film and video. Exposure meters generally provide data on the assumption that whatever you are measuring should ultimately print as "middle gray," defined in the Zone System as Zone V.

DETERMINING EXPOSURE
So we have two basic tasks:

- To manipulate the brightness ratio of the scene so that it can be properly reproduced on film or video.
- To set the aperture so that the scene values fall on the appropriate part of the curve.

In practice these often turn out to be two sides of the same coin. The first task is essentially the work of lighting and lighting control, the second task involves measuring the scene and making a judgment about the best setting for the lens.

Figure 6.16 shows how film speed is determined by the manufacturer. Strictly speaking, this method applies only to black-and-white film. The speed of color film is determined by testing and is expressed as either EI (Exposure Index) or ISO number (International Standards Organization) for black-and-white film and as EI (Exposure Index) for color film. Although they are not as commonly used as they once were, you will still hear reference to "lighting ratio." The lighting ratio is the relationship of the key light to the fill light. If we consider the average face, it is the difference between the lighter side and the darker side.

THE TOOLS
The two most basic tools of the cameraman's trade are the incident meter and the spot meter. There is a third type of meter, the wide angle reflectance meter (what still photographers would simply call a "light meter"), but it has extremely limited use in film.

THE INCIDENT METER
The incident meter measures scene illumination only. In other words: the amount of light falling on the scene. To accomplish this purpose,

6.14. Deliberate overexposure of the main subject adds menace and mystery in this shot from *The Lost Boys* (Warner Bros., 1987), photographed by Michael Chapman.

6.15. Lee Garmes regularly lit Marlene Dietrich one stop hotter than everyone else, as in this scene from *Shanghai Express* (Paramount Publix Corp., 1932).

most incident meters use a hemispherical white plastic dome which covers the actual sensing cell.

The diffusing dome accomplishes several purposes. It diffuses and hence "averages" the light which is falling on it. It also approximates the geometry of a typical three-dimensional subject. Unshielded, the dome will read all of the front lights and even some of the side-back and back light that might be falling on the subject. Left to itself, the hemisphere would provide a reasonable average of all the sources falling on the subject. In practice, many people use their hand to shield the back light off the reading and use a combination of hand shielding and turning the meter to read the backlight and sometimes the key, fill, side lights and back lights separately (Figure 6.17).

The classical practice, however, is to point the hemisphere directly at the lens and eliminate only the backlights, then take a reading exactly at the subject position. Reading key, fill and backlight separately is in fact only a way of determining the ratios and looking for out of balance sources. The actual reading which will determine the aperture setting is the averaging one. Later we will look at applications which go beyond the simple classical approach and are useful in dealing with unusual situations. Most meters which are used with the diffusing dome also come with a flat diffusing plate which has a

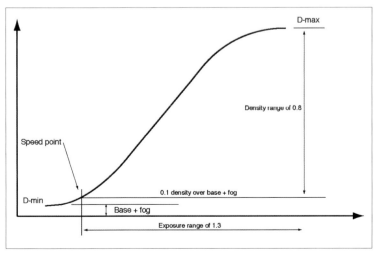

6.16. How speed (ASA or ISO) is determined in black-and-white film.

exposure

6.17. An incident meter with dome receptor. This one also functions as a flash meter, wide-angle reflectance meter and has a mini-receptor for macro work.

much smaller acceptance angle (about 45° to 55°) and has a cosine response rather than an averaging one. This means that the angle of the light falling on the plate has an effect on the reading, just as it does in illuminating a subject.

The flat plate makes taking readings for individual lights simpler and is also useful for measuring illumination on flat surfaces, such as in art copy work, animation plates, etc. Incident meters are generally also supplied with a lenticular glass plate which convert them to wide acceptance reflectance meters. These see little use on most sets as they have very wide acceptance angles and it is difficult to exclude extraneous sources from the reading.

For the most part, incident meters are set for the film speed and shutter speed being used (either electronically or by using slide-in plates) and then read out directly in f/numbers. Some meters have an alternate mode which reads foot-candles directly; the user is then able to calculate exposure separately. This is useful if there is no slide for the exposure index (EI) being used.

THE REFLECTANCE METER

Reflectance meters read the actual luminance of the subject, which is itself an integration of two factors: the light level falling on the scene and the reflectivity of the subject. (Figure 6.18).

On the face of it, this would seem to be the most logical method of reading the scene, but there is a catch. Simply put, a reflectance or "spot" meter will tell us how much light a subject is reflecting but this leaves one very big unanswered question: how much light do you want it to reflect? In other words: incident meters provide absolute readouts (f/stops) while spot meters provide relative readouts which require interpretation. While most spot meters were formerly calibrated in exposure value (EV) units, some of the new electronic spot meters provide direct readout in f/stops, but it would probably be better if they didn't as they are a source of much confusion.

Think of it this way: you are using such a meter and photographing a very fair skinned girl holding a box of detergent in front of a sunset. You read the girl's face: f/5.6, the box reads f/4, the sky is f/22. So where are you? Not only do we not know where to set the aperture, we don't even know if the situation is good or bad. Let's step back a moment and think about what it is that light meters are telling us. To do this we have to understand the cycle of tone reproduction and lay down a basic system of thinking about it.

THE ZONE SYSTEM

We must remember that the exposure values of a scene are not represented by one simple number: most scenes contain a wide range of light values and reflectances. In evaluating exposure we must look at a subject in terms of its light and dark values: the subject range of brightness. For purposes of simplicity we will ignore its color values for the moment and analyze the subject in terms of its monochromatic values.

Let's visualize a continuous scale of gray values from completely black to completely white (Figure 6.20). Each point on the gray scale represents a certain value which is equivalent to a tonal value in the scene. In everyday language we have only vague adjectives with which to describe the tones: "dark gray," "medium gray," "blinding white" and so on. We need more precise descriptions. Using Ansel Adam's classic terminology we will call the most completely black section Zone 0 and each tone which is one f/stop lighter is one zone "higher." For example, a subject area which reflects three stops more light than the darkest area in the scene would be designated Zone IV. It is crucial to remember that these are all relative. Zone 0 is not some predetermined number of foot-candles — it is the darkest area in this scene.

Still photographers might be accustomed to thinking of ten zones in all, but if there is a great contrast range in the scene, there might well be zones XII, XIII or more. (Zone system purists will no doubt object to such an extreme simplification of the method, but it is sufficient for the present discussion since few cinematographers do their own darkroom work). What we are measuring is subject brightness (luminance), which can vary in two ways: its inherent reflectance and the amount of light that falls on it. Reflectance is a property of the material itself. Black velvet reflects about 2% of the light that falls on it. A very shiny surface can reflect up to 98% of the light that falls on it. This is a brightness ratio (BR) of 1:48.

However, this is the reflectance ratio if the same amount of light falls on both objects. In reality, different amounts of light fall on different areas in the same frame (indeed, we make our living making sure they do). In natural light situations the reflectance ratio can be as much as 3200:1. Picture the most extreme example possible: a piece of extremely absorbent velvet in deep shadow in the same scene with a mirror reflecting the sun.

The brightness range of a typical outdoor subject is about 1000:1. This is 15 stops and here's the rub: imaging systems cannot reproduce this range of subject brightness, just as the human eye cannot accommodate such a range. Recall that the human eye reacts in two different ways. First, the iris (the aperture of the eye) expands or contracts to allow more or less light to pass. Second, the eye shifts it's imaging from the cones to the rods. This is like switching to a higher speed film. (It is also, in essence, switching to black-and-white film; see the chapter on *Color Theory.*)

6.18. The reflectance or spot meter.

ZONES IN A SCENE

Examine a typical scene with the spot meter — see Figure 6.21. If you assign the darkest value to Zone 0 you can then find areas which are 1, 2, 3, 4, 5, 6, 7 and perhaps 8 stops brighter than the darkest area. These are Zones I through IX. This is an important exercise and is vital to understanding exposure control. Ignoring the effect of color contrast can be cumbersome. It can be helped by viewing the scene through a viewing glass, which is a neutral density filter.

Now picture each of these tonal values arranged in ascending order. What you have is a gray scale, and fortunately it is a commonly available item. Most gray scales are made to reasonable rigorous densitometric standards and are useful calibration tools. Let's take a look at what it really is (Figure 6.20).

6.19. The secret of a good silhouette shot is to properly expose for the background, as in this frame from *Nine 1/2 Weeks*, shot by Peter Biziou.

6.20. Zones 0 through IX, a stepped gray scale and a continuous gray scale. By convention zones are represented in Roman numerals.

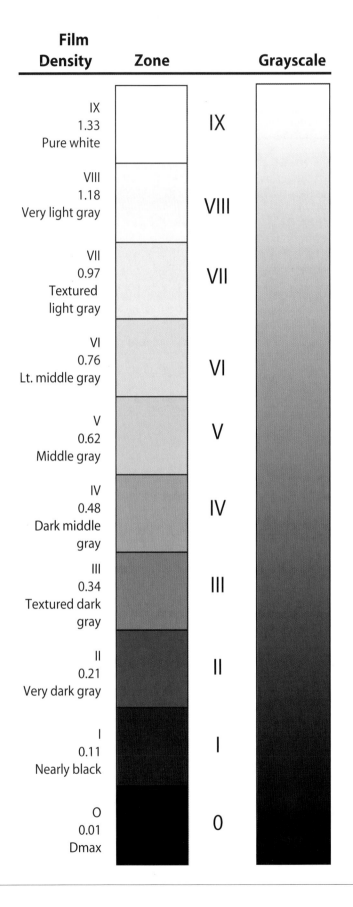

Film Density	Zone	Grayscale
IX 1.33 Pure white	IX	
VIII 1.18 Very light gray	VIII	
VII 0.97 Textured light gray	VII	
VI 0.76 Lt. middle gray	VI	
V 0.62 Middle gray	V	
IV 0.48 Dark middle gray	IV	
III 0.34 Textured dark gray	III	
II 0.21 Very dark gray	II	
I 0.11 Nearly black	I	
O 0.01 Dmax	0	

THE GRAY SCALE

There are a great many gray scales but they all have one thing in common: they vary from black to white. Most are divided into six to ten steps but they certainly don't have to be: many are 20 steps or more. How white the white is and how black the black is varies somewhat depending on the printing quality and the materials involved. Some scales include a piece of black velvet since black paper can never be truly black. For our purposes, we will consider only gray scales where each step represents one full "stop" increment over the previous, that is: where each step is $\sqrt{2}$ times the reflectance of the previous one (Table 6.7).

WHY 18%?

Zone V is the middle zone of a ten-zone scale and we would therefore assume it to be 50% reflectance. It isn't — it is 18% reflectance. The reason for this is that the eye perceives changes in tone logarithmically rather than arithmetically, as we saw above. If each zone were, for example, 10% more reflective than the previous, the eye would not read it as a smooth spectrum.

Discussion of the zone system is always in terms of grays, but any color can be interpreted in terms of its gray scale value. The importance of value cannot be stressed too much. The value relationships between colors carry about ninety percent of the information in any picture. In a black-and-white photograph the gradients of light and shadow on surfaces contains the information about form, clearly defining all the objects. The black-and-white photo also contains the information about the amount and direction of light in the scene. Color contributes a small amount of information, but a great deal of the beauty and interest of the picture.

In fact it works out as in Table 6.7. Each step is greater than the previous by $\sqrt{2}$; a familiar number, no? The square root of 2 is also the derivation of the f/stop series. What appears middle gray (Zone V) to the eye is actually 17-1/2% reflectance, which is universally rounded off to 18%. There's more: it turns out that if you take dozens of spot readings of typical scenes, most will turn out to have an average reflectance of about 18%. Simply put: 18% is the average reflectance of the normal world. Clearly it is not the average reflectance in a coal mine or in the Sahara at mid-day, but in the most of the rest of the world it is a reasonable working average. This gives us a solid ground on which to build. In fact, it is the standard on which incident meters are built. As you recall, in the introduction to incident meters we noted that most incident meters, when set for film speed and shutter speed, read out directly in f/stops.

Zone	Reflectance
Zone X	100%
Zone IX	70%
Zone VIII	50%
Zone VII	35%
Zone VI	25%
Zone V	17.5%
Zone IV	12.5%
Zone III	9%
Zone II	6%
Zone I	4.5%
Zone 0	3.5%

Table 6.7. Percentage of reflectance for zones.

ZONE	DENSITY	DESCRIPTION
0	0.02	Dmax.
I	0.11	1st perceptible value lighter than black.
II	0.21	Very, very dark gray
III	0.34	Fully textured dark gray
IV	0.48	Dark middle gray
V	0.62	Middle gray - 18% reflectance
VI	0.76	Light middle gray
VII	0.97	Fully textured light gray
VIII	1.18	Very light gray
IX	1.33	First perceptible gray darker than pure white
X	1.44	Pure white

Table 6.8. Zones, negative density and description.

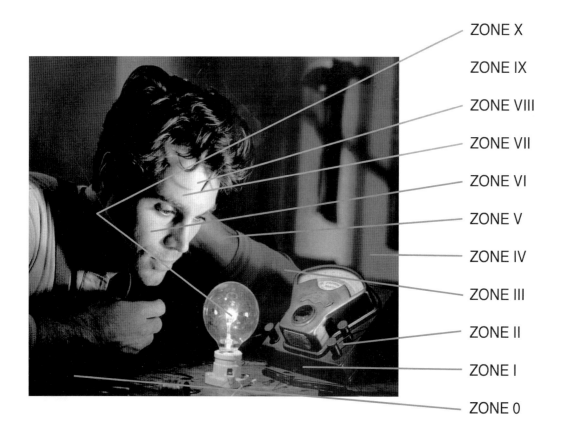

ZONE X

ZONE IX

ZONE VIII

ZONE VII

ZONE VI

ZONE V

ZONE IV

ZONE III

ZONE II

ZONE I

ZONE 0

6.21. Zones in a black-and-white print. (Photo by author.)

How do they do this? How can they know if we are photographing diamonds on a white background or a chimney-sweep in the basement? They don't know, they just assume that we are photographing a scene of average reflectances and the diffusing dome averages the light and the meter calculates the f/stop needed to photograph the scene for good exposure based on these assumptions. More simply: if we are photographing a card that is exactly 18% reflectance (a photographic gray card) and we read the light with an incident meter, then set the aperture to the stop the meter indicates, the print will in fact come out to be Zone V.

Try this experiment. Set a photographic gray card in even, uniform light. Read it with a spot meter and note the f/stop the meter indicates. Then read the light with an incident meter. The readings should be exactly the same. If they're not, have your meters checked. Now try a reverse experiment. Read a uniformly lit scene with an incident meter and notice the indicated stop. Now take the spot meter and read various parts of the scene until you find something that the spot meter indicates as the same f/stop. You have just found a Zone V subject brightness.

Now photograph the scene with a black-and-white Polaroid or with black-and-white film. Compare the Zone V subject with the gray card: they should be roughly the same. This is the simple key which unlocks the world of exposure control:

- an incident reading,
- an average 18% reflectance,
- a spot meter reading of a gray card and

- Zone V

are all the same thing looked at from different perspective.

The result of this is that there are many different ways to read the exposure of a scene and arrive at the same result.

- You can read it with an incident meter.
- You can place a gray card in the scene and read it with a spot meter.
- You can find something in the scene that is "Zone V" and read it with the spot meter.

Let's think about that last one, because it really points us in a whole new direction. It depends on you making a certain judgment: you have to look at a scene in the real world of color and decide that it is about Zone V or middle gray. (It takes some practice to do this, but it is an incredibly important exercise; I urge you to do it often.) What about the next logical step: what if there isn't anything in the scene that is middle gray? What do we do then? Let's remember that each step on the gray scale is one stop different from its neighbor (remember, this is a simplified version of the zone system). So if Zone V equals f/4 (given a particular film and shutter speed) then Zone VI must be f/5.6 and Zone IV must be f/2.8, right?

So if there is nothing in the scene that equals Zone V, but there is something in the scene that equals Zone VI, we're still in business. If we read it and it equals f/5.6 then we know that Zone V would be f/4. We also know that Zone V (f/4 in this example) is the same as an incident or average reading and is therefore the correct f/stop to set on the lens.

So what is there that we can count on to be roughly Zone VI under most conditions? Easy one: Caucasian skin. Average Caucasian skin is around Zone VI, it is in fact one of the few constants we can count on. Get out your light meter and check it out. If you are ever stuck without an incident meter, or worse, even without a spot meter you can always use the old "palm trick." Use your spot meter or any reflecting meter to read the palm of your hand. This equals Zone VI. Then open up one stop to get Zone V and you have your reading. There is a greater variation in non-caucasian skin and so there is no one standard, however many DP's take Zone V as a starting point for African-Americans.

I think you can see where this leads us. We don't have to confine ourselves to just reading things that equal Zone V and Zone VI: in fact we can do it with any zone. It all depends on your judgment of what gray tone a subject brightness should be. In real life, it takes years of practice and mental discipline to accurately determine subject brightnesses in terms of gray scale values, but in the long run it is a useful skill. If you can pre-visualize what gray-scale value you want a particular subject to be in the final print, you then have the power to "place" it where you want it in the exposure range. This turns out to be a powerful analytical and design tool.

PLACE AND FALL

What do we mean by "placement?" We just saw its simplest form. We "placed" the skin-tone value of the hand on Zone VI. We can, if we want, place any value in the scene. Say we have a gray background in the scene which the director wants to be "light gray." We decide that by light gray, she means Zone VII (two stops above middle gray). We then read the background with a spot meter and it indicates f/4. We then count down two stops and get f/2. If we set the lens at f/2, that gray background will photograph as "light gray" or Zone VII.

Let's try the reverse as a thought experiment. Say we had the same background under exactly the same lighting conditions, but the director decided she wanted it to be dark gray, which we take to mean Zone III. We read it with the spot meter and of course nothing has changed, the spot meter still indicates f/4, only now we want the gray background to appear much darker, so we "place" it on Zone III, which we do by counting "up" two stops to get f/8. Common sense tells us that if we photograph the same scene at f/8 instead of f/2, it is going to come out much darker in the final print: the gray background will not be Zone III (dark gray) instead of Zone VII (light gray).

Nothing has changed in the actual set; we have changed the value of the final print by "placing" the value of the background differently. But what's the flaw in this ointment? There is more in the scene than just a gray background, and whatever else is there is going to be photographing lighter or darker at the same time. This brings us to the second half of the process: "fall."

If you place a certain value in a scene on a certain zone, other values in that scene are going to fall on the gray scale according to how much different they are in illumination and reflectance. For our example, let's assume we are using a Pentax Spotmeter which has a zone dial attached to it. The Pentax reads in EVs. Typical white skin tone is a Zone VI. You read an actor's face and find that it reads EV 10. Turn the dial so that 10 aligns with Zone VI. Now read the exposure indicated opposite Zone V: this is the exposure to set the lens aperture, adding adjustments for filter factors, etc.

Let's try an example. We are lighting a set with a window. We set a 10K to simulate sunlight streaming in through the window. We then read the curtains and the spot meter indicates f/11. We have decided that we want the curtains to be very "hot" but not burned out. On the film stock we are using today, we know that white "burns out" at about three stops hotter than Zone V. So we want to "place" the curtains on Zone VIII (three stops hotter than the average exposure). By placing the curtains on Zone VIII, we have determined the f/stop of the camera: it will be f/4, right?

We then take an incident reading in the room where the people will be standing. The incident reading is f/2.8. This means that people standing in that position will photograph one zone too dark. Maybe for this scene that's OK, but let's assume we want to actors to have normal exposure which will result in normal skin tone values. In other words Zone VI "falls" at f/4 (one stop above the incident reading, which equals Zone V). Their skin tone will come out as Zone V instead of Zone VI.

To correct the situation we have to change the balance. If we just open up the lens, we are shifting the placement of the curtains and they will burn out. We must change the ratio of the illumination, not just shift the aperture of the camera. We can either tone down the 10K hitting the window with a double scrim (reducing it one stop) or we can raise the exposure of the subject area by increasing the light level there one stop. Either way are manipulating the subject values of the foreground to "fall" where we want them, based on our "placement" of the curtains on Zone VIII. We could have just as easily approached it from another direction, of course. We could "place" the foreground values where we want them and then see where the curtains "fall." It's the same thing. By reading the scene in different ways you can "place" the values of the negative where you want them to fall.

Placement is important in determining subject brightness ranges and contrast ratios and in reading subjects which you can't get to for an incident reading. In order to expose by placement you must pre-visualize which zone you want a subject value to reproduce as. For Ansel Adams, the godfather of exposure, pre-visualization was what it was all about, and remember, he dealt mostly with landscapes where he had no control over lighting. Since we usually control the lighting we can take pre-visualization one step further.

READING EXPOSURE WITH ULTRAVIOLET

Ultraviolet lights present a special problem. Several companies make ultraviolet light sources. They include Wildfire and Nocturn. When combined with props or clothing painted with UV sensitive fluorescent paints or dyes or with objects that naturally fluoresce such as your old Jimi Hendrix poster, an incident reading is meaningless. The only valid means of assessing exposure is a reflected reading. A wide angle reflectance meter will work if you have one, or have an adapter for your incident meter. If that is not available, a spot reading will work. Here, it is important to consider the Zone values and use judgment and calculate the exposure accordingly.

EXPOSURE AND THE CAMERA

Nearly all film cameras have rotating reflex shutters, which control exposure by alternately rotating closed and open sections past the film plane: while the closed section is in front of the film gate, the film moves, while the open section is in front of the gate, the film is exposed (Figures 6.12 and 6.13). Some video cameras also have variable exposure times.

The exposure time of the camera is determined by two factors: the speed at which the shutter is operating and the size of the open section. The speed is determined by the frame rate at which the camera is operating. The U.S. standard is 24 frames per second for sync sound filming and the European standard is 25 frames per second (based on the 50 cycles per second power supply). This carries over to High Def shooting as well in 24P or 25P mode. The open section of the rotating shutter assembly is referred to as the "shutter angle" and is measured in degrees. Sensibly, most shutters are half open and half closed, which makes the shutter angle 180°. Some shutters are 165° and many are adjustable (Table 6.11).

With the camera operating at 24 fps and a 180° shutter, the exposure time is 1/48th of a second (1/50th at European 25 fps). This is commonly rounded off to 1/50th of a second and is considered the standard motion picture exposure time.

Light meters that use different slides for various ASAs (such as the venerable Spectra or Studio Sekonic), just assume a 1/50th of a second exposure. Exposure time can then vary in two ways: by changing the frame rate (which is common) and by varying the shutter angle (which is less common). Exposure is determined by this formula:

Shutter speed for 180° shutter =

$$\frac{1}{2 \times \text{fps}}$$

Exposure in seconds =

$$\frac{\text{shutter opening (degrees)}}{360 \times \text{frames per second}}$$

MORE INFORMATION

For more on exposure, including detailed tables for exposure with filters, macro, miniatures, shutter changes, shutter angle, ramping, various film stocks, high and low speed shooting, special effects and other data, see *The Filmmaker's Pocket Reference*.

FPS	24	25	30	32	38	48	60	76	96	120	150	190	240	300	380	480
Stops	Normal	1/3	1/2	2/3	1	1	$1^{1/3}$	$1^{2/3}$	2	$2^{1/3}$	$2^{2/3}$	3	$3^{1/3}$	$3^{2/3}$	4	$4^{1/3}$

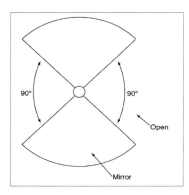

FPS	8	12	16	24	25	32	48	96	120	240
	1/16	1/24	1/32	1/50	1/50	1/60	1/100	1/200	1/250	1/500

180° SHUTTER	EXPOSURE (in stops)	165° SHUTTER	120° SHUTTER
180	No change	165	120
140	- 1/3	130	100
110	2/3	100	80
90	1	80	60
70	1 1/3	65	50
55	1 2/3	50	40
45	2	40	30
35	2 1/3	30	
30	2 2/3	25	
22	3	20	
18	3 1/3	15	

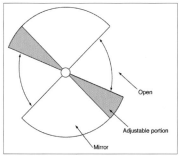

Table 6.9. (top) Exposure changes for high speed shooting.

Table 6.10. (above, right) Exposure changes for low speed shooting. Both this chart and table 6.9 apply equally to film and video.

6.22. (above middle) Butterfly rotating shutter from a reflex film camera.

6.23. (above) Adjustable rotating shutter. Shutter angle adjustment in video or High Def cameras is done electronically.

Table 6.11. (right) Exposure changes with various shutter angles. These shutter angles are typical for various makes of film cameras.

For a more detailed discussion of exposure in regard to lighting with scene lighting examples, see *Motion Picture and Video Lighting*, both published by Focal Press.

color theory

THE NATURE OF LIGHT

As we recall from the chapter on exposure, light is composed of photons, which have the properties of both matter and light. Even Newton recognized that individual photons don't have "color", but they do have different properties of energy which cause them to interact in different ways with physical matter, which, when reflected is perceived by the eye/brain combination as "color."

Every beam of light has a characteristic color which can vary if the observer is moving toward or away from the light source. Visible light is a small part of the continuous spectrum of electromagnetic radiation most of which is not directly observable, and was unknown until the last century. At the low frequency (long wavelength) end of the spectrum we find radio, television, microwave, and infra-red radiation. (Figure 7.2).

Then we encounter a tiny slice of the spectrum which we can see with our eyes; this extends from red to violet — the colors of the rainbow. They were originally classified as Red, Orange, Yellow, Green, Blue, Indigo and Violet. (R-O-Y-G-B-I-V). Above violet the high frequency are ultra-violet, x-rays, and gamma rays.

Indigo is no longer recognized as a color of the spectrum so the I is no longer used. Where formerly it could be memorized as Roy G. Biv, Roy no long has a vowel in his last name and it is now Roy G. Bv. Visible light is only produced when an electron falls into the second shell of an atom. Different colors happen because atoms have different sizes, different nuclear charges, and influences on each other when they are close together. For our purposes, it is conventional to consider visible light as a wave, as it exhibits all properties of a wave and follows the same rules as all electromagnetic waves.

Waves have four major properties:

- Amplitude
- Frequency
- Wavelength
- Speed

Amplitude is the height of the wave. (Figure 7.3). It shows the energy of the event that started the wave. In the previous pond example, if we had hoisted a large boulder and (with the help of a friend) launched it into the pond, we would have seen much higher waves come crashing toward us. For example, in audio, loud sounds have high amplitude.

Frequency is a measure of the number of waves that pass a point in a given amount of time. It is usually measured in Hertz (Hz). One hertz means one wave (peak to peak) passes every second. When we count waves, we have to divide the whole waveform into parts. The easiest way to do this is to go from one crest to another. This is one wave. We can now count the number of crests passing in a second to find our frequency. Again, to use an audio analogy: a short frequency wave is a very high pitched sound — like a dog whistle. A long frequency wave is a low pitched sound, like a bass note on a guitar. Wavelength is just that: the length of the wave. It is measured in units of distance, which can be anything from meters to

7.1. (previous page) Color theory played a key role in the selection of wardrode and props, graphic impact and harmony in this shot staged in front of a New York City firehouse. (Photo by author.)

7.2. (right)The naturally occuring color spectrum and respective wavelengths in nanometers.

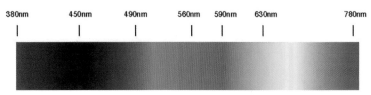

nanometers. A nanometer is one thousand-millionth of a meter. (A meter, just for reference, is one one-millionth of the distance from the equator to the North Pole.)

COLOR PERCEPTION

The perception of color is a complex phenomenon which involves the physics of light, the nature of physical matter, the physiology of the eye and it's interaction with the brain and even social and cultural factors. We can break it down to five aspects:

- Abstract relationships: purely abstract manipulation of color for it's own sake.
- Representation: e.g., a sky is blue, an apple is red.
- Material concerns: texture: chalky, shiny, reflective, dull, etc.
- Connotation and symbolism: Associative meanings, memory, cultural significance, mythical reference. The red, white and blue of the flag.
- Emotional expression: the fiery red of passion, the cold blue of night, etc.

Most people can tell you that the three primaries are red, green and blue, but few can say why these, of all colors are the primaries. The reason is in our eyes.

THE TRISTIMULUS THEORY

The human retina is filled with two kinds of light receptors which are called rods and cones. (Figure 7.4). The rods are primarily responsible for the perception of light and dark: value or grayscale. The cones primarily perceive color. The retina has 3 kinds of cones. The response of each type of cone as a function of the wavelength of the incident light is shown below. The peaks for each curve are at 440nm (blue), 545nm (green) and 580nm (red). Note that the last two actually peak in the yellow part of the spectrum.

FUNCTIONS OF THE EYE

There are many theories to explain the phenomenon of color vision. The most easily understood is the three-component theory which assumes three kinds of light sensitive elements (cones) — each receptive to one of the primary colors of light — an extreme spectrum red. (Figure 7.5), an extreme spectrum violet and an imaginary green. There are about seven million cone in each eye. They are located primarily in the central portion of the retina called the fovea, and are highly sensitive to color. People can resolve fine details with these cones largely because each one is connected to its own nerve end. Muscles controlling the eye always rotate the eyeball until the image of the object of our interest falls on the fovea. Cone vision is known as photopic or daytime vision.

Other light receptors, called rods, are also present in the eye but they are not involved in color vision. Rods serve to give a general, overall picture of the field of view, and are receptive only to the

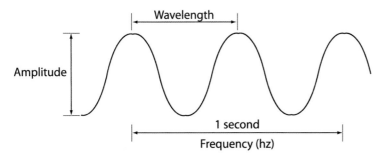

7.3. Components of a wave.

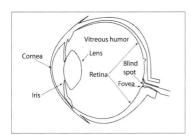

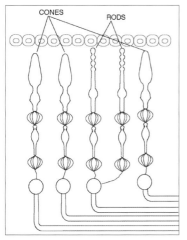

7.4. (top) Physiology of the eye.

7.5. (above) Rods and cones in the retina.

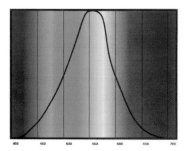

7.6. Spectral response of the human eye.

quantity of light waves entering the eye. Several rods are connected to a single nerve end; thus they cannot resolve fine detail. Rods are sensitive to low levels of illumination and enable the eye to see at night or under extremely low lighting conditions. Therefore, objects which appear brightly colored in daylight when seen by the color-sensitive cones appear only as colorless forms by moonlight because only the rods are stimulated. This is known as scotopic vision.

THE PURKINJE EFFECT AND MOVIE MOONLIGHT
As the adjacent spectral sensitivity curves show, the eye is not equally sensitive to all wavelength. In dim light particularly, there is a definite shift in the apparent brightness of different colors. This was discovered by Johannes von Purkinje. While walking at dawn one day, von Purkinje observed that blue flowers appeared brighter than red, while in full daylight the red flowers were brighter than the blue. This is now called the Purkinje effect and is particularly important in photometry — the measurement of light. The Purkinje effect fools the brain into perceiving moonlight as slightly blueish, even though as reflected sunlight, it is the same color as daylight. This is the reason it is a convention to light night scenes blue.

LIGHT AND COLOR
Color is light, but the color of objects is a combination of the color of the light and the nature of the material it is falling on and being reflected by. Essentially, the color of an object is the wavelenghts of light which it does not absorb. Sunlight appears white — it contains all colors. Light is an additive system of color. Red, Green and Blue are the primaries. When mixed in pairs they produce Magenta, Cyan and Yellow (a hot red, a blue/green, a bright yellow). The mixture of all colors in light creates white. The human eye has receptors (cones) Red/Green, Blue/Yellow which translate light waves of differing length to the optic nerve. The eye is not equally sensitve to all colors, (Figure 7.6) this has far ranging implications in color theory, exposure and even light meters.

Paint is a subtractive system of color. The primaries are Red, Blue and Yellow. The mixing of paint removes subtracts light, All colors mixed would produce a muddy gray brown, or theoretically black. For our purposes we will be discussing the subtractive system of color, but painters need to understand both, since the world they try to capture in paint and their actual paintings are affected by light and the additive system of color. Color has four basic qualities: Hue, Value, Chroma and Temperature. The first three are physical properties and are often called the dimensions of color. The last is a psychological aspect of a color.

The First Dimension: Hue — A hue is a wavelength of light. It is that quality by which we give names to color (i.e., red, yellow, blue, etc.) The average person can distinguish around 150 distinct hues. The hue of a color is simply a definition of it's wavelength: it's place on the natural color spectrum.

Hue, along with Chroma (saturation) and Value (lightness/darkness) make up the three distinct attributes of color. The terms "red" and "blue" are primarily describing hue — hue is related to wavelength for spectral colors. It is convenient to arrange the saturated hues around a Newton Color Circle. Starting from red and proceeding clockwise around the circle below to blue proceeds from long to shorter wavelengths. However it shows that not all hues can be represented by spectral colors since there is no single wavelength of light which has the magenta hue — it may be produced by an equal mixture of red and blue. Newton created the color he called purple by mixing red and blue pigments, thus creating a wheel of colors.

7.7. Color is a crucial component of this frame from *Days of Heaven*. The primary red and the orange tones function not only as pure color but also have strong associations with mood and time of day — both of which are important in the story of this film. The shooting schedule of the film was built around times of day when shots like this could be captured — there is no way you can fake a shot like this with a special filter or "fix it up in post."

The Second Dimension is Value — Relative lightness of darkness of color. A lightened color is called a Tint; created by adding white to a color. A darkened color is called a Shade, created by adding either black or a complement to a color. Dark colors are often called Low Key Colors, pale colors are High Key Colors.

VALUE

Value, along with Chroma (saturation) and Hue make up the three distinct attributes of color. (Figure 7.8). The relative lightness of a colored surface depends upon the illuminance and upon its reflectivity. Since the perceived lightness is not linearly proportional to the reflectivity, a scale from 0 to 10 is used to represent perceived lightness in color measurement systems like the Munsell system. It is found that equal surfaces with differing spectral characteristics but which emit the same number of lumens will be perceived to be equally light. If one surface emits or reflects more lumens, it will be perceived to be lighter in a logarithmic relationship which yields a constant increase in lightness of about 1.5 units with each doubling of lightness.

Every pure hue has its own value before mixing. No color is as dark as black or as light as white, but pure violet is darker than pure orange; yellow is lighter than green. By arranging the color wheel as a color-value wheel, according to the value of each hue, we develop a simple curve, with violet as the darkest hue and yellow as the lightest. The average person can distinguish about 200 distinct value changes. Value is not equal for all hues.

The Third Dimension: Chroma, (also called Intensity and Saturation) — The strength of the color. or relative purity of a color — its brilliance or dullness (grayness). Any hue is most bright in its pure state when no black or white has been added to it. Adding black or white or both (gray), or adding the color's complement (the color opposite it on the color wheel) lowers the intensity, making a color duller. A color at its lowest possible intensity is said to be neutral. Here the average person can see only about 20 levels of chroma change.

Temperature: Another aspect of a color is temperature. The temperature is the relative warmth or coolness of a hue. This derives from the psychological reaction to color — red or red/orange the warmest and blue or blue/green the coolest. It has been proven that people coming in from the cold to a room panted in cool colors

7.8. Value is the relative lightness or darkness of a particular hue as shown here.

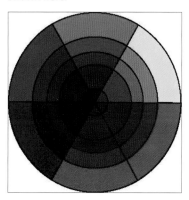

color theory

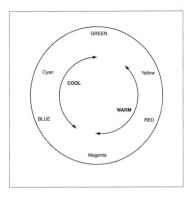

7.9. (above) Warm and cool colors.

7.10. (right) The derivation of the color wheel from the spectrum, as devised by Newton.

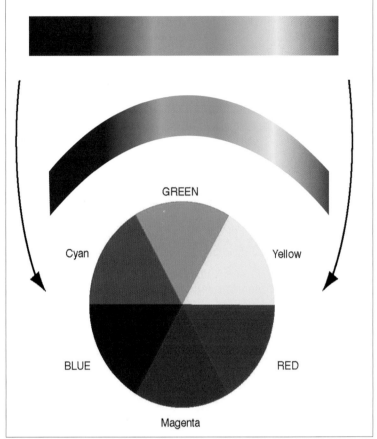

7.11. Primary, secondary and tertiary divisions on the color wheel.

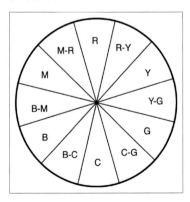

take longer to feel warm than those coming into a room painted in warm colors. Even body temperature has been found to differ by a few degrees in rooms painted warm to those painted cool. Color temperature is derived from physical temperature — a neutral body when heated will first glow red, then orange and eventually white.

THE COLOR WHEEL

Artists have found it helpful to bend the linear spectrum around in a circle called the color wheel. The British scientist Sir Isaac Newton, who discovered the spectrum in the seventeenth century, also turned it into a color wheel. (Figure 7.10) On the color wheel, instead of being at opposite extremes, red and violet lie next to one another. A circular spectrum better describes our perception of the continuous flow of hues, and it establishes opposites across the diameters. The color wheel is created by wrapping the visible spectrum into a circle and joining the far red end (loing wavelengths) to the far violet end (short wavelengths).

Primary Colors are hues which cannot be mixed and from which all other colors can be mixed. In light they are red, green and blue. Secondary Colors are hues made by mixing two primaries

RED + BLUE = Magenta

BLUE + GREEN = Cyan

RED + GREEN = Yellow

Tertiary Colors are combinations of the secondary colors. The primary, secondary and tertiary colors together make up the twelve colors of the basic color wheel. (Figure 7.11)

BEYOND THE COLOR WHEEL

The color wheel is very useful but it deals only with hue, the spectral color. It tells us nothing about how bright the color is or how light or dark it is in terms of the gray scale.

THE MUNSELL SYSTEM

One of the most influential color-modeling systems was devised by Albert Henry Munsell, an American artist. Munsell desired to create a "rational way to describe color" that would use clear decimal notation instead of arbitrary color names. The Munsell system describes color in three dimensional form. The hues are arranged in a circle. Variations in chroma are away from or towards the central axis and variations in value are up and down the central axis. His system, which he began in 1898 with the creation of his color sphere, or tree, saw its full expression with his publication, *A Color Notation*, in 1905. This work has been reprinted several times and is still a standard for colorimetry (the measuring of color).

Munsell modeled his system as a globe around whose equator runs a band of colors. (Figures 7.12 and 7.13). The axis of the orb is a scale of neutral gray values with white as the north pole and black as the south pole. Extending horizontally from the axis at each gray value is a gradation of color progressing from neutral gray to full saturation.

HUE, CHROMA AND VALUE

Munsell named these aspects, or qualities, Hue, Value, and Chroma. They are similar to the traditional uses of these terms, but slightly different in some ways.

HUE

Munsell defined hue as "the quality by which we distinguish one color from another." Hue is the spectral color: it can be defined by its wavelength on the electromagnetic spectrum. It is what, in everyday language, we call "color."

Munsell selected five principle colors (this is slightly different from the "primary" colors): red, yellow, green, blue, and purple; and five intermediate colors: yellow-red, green-yellow, blue-green, purple-blue, and red-purple; and he arranged these in a wheel measured off in 100 compass points:

The colors were simply identified as R for red, YR for red-yellow, Y for yellow, etc. Each primary and intermediate color was allotted ten degrees around the compass and then further identified by its place in the segment. For example, primary red would be identified as 5R since it stands at the mid-point of the red segment. 2.5R would be a red tending more toward red-purple, while 7.5R is a red tending more toward yellow-red.

VALUE

Value was defined by Munsell as "the quality by which we distinguish a light color from a dark one." In common language it might be referred to as "dark red" or "light red." Value is a neutral axis that refers to the gray level of the color which ranges from white to black. As notations such as 10R, 5YR, 7.5PB, etc. denote particular hues, the notation N is used to denote the gray value at any point on the axis. Thus a value of 5N would denote a middle gray, 2N a dark gray, and 7N a light gray. In Munsell's original system, values 1N and 9N are, respectively, black and white, though this was later expanded to values of 0 (black) through 10 (white). We can, of course, see precise parallels to the Zone System. Remember the zone system is a way of considering all visible things in terms of their light and dark value without regard to their color. Here we are just adding the elements of color.

The value of a particular hue would be noted with the value after the hue designation. For example, 5PB 6/ indicates a middle purple-blue at the value level of 6. It should be noted, too, that Munsell's scale of value is visual, or perceptual. That is, it's based on how we *see* differences in relative light, not on a strict set of mathematical values from a light source or illuminant. This is because the eye/brain combination does not perceive all hues and values equally. (The CIE system described below is a more mathematical method of describing color; a method which can be more closely associated with color emulsion or electronic representations of color.)

CHROMA
Chroma is the quality that distinguishes the difference from a pure hue to a gray shade. The chroma axis extends from the value axis at a right angle and the amount of chroma is noted after the value designation. We can, of course, see precise parallels to the zone system. Remember the zone system is a way of considering all visible things in terms of their light and dark values. However, chroma is not uniform for every hue at every value. Munsell recognized that full chroma for individual hues might be achieved at very different places in the color sphere. For example, the fullest chroma for hue 5RP (red-purple) is achieved at 5/26: Another color such as 10YR (yellowish yellow-red) has a much shorter chroma axis and reaches fullest chroma at 7/10 and 6/10:

7.12. (top, right) and 7.13 (bottom, right) Advancing and retreating color in *Barry Lyndon*. Viewed as individual segments within the film, the color just becomes part of the scene. When you look at them in direct opposition we can more clearly see how they play a role in the storytelling of each moment in the film.

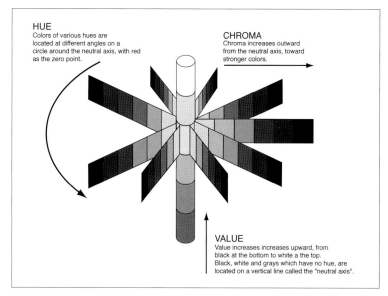

HUE
Colors of various hues are located at different angles on a circle around the neutral axis, with red as the zero point.

CHROMA
Chroma increases outward from the neutral axis, toward stronger colors.

VALUE
Value increases increases upward, from black at the bottom to white a the top. Black, white and grays which have no hue, are located on a vertical line called the "neutral axis".

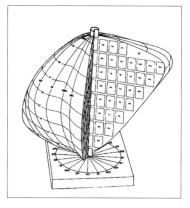

7.14. (above) The Munsell system is formed as a tree structure; the variations in horizontal size are due to the fact that some hues reach full saturation sooner than others.

7.15. (left)The Munsell system represents hue, chroma and value as three axes of a tree structure.

In the Munsell System, reds, blues, and purples tend to be stronger hues that average higher chroma values at full saturation, while yellows and greens are weaker hues that average fullest chroma saturation relatively close to the neutral axis. Reds, blues, and purples reach fullest saturation at mid-levels on the value scale, while yellows and greens reach it at higher values. The result of these differences is that what Munsell originally envisioned as a sphere is radically asymmetrical. A three-dimensional solid representation of Munsell's system is shown in Figures 7.14 and 7.15.

COLOR MIXING

COMPLEMENTARY
Hues directly opposite one another on the color wheel are called complements. They are called complements because they contain or complete the triad of primary colors — for example, the primary red is opposite the secondary green, which contains the primaries yellow and blue.

ADVANCING AND RETREATING COLOR
Another psychological response: hottest, darkest colors move forward aggressively as do black, brown, dark blue and dark green. Pale tones retreat. Pale green and blue the furthest. Pale reds, oranges and yellows recede but not as far as cools. Yellow though light, advances when intense. (Figures 7.12 and 7.13).

Weight and Balance — The way we see color depends not only on the color themselves, but also on the size of each color area, on the shapes that contain the color, and on the interaction between neighboring colors. Darker hues, like darker values, tend to be heavier looking than lighter ones, yet, warm intense colors like yellow and orange and can overpower a darker color.

FILM AND VIDEO COLORSPACE
The medium, whether it is paint, television, film, fabric or printed matter, also affects the possible range of colors, i.e., all the possible variations in hue, value and chroma that can be achieved in a medium, is referred to as its color gamut. In monitors and video systems, it is often referred to as colorspace.

7.16. Relative colorspace of film and video.

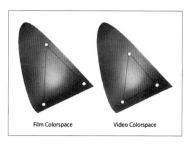

Film Colorspace   Video Colorspace

7.17. Triadic harmonies.

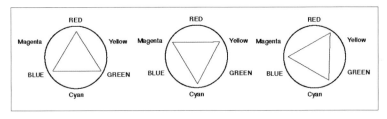

TRANSPARENCY AND REFLECTION

These tend to lighten color. Transparency is the ability to see through the color to another under it. Reflection on a form as well as transparency will lighten it. In paint the transparency and reflective quality of the paint will affect the value and intensity of the color as well, this principle is used in set painting, prop and wardrobe and can affect lighting choices.

COLOR HARMONIES & THE INTERACTION OF COLOR

Color Harmony — Like music, color can be strongly emotive and expressive. Certain combinations of color, as of sound, have seemed to have special beauty or be intrinsically pleasing in ways most people recognize intuitively. The notions of balance and resolution are implied in color harmony. Harmony refers to clear relationships based on divisions of the color wheel, see Figures 7.17, 7.18 and 7.19. Some examples of color harmony follow:

- Monochrome Color Harmony — refers to a harmony of tones of all the same hue but at different values and intensity (i.e. tints and shades of blue).
- Analogous Color Harmony — is a harmony of hues close to or touching one another on the color wheel, although of different values and intensities. (i.e. yellow-green, green and blue-green or yellow, green and blue).
- Triadic Harmonies — are based on groups of three colors more or less equidistant from one another on the color wheel. The three primary or the three secondary colors form triadic harmonies, but any group of three will serve, if they are evenly spaced around the color wheel.
- Complementary Harmonies — involve the pairing of any two colors that sit opposite one another on the color wheel. (i.e. red with green, yellow with violet)
- Split Complementary Harmonies — group a color not with its complement, but with the pair of colors adjacent to its complement. (i.e. yellow with red-violet and blue-violet, blue with yellow orange and red orange, red with yellow-green and blue-green).
- Discord and Discordant Colors — Colors can be mismatched or out of harmony, often referred to clashing colors. This happens when a grouping of harmonious colors are placed next to a color outside the harmony.

7.18. (below) Complimentaries.

7.19. (bottom) Split complimentaries.

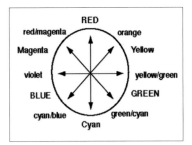

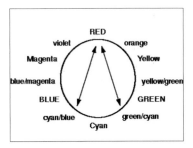

INTERACTION OF COLOR AND VISUAL PHENOMENA

All perception of color is based on an interaction of color. One color cannot be seen unless it has others around it. Scientists have put individuals in a room painted in one color. The subject could not distinguish what color the room was, instead they saw white. Only when another color was introduced to the environment were they able to see color. More important is the understanding of how color changes when surrounded by or touching other colors. The effect of simultaneous contrast is greatest at the edges between colors or on patterns of small scale.

Degradation of Colors: One color adjacent to another color will give a tinge of its complement to the other color. Therefore, two adjacent complementary colors brighten each other. Therefore non-complementary colors will have the opposite effect. A yellow next to a green will give the green a violet tinge, making the latter appear muddy. This is known as the degradation of color.

7.20. Simultaneous contrast in practice.

AFTERIMAGES
Eye fatigue by staring at a color or a bright light can occur; this causes us to see an image in opposition of what we were looking at as relaxation from the stress of one color. A red dot will give a green afterimage. One can train their eyes to look into the shadow of a color and you can find its complement.

THE LAWS OF SIMULTANEOUS CONTRAST
Devised by the French chemist Michel-Eugene Chevreul, the law of simultaneous contrast was first described in his book "The Law of Simultaneous Contrast" written in 1839. When one object is next to another it is useful if any color difference between them is emphasized. Think of a man in a brown jacket standing in front of a brick wall. He is easier to distinguish if the eye/brain combination emphasizes whatever color difference exists between the jacket and the wall. To do this, the visual system modifies our perception of the red in both the jacket and the wall, but the adjustment is larger in the jacket since it is smaller and surrounded by the wall. The result of this adjustment is called simultaneous contrast. Put more simply: our perception of a color is changed by a color that surrounds and touches it. Both colors are actually changed by being next to each other. When two different colors come into direct contact, the contrast intensifies the difference between them. (Figure 7.20).

A light color next to a dark color will appear lighter and the dark will appear darker. The same is true for hue (i.e. yellow/greener), temperature (hotter/cooler) and chroma (brighter/duller).

- Colors are modified in appearance by their proximity to other colors.
- All light colors seem most striking against black.
- Dark colors seem most striking against white.
- Dark colors upon light colors look darker than on dark colors.
- Light colors upon dark colors look lighter than light colors.
- Colors are influenced in hue by adjacent colors, each tinting its neighbors with its own complement.
- If two complementary colors lie side by side, each seems more intense than by itself.
- Dark Hues on a dark ground which is not complementary will appear weaker than on a complementary ground.
- Light colors on a light ground which is not complementary will seem weaker than on a complementary ground.
- A bright color against a dull color of the same hue will further deaden the color.
- When a bright color is used against a dull color, the contrast will be strongest when the latter is complementary.
- Light colors on light grounds (not complementary) can be greatly strengthened if bounded by narrow bands of black or complementary colors.
- Dark colors on dark grounds (not complementary) can be strengthened if similarly bounded by white or light colors.

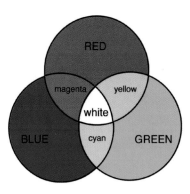

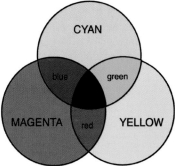

7.21. Additive color.
7.22. Subtractive color.

METAMERISM

All this is closely related to metamerism. Two colors that match under one light source, but do not match under a different light source are called metamers. They are said to be a metameric match. Metamerism occurs because the appearance of a color depends on the wavelengths it reflects which, in turn, depend on the wavelengths of the light source.

This can have an important influence of the selection of colors for sets or props, especially in the case of green screen or blue screen work. Always take the light source into consideration when previewing paint chips, wardrobe, makeup, etc. Obviously, this is the reason that the makeup room and wardrobe trailer should have a light source which approximates what will be used on the set.

COLOR MODELS

In addition to the pioneering Munsell system, several different color models are used to classify colors and to qualify them according to such attributes as hue, saturation, chroma, lightness, or brightness. There are a number of models which are relevant to film and video:

THE RGB (CMY) COLOR MODEL

The red, green, blue (RGB) and cyan, magenta, yellow (CMY) models are closely related; one is based on the additive primaries and the other on the additive secondaries. These are also the most representative models for additive and subtractive colors, respectively. RGB is also the basic color model for video and computer monitors.

CMY is most commonly referred to as CMYK. The K stands for black (since B is already used for Blue). In subtractive colors (inks and paints) adding all three primaries together theoretically produces black. In additive color, mixing the three primaries together produces white light. So black has to be considered as a separate color.

ADDITIVE COLORS

Additive colors are those relevant to light and mixing colors in light. (Figure 7.21). The most common examples of this are television screens and computer monitors, which produce colored pixels by firing red, green, and blue electron guns at phosphors on the television or monitor screen. Additive color can be produced by mixing two beams of colored light, or by layering two or more colored gels or by showing the two colors in rapid sucession.

This can be illustrated by a technique used in the earliest experiments with additive colors: color wheels. These are disks whose surface is divided into areas of solid color. When attached to a motor and spun at high speed, the human eye cannot distinguish between the separate colors and sees them instead as a composite of the colors on the disk. Color can also be mixed by showing small bits of color closely spaced together — such as pixels on a video screen.

SUBTRACTIVE COLORS

Subtractive colors are used to describe when pigments in an object absorb certain wavelengths of white light while reflecting the rest. (Figure 7.22). Any colored object, whether natural or man-made, absorbs some wavelengths of light and reflects or transmits others; the wavelengths left in the reflected/transmitted light make up the color we see. This is the nature of print color and cyan, magenta, and yellow, as used in four-color process printing, are considered to be the subtractive primaries. The subtractive color model in printing operates not only with CMY(K), but also with printing inks.

RGB

Red, green, and blue are the primary stimuli for human color perception and are the primary additive colors. The importance of RGB as a color model is that it relates very closely to the way we perceive color with the cone receptors in our retinas. RGB is the color model used in video or any other medium that projects the color. It is the basic color model on computers and is used for web graphics.

CMY(K)

Cyan, magenta, and yellow correspond roughly to the primary colors in art production: red, blue, and yellow — they are the secondary colors of the additive system.

Both models fall short of reproducing all the colors we can see. Furthermore, they differ to such an extent that there are many RGB colors that cannot be produced using CMY(K), and similarly, there are some CMY colors that cannot be produced using RGB. The exact RGB or CMY gamut depends on other factors as well. Every RGB device, whether it be color negative, transparency film, video camera, display monitor, color printer, color scanner, etc., has it's own unique gamut — it's own colorspace, there will always be some variation as an image moves from system to system.

THE HSB/HLS MODEL

Hue, saturation, and brightness and hue, lightness, and saturation are two variations of a similar model that is a standard for computer graphics and some video applications. It closely approximates the qualities most apparent to human perception of color.

HSB/HLS are two variations of a very basic color model for defining colors in desktop graphics programs that closely matches the way we perceive color. This model is somewhat analogous to Munsell's system of hue, value, and chroma in that it uses three similar axes to define a color. In HSB, these are hue, saturation, and brightness; in HLS, they are defined by hue, lightness, and saturation.

HUE

The values for the hue axis run from 0-360° beginning and ending with red and running through green, blue and all intermediary colors like greenish-blue, orange, purple, etc. In this respect, HLS is very similar to Munsell's color wheel. Although Munsell used a different method for indicating hue, both arrange the colors in a circular pattern and progress them through compass points. Saturation indicates the degree to which the hue differs from a neutral gray. The values run from 0%, which is no color saturation, to 100%, which is the fullest saturation of a given hue at a given percentage of illumination. This is similar to Munsell's concept of chroma.

Lightness (value) indicates the level of illumination. The values run as percentages; 0% appears black (no light) while 100% is full illumination, which washes out the color (it appears white). In this respect, the lightness axis is similar to Munsell's value axis. Colors at percentages less than 50% appear darker while colors at greater than 50% appear lighter.

THE CIE COLOR SYSTEM

The CIE color models are highly influential systems for measuring color and distinguishing between colors. The C.I.E. color system was devised by the C.I.E. (Commission International de l'Eclairage — the International Commission on Illumination) in 1931 and has since become an international standard for measuring, designating, and matching colors. (Figure 7.23). In the C.I.E. system, the relative percentages of each of the theoretical primary colors (red, green,

7.23. A diagram of the CIE color system.

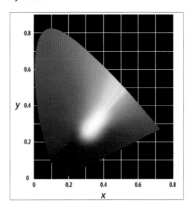

color theory

139

blue) of a color to be identified are mathematically derived, then plotted on a Chromaticity Diagram as one chromaticity point, the dominant wavelength and purity can be determined. All possible colors may be designated on the Chromaticity Diagram, whether they are emitted, transmitted, or reflected. Thus, the C.I.E. system may be coordinated with all other color designation systems. Any color on the CIE chromaticity diagram can be considered to be a mixture of the three CIE primaries, X,Y and Z. That mixture may be specified by three numbers X,Y and Z, called tristimulus values

The light from a colored object is measured to obtain its Spectral Power Density (SPD) and the value for the SPD at each wavelength is multiplied times the three color matching functions and summed to obtain X, Y, and Z. These values are then used to calculate the CIE chromaticity coordinates.

STANDARD LIGHT SOURCES IN CIE
The following CIE standard sources were defined in 1931:
- Source A — A tungsten-filament lamp with a color temperature of 2854K
- Source B — A model of noon sunlight with a temperature of 4800K
- Source C — A model of average daylight with a temperature of 6500K.

This is slightly different from the standard 5500K daylight as defined by the U.S. government. The 5500K standard is still widely used for lighting instruments, globes and correction gels.

DIGITAL AND ELECTRONIC COLOR
Electronic color is displayed on television and computer screens through the use of a cathode-ray tube (CRT). A CRT works by moving back and forth behind the screen to illuminate or activate the phosphor dots on the inside of the glass tube. Color monitors use three different types of phosphors that appear red, green, and blue when activated. These phosphors are placed close together, and when combined in differing intensities can produce many different colors. The primaries of electronic color are therefore red, green, and blue, and other colors can be made by combining different intensities of these three colors. There are differences in the measurement system of analog and digital video. The intensity of each color is measured on a scale from 0 to 255 (in the digital system), and a color is specified by telling the monitor the RGB values. For instance, yellow is specified by telling the computer to add 255 red, 255 green, and 0 blue. Video color is analysed on the vectorscope, which is discussed in detail in the chapter on *Video and High Def.*

the tools of lighting

THE SEVEN TYPES OF LIGHTING EQUIPMENT

DP's and directors do not need to know all the details of how each piece of lighting equipment works but it is essential that they know the capabilities and possibilities of each unit as well as its limitations. A great deal of time can be wasted by using a light or piece of grip equipment which is inappropriate for the job. One of the DP's most important functions is ordering the right lighting equipment for the job and using it appropriately. Motion picture lights fall into seven general categories: HMIs, tungsten fresnels, tungsten open face lights, fluorescent, xenons, practicals and sunguns.

HMI

HMIs generate three to four times the light of tungsten halogen, but consume up to 75% less energy for the same output. When a tungsten bulb is color corrected to match daylight, the advantage increases to seven times as a great deal of the spectrum is absorbed by the blue gel (color temperature blue or CTB. See the chapter on color balance). Because HMIs are more efficient in converting power to light, they generate less heat than a tungsten lamp with the same output (Figure 8.2).

HMI stands for the basic components: H is from the Latin symbol for mercury (Hg) which is used primarily to create the lamp voltage. M is for the many rare earth metals such as sysporsium, thulium and homium which control the color temperature of the output. I stands for iodine and bromine which are halogen compounds. The halogen serves much the same function as in a tungsten halogen lamp in prolonging the useful life of the bulb and ensures that the rare earth metals remain concentrated in the hot zone of the arc.

HMI lamps have two electrodes made from tungsten which project into a cylindrical or ellipsoidal discharge chamber. Unlike tungsten bulbs which have a continuous filament of tungsten wire, HMIs create an electrical arc which jumps from one electrode to another and generate light and heat in the process. Color temperature as it is measured for tungsten bulbs or sunlight does not technically apply to HMIs (or to other types of discharge lighting such as fluorescents) because they produce a quasi-continuous spectrum. In actual practice though, the same measurements and color temperature meters are used for all types of video and motion picture lighting sources.

In an HMI lamp the basic mercury discharge spectrum is very discontinuous and concentrated in a few narrow bands. The output of the rare earths fills out the spectrum and produces a spectrum very close to daylight. Sources, especially those with other than continuous "natural" spectrums, can vary in how well they "show" the color of an object. Recall our discussion of metamerism in the chapter on color theory. Metamerism is where an object appears to be a certain color under one light source but looks quite different under another. The farther a source is from a true spectrum, the greater this mismatch will be.

COLOR RENDERING INDEX

Lights are classified according to Color Rendering Index (CRI). This is a method of quantifying how accurately a lighting source displays the color of an object (see the discussion of metamerism in the chapter *Color Theory*). A CRI of 90 or above (on a scale of 0 to 100) is considered necessary for film and video work. The CRI is especially important when judging fluorescent and other gas discharge sources. For most HMIs the color rendering index is greater than 90, and thus above the minimum for film and video. When first developed, HMIs were not dimmable but units have become available which can be dimmed to 40% of their rated output which cor-

8.1. (previous page) Lighting can be a character in the story as well as merely illumination for the subject and the sets: *Bladerunner* (Warner Bros.,1982).

8.2. Below, a 12K HMI with desert wheels. (Photo courtesy of Backstage Equipment Inc.)

responds to 30% of their light output. There is some slight shift of color temperature under these conditions. Under normal conditions a decrease in voltage to the ballast will make the light shift slightly cooler. This is the opposite of a tungsten bulb which gets warmer as the voltage drops.

BALLASTS

All HMIs require a ballast. As with a carbon arc or an arc welder, the ballast includes a choke which acts as a current limiter. The reason for this is simple: an arc is basically a dead short; if the current were allowed to flow freely, the circuit would overload and either blow the fuse or burn up. Early ballasts for HMIs were extremely heavy and bulky (200 pounds or more) as they contained current limiters which consisted of heavy copper wire wound in a coil like a transformer. This coil ballast works on the principle of reactance (Figure 8.3).

The invention of the smaller and lighter electronic ballast was a major improvement. Electronic ballasts also allow the unit to operate on a square-wave, which solves the flicker problem as we will see in the chapter on technical issues. The square-wave also increases light efficiency by about 8%.

Voltages as high as 12,000 VAC or more are needed to start the arc, which is provided by a separate ignitor circuit in the ballast. This creates the power needed for the electric current to jump across the gap between the two electrodes. The typical operating voltage is around 200V. When a lamp is already hot, much higher voltages are needed in order to ionize the pressurized gap between the electrodes. This can be from 20kV to more than 65 kV. For this reason, some HMIs cannot be restruck while hot. Hot restrike, which generates a higher voltage to overcome this resistance is a feature on most newer HMIs. The reason for this is that once an HMI is hot, the gases inside the bulb are pressurized and ionized; they provide greater resistance and therefore a high voltage is necessary to jump the gap.

Due to devitrification (deterioration of the glass of the bulb), which increases as the lamp ages, the color temperature falls by about 0.5 to 1K per hour burned, depending on the wattage. HMI bulbs should not be operated more than 25% past their rated life as there is a danger of explosion.

18K'S AND 12K'S

The 18K and the 12K HMIs are the most powerful fresnel lights currently available. Like all HMIs they are extremely efficient in luminous output per watt of input power. They produce a very sharp, clean light which is the result of having a very small source (the gas arc) which is focused through a very large lens (usually a 24" lens for both types) (Figure 8.4).

These large lights are invaluable where very large areas are being covered or there is a need for high light levels for high-speed shooting. They are also a natural for sunlight effects such as sun beams through a window or any other situation where a strong well defined beam is needed. They are also among the few sources (along with HMI PARs) which will balance daylight and fill in the shadows sufficiently to permit shooting in the bare sun without silks or reflectors. The fact that they burn approximately "daylight blue" (5500 degrees kelvin) is a tremendous advantage in these situations: no light is lost to filters. Often when a 12K or 18K is used to fill in sunlight it is the only unit operating on a generator. If it was drawing on one leg only, the load would be extremely difficult to balance and might damage the generator.

8.3. The ballast acts as a transformer to provide operating voltage and also starting voltage which can be as high as 20,000V. It is also a current limiter.

8.4. A 12K/18K HMI, currently the most powerful fresnel light available. (Photo courtesy of Arri Group.)

Most 12 and 18Ks are 220 volt lights but some are 110 volt units which can make load balancing difficult. As with any large light, coordinate with the gennie operator before firing it up or shutting it down. Be sure to clarify with the rental house what type of power connectors are used on the lights when you are placing your lighting and grip order for the job.

The most significant new development in HMIs is the new "flicker-free" ballasts which use square-wave technology to provide flicker-less shooting at any frame rate. With some units there is a penalty paid for flicker-free shooting at frame rates other than sync sound speed — when the high speed flicker-free button is selected on these units they operate at a significantly higher noise level. If the ballasts can be placed outside or shooting is MOS, this is not a problem. Header cables are the power connection from the ballast to the light head itself. Many larger HMIs can only take two header cables; a third header will usually result in a voltage loss too great to get the lamp to fire up.

Square-wave refers to the shape of the sine wave of the alternating current after it has been reshaped by the electronics of the ballast. Flicker is discussed in more detail in the chapter on *Technical Issues* but suffice it to say here that the normal sine wave of AC current leaves too many "gaps" which become visible if the camera shutter is not synchronized to its rhythm. By squaring the wave, these gaps are minimized and there is less chance of flicker. This is especially important if you are shooting at anything other than normal speed; high speed photography in particular will create problems. It is important to note that flicker can be a problem in video also, just as with film cameras.

6K & 8K

6K and 8K HMIs can handle many of the same jobs as the bigger lights, particularly where the area covered is smaller. Although they generally have a smaller lens they still produce a sharp, clean beam with good spread. In many applications they perform admirably as the main light: serving as key, window light, sun balance, etc. Some 6Ks and 8K's are 110 volts and some are 220, depending on the manufacturer and the rental house. They may require a variety of connectors or a set of Siamese splitters.

When ordering any large lamp, it is crucial to ask these questions and be sure the rental house will provide the appropriate distribution equipment or adapters. Failure to do so may result in the light not being functional. Some makes of HMIs provide for head balancing. This is accomplished by sliding the yoke support backwards or forwards on the head. This is a useful feature when adding or subtracting barndoors, frames or other items which radically alter the balance of the light.

4K & 2.5K

The smaller HMIs, the 4K and 2.5K are general purpose lights, doing much of the work that used to be assigned to 5K and 10K tungsten lights. Slightly smaller than the bigger HMIs, they can be easily flown and rigged and will fit in some fairly tight spots.

1.2K AND SMALLER UNITS

The smallest lamps, the 1.2K and 575 HMI, are versatile units. Lightweight and fairly compact, they can be used in a variety of situations. The electronics ballasts for the small units have become portable enough to be hidden in places where larger units might be visible.

RULES FOR USING HMI UNITS

- Always ground the light and the ballast with appropriate grounding equipment.
- Check the stand and ballast with a VOM meter for leakage by measuring the voltage between the stand and any ground. There will usually be a few volts, but anything above 10 or 15 volts indicates a potential problem.
- Keep the ballast dry. On wet ground, use boxes or rubber mats.
- Avoid getting dirt or finger marks on the lamps: oil from the skin will degrade the glass and create a potential failure point. Many lamps come provided with a special cleaning cloth.
- Ensure that there is good contact between the lamp base and the holder. Contamination will increase resistance and impair proper cooling.
- The filling tip (nipple) should always be above the discharge, otherwise there is a risk of a cold spot developing inside the discharge chamber where the filler substances may condense and change the photometric properties.
- Prolonged running at above rated voltage may result in premature failure.
- Extended cable runs may reduce the voltage to a point which affects the output and may result in the lamp not firing.
- Excessive cooling or direct airflow on the lamp may cool the lamp below its operating temperature which can result in a light with a high color temperature and inferior CRI.
- All bulbs are rated for certain burning positions which vary from plus or minus 15 degrees to plus or minus 45 degrees. In general, bulbs 4K and above have a 15 degree tolerance while smaller bulbs have a greater range.

POTENTIAL PROBLEMS

HMIs may sometimes fail to function properly. Be sure to have a few extra header cables on hand: they are the most common cause of malfunctions. The safety switch on the lens can also cause trouble. Never try to bypass it, however; it serves an important function. HMIs should never be operated without the glass lens. The glass filters out harmful ultraviolet radiation which can damage someone's eyes and give them a sunburn. When they do fail to fire:

- Check that the breakers are on. Most HMIs have more than one breaker.
- After killing the power, open the lens and check the micro-switch which contacts the lens housing. Make sure it is operating properly and making contact. Wiggle it, but don't be violent — the light won't operate without it.
- If that fails, try another header cable. If you are running more than one header to a light, disconnect and try each one individually. Look for broken pins, garbage in the receptacle, etc.
- Check the power. HMIs won't fire if the voltage is low. Generally they need at least 108 volts to fire. Some have a voltage switch (110, 120, 220); be sure it's in the right position.
- Try the head with a different ballast and vice-versa.
- Let the light cool. Many lights won't do a hot restrike.

XENONS

Xenons are similar to HMIs as they are a gas discharge arc with a ballast. They feature a polished parabolic reflector which gives them

8.5. Xenons produce an incredibly powerful and focused beam — they will break most ordinary windows and mirrors if placed too close. Matthews makes this mirror specifically for Xenons. It is not designed to be used for other applications. (Photo courtesy of Matthews Studio Equipment, Inc.)

amazing throw and almost laser-like beam collimation. At full spot they can project a tight beam several blocks with a relatively small mount of spread (Figures 8.5 and 8.6).

Xenons are very efficient with the highest lumens per watt output of any light. Xenons currently come in five sizes: a 1K, 2K, 4K, 7K and 10K. There is also a 75 watt sun-gun unit. The 1K and 2K units come in 110 and 220 volt models, some of which can be wall-plugged. This produces a high output light which can be plugged into a wall outlet or a small portable generator. The larger xenons are extremely powerful, and must be used cautiously: at full spot they can quickly crack a window. Just one example of their power: with ASA 320 film stock and the light set at full spot, a 4K delivers f/64 at 40 feet from the light.

The current supplied by the ballast to the bulb is pulsed DC; as a result flicker is not a problem for xenons and they can be used for high speed filming up to 10,000 fps. Xenons do, however, have some disadvantages: all xenons are expensive to rent and have a cooling fan which makes them very difficult to use in sound filming. Also, because of the bulb placement and reflector design, there is always a hole in the middle of the round beam, which can be minimized but never entirely eliminated.

Due to the parabolic reflectors, flagging and cutting are difficult close to the light: flags cast bizarre symmetrical shadows. Also, the extremely high and concentrated output means that they burn through gel very quickly. Many people try to compensate by placing the gel as far as possible from the light. This is a mistake: the safest place to gel is actually right on the face of the light.

Seventy-five watt xenon sunguns were developed for the Navy. They are excellent for flashlight effects. They come in both AC (110 volt) and DC configurations. Most have motorized flood /spot controls which can be operated during the shot. As with larger xenons, there is a hole or a hot spot in the center of the beam (depending on the focus) which cannot be eliminated. Xenon bulbs do not shift in temperature as they age or as voltage shifts.

CARBON ARCS

For many years, the Brute Arc was the most powerful light available. It was the standard for fill to balance sunlight, night exteriors and sun effects through windows. Dating back to 1801, the arc was the first high intensity electric light. It was used in theaters and then adopted by the film industry as the only source bright enough to

8.6. *Bladerunner* (1982) was the first use of xenons in a feature film. Jordan Cronenweth used them very effectively as powerful and evocative story and design elements.

use with the extremely slow emulsions available then. It was the only artificial alternative to the all glass or all sky-light studios that were then necessary.

They produce light by creating an actual arc between two carbon electrodes. Since they are not enclosed in glass and surrounded by special gases, as the arc burns the negative and positive electrode are consumed and so have to be continuously adjusted to keep them in the correct position. This is done with small electric motors. Even with feed motors and complex geared mechanisms, arcs require an operator to monitor them constantly and adjust the speed of the motors to maximize output and prevent the arc from "flaming out." Arcs require a huge amount of power (225 amps for the standard Brute) which calls for a #00 cable run for each light) and the fact that it must be DC, which dictates either a studio with DC power or a large DC generator (Figure 8.7).

The Brute Arc has a lighting quality which is distinctive and quite beautiful. Because the plasma arc which creates the light output is quite small, the arc is almost a point source. The very small source of the plasma arc, combined with the very large lens, produces a sharp, specular light which has a very clean, "wrapping" quality. This combined with ability to change the color of the arc makes it unfortunate that they are no longer economically feasible. Arcs can be either daylight or tungsten balance without gels, something that no other light can do. This is accomplished by using either "white-flame" carbons (daylight balance) or "yellow-flame" carbons (tungsten balance). For daylight balance use, the white-flame carbons run high in ultraviolet and a Y-1 filter is usually added to counteract this. MT-2 converts the white-flame carbons to tungsten color balance.

All arcs have their power supplied through a ballast, which is also called a grid. The grid serves two purposes: it is a giant resistor which limits current flow across the arc and reduces the voltage to the optimum 73 volts without reducing the amperage. Voltage that is too high or too low can cause the electrodes to burn improperly and inefficiently. While the 225 amp Litewate Brute is by far the most common type of DC arc, other sizes are available. These include the 150 (150 amps), the Baby Brute (225 amps) and the Titan (350 amps). Only a few Titans ever existed. Arcs create a good deal of ultraviolet. To correct this, warming gels are used: a Y-1 for daylight balance carbons and a YF-101 or an MT-2 plus a Y-1 for tungsten balance (yellow flame carbons).

Arcs are unfortunately expensive to operate as they require not only a very large generator but also each one needs its own operator to feed and trim the carbons. In addition, the supplied power must be DC (direct current) and so it must either be a dedicated gennie or one which can supply AC and DC at the same time — called a "concurrent" gennie.

8.7. The carbon arc was for decades the only really big light in motion picture production. For a history of film lighting, see *Motion Picture and Video Lighting*, by the same author, also published by Focal Press.

TUNGSTEN FRESNELS

Tungsten lamps are just bigger versions of ordinary household bulbs; they all have a filament of tungsten wire just as invented by Thomas Edison. There are two types of tungsten fresnels: studio and baby. The "studio" light is the full size unit, the "baby" is a smaller housing and lens, making it more compact for location use (Figure 8.8). As a rule the baby version is the housing of the next smaller size (for example the 5K is similar to a studio 2K). The baby lights are much favored for location work.

8.8. A head cart with a standard assortment of tungsten fresnels. (Photo courtesy of Backstage Equipment.)

8.9. A 20K fresnel tungsten. (Photo courtesy of Cinemills.)

TWENTY

The biggest tungsten light now in use is the 20K. It is a large unit with tremendous output. Many jobs that were formerly done by the 10K are now done with this light. Most run at 220 volts and several models come with a built-in dimmer (Figure 8.9).

TENNERS

The 10K fresnel comes in three basic versions:
- The baby 10K provides high intensity output with a fairly compact, easily transportable unit with a 14″ fresnel lens.
- The basic 10K, known as a "tenner" or studio 10K, has a 20″ fresnel.
- The largest light of this group is the "Big Eye" tenner which has a 24″ lens. The Big Eye is a very special light with quality all its own. The DTY (10K) bulb provides a fairly small source, while the extremely large fresnel is a large radiator. The result is a sharp hard light with real bite but with a wrap around quality which gives it a soft light quality on subjects close to the light. This is a characteristic of all very big lights which gives them a unique quality.

It is important to never use a 20K, 10K or a 5K pointing straight up (this applies to large HMIs and xenons as well). The lens blocks proper ventilation and the unit will overheat. Also, the filament will not be properly supported and will sag and possibly touch the glass. Either condition will cause the bulb to fail and overheating may crack the lens. The failure will cost somebody hundreds of dollars and put the light out of commission.

FIVE K

Although it is available in both versions, the baby 5K is far more popular than the larger unit. It can work as a general purpose "big light" and a fill used against a 10K. The 5K is also called a senior.

JUNIORS

The 2K fresnel is also known as a deuce or a junior. It has enough power to bring a single subject or actor up to a reasonable exposure, even with diffusion in front of the lens. Deuces are also useful as backlights, rims and kickers. Baby juniors (called BJs) are the more compact and an extraordinarily versatile unit.

BABIES

Thousand watt units (1Ks) are also known babies, aces or 750s. The 1K is used as an accent light, a splash on the wall, a small back light, a hard fill and for dozens of other uses. The baby can use either a 750 watt bulb (EGR) or a 1000 watt bulb (EGT) the widely used name of 750 comes from the days before quartz halogen when the 750 tungsten bulb was the most common. Most are now used with the 1K quartz bulb, but are still called 750s. The Baby 1K, also called a Baby Baby, is the small size version. Because of its smaller lens and box, it has a wider spread than the studio 750 and this can be a useful feature when hiding small units in nooks and crannies.

TWEENIE / PEPPER

The tweenie is "between" the 1K and the inkie. With the new high speed films, the tweenie is often just the right light for the small jobs a baby used to do. It is very useful for a number of small jobs, easily hidden and can function as a quick accent, a slate light or an eyesight. There is also a 400w Pepper which is similar to an inkie (Figure 8.10).

INKIE / PEPPER

At 200 or 250 watts (depending on the bulb), the inkie or Pepper is not a powerful unit, but up close it can deliver a surprising amount of light. The inkie is great for a tiny spritz of light on the set, as an eye light, a small fill, or for an emergency last minute light to just raise the exposure a bit on a small area.

OPEN FACE

Some 2K, 1K and 650 units are available as "open face" lights, that is, they have no lenses but they do have some spot flood focusing. They are raw but they do have a tremendous output for their size. They are good for bounce or shooting through diffusion (Figure 6.11).

PARS

PAR stands for parabolic — the shape of the reflector. A parabola is the only shape which collects all of the light rays and projects them out in the same direction. In conjunction with this, all PAR units have a lens, which functions primarily to concentrate or spread the beam. Tungsten parts generally come with a fixed lens which is part of the unit: they are pretty much the same as a car headlight. HMI PARs always come with a set of interchangeable lenses: these go from a very wide beam to a very narrow beam. The disadvantage of PARs is that the beam generally covers only a very small area and is not a very complimentary light nor is it easily controllable but it is useful for many purposes which call for just raw light power.

PARs come in two basic varieties: film versions come in a solid rotatable housing such as Mole Richardson's MolePar (Figure 8.12) or CineQueen (Colortran), which feature barndoors and scrim holders; and in a flimsier theatrical version called a PAR can. Theatrical lights are not generally as sturdily built because they are generally hung in a theater and then left alone. They don't get the rough treatment and adverse conditions that film and video lights do. PARs (especially NSPs) can quickly burn through even the toughest gels, melt bead board and set muslin diffusion on fire.

PARs with a dichroic coating have an output which is very close to daylight (blue) balance. Small PAR 48s and 36s are also available at lower voltages as well as 110v. Nearly all types of bulbs are also available in 220 volts, which is the standard in Europe and much of the rest of the world.

PAR GROUPS

PARs are also made in groups, the best known being the Maxi Brute, a powerful unit with tremendous punch and throw. They are used in large night exteriors and in large scale interior applications: aircraft hangars, arenas, etc. They can also be used directly or through gel, muslin, etc., when very high light levels are needed to get through heavy diffusion.

Maxi Brutes and Dinos are similar in design but different in size. Maxi's come in configurations of 6, 9 or 12 x PAR 64 lamps; the most common being the 9 lamp head. A Dino is 36 x PAR 64 lamps. Other variations of this design exist as well (Figure 8.14).

Fay lights are clusters of 650 watt PAR 36s and come in single lamps up to 9 (or 12) lamp configurations. The Wendy lights come in panels with the same PAR 36 lamps (usually DWE) and are 49 lamps in the largest configuration. They can be ordered with flood (FL), medium flood (MF), spot (SP) or very narrow spot (VNS) lamps. Same goes with the MolePar or Parcan which use the same PAR 64 as the Dinos and Maxi Brutes but are single lamp fixtures. The bulbs are housed in banks which are individually orientable

8.10. (top) The Pepper, a compact and versatile small light. (Photo courtesy of LTM.)

8.11. (above) The Mole Richardson open face 2K, usually called a Mighty Mole. (Photo courtesy of Mole Richardson.)

8.12. Mole's 1K MolePar. (Photo courtesy of Mole Richardson.)

8.13. A Ruby Seven working along side some 24K multi-Par units. (Photo courtesy of Luminaria.)

for some control. All the bulbs are individually switchable, which makes for very simple intensity control. All PAR group lights allow for spot, medium and flood bulbs to be interchanged for different coverages. Also called 5-lights, 9-lights or 12-lights, depending on how many bulbs are incorporated, FAY lights use PAR 36 bulbs (650 watts). The FAY bulbs are dichroic daylight bulbs; tungsten bulbs can also be used. They can be used as daylight fill in combination with or in place of HMIs. They are not exactly daylight balance but are very close and can be corrected with gels.

Most people refer to any PAR 36 dichroic bulb as a FAY, but in fact there are several types. FAY is the ANSI code for a 650 watt PAR-36 dichroic daylight bulb with ferrule contacts. If the bulb has screw terminals it is an FBE/FGK. With heavy diffusion these units can be used as a large-source soft light (Figure 8.16).

THE RUBY

Multi-PAR units are an outstanding source of raw "firepower." They provide a lot of output per watt that can be concentrated into a small area or flooded with some degree of precision. They have nowhere the degree of control of a fresnel, however.

In particular, it is difficult if not impossible to "spot" them. The individual banks can be panned left and right and the whole unit can be tilted up and down, but there is no way to focus all of the heads or flood them in a truly uniform way. The Ruby Seven solves this problem with an ingenious mechanism that tilts the outer ring in or out, moving on the axis of the center bulb (Figure 8.13 and 8.15).

HMI PARS

8.14. The Dino, or in this illustration, Mole Richardson's Moleeno, consists of 36 1K PAR bulbs. (Photo courtesy of Mole Richardson.)

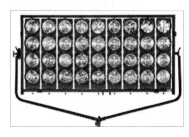

HMI PARs are available as 2.5K, 1.2K and 575s. These are extremely popular as bounce units, to create shafts and for raw power. The smaller ones can be moved easily, where moving a scaffold and heavy light is a major operation. HMI PARs are different from tungsten units in that they have changeable lenses which can be added to make a narrow spot, a medium flood, wide flood and an extra wide flood. As with tungsten PARs, the beam is oval and the unit can be rotated within its housing to orient the pattern. Every HMI PAR will come with its own set of lenses.

SOFT LIGHTS

Studio soft lights consist of one or more 1000 watt or 1500 watt bulbs directed into a "clamshell" white painted reflector which bounces light in a random pattern, making a light which is apparently as large as the front opening. They vary from the 1K studio soft (the Baby soft, also known as a 750 soft) up to the powerful 8K Studio Soft, which has eight individually switchable bulbs (Figure 8.17).

All soft lights have certain basic problems: they are extremely inefficient in light output; they are bulky and hard to transport; like all soft lights they are difficult to control, while the large reflector does make the light "soft," the random bounce pattern makes the light still somewhat raw and unpleasant.

As a result of this rawness, some people put some diffusion over the soft light for any close-up work. Big studio softs through a large frame of 216 is probably the easiest and quickest way to create a large soft source in the studio. Often used with the studio is the eggcrate, which minimizes side spill and does make the beam a bit more controllable. Soft lights see most of their use in television studios where they provide a soft source without additional rigging. Since they are more or less permanently flown, their bulkiness is not a problem. Small compact versions of the 2K and 1K soft lights are called zip lights. They have the same width but half the height of a soft light of similar wattage. Because of their compactness, zips are great for slipping into tight spaces.

COLOR CORRECTED FLUORESCENTS

Color corrected fluorescent tubes have gained enormous popularity in recent years. Pioneered by the Kino Flo company, they are extremely lightweight, compact and portable sources. Achieving a truly soft light can be difficult and time consuming. If it's done by bouncing off a large white surface or by punching big lights through heavy diffusion — either way takes up a lot of room and calls for a lot of flagging to control it.

Kino Flos had their origin in 1987. While working on the film *Barfly*, DP Robby Mueller was shooting in a cramped interior that didn't leave much room for a conventional bounce or diffusion soft source. His gaffer Frieder Hochheim and best boy Gary Swink came up with an answer: for fill and accent lighting, they constructed high-frequency fluorescent lights. By using remote ballasts, the fixtures were maneuverable enough to be taped to walls, hidden behind drapes and mounted behind the bar. Kino Flos were born (Figures 8.18, 8.19 and 8.21).

8.15. (above, left) The Ruby Seven, a PAR based unit that offers additional controllability. (Photo courtesy of Luminaria.)

8.16. (top) Two Mole FAY lights boxed in with some 4x8 floppies for control.

8.17. The 8K soft light — useful, but strictly for studio use. Big softlights are very popular in television lighting.

Unlike conventional fluorescent ballasts which can be quite noisy especially as they age, their ballasts were dead quiet and their light was flicker free due to the higher than normal frequency. There are now several companies that make these types of lights. Their secret is two-fold: first, the ballasts are high-frequency, which eliminates the potential problem of flicker which is always present with fluorescent type sources. Second, the bulbs are truly color correct. They precisely match daylight and tungsten. Colored bulbs are also available for various effects as well as for greenscreen, bluescreen or red screen. Kino makes a variety of extremely large rigs which can either front light or backlight an effects screen.

An added bonus of color correct, high-frequency fluorescents is that they generate considerably less heat than either tungsten or HMI. For this reason they have become very popular for lighting television sets for news and other types of programming. Portable fluorescent arrays are available from several sources. The Lowell unit, for example, uses 6 120 volt, 4 foot, 2-pin tubes, and the flicker free ballast serves as a counter-balance for the head. The unit draws only 3 amps and folds down to a compact, highly portable package. Fluorescent rigs are often used as a front fill when shooting in a fluorescent-lit industrial situation.

CYCS, STRIPS, NOOKS AND BROADS

When just plain output is needed, broad lights are strictly no-frills, utilitarian lights. They are just a box with a double-ended bulb. As simple as it is, the broad light has an important place in film history. In classical Hollywood hardlighting, the fill near the camera was generally a broad light with a diffuser. The distinctive feature of the broad light is its rectangular beam pattern, which makes blending them on a flat wall or cyc much easier: imagine how difficult if would to be smoothly combine the round, spotty beams of mighties or fresnel lights.

The smallest version of the broad is the nook, which, as its name implies, is designed for fitting into nooks and crannies (Figure 8.20). The nook light is a compact, raw-light unit, usually fitted with an FCM or FHM 1000 watt bulb. The nook is just a bulb holder with a reflector. Although barndoors are usually available, nooks aren't generally called on for much subtlety, but they are an efficient and versatile source for box light rigs, large silk overhead lights and for large arrays to punch through frames.

A number of units are specifically designed for illuminating cycs and large backdrops. For the most part they are open face 1K and 1.5K units in small boxes; these are call cycs, cyc strips or Far Cycs (which create a more even distribution up and down the background. Their primary characteristic is the asymmetrical throw which puts

8.18. (below) The Wall-O-Light from Kino Flo. Kinos can be rebulbed for tungsten, day light, bluescreen, greenscreen and other color conditions.

8.19. (below, right) Photometrics for a 2 ft., 4 bank Kino Flo.

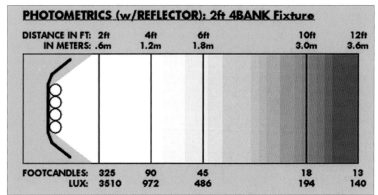

PHOTOMETRICS (w/REFLECTOR): 2ft 4BANK Fixture					
DISTANCE IN FT: 2ft	4ft	6ft		10ft	12ft
IN METERS: .6m	1.2m	1.8m		3.0m	3.6m
FOOTCANDLES: 325	90	45		18	13
LUX: 3510	972	486		194	140

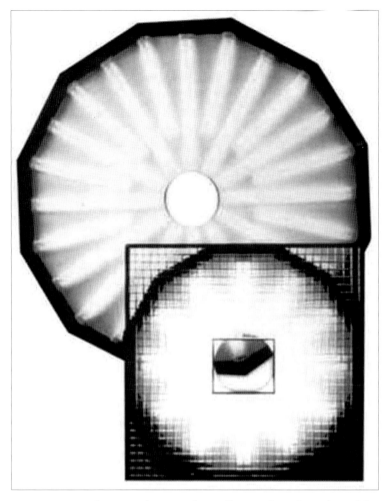

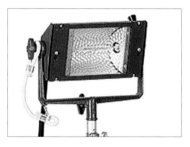

8.20. (above) The Mole nook light; a very handy compact unit that can be tucked into a variety of spaces. (Photo courtesy of Mole Richardson.)

8.21. (left) Color correct fluorescents in the form of a ring light for the camera. This is the Iris, made by Softlights. (Photo courtesy of Softlights.)

more output at the top or bottom, depending on the orientation of the unit. The reason for this is that cyc lights must be either placed at the top or bottom of the cyc but the coverage must be even. Placing cyc lights must be done carefully to achieve this coverage.

Strip lights are gangs of PARs or broad lights, originally used as theatrical footlights and cyc lights. They are often circuited in groups of three. With each circuit gelled a different color and on a dimmer, a wide range of colors can be obtained by mixing. This can be a quick way to alter background colors and intensities.

The Lowell Tota Lite deserves special mention. Small, cheap and fundamental, its no-nonsense reflector design and 1000 watt double-end bulb provide tremendous bang for the buck. Practically a back pocket light, the Tota can be used as an umbrella bounce, hidden in odd places or used in groups for a frog light or cyc illumination. Two Totas can be ganged by simply inserting the male end of the stand clamp into the female side of the other Tota. Adding more lights to the stack is a problem: they are too close together to allow the doors to open fully.

CHINESE LANTERNS AND SPACELIGHTS

Chinese lanterns are the ordinary paper globe lamps available at houseware stores. A socket is suspended inside which holds either a medium base bulb (household, ECA, ECT, BBA, BCA, etc.) or a 1K or 2K bi-post. Just about any rig is possible if the globe is large

8.22. (top) Spacelights and lekos in use on a miniatures shoot. (Photo courtesy of Mark Weingartner.)

8.23. (right) Two Musco lights set up to light a large background for a water shot. (Photo courtesy of Musco Lighting, Inc.)

enough to keep the paper a safe distance from the hot bulb. Control is accomplished by painting the paper or taping gel or diffusion to it. Similar in principle are spacelights (Figure 8.22), which are basically big silk bags with several 1K nook lights inside. For establishing an even overall base level on a set, they can be quite useful. With a bit of rigging, they can be made dimmable, although it is not convenient. When cabling, you will want to separate them into different circuits to give you some degree of control over the level.

SELF CONTAINED CRANE RIGS
There are a number of units which consist of several large HMIs rigged on a crane (Figure 8.23). Most also carry their own generator. Musco was the first of these, but now there are several to choose from. These units can provide workable illumination up to a half mile away and are used for moonlight effects and broad illumination of large areas. The main Musco unit comes with its own 1000 amp generator, which is typical of this type of unit. The 6K heads are individually aimable by a handheld remote control which operates up to 1000 feet away from the truck. The boom allows placement of the heads at up to 100 feet in the air.

LEKOS
The ellipsoidal reflector spot (Leko) is a theatrical light, but is used occasionally as a small effects light because of its precise beam control by the blades. Because the blades and gobo holder are located at the focal point of the lens, the leko can be focused sharply and patterned gobos can be inserted to give sharply detailed shadow effects. Not all lekos have gobo holder slots and if you need one you must specify when ordering (Figure 8.24). Lekos come in a size defined by their lens size and focal length (such as 6x9). The longer the focal length the narrower the beam.

BALLOON LIGHTS
Balloon lights are a recent development which provide a powerful and flexible new tool for night exteriors (Figures 8.25, 8.26 and 8.27). They generate a soft, general fill light for large areas. Perhaps their greatest advantage is that they are much easier to hide than a crane or scaffolding. They are also faster to set up. The disadvantage is that they can be very time consuming and expensive to gel. Wind is a factor when flying balloon lights. The smaller the balloon, the lower the acceptable wind speeds for keeping the balloon aloft. 15-20 mph for the smaller balloons (25 mph for the large ones) is a general upper limit of safety. A good reference is to observe flags — if they're flapping straight out, it's too windy.

8.24. (above) A leko being used as an on-camera light.

8.25. (left) Balloon lights in use on a boat movie. (Photo courtesy of Airstar.)

PORTABLE UNITS

Portable handheld, battery operated units are generally called sunguns. There are two basic types: tungsten and HMI. Tungsten sunguns are usually either 12 volt or 30 volt and powered from battery belts. Some are specifically designed as sunguns, but some are 120 volt lights converted by changing the bulb and power cable (Figure 8.28.) Typically, a tungsten sungun will run for about fifteen to twenty minutes. Sunguns with HMI bulbs are daylight balance and more efficient than tungsten units.

DAY EXTERIORS

Day exteriors can be approached in three ways: filling with large units such as a Brute Arc or 12K HMI, bouncing the existing light with reflectors or covering the scene with a large silk to control the contrast. Usually it is some combination of the three (Figure 8.29.)

CONTROLLING LIGHT WITH GRIP EQUIPMENT

Once you have a light working you have to control it. As soon as you get beyond what can be done with the barndoors, it becomes the province of the grip department. Grip equipment is wide and varied, but in relation to lighting control it falls into three basic categories: reduction, shadow casting and diffusion. Reducing the amount of light without altering the quality is done with nets. The same frames

8.26. (below, left) Photometrics for a 16K HMI balloon light. (Photo courtesy of Airstar.)

8.27. (below) A balloon light on a night shot for a car commercial. (Photo courtesy of Fisher Lights.)

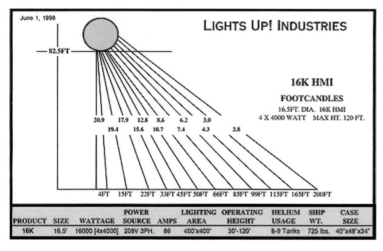

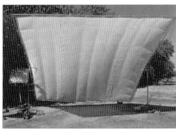

used for nets can be covered with white silk-like material which is a medium heavy diffusion. When they are covered with black duvetyne they are flags and cutters, which can control spill, cast shadows or block off flares from the lens. The same silk-like material also comes in larger sizes for butterflies and overheads. These come in various sizes, commonly: 4x4, 6x6, 8x8, 12x12 and 20x20. These are referred to as 8by, 12by, etc. (Figure 8.30).

FOR MORE INFORMATION ON LIGHTING

Lighting is a vast subject; here we have room only to cover the basic tools. For more on lighting techniques, photometric data, grip equipment and methods, electrical distribution, bulbs and scene lighting examples see *Motion Picture and Video Lighting* by the same author, also published by Focal Press. Photometric data, bulb designations for all types of lights, gel charts and color correction data can also be found in *The Filmmaker's Pocket Reference*, also a Focal Press book.

8.28. (top) A sungun with handle.

8.29. (top, right) Lighting a "walk-and-talk" is often a tricky business. Here, the gaffer and key grip are "Hollywooding" (hand holding) a slight diffusion and a reflector card.

8.30. (above, middle) Flying a 20x20 silk requires an experienced crew. (Photo courtesy of Matthews Studio Equipment.)

8.31. (above) The soft side of a reflector board. (Photo courtesy of Matthews Studio Equipment.)

lighting as storytelling

STORYTELLING

In previous chapters we have looked at the technical and practical aspects of lighting. In this chapter we will look at lighting as a key element of storytelling.

Let's divert our attention from film for a moment and look at two paintings. Studying classical art is useful in that the painter must tell the whole story in a single frame (not to mention without dialog or subtitles). Thus the painter must employ every aspect of visual language to tell the story of the painting as well as layer it with subtext, symbolism and emotional content. As with the films of Kubrick, Welles and Kurosawa, it is also useful to study the visual design as nothing in the frame is accidental. Every element, every color, every shadow is there for a purpose and its part in the visual and storytelling scheme has been carefully thought out.

First, let's look at this beautiful painting by Joseph of Derry, Figure 9.1 on the previous page. It is called *A Philosopher Giving A Lecture On The Orrery*. The orrery is a mechanical model of the solar system, sort of like a small planetarium. This painting was made at around the same time that Newton published his new theories of physics and gravitation. The philosopher has placed a lamp in the center of the device to represent the sun for his students. The beautiful single source casts a light so reminiscent of many of the paintings of de La Tour. It is a clean, simple light which makes the faces glow with fascination and the excitement of learning.

Light also has a great power to form space. In this case, the central source forms a sphere of space which envelops the students. Outside it is another space, sharply delineated. Within the sphere of light is knowledge, outside is darkness — ignorance. As Newton said, "What we know is a drop, what we don't know is an ocean."

Clearly the light represents knowledge, the illuminating power of the great mystery of the universe, but it is not just a symbol — it tells the story itself. Let's go back briefly to our primary example, Caravaggio's *The Calling of St. Matthew* (Figure 9.2). As we mentioned briefly in the chapter on *Visual Language*, the light is a crucial part of the design. It carries a major portion of the storytelling as well.

The boldness of Caravaggio's vision (and what makes this painting the genesis of the Baroque as opposed to merely an extension of the Renaissance) is that he sets this tale from the Bible in common settings (and contemporary for his time) — a dimly lit tavern; some local lowlifes are drinking and playing cards. Christ, who is giving Matthew his calling as a disciple, is mostly in shadow, almost a background character, barely seen in the back at the far right, his outstretched hand bridging the gap between the two groups. The fact that he is in shadow is important, as is the small slash of light that falls across his face.

H.W. Janson discusses the painting in his *The History of Art*: "Most decisive is the strong beam of light above Christ that illuminates his face and hand in the gloomy interior, thus carrying his call across to Matthew. Without this light, so natural yet so charged with symbolic meaning, the picture would lose its magic, its power to make us aware of the divine presence."

The lighting is chiaroscuro at its best; not only does it create strong contrasts and clearly delineate the characters in sharp relief (the figures almost jump out at us), the strong directionality of the light guides the eye and unifies the composition. What is unimportant falls into shadow and thus does not distract the eye. According to Edmund Burke Feldman in *Varieties of Visual Experience*, "In Baroque painting, light is an aggressive liberating force. A small

9.1. (previous page) *Philosopher Giving A Lecture On The Orrery*, Joseph of Derry. (Photo courtesy of the Derry Museum, Derry, England.)

9.2. (below) Caravaggio's *The Calling of St. Matthew*. The lighting carries a great deal of the storytelling power of the image.

amount of it is enough to reveal the spiritual opportunities that lie hidden." Here the strong beam of sunlight is the hand of God itself, reaching into the dusky tavern to pluck Matthew out of the darkness. The light coming from outside is clearly the presence of the divine truth; it penetrates the dusty darkness of ignorance in the tavern, thus the shadows are equally important — ignorance, lethargy and wasted lives. As we discussed in *Visual Language* they also form negative spaces which are important compositionally.

They are both powerful, enigmatic paintings that carry depths of meaning and content far beyond their mere visual beauty — the kind of thing we strive for every day on the set. All that is missing is a producer in the background saying, "It's awfully dark, couldn't we add some fill light?"

ORIGINS OF MOTION PICTURE LIGHTING

Historically, motion picture lighting has gone through a number of periods. At first it was purely functional. The low speed of the film and the lenses together with lack of high-power, controllable light sources made it a necessity to just pour as much light as possible onto the scenes. As a result, most films were filmed outdoors in broad daylight.

Even studios were outdoors: sets were built on the backlots in open air, using the sun as the luminaire. The very first studio was developed by K.L. Dickson, the co-creator (with Thomas Edison) of motion picture technology. Called "Black Maria," it was built on a revolving platform, so that it could be rotated to follow the sun as it crossed the sky during the day (Figure 9.3).

In New York, where the film industry was born, studios were built with glass ceilings on the top floor of buildings. The only form of control was huge tents of muslin, which could be stretched across the ceiling to soften and modulate the light. Later, adaptations of arc lamps were used to provide a degree of illumination, but with little control. Gas discharge tubes very similar to modern fluorescents (Figure 9.4) were also used, but they too were just raw sources. This was not considered a problem, however. At that time, in the theater, "natural" lighting was considered to be broad, flat lighting which merely illuminated the elaborate sets.

It was the brash talent of theater impresario David Belasco and his lighting designer Louis Harttman who turned this trend around. Belasco's emphasis was on realistic effects to underscore the drama. Also working at that time was Adophe Appia, who believed that the shadows were as important as the light, and that the manipulation of light and shadow was a means of expressing ideas.

It was an actor who had worked for Belasco who translated many of these ideas in to the world of film: a young man named Cecil B. DeMille. Working with cameraman Alvin Wycoff, he employed expressive single source lighting that was both naturalistic and visually involving. When Technicolor was introduced, the necessity of huge amounts of light was a setback for natural, expressive lighting, but black-and-white films still continued to use lighting creatively and effectively.

FILM NOIR

Certainly, one of the highlights of lighting as storytelling is the era of film noir: American films of the forties and fifties, primarily in the mystery, suspense and detective genres, nearly all of them in black-and-white. The noir genre is best known for its low-key lighting style: side light, chiaroscuro, shadowy (Figure 9.5). This was, of course, only one of the various elements of visual style: they also

9.3. (top) The Black Maria, developed by Edison and Dickson, the first method of controlling lighting for filmmaking.

9.4. (above) D.W. Griffith and his cameraman Billy Bitzer examine a piece of negative in front of some Cooper-Hewitt tubes, one of the earliest artificial lighting sources. (For a more extensive discussion of the history of film lighting see *Motion Picture and Video Lighting*, by the same author, also published by Focal Press).

9.5. The black-and-white noir period is one of the highest achievements of film lighting as a story element — this frame from *Mildred Pierce* (Warner Bros., 1945).

9.6. Although not strictly a noir film, *Citizen Kane* is of the same era and employs the same techniques of visual storytelling with lighting that is expressive, visually striking and makes specific story points. Here the reporter has come to the vault where Kane's memoirs are kept. As the guard brings forward the sacred book which we hope will contain the ultimate secrets, the single beam of light represents knowledge reaching into the darkened space in much the same way that it does in the Caravaggio (Figure 9.2).

Being a backlight with no fill, it leaves the characters in complete silhouette, representing their ignorance of the knowledge. (*Citizen Kane*, RKO, 1941. Now owned by Turner Classic Movies).

used angle, composition, lighting, montage, depth and movement in expressive new ways. Many factors came together to influence this style: technical innovations such as faster, finer grained black-and-white negative, faster lenses, smaller, more mobile camera dollies, cameras light enough to hand-hold and portable power supplies, all perfected during World War II, alleviated many of the logistical problems previously connected with location filming.

This enabled filmmakers to get out to the dark, mean streets of the city with its shadowy alleys fraught with unknown dangers, blinking neon lights reflected on rain-soaked pavement and all of the mystery and menace of the city after dark. Beyond just the gritty reality and groundedness that come with actual locations, the challenges and various difficulties of lighting in and around real structures tend to force cinematographers to experiment and be bolder with their lighting — there is less of a tendency to just do it the same old way it's always been done back in the studio.

9.7. An example of the classic metaphor of noir — the characters trapped somewhere between the dark and the light, good or evil, knowledge or ignorance. In this frame from *The Big Combo*, which we previously looked at in *Visual Language*, the detective and the woman have triumphed over the bad guy and are emerging from the darkness into the light.

As in the shot from *Citizen Kane* (Figure 9.6), the light seems to exert an almost palpable pull on them. Backlit and glowing, the fog forms a concrete space distinct from the foreground space of blackness and emptiness. Silhouetted and faceless, the shot is about their situation and the resolution of their conflict, not about their individual thoughts or expressions at this moment.

The second result of the war was the influx of European directors and cinematographers who brought with them the "...full heritage of German Expressionism: moving camera; oddly angled shots; a chiaroscuro frame inscribed with wedges of light or shadowy mazes, truncated by foreground objects or punctuated with glinting headlights bounced off mirrors, wet surfaces, or the polished steel of a gun barrel." (Alain Silver and Elizabeth Ward, *Film Noir*).

But all of this is more that just visual style: it is inherently a part of the storytelling, an integral narrative device. "A side-lit close-up may reveal a face, half in shadow, half in light, at the precise moment of indecision." (Silver and Ward). Beyond narrative, it becomes part of character as well — noir was the birth of the protagonist who is not so clearly defined as purely good or evil. As with Walter Neff in *Double Indemnity* or Johnny Clay (the Sterling Hayden character) in *The Killing* and so many others, they are characters full of contradiction and alienation. In their very being they may be pulled between good and evil, light and dark, illumination and shadow. This reflects the confusion and sense of lost ideals that returned with the veterans and survivors of the war. It also reflects the "zeitgeist" of the times: the growing undercurrent that not all things can be known, "...the impossibility of a single, stable point of view, and thus the limits to all seeing and knowing." (J.P. Tellotte, *Voices In the Dark*) — that what is unseen in the shadows may be as significant as what is seen in the light.

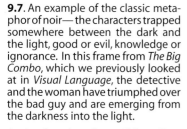

LIGHT AS VISUAL METAPHOR

Let's turn now to a more recent example, a film that uses light as a metaphor and as storytelling perhaps better than any other of the modern era: Barry Levinson's *The Natural*. Masterfully photographed by Caleb Deschanel, the film is so visually unified and well thought out that it would be possible to comment on the metaphoric or narrative use of lighting in almost every scene; here we will examine only the high points.

In the opening shot we see the title character alone, dejected and older, sitting at a railroad station. He is half in light and half in shadow, a metaphor for his uncertain future and his dark, unclear past. The train arrives and blacks out the screen. He gets on. End of title sequence. It is mysterious, suggestive and supremely simple (Figure 9.8).

The Natural is the tale of a talented young baseball player Roy Hobbes (Robert Redford) who is diverted from his career by a chance encounter with a dark and mysterious young lady, but makes a comeback years later as he simultaneously finds love with his long lost childhood sweetheart. It is a story of good versus evil in the classic sense and Levinson and Deschanel use a wide variety of cinematic and narrative devices to tell it.

As the story begins, Roy is a young farm boy full of energy, talent, promise and infatuation for his sweetheart Iris (Glenn Close) who always wears white. This section is shot in bright afternoon sunlight: the vibrant energy of nature with just a hint of a soft filter. It is backlit with the sun and everything is warm and golden.

His father dies of a heart attack in the shade of a tree and that night there is a ferocious storm: inky blue punctuated with stabs of violent lightning. A bolt splits the tree and Roy uses the heart of the tree to make his own bat which he inscribes with a lightning bolt: a symbol of the power of nature: light in its most intense, primitive and pure form. He gets a call from the majors and asks Iris out for a last meeting. They are silhouetted on a ridge against a glowing ultramarine blue sky which represents night and the temptations of eros (Figure 9.9). If you look closely, it is completely unnatural (it's day-for-night with a blue filter) but beautiful and perfectly portrays their mental state. In the barn, as they make love they are engulfed in stripes of moonlight alternating with darkness: it is a radiant

9.8. The opening shot from *The Natural* — a faceless character lost somewhere in the light and the dark, suspended in time: the past is uncertain and the future is unclear. This purgatory of being caught between them establishes the mood and tone of uncertainty and conflict between two worlds that is carried through the rest of the film. (*The Natural*, Tristar Pictures/RCA/Columbia, 1984.)

9.9. (top) Early in the film, Roy and Iris are young and innocent, but their purity is disrupted when they meet in the blue moonlight and make love. We will only find out at nearly the end of the film that this loss of innocence leads to a son, which Roy does not know about until he is redeemed and recovers this purity which is represented by the golden sunlight of a wheat field where he plays catch with his newly discovered son. Here and in his love tryst with Memo Paris (Figure 9.13) blue represents the danger of succumbing to temptation.

9.10. (above) The Lady In Black — the temptation that leads to Roy's downfall. She is always lit dimly and is somewhat shadowy — an ephemeral figure; in this shot underlit for a mysterious look.

9.11. After years of foundering in the narrow darkness of obscurity, Roy emerges into the light of the one thing that gives him power — the bright sunny open space of a baseball field.

moment but there are hints of danger (we will learn much later in the film that she is made pregnant by this encounter). As he boards a train to travel to his major league tryout, things darken a bit. The only light source is the relatively small windows of the train and while they admit plenty of light, it is low angle and somewhat shadowy and malevolent.

LIGHT AND SHADOW — GOOD AND EVIL

It is here that he first sees the woman who is to bring evil and temptation into his life — The Lady In Black (Figure. 9.10), who we first see in silhouette and from the back. Usually portrayed backlit or in shadow, as befits her evil nature, she invites him to her hotel room, shoots him and then jumps to her death, ending his baseball hopes.

Sixteen years later, we see him arrive at the stadium of the New York Knights. He is in total darkness as he walks up the ramp, then emerges into sunlight as he enters the ballpark: he is home, where he belongs (Figure 9.11). Given his first chance to play, the sequence opens with a shot of what will become an important symbol: the lighting towers of the field. They are dark and silhouetted against black storm clouds. It is twilight, halfway between day and night. As he literally "knocks the cover off the ball" there is a bolt of lightning and it begins to rain. Lightning, the most powerful form of light, is a recurring symbol throughout the film — light as pure energy, bringing the power of nature. Coming back into the dugout, we are introduced to a second visual theme: the flashbulbs of news photographers (Figures 9.14, 9.15 and 9.16).

As one of his teammates adopts the lightning bolt as a shoulder insignia, the team takes off; a symbol of the power of light and energy that Roy has brought to the squad. They are on a hot streak. Now we meet the Judge, half owner of the team. Slimy and evil, his office is completely dark, lit only by the dim light that seeps through the closed venetian blinds (Figure 9.12). His face is obscured in shadow. After the Judge tries to get him to lose so he can buy the team, Roy rebuffs him and on his way out defiantly flips the room lights on. Then the bookie emerges from the shadows.

Their attempt at bribery having failed, they contrive to set him up with Memo (Kim Basinger, who always wears black) at a fancy restaurant, where the only illumination is the table lamps which cast an ominous underlight on the characters, although fill is added for Roy (purity) and Memo (raw beauty). She takes him to the beach and in a reprise of the love scene between Roy and Iris they are bathed in blue moonlight. But this is a slightly different moonlight than we saw with his boyhood girl: colder and harsher; sensuous, but not romantic (Figure 9.13). She comes to seduce him and she is completely in silhouette, sexy but still mysterious.

9.12. The Judge, the most elemental evil in the film, claims to abhor sunlight — he stays always in the dark; only a few meager slits of light manage to seep into his darkened den.

9.13. As Roy begins to fall victim to the temptations of fame and the glamour of the big city, he once again is silhouetted in dark blue — even the car headlights seem to be glowering at him as he falls for the seductive Memo Paris.

FADING FLASHBULBS

Next comes a montage sequence of flashbulbs popping, symbolizing fame, celebrity, glamour and the seduction of the fast life which will distract him from baseball. Roy descends into a slump, bringing the team down with him. In his decline, the flashbulbs still go off, but in marvelous subtlety we see them in slow-motion at the end of their burn cycle as they fade out. Iris comes to a game to watch, unbeknownst to Roy. As the team is losing and Roy is striking out, Iris stands up (Figure 9.19). Her translucent white hat is backlit by a single shaft of sunlight, making her appear angelic. Roy hits a home run that breaks the stadium clock — stopping time. Photographers' flashbulbs go off and as Roy peers into the crowd looking for Iris he is blinded by them and can't see her (Figure 9.17). Later, they meet and go for a walk. As he tells her the story of his dark past, they are in complete silhouette, in darkness even though it is midday. As he ends his confession they emerge into full daylight. Later, the silver bullet that has been in his stomach sends him to the hospital.

9.14. (below, left) Throughout the film, flashbulbs represent the glare of fame, fortune and celebrity. For Roy, as the new hero of the team, the newspaper flashbulbs are everywhere.

9.15. (below) They quickly become the flashbulbs of the paparazzi as he paints the town red with his glamourous girlfriend Memo.

9.16. As the nonstop nightlife hurts Roy's performance on the field, a slowmo shot of a flashbulb fading to black represents Roys loss of power — the dimming of his light.

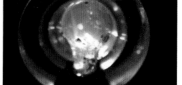

9.17. (above) His long lost love Iris comes to a game. Roy seems to sense her presence, but as he turns to look for her, he is blinded by the glare of the photographer's flashes.

9.18. (above, right) As Roy's light on the field promises to rescue the team and spoil the Judge's plans, he watches from his shadowy lair. This image is repeated at the end of the film when Roy's home run seals the Judge's fate and the fireworks of exploding bulbs glare on the Judge's glasses.

9.19. (right) As Roy is faltering on the field, near defeat, Iris stands up and a single beam of light illuminates her so that she is visible in the crowd — it gives him the power to hit a home run and win the game. The angelic glow makes her hat a halo to supplement the white dress and the standing pose. To reinforce the lighting effect, she is surrounded by men only, all in dark clothes and hats.

9.20. (below) As a reporter comes close to uncovering Roy's dark secret, he sneaks onto the field to photograph him at batting practice. To stop him, Roy hits a ball with perfect aim that breaks the reporter's camera; the flashbulb fires as it falls to the ground — the glare of disclosure, of secrets being brought to light, is prevented by Roy's sheer talent with the bat.

9.21. (right) As Roy lays ill in the hospital before the playoffs, the Judge comes to offer him a bribe. Rather than rendering the Judge in shadow as might be the obvious choice, Deschanel arranges for the warm glow of the otherwise benevolent hospital lamps to glare on the Judge's glasses — thus the light itself manages to obscure his eyes and partly disguise his evil. This is appropriate as he appears here not as the intimidating force of evil but as a silky voiced cajoler.

Against doctor's orders, he tries to practice in secret, but the reporter attempts to take a picture of him. Roy hits a ball that smashes his camera which falls to the ground and the flashbulb fires as it breaks: he is striking back at the glare of publicity that has nearly destroyed him (Figure 9.20).

The final climactic game is at night and the stadium tower lights burn brightly. The Judge and the bookie watch the game from his skybox, which we see from below as just a pale yellow glow on the partially closed blinds: an image of evil and corruption hovering over the game (Figure 9.18).

Roy is struggling as his injury plagues him and it all comes down to one final pitch which will win or lose the pennant. Having it all rest on the final pitch is, of course, a given in any baseball movie, but the cinematography and the metaphor of lighting and lightning together with the mystical glow of the dying sparks gives this scene a magical quality which makes it one of the most memorable final scenes in American cinema and visually one of the most moving.

9.22. (above) The moment before the do-or-die climactic pitch is thrown, lightning (which has always brought the power of good to Roy) strikes the light towers of the baseball field.

9.23. (above, left) As Roy connects powerfully with the ball, he is framed so that the lights of the field (representing the ennobling power of baseball) are in the shot with him.

9.24. (left, below) Roy's home run strikes the lights of the field; one shatters, short circuiting them all and they explode in a shower of fireworks.

VISUAL POETRY

Roy slams a home run right into the stadium lights (Figure 9.23), which shatter and short-circuit, sending a shower of sparks onto the field (Figures 9.24 and 9.25). In one of the truly great images of contemporary cinema, as he rounds the bases in slow-motion triumph, Roy and his celebrating teammates are enveloped in these glowing fireworks, as if miniature stars of glory are raining on them. A soft, golden glow of light personified engulfs them as the film ends. It is the light of pure good; Roy and the power of his talent as symbolized by the bat carved from the tree struck by lightning have transformed them and invigorated them with the essence of all that is good about baseball (and all that it symbolizes about American democracy).

The firefly-like glow comes from the exploding lights of the field (the illuminating spirit of baseball), shattered by Roy's home run (his talent) which have just been struck by a bolt of lightning — the same lightning that has brought Roy the power of his unsullied talent). These are symbols and they work, but there is a more subtle visual metaphor at work and it is what makes the shot so hauntingly evocative. What is magical about this shot is that the light is everywhere, it is an omnipresent bathing glow, it is all around them, it almost seems to emanate from within them as they bask in the beauty of a pure and simple moment of triumph in baseball and the triumph of right over the insidious attempts of the Judge to infect baseball with his money-hungry infestation.

With this elegantly simple but visceral and expressive visual image system, Levinson and Deschanel make the most of and add extra layers of meaning onto a great story, a great script and a superlative cast. In this particular film, light is used as a metaphor in a very clear and sustained way. In most films, lighting is a part of storytelling in more limited and less overtly metaphorical ways, but it can always

9.25. As Roy rounds the bases, the sparks from the exploding bulbs surround him and his jubilant teammates in a soft gentle wash of light- they are enveloped in an omnipresent glow of the power of pure good triumphant over evil — one of the most beautiful and haunting images in modern cinema. The light is non-directional — it is all around them, part of them, within them.

be a factor in underlying story points, character and particularly the perception of time and space. Filmmakers who take a rejectionist attitude toward lighting are depriving themselves of one of the most important, subtle and powerful tools of visual storytelling. Those who reject lighting are often those who least understand its usefulness and eloquence as a cinematic tool.

controlling color

WHAT IS WHITE?

The eye will accept a wide range of light as "white," depending on external clues and adaptation. The phenomenon is both psychological (adaptation) and environmental. The color meter (and color film, which is very objective about these things) will tell us that there are enormous differences in the color of light in a room lit with tungsten light, one lit with ordinary fluorescents and one flooded with noon daylight. Our perception tells us that all three are "white light," mostly because we are psychologically conditioned to think of them as white and physiologically, the eye adapts. Without a side-by-side comparison, the eye is an unreliable indicator of what is neutral light. Unfortunately, color film emulsions and video CCD's are extremely sensitive and unforgiving. An absolute color reference is essential.

COLOR TEMPERATURE

In film and video production, the most common system used in describing the color of light is color "temperature." This scale is derived from the color of a theoretical black body (a metal object having no inherent color of its own, technically known as a Planckian radiator). When heated to incandescence, the black body glows at varying colors depending on the temperature (Table 10.1). Color temperature is a quantification of the terms "red hot," "white hot," etc.

Developed by Lord Kelvin, the 19th century British scientific pioneer, color temperature is expressed in degrees Kelvin in his honor. On the Celsius scale, the freezing point of water equals 0°. The Kelvin scale takes absolute zero as the zero point. Absolute zero is -273° Celsius on the Kelvin scale, thus 5500° Kelvin is actually 5227° Celsius. Degrees Kelvin is abbreviated "K" and the degree symbol is omitted. Because a tungsten filament heated to incandescence is very similar to a Planckian radiator, the color temperature equivalence is very close for tungsten halogen lamps, but not for HMIs, CIDs and fluorescents (Figure 10.2). A graphic representation of the various wavelengths is called an SED (Spectral Energy Distribution) or SPD (Spectral Power Distribution).

When a metal object (such as the tungsten filament of a light bulb) is heated to incandescence, its SED is quite similar to that of a Planckian radiator and is fairly smooth across all wavelengths, even if some are stronger than others. This is not necessarily true for all light sources. Fluorescent lights, for example, have very "spiky" outputs, which tend to be very heavy in green (Figure 10.3)

Color temperatures can be very misleading; for many sources (especially those which exhibit discontinuous SEDs), it is only an approximation and is referred to as "correlated color temperature." Color temperature tells us a great deal about the blue/orange component of light and very little about the magenta/green component, which can produce extremely unpleasant casts in the film even if the meter indicates a correct reading for the color temperature.

An approximate measure of how close a source is to a pure black body radiator is the Color Rendering Index (CRI), a scale of 1 to 100 which gives some indication of the ability of a source to render color accurately. For photographic purposes, only sources with a CRI of 90 or above are generally considered acceptable.

COLOR METERS

Most light sources are not a narrow band of the spectrum; hence they are not a pure hue. Most colored light is a combination of various wavelengths; there is no one number that can describe the color

10.1. (previous page) Bold use of color in *Bladerunner*. Throughout the film, color is tightly controlled for maximum effectiveness.

Table 10.1. (below) Color, wavelength and frequency of the major bands of the spectrum.

10.2. (bottom) Color and wavelength of typical sources.

COLOR	WAVELENGTH (nanometers)	FREQUENCY
Red	800-650	400-470
Orange	640-590	470-520
Yellow	580-550	520-590
Green	530-490	590-650
Blue	480-460	650-700
Indigo	450-440	700-760
Violet	430-390	760-800

1 nanometer = 0.0000001 mm

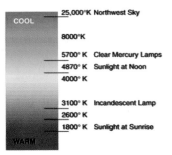

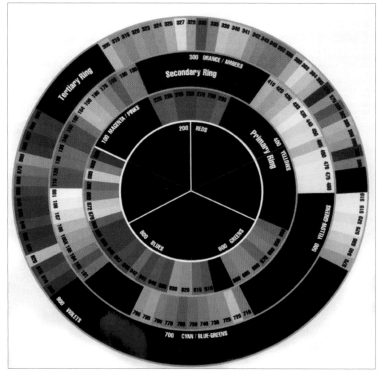

Candle	2000K
Sunlight at dawn	2000K
Low wattage tungsten bulb	2900K
Tungsten-halogen bulb	3200K
Photo bulbs	3400K
Morning/afternoon sun	4400K
Arc with WF carbon	5000K
Midday sun	5500K
HMIs	5600-6500K
Midday sunlight + skylight	6500K
Cloudy sky	6800K
Clear blue sky	10,000+ K

10.3. (left) GAM color filters displayed as a color wheel. (Photo courtesy of Great American Market.)

Table 10.2. (above) Color temperatures of common film and natural sources.

accurately. Rather, it is defined on two scales: red/blue and magenta/green. As a result, most meters give two readouts (they are called three color meters, since they measure red, blue and green), one for the warm/cool scale and one for the magenta/green scale. In the case of the Minolta color meter, the magenta/green readout is not in absolute numbers, but directly in amount of filtration needed to correct the color to "normal" on the magenta/green scale.

Rosco Laboratories makes the following recommendations for gels based on reading from a Minolta Color Temperature meter. LB is the Light Balancing index. Its use is based on whether you are using daylight or tungsten balance film. Light balancing values are shown in Table 10.3.

CC index is Color Correction. It describes the green/magenta aspects of the color source. It is most relevant when shooting with fluorescents, sodium vapor, mercury vapor or other types of discharge sources which usually have a large green component. The newer Minolta Color Meter III has an expanded green-magenta scale. Recommended corrections are shown in Table 10.4 and 10.5.)

MIREDS

Another problem with color temperature is that equal changes in color temperature are not necessarily perceived as equal changes in color. A change of 50K from 2000K to 2050K will be a noticeable difference in color. For an equivalent change in color perception at 5500K, the color temperature would need to shift 150K and about 500K at 10,000K.

For this reason, the mired system has been devised. Mired stands for micro-reciprocal degrees. Mireds are derived by dividing 1,000,000 by the Kelvin value. For example, 3200K equals 1,000,000/3200 = 312 mireds. To compute how much color correction is required, you use the mired values of the source and the final

10.4. (below) These SED charts illustrate the uneven output typical of gas discharge sources which makes them difficult to control for film and video use.

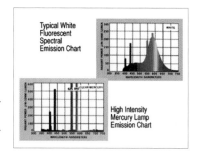

85 (Full CTO)	+131
1/2 CTO	+81
1/4 CTO	+42
1/8 CTO	+20
CTB	-131
1/2 CTB	-68
1/3 Blue	-49
1/4 Blue	-30
1/8 Blue	-12

+ 167	Full CTO	- 131	Full Blue
+ 131	Sun 85	- 68	Half Blue
+ 81	Half CTO	- 49	Third Blue
+ 40	Quarter CTO	- 30	Quarter Blue
+ 20	Eighth CTO	- 12	Eighth Blue
+ 12	UV filter		

8M	1/4 Minusgreen	5G	1/4 Plusgreen
15M	1/2 Minusgreen	13G	1/2 Plusgreen
30M	Full Minusgreen	37G	Full Plusgreen

+ 3	1/4 Minusgreen	- 2	1/4 Plusgreen
+ 6	1/2 Minusgreen	- 5	1/2 Plusgreen
+ 13	Minusgreen	-12	Plusgreen

Table 10.3. (top) Light Balancing Index for the most common correction gels.

Table 10.4. (middle) Color compensating as indicated by the Minolta Color Meter II. Color correction applies only to the magenta-green balance.

Table 10.5. (bottom) Color compensating values as indicated by the Minolta Color Meter III.

desired color. If you have source at 5500K and wish to convert it to 3200K, subtract the mired value of the desired color from that of the source. 5000K = 200 mireds. 3200K = 312 mireds and then 312-200= 112 mireds. 85 orange has a mired value of +112. On the mired scale, a plus shift value means the filter is yellowish, a minus value means the filter will give a blue shift. When combining filters, add the mired values.

COLOR BALANCE OF FILM
No color film can accurately render color under all lighting conditions. In manufacture, the film is adjusted to render color accurately under a particular condition, the two most common being average daylight (type D film), which is set for 5500K and average tungsten illumination (type B film) designed for 3200K. There is a third, which is based on the now disused "photo" bulbs, which were 3400K (type A film), rather than 3200K; these are rare now.

Given the fact that providing tungsten light is costly and electricity intensive, while sunlight is usually far more abundant, most motion picture films are type B, balanced for tungsten. The idea is that we put a correcting filter on when we can most afford to lose light to a filter factor — in the sunlight. Kodak and Fuji now have several daylight balance films available.

COLOR BALANCE WITH CAMERA FILTERS
There are three basic reasons to change the color of lights:
- To correct the color of the lights to match the film type (instead of using a camera filter)
- To match various lighting sources
- For effect or mood

To shoot with type B film under "blue" light (in the 5500° degree area) an 85 orange filter is used. The 80A or 80B blue filters for shooting daylight film with warm light are rarely used, and in most cases should be combined with a UV filter because tungsten film cannot tolerate the high proportion of UV in daylight and HMIs. There is some light loss when using a correction filter and the filter factor must be used to adjust the T/stop. For convenience, most manufacturers list an adjusted Exposure Index which allows for the filter loss.

When using this adjusted EI, do not also use the filter factor. EI is not technically the same as ASA (American Standards Association) which is the scale used to rate film for still photography, but in practice they are the same. This is because the speed of color film is not measured in the same way as black-and-white emulsion (see the chapter on *Exposure*). Color film speed is determined by testing.

You will also notice two different EIs on cans of black-and-white film, as well. This is not related to correction filters, since none are needed. It has to do with the fact that black-and-white films vary in their sensitivity to colors. In most cases the EI for tungsten light will be 1/3 stop lower. Most black-and-white films available today are panchromatic, meaning they are relatively sensitive to most of the visible spectrum. Early black-and-white films were orthochromatic; they were not sensitive to blue light at all. This meant that actors with blue eyes appeared to have white eyes. Smaller color mismatches can also be corrected with color filters, as well. If the scene lighting is 2800K, for example (too warm), then an 82C filter will correct the light reaching the film to 3200K.

There are three basic filter families used in film and video production: conversion, light balancing and color compensating. This applies to both lighting gels and camera filters.

10.5. (left) Extension frames make it possible to gel these Muscos for a car shot. (Photo courtesy of Musco Lighting, Inc.)

10.6. (above) The Minolta Color Temperature Meter II.

CONVERSION FILTERS
Conversion filters work in the Blue-Orange axis and deal with fundamental color balance in relation to the color sensitivity of the emulsion. Conversion filters affect all parts of the SED for smooth color rendition. Although there used to be more, currently there are only two types of color emulsion: daylight and tungsten. The basic filter families are shown in Table 10.7. The conversion filters we use in film and video are called CTO and CTB (see below).

LIGHT BALANCING FILTERS
Light Balancing filters are warming and cooling filters; they work on the entire SED as with the conversion filters, but they are used to make smaller shifts in the Blue-Orange axis.

CORRECTING LIGHT BALANCE
Daylight sources include:
- Daylight itself (daylight is a combination of direct sun and open sky).
- HMIs.
- Cool-white or daylight type fluorescents.
- Color correct fluorescents.
- Dichroic sources such as FAYs.
- Arcs with white-flame carbons.

In general, daylight sources are in the range of 5400K to 6500K, although they can range much higher. Near sunrise and sunset they

10.7. Gel taped to a 4x4 open frame is usually the best way to add color to an intense source such as these Ruby Sevens. Care must be taken not to get it too close or the gel will burn. (Photo courtesy of Luminaria, Inc.)

are much warmer as the sun is traveling through a much thicker layer of atmosphere and more of the blue wavelengths are filtered out. The amount of dust and humidity in the air are also factors, which accounts for the different colorings of light prevalent in different locales. Perhaps most famous is the translucent blue light of Venice made famous by the painter Canaletto.

Correction is achieved with either "85" or CTO, both of which are orange filters. The Rosco product is Roscosun 85 (85 refers to the Wratten number equivalent), it has a mired shift value of 131 which will convert 5500K to 3200K. (Technically, this is equivalent to a Wratten 85B; Wratten 85 has a mired shift value of 112, which converts 5500 to 3400, slightly cool for tungsten balance.)

CTO

CTO is the acronym for Color Temperature Orange. CTO is warmer than 85 and has a higher mired shift value: 159. This means that it will convert 6500K to 3200K, which is excellent when correcting cooler sources such as HMIs, which are running blue or heavily skylit situations. It is also useful when going for a warmer look, as it will convert 5500K to 2940K. (5500K = mired 181, shift value of 159. Warmer equals positive. 181+159 = 340 mired. Divide 1,000,000 by 340 = 2940K.) The difference is basically American vs. European: probably due to the fact that European skylight is generally bluer than American skylight (Table 10.7).

An important variation of 85 is the combination of color correction and neutral density. The purpose of this is to avoid having to put two separate gels on a window, which might increase the possibility for gel noise and reflections, not to mention the additional cost (which is substantial). The variations are shown in table 10.9: Unfortunately, no one makes a 1/2 85 plus ND filter, which would be useful to preserve a natural blueness in the windows.

TUNGSTEN TO DAYLIGHT

Filters for converting warm tungsten sources to nominal daylight are called full blue, Tough Blue or CTB (Color Temperature Blue) (Table 10.8).

Table 10.6. The basic filter families and their designations.

85:	Conversion	Daylight to tungsten.
80:	Conversion	Tungsten to daylight.
82:	Light balancing	Cooling filters.
81:	Light balancing	Warming filters.
CC's	Color Compensating	Primary & secondary colors.

The problem with "blueing the lights" is that CTB has a transmission of 36% while 85 has a transmission of 58%. This means that while you lose almost a stop and a half with CTB, you lose only about 2/3 of a stop with CTO. CTB is very inefficient; its most common use is to balance tungsten lights inside a room with the daylight blue window light that is coming in. This is a losing situation from the start: the window light is liable to be far more powerful than the tungsten lights to begin with. If we then lose 2 stops off the tungsten by adding CTB we are really in trouble (not to mention the fact that we also have to put an 80B filter on the lens with tungsten balance film and we lose heavily there too). In practice most people try to avoid this solution; the alternatives are:

10.8. For this music video we wanted vivid color and a dreamlike effect. One tungsten bounce was gelled double CTO and the other flame red, the two were on separate flicker boxes and the shot was overcranked. The result was a nightmare-in-hell feeling that fit the tone of the video.

- Put 85 on the windows and shoot at tungsten balance. By doing this we avoid killing the tungsten lights, we don't have to use an 80B on the camera and we lose 2/3 of a stop off the windows, which may keep them more in balance with the inside exposure.
- Put 1/2 85 on the windows and 1/2 blue on the lights.
- Put 1/2 CTB on the lights and let the windows go slightly blue. This is actually a more realistic color effect and is much preferred these days.
- Use daylight balance lights (FAYs, HMIs or Kinos) inside.

FLUORESCENT LIGHTING

One of the most common color problems we face today is shooting in locations where the dominant source is fluorescent. The problem with fluorescents is that they are not a continuous spectrum source: in most cases they are very heavy in green. Another problem is that even if they may appear to be approximately correct in color, their discontinuous spectra may cause them to render color very poorly. (Recall our discussion of metamerism in the chapter on *Color Theory.*) This is measured as the Color Rendering Index (CRI). A CRI of 90 or better is considered necessary for film and video work. As a result, fluorescents cannot be corrected only by changing the color with a gel on the lighting unit or filter on the camera lens.

Also because of their discontinuous spectra, discharge sources (of which fluorescents are one example) can't be considered to have a true color temperature. The black body color temperature that they approximate is called the Correlated Color Temperature (CCT). On

NAME	TYPICAL CONVERSION	MIRED VALUE	STOP LOSS
85	5500K >3200K	+131	3/4 stop
Full CTO	5500K > 2900K, 6500K > 3125K	+167	2/3 stop
1/2 CTO	5500K > 3800K, 4400K > 3200K	+81	1/2
1/4 CTO	5500K > 4500K, 3800K > 3200K	+42	1/3
1/8 CTO	5500K > 4900K, 3400K > 3200K	+20	1/3

NAME	TYPICAL CONVERSION	MIRED VALUE	STOP LOSS
CTB, Full Blue	3200K > 5500K	-131	1-1/2
1/2 CTB, Half Blue	3200K > 4100K	-68	1
1/3 CTB, 1/3 Blue	3200K > 3800K	-49	2/3
1/4 CTB, 1/4 Blue	3200K > 3500K	-30	1/2
1/8 CTB, 1/8 Blue	3200K > 3300K	-12	1/3

Table 10.7. (left) CTO filters, conversion vales and light loss.

Table 10.8. (left, below) CTB filters, conversion values and light loss.

NAME	CONVERSION	LOSS
85N3	Daylight to tungsten	1-2/3
85N6	Daylight to tungsten	2-2/3
85N9	Daylight to tungsten	3-2/3

TO REDUCE GREEN	NOMINAL CC EQUIVALENT	FOR USE WHEN CC INDEX IS APPROX
Minusgreen	30	-12
1/2 Minusgreen	15	-5
1/4 Minusgreen	075	-2

TO ADD GREEN	NOMINAL CC EQUIVALENT	FOR USE WHEN CC INDEX IS APPROX
Plusgreen	30	+13
1/2 Plusgreen	15	-5
1/4 plusgreen	075	-3

Table 10.9. (top) Combination 85s.

Table 10.10. (above) Gels for correcting green sources

practical locations it is not always possible to turn off the fluorescents and replace them with our own lights. The many options and combinations can get to be a bit confusing sometimes. Table 10.11 shows a decision chart for dealing with these situations. Additional tips on shooting with fluorescents include:

- In the field, it may be necessary to use a combination of these techniques. Whatever you do, SHOOT A GRAY SCALE to give the lab a starting point for correction.
- Shooting with ordinary fluorescents alone and letting the lab remove the green results in a very flat color rendition. Adding some lights (such as tungsten with plusgreen) gives a much fuller color feeling to the image.
- Several high output units are available which use color corrected (full spectrum) fluorescents and can be used in conjunction with HMI or tungsten lighting (with either daylight or 3200K fluorescent tubes) and provide perfect color. They are very efficient in power usage and give a soft even light.
- Full minusgreen is equivalent to CC30M (30 magenta). In an emergency, it is possible to use a piece of CC30M.
- Don't forget that most backlighted advertising signs (such as those in bus shelters) have fluorescent tubes in them. The scene may look fine but the fluorescent cast of the lighted signs will be very ugly.
- If you are shooting a large area such as a supermarket, factory or office, it is far more efficient to add green to your lights than to have the crew spend hours on ladders gelling or changing bulbs.
- When you add plusgreen or fluorofilter to lights they give a very strongly colored light which to the eye looks very wrong and doesn't appear to visually match either HMI or tungsten light. It looks absolutely awful. You will often find it difficult to convince a director that this the right thing to do. Try taking a color Polaroid.

CORRECTING OFF-COLOR LIGHTS

ARCS
Carbon arcs give off heavy ultraviolet. Rosco Y-1 or Lee L.C.T. Yellow reduces the UV output. Correction of white flame carbon arcs to tungsten balance: use Rosco MT2 (together with Y-1) or Lee 232. Rosco MTY is a combination of MT2 and Y-1.

10.9. This pool room shot needed to feel degenerate and raw. A 24K Lightwave (similar to a Dino) was outside the window. The existing daylight was allowed to leak in and was uncorrected. The combination of the two contributed to the sleazy, honky-tonk feel which was appropriate for the scene.

EXISTING SOURCE	YOUR LIGHTS	STRATEGY	COMMENTS
Any fluorescents	None or fluorescents	Shoot Fluorescent balance	Use fluorescents only (adding fluorescent fill if necessary) and let the lab time the green out of the print
Any fluorescents	Tungsten or HMI	Replace the lamps	Remove existing fluorescent lamps and replace with "full spectrum" fluorescent bulbs which provide photographic daylight or tungsten balance
Cool white fluorescents	HMIs	Gel the fluorescents (daylight balance)	Add minusgreen gel to the existing fluorescents which removes the green. With cool white fluorescents this will result in daylight balance. Tungsten lights can be blued or HMIs used.
Warm white fluorescents	Tungsten	Gel the fluorescents (tungsten balance	Add minusgreen gel. With warm white fluorescents this will result in a tungsten balance. Tungsten lights may be used or HMIs with 85.
Cool white fluorescents	HMIs	Gel the HMIs	Add plusgreen to the HMIs which matches them to the heavy green output of the fluorescents. Then use a camera filter to remove the green or have the lab time it out.

Table 10.11. (left) Strategies for dealing with off-color sources.

HMI
HMIs generally run a little too blue and are voltage dependent. Unlike tungsten, their color temperature goes up as voltage decreases. It is important to check each lamp with a color temperature meter or color Polaroid and write the actual color temp on a piece of tape attached to the side. For slight correction Y-1 or Rosco MT 54 can be used. For more correction, use 1/8 or 1/4 CTO. Many HMIs also run a little green. Have 1/8 and 1/4 minusgreen available.

INDUSTRIAL LAMPS
Various types of high efficiency lamps are found in industrial and public space situations. They fall into three general categories: Sodium Vapor, Metal Halide and Mercury Vapor. All of these lights have discontinuous spectrums and are dominant in one color. They all have very low CRIs. It is possible to shoot with them if some corrections are made. High pressure sodium lamps are very orange and contain a great deal of green. Low pressure sodium is a monochromatic light: they are impossible to correct.

CAMERA FILTRATION FOR INDUSTRIAL SOURCES
The following are recommended starting points for using camera filtration to correct off-balance industrial sources. They are approxima-

Film Type	Existing Source	Camera Filters
Tungsten	High Pressure Sodium	80B + CC 30M
	Metal Halide	85 + CC50M
	Mercury Vapor	85 + CC50M
Daylight	High Pressure Sodium	80B + CC50B
	Metal Halide	81A + CC30M
	Mercury Vapor	81A + CC 50M

Table 10.12. Typical camera filtration for common industrial sources. Always confirm with film testing or a Polaroid.

Cool White
Fluorescent | Daylight
5500K

Cool White
Fluorescent | Tungsten
3200K

Plusgreen 50

Cool White
Fluorescent | Tungsten
3200K

Fluorofilter

Cool White
Fluorescent | Daylight
5500K

Minusgreen

Warm White
Fluorescent | Tungsten
3200K

Minusgreen

1/4 CTO

Optima 32 | Tungsten
3200K

10.10. (top, left) Cool White fluorescent with normal daylight. Notice how green the left side of her face is.

10.11. (top, middle) Cool White fluorescent balanced against a tungsten source with Rosco Plusgreen 50. Green is then removed by the lab.

10.12. (top, right) Cool White fluorescent with Rosco Fluorofilter, which converts them to tungsten balance.

10.13. (above, left) Cool White fluorescent with Minusgreen (CC 30M) balanced with a daylight source.

10.14. (above, middle) A Warm White fluorescent with Rosco Minusgreen and 1/4 CTO to match a tungsten source.

10.15. (above, right) An Optima 32 (color correct fluorescent) matched with a tungsten source.

tions only and should be confirmed with metering and testing. *Never* fail to shoot a gray scale and some skin tone for a timer's guide. Only with these references will the color timer or video transfer colorist be able to quickly and accurately correct the color. For more on shooting the gray scale reference see the chapter on *Image Control*. Pay close attention to how the gray scale is shot — an incorrectly done gray scale can do more damage than none at all; if the telecine transfer artist or film color timer adheres to it, your dailies will be very different than you expected. Some starting points for testing are shown in Table 10.12.

STYLISTIC CHOICES IN COLOR CONTROL

As with everything in film and video production, stylistic choices affect the technical choices and vice versa. This is especially true with color correction. Until a few years ago, considerable time and money were spent on correcting every single source on the set and every light or fixture that appeared in the frame to precisely 3200K (for tungsten) or 5500K (for daylight or HMIs) with no green. As a result of the influence of commercials and music videos, there is more of a tendency to "let them go green" and even let many different mixed sources appear in the frame. This is a much more naturalistic look and has become a style all its own. It has been said that "green is the new orange." Some commercials and features even go out of their way to establish the green fluorescent look.

optics

Except for certain minor differences, the principles of optics and the use of lenses is the same for film and video. Nearly all principles of optics and optical design are based on a few laws of physics. The two most basic are reflection and refraction. There are a few things we need to know about the basic behavior of light in order to understand the fundamentals of optics.

PHYSICAL BASIS OF OPTICS

Aside from lighting sources most things in the real world do not emit visible light but reflect natural or artificial light. For instance, an apple appears a shiny red color because it has a relatively smooth surface that absorbs other non-red (such as green, blue, yellow) wavelengths of light. The reflection of light can be roughly categorized into two types of reflection: specular reflection is defined as light reflected from a smooth surface at a definite angle, and diffuse reflection, which is produced by rough surfaces that tend to reflect light in all directions. There are far more occurrences of diffuse reflection than specular reflection in our everyday environment.

The basic rule of reflection, known to any schoolchild is: the angle of incidence equals the angle of reflection (Figure 11.2). The amount of light reflected by an object is dependent upon the texture of the surface. When surface imperfections are smaller than the wavelength of the incident light (as in the case of a mirror), virtually all of the light is reflected. In everyday language — it's shiny. However, in the real world most objects have convoluted surfaces that exhibit a diffuse reflection, with the incident light being reflected in all directions.

As will be discussed in the chapter on lighting, diffusion is also a key element in controlling light that is transmitted through things: namely diffusion materials. In both cases, diffusion means the same thing; the light rays are more scattered in all directions after they are reflected or transmitted than they were before. The opposite of reflection, absorption, is of interest in two ways. First of all it is how objects have "color" (see chapter on *Color Theory*) and secondly it is how we control light on the set.

REFRACTION

The refraction of visible light is an important characteristic of lenses that allows them to focus a beam of light onto a single point. Refraction, or bending of the light, occurs as light passes from one medium to another when there is a difference in the index of refraction between the two materials.

Refractive index is defined as the relative speed at which light moves through a material with respect to its speed in a vacuum. By definition, the refractive index of a vacuum is defined as having a value of 1.0. The refractive indices of all transparent materials are therefore greater than 1.0.

11.1. (previous page) One of the best known and most fascinating uses of optics — the mirage shot from *Lawrence of Arabia* (Columbia Pictures, 1962.)

11.2. (below) Angle of incidence equals angle of reflection.

When light passes from a less dense medium such as air to a more dense medium such as glass, the speed of the wave decreases. Conversely, when light passes from a more dense medium to a less dense medium, the speed of the wave increases. The angle of refracted light is dependent upon both the angle of incidence and the composition of the material into which it is entering. We can define the normal as a line perpendicular to the boundary between two substances.

The concept of refractive index is illustrated in Figure 11.3 for the case of light passing from air through both glass and water. Notice that while both beams enter the denser material through the same angle of incidence with respect to the normal (60 degrees),

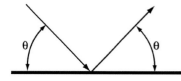

the refraction for glass is almost 6 degrees more than that for water due to the higher refractive index of glass. The index of refraction varies with the frequency of radiation (or wavelength) of light. This occurs with all transparent media and is called dispersion.

As the wavelength of light increases, the refractive index decreases. It is the dispersion of light by glass that is responsible for the familiar splitting of light into its component colors by a prism.

This is important in optics for film and video in that it means that the various wavelengths, that is colors, of light do not interact with the glass of the lens in exactly the same way. Poorly designed lenses will not focus all colors on exactly the same plane. Modern lenses, however, are designed to deal with this and it is not a significant problem.

When measuring the refractive index of a transparent material, the particular wavelength used in the measurement must be identified. This is because dispersion is wavelength-dependent. When the beams exit the glass and water, they are again refracted at the same angle that they entered the materials.

Refraction of light is important in the construction and physics of lenses. In a convex lens, as illustrated below, light waves reflected from the object are bent towards the optical center of the lens and converge on the focal point.

The relative position of the object with respect to the front focal point of the lens determines how the object is imaged. If the object is beyond twice the length of the focal point, then it appears smaller and inverted and must be imaged by an additional lens in order to magnify the size. However, when the image is closer to the lens than the focal point, the image appears upright and larger, as can be easily demonstrated with a simple magnifying glass.

It is one thing to have the lens form an image on the focal plane but the amount of light that reaches it must be controlled. This is done with an aperture, which is nothing more than a variable size hole that is placed in the optical axis.

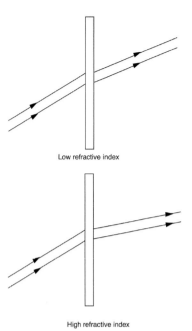

Low refractive index

High refractive index

11.3. Refraction.

F/STOP

The f/number or f/stop of a lens is a measure of its ability to pass light. A lens with an f/stop of 1.0 would theoretically pass all of the light reaching through to the focal plane. The f/stop is the ratio of the focal length of a lens to the diameter of the entrance pupil. However this is a purely mathematical calculation that does not account for the varying efficiency of different lens designs.

T/stop (true stop) is a measurement of actual light transmission as measured on an optical bench. F/stops are used in depth-of-field and hyperfocal calculations and T/stops are used in setting exposure.

When setting the aperture on a lens never go backwards. Most apertures have a certain amount of backlash which must be compensated for. If it is necessary to go to a larger stop (i.e., "open up") open the lens all the way up and then reset the stop.

BASIC MATHEMATICS OF OPTICS

The fundamental optical equations use these terms:

> D = distance
> O = object size
> F = focal length
> A = aperture size (the diaphragm)

Optical equations can get quite complex but the basics that we need to understand as working cinematographers and videographers are simple.

The fundamental formula is:

$$O = \frac{D}{A*F}$$

Variations on this are:

$$D = \frac{O \times F}{A}$$

$$\text{Distance} = \frac{\text{object size x focal length}}{\text{aperture size}}$$

$$O = \frac{D \times A}{F}$$

$$\text{Object Size} = \frac{\text{distance x aperture size}}{\text{focal length}}$$

$$F = \frac{D \times A}{O}$$

$$\text{Focal Length} = \frac{\text{distance x aperture size}}{\text{object size}}$$

$$A = \frac{F \times O}{D}$$

$$\text{Aperture size} = \frac{\text{focal length x object size}}{\text{distance}}$$

In anamorphic photography the aperture width is equal to 2A.

FOCUS

Focus is a much misunderstood aspect of filmmaking. What is "in focus?" Theoretically, it means that the actual object is projected onto the film or video "as it appears in real life."

The human eye tends to perceive everything as in focus, but this is a result of the eye/brain interaction. The eye is basically an f/2 optic and may be considered a fairly "wide angle" lens, so much of the world actually is in focus, certainly in brightly lit situations. But, nearly imperceptible to us, the focus is constantly shifting. This is accomplished by the muscles that control the lens of the eye. They distort its shape to shift the focus. If you look at something very close in a dimly lit situation, the background will be out of focus, but most likely you will not perceive it - because you are "looking" at the near object. By "looking" I mean that your brain is focusing your attention on the near object. This is what differentiates the eye from a camera: our mental focus is a condition of our consciousness and attention — the camera simply records everything.

As we will see later, a great number of the practices of focus: focal length, composing the frame and even lighting, are attempts to re-create this mental aspect of focus and attention. We are using the camera to imitate how the eye and brain work together to tell a visual story in an imitation of how life is perceived by the mind.

First, the technical basics: the taking lens is the optical system that projects the image onto the film or video sensor, which is called the image plane. The image plane is two-dimensional. As we discussed in the chapter on *Filmspace*, all imaging, whether photography, cinema, video or even painting is the act of taking a three-dimensional world and rendering it onto this two-dimensional plane.

When discussing focus, we often tend to think only in terms of the flat image plane, but it is more useful to remember that the lens is forming a three dimensional image in space: not a flat picture plane. It is the flat picture plane that must be "focused" onto. It is the only part of the image that gets recorded. This will be especially relevant when we get to the circle of confusion. (Some may think we are in the circle of confusion already, but stick with it, this is important.)

The image plane is also called the Principal Plane of Focus; sort of the uptown business address for what we commonly call the focal plane. Think of it this way: we are shooting a scene that has some foreground bushes, a woman standing in the middle and some mountains behind her. The woman is our subject. We focus the lens so that she is sharply projected onto the image plane.

In our three-dimensional model, the bushes and the mountains are projected behind the lens, but in front of her and behind her. In other words they are being projected into the camera, but in front of and behind the Principal Plane of Focus. As a result they are out of focus. By shifting the focus of the lens, or by stopping down, or using a wider angle lens we can bring them into focus, but let's assume we are shooting wide open with a fairly long lens. By changing the focus of the lens, what we are actually doing is shifting that three-dimensional image backwards and forwards. If we shift it backwards, the mountains are focused on the image plane; if we shift forwards, the bushes are focused. Only objects that are projected sharply on the image plane are actually in "critical focus." But there are many objects that are only slightly in front of or behind the principal subject. If we stop down a little, thus increasing depth-of-field, they appear sharp (Figures 11.4 and 11.5). Note also that depth-of-field is different from depth-of-focus, as in Figure 11.6.

But they are not actually sharp. This is called apparent focus. What is the boundary line between actual focus and apparent focus. There is none; at least not technically definable. It is a very subjective call that depends on many factors: perception, critical judgment, the resolving power of the lens, the resolving power of the film or video, the amount of diffusion, the surface qualities of the subject, lighting and so on. Also very important is the end use of the footage. Something that appears in focus on a small television might be horribly soft on an Imax screen. There is a technical measurement of critical focus which is discussed below — it is called the circle of confusion but as we will see, it is a mathematical measurement which is based on certain judgment calls.

MENTAL FOCUS

As we discussed in the eye/brain phenomenon, the viewing audience is subject to the same tendency: they will focus their attention on the part of the image that is "in focus." This is an important psychological function that is extremely valuable in visual imagery and storytelling with a lens.

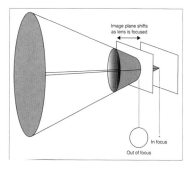

11.4. (top) The cone of focus on the imaging side of a converging lens.

11.5. (above) As the lens is focused, the cone of focus moves back and forth. The goal is to put the smallest point of the cone exactly at the imaging plane.

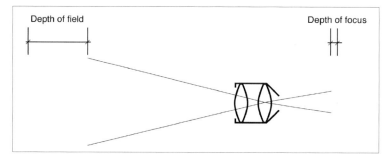

11.6. Depth-of-field is on the subject side of the lens, depth-of-focus is at the image plane.

There is a long history of the shift from deep focus so much favored in the black-and-white era (used most notably by Orson Welles and Gregg Toland in *Citizen Kane* and *The Magnificent Ambersons*) and the current trend to limited depth-of-field favored today, not to mention the recent use of "tilted focus" so much favored by music video and commercial directors. More on that later.

But cinematographers and videographers are engaged not only in shaping mental perception; they are technicians also. We need some way of quantifying focus, however arbitrary that might be. Let's think about a single ray of light, for example an infinitely small (or at least a very tiny) point of light that is the only thing in the field of view. This sends a single ray of light toward the lens. As the ray of light leaves the object, it expands outward; no set of light rays is truly parallel, not even a laser or the light from a distant start. The lens captures these slightly expanding rays of light and reconcentrates them: this bends them back toward each other. This forms a cone behind the lens. Where these rays actually meet (and keep in mind that we are talking about the rays of a single point of light) is where the image is in focus. The lens can then be adjusted so that this single point of light is sharply focused on the image plane: that is, it appears to be just as small on the image plane as it does in life.

Now, we shift the lens so that the image of the dot of light is not exactly at the image plane. What happens? The image of the dot gets larger because we are no longer at the confluence of the rays of light as concentrated by the lens. If we do this only slightly, no one may notice. We say that this is still acceptable focus. If we shift a lot, most people would then perceive it as not acceptable focus, but as we have pointed out, this is all subjective. Based on a general consensus taking into account the various factors involved, imaging scientists have quantified how much bigger that dot can get and still be deemed acceptable focus for most general use purposes.

CIRCLE OF CONFUSION

The term for this is "circle of confusion" (it is not to be confused with the circle of confusion created when several producers gather round and start talking about cinematography). The circle of confusion is basically a measure of how large the projected image of a true point source can be before it is considered to be unacceptably out of focus. Theoretically, of course, the point of light projected

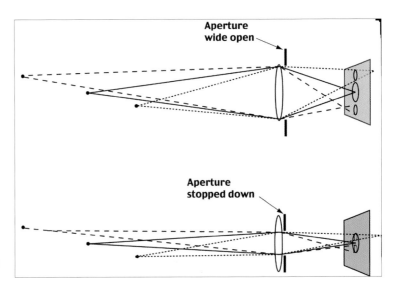

11.7. How stopping down affects the circle of confusion.

onto the film plane should be the same size as the infinitely small point of light it is seeing, but due to the nature of optics it can never be perfect. For film work in 16mm, the circle of confusion varies from 1/2000" (.0005") for critical applications to 1/1000" (.0001"). For 35mm it ranges from 1/700" (.00014") to 1/500" (.002").

The circle of confusion is smaller for 16mm because 16mm has to be blown-up more to achieve the same image size on the screen or monitor. The circle of confusion is most important in the calculation of depth-of-field. Whenever you look at a depth-of-field chart, you will see listed the circle of confusion used in the calculations. It is important to remember that the end use of the footage is an important consideration in making these judgments.

DEPTH-OF-FIELD

Back to our model of a three dimensional projected image. The portion of this image that falls on the image plane and is within the circle of confusion is called the depth-of-field. It has a near and far limit. A number of factors affect depth-of-field:

- Focal length of the taking lens. The shorter the focal length, the more the depth-of-field.
- The aperture of the lens. The smaller the aperture, the greater the depth-of-field.
- Image magnification (object distance). The closer the subject is to the image plane, the less the depth-of-field.
- The circle of confusion selected for the situation. (Remember, they are different for 16mm and 35mm).
- Indirectly: the resolving power of lens and film, end use, diffusion, fog, smoke, the type of subject.

With a tendency to use faster films and longer lenses in darker, "low-key" light, depth-of-field is a critical issue. With a 150mm lens doing a tight close-up of a face, it is not unusual for your focus puller to ask, "which eye do you want in focus?" The general practice is that critical focus should be on the pupils of the eyes, but it may not be necessary to get them both; in this case it is your judgment call to decide which one is more important. As a general rule: depth-of-field is not evenly distributed in front of and in back of the plane of critical focus. Usually, it is one third in front and 2/3 behind. This is because behind the plane of focus is, of course, farther away.

DEPTH-OF-FIELD CALCULATIONS

Depth-of-field is a plane of focus perpendicular to the optical axis where objects are focused to acceptable sharpness. The near and far planes of sharpness are calculated:

$$ND = \frac{H \times S}{H + (S-F)}$$

$$FD = \frac{H \times S}{H - (S-F)}$$

ND = Near distance
FD = Far distance
H = Hyperfocal distance
S = Distance from camera to object
F = Focal length of the lens

HOW *NOT* TO GET MORE DEPTH-OF-FIELD

As a result of the basic principles of physics, wide angle lenses will have more depth-of-field at a given f/stop. Here we must dispel one of the most persistent and pernicious myths of filmmaking. Many people still believe that if you are having trouble getting the important elements in focus, the answer is to put on a wider angle lens and you will have greater depth-of-field. Technically true, but in actual practice, they then move the camera forward so they have the same frame size. The actual result? You end up with exactly the same depth-of-field you started with! This is because you have moved the camera forward and end up with same image magnification. It is image magnification that is the critical factor. If you have a 6' tall person from head to toe in the frame with a 50mm lens and you then put on a 24mm lens, you have to move the camera significantly forward. You are decreasing subject distance and increasing image magnification, both of which decrease depth-of-field.

DEPTH-OF-FIELD
Depth-of-field is another term that occasionally creates confusion. Depth-of-field is a measure of how much in front of or behind the critically focused subject is also deemed to be in acceptable focus. It is a measure of distance at the subject. Depth-of-field is a measure of distance at the image plane. Think back to our three-dimensional projected image. Depth-of-field relates to how much of the projected image is in apparent focus (Figure 11.6).

HYPERFOCAL DISTANCE
For every focal length and f/stop there is a particular focus distance which is special: the hyperfocal distance. This is the closest focus distance at which both objects at infinity and closer objects are in focus. When a lens is set at the hyperfocal distance, everything from 1/2 of the hyperfocal distance to infinity will be in focus.

The formula for hyperfocal distance is

$$H = \frac{F^2}{f*Cc}$$

F   = focal length of lens
f   = f/stop number
Cc = circle of confusion

There are two ways of defining hyperfocal distance (HD).

First: Hyperfocal distance is the focus setting of the lens when objects at infinity and objects at the nearest point to the camera are both in acceptable focus.

Second: If the lens is set at the hyperfocal distance, both objects at infinity and at 1/2 of that hyperfocal distance will be in acceptable focus. Most lens charts will list the hyperfocal distance for various lenses at any given f/stop. (Remember, f/stops are used for optical calculations and t/stops are used for setting the aperture.) For example: for a 50mm lens at f/8 with a circle of confusion of .0001", the hyperfocal distance is 40 feet. Thus if you set the focus distance at 40 feet, everything from 20 feet to infinity will be in focus.

Opening up two stops doubles the hyperfocal distance. e.g., it goes from 40 feet at f/8 to 80 feet at f/4. Conversely closing down two stops decreases the hyperfocal distance by one half. Another characteristic of hyperfocal distance is this. When the lens is set at HD, depth-of-field extends from 1/2 HD to infinity. When the lens is set at 1/2 of HD, the DOF is from 1/3 of HD to infinity and so on.

NODAL POINTS
Another enduring myth of depth-of-field is that all depth-of-field calculations are from the image plane. Even some of the most experienced camera assistants will tell you this. It's not true. Depth-of-field is calculated from the Front Nodal Point. This is accounted for in most depth-of-field charts.

"Nodal points" are the two points such that a light ray entering the

11.8. A true nodal point head by Cartoni. (Photo courtesy of Cartoni, S.p.A.)

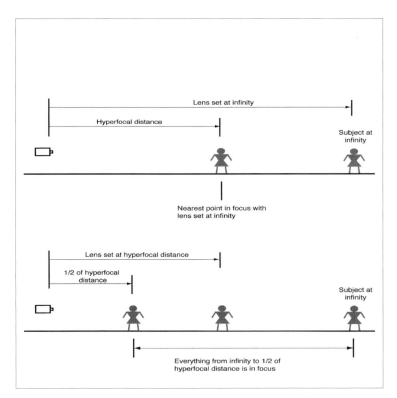

Lens set at infinity

Hyperfocal distance

Subject at infinity

Nearest point in focus with lens set at infinity

Lens set at hyperfocal distance

1/2 of hyperfocal distance

Subject at infinity

Everything from infinity to 1/2 of hyperfocal distance is in focus

front of the lens and headed straight toward the front nodal point will emerge going straight away from the rear nodal point at exactly the same angle to the lens axis as the entering ray had. The nodal points are identical to the principal points when the front and rear media are the same, e.g., air, so for most practical purposes the terms can be used interchangeably.

In simple double convex lenses the two principal points are somewhere inside the lens (actually 1/n-th the way from the surface to the center, where n is the index of refraction), but in a complex lens they can be almost anywhere, including outside the lens, or with the rear principal point in front of the front principal point. In a lens with elements that are fixed relative to each other, the principal points are fixed relative to the glass. In zoom or internal focusing lenses the principal points may move relative to the glass and each other when zooming or focusing.

When a camera lens is focused at infinity, the rear principal point is exactly one focal length in front of the film. To find the front principal point, take the lens off the camera and let light from a distant object pass through it "backwards." Find the point where the image is formed, and measure toward the lens one focal length. With some lenses, particularly ultra wides, you can't do this, since the image is not formed in front of the front element.

Entrance pupil and exit pupils are not often where we think they should be — at the front and back of the lens. The accompanying diagram shows how they are calculated. In fact, for some lens designs, it is possible for the front entrance pupil to actually be behind the film plane. An example: on a Zeiss 50mm lens at f/2.1 the FNP is 34.5mm back from the front vertex of the lens and the lens is a total of 77.9mm from the front vertex to the focal plane.

This means that for this lens at this f/stop, focus and depth-of-field are measured starting at 34.5mm back from the middle of the front element. Don't panic — in actual practice this is compensated for in

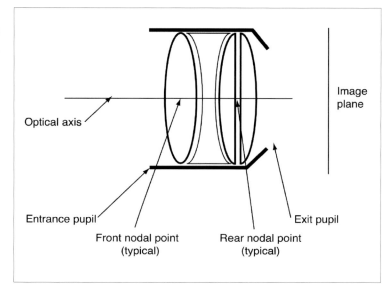

Optical axis

Image plane

Entrance pupil

Exit pupil

Front nodal point (typical)

Rear nodal point (typical)

depth-of-field charts, which add a fixed distance in front of the focal plane which varies for prime lenses and zooms. This also explains why there might be very slight differences between focus charts from different manufacturers.

For simplicity, all actual distance measurements in the field are from the focal plane. All cameras have either a mark at the focal plane and usually also a protruding screw to which the camera assistant can attach a measuring tape. The discrepancy may only become a factor in extreme macro work, in which case it is often best to rely on eye focus wherever possible.

THE REAR NODAL POINT AND SPECIAL EFFECTS SHOTS
The Rear Nodal Point is also important for lining up special effects shots through half silvered mirrors, certain types of panning shots where the camera must be panned or tilted without shifting the image and also in front projection.

If manufacturers data are not available, the nodal point on which the camera must rotate can be determined in the field by mounting the camera on a head which has a slide plate. Then mount a cross on a c-stand in front of the camera. On the wall behind, mount a same-size cross so that the two are congruent, i.e., the front cross perfectly covers the back one. Then experiment with sliding the camera back and forth until you find a position where you can pan the camera and the rear cross stays centered behind the front cross. You have found the nodal point of the lens and centered it over the pivot point of the panning head. In some cases, side to side alignment may also be necessary, for example, when a small camera is mounted on a larger head such as the old "aircraft carrier" Worral geared head.

11.11. A typical zoom. (Photo courtesy of Century Precision Optics.)

With all but the simplest single element lenses, the FNP and Entrance Pupil have no relation to the position of the front element, type of lens or who made it. They are all different and can only be determined by complex optical formulae. For this reason, it is often necessary to obtain this information from the lens manufacturer. On these charts, the FNP is measured from the vertex of the front element backwards towards the focal plane.

ZOOMS AND DEPTH-OF-FIELD
Zooms (Figure 11.11) have some special characteristics when it comes to depth-of-field. As we discussed previously, depth-of-field is not measured from the film plane or video receptor. In fact it is

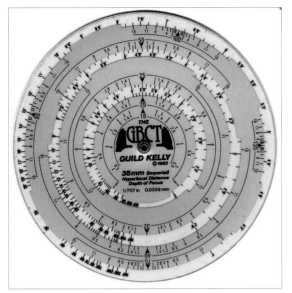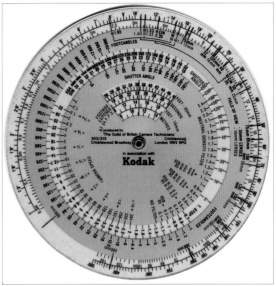

11.12. Front and back of the Guild Kelly calculator.

measured from the nodal point of the lens. Depth-of-field charts compensate for this in a general way by adding a fixed amount in front of the focal plane. This is why you may see different DOF charts for zooms and primes at equivalent focal lengths.

The issue with variable focal length lenses is that as they are zoomed, the nodal point may actually shift. With some zooms the nodal point actually ends up 5″ behind the film plane at its long end. With the old Cooke 20/100 the range was about 10.5″ in front of the film plane at 20mm, and 5″ in front of the film plane at 100mm.

Motion control rigs that keep the nodal point over the pan center use a long worm gear that moves the camera/zoom back and forth over the center point as you zoom. In practical depth-of-field applications with zoom lenses the only thing that is really of any consequence to us is at the wide end, where the nodal point is typically around 10″ in front of the film plane. Thus if you are shooting a close-up at the wide end of a zoom it's as if you were 10″ closer to your subject matter. Being closer you of course have less depth-of-field. This is one of the reasons that zooms are seldom used in macro, table-top and other critical focus applications.

MACROPHOTOGRAPHY

For extreme close-up work, called macrophotography, it is more useful to think in terms of image magnification instead of depth-of-field. Macrophotography is any imaging where the image size is near to or greater than the actual size of the object. For example, photographing a postage stamp full frame is macro work.

Regular prime lenses can seldom focus closer than 9 or 10 inches; zooms generally have a minimum of around 2 to 3 feet. Extreme close-up photography has a set of problems all its own. The most critical aspect of macro work is the degree of magnification. A magnification of 1:1 means that the object will be reproduced on film actual size, that is an object that is 1/2″ in reality will produce an image on the negative (or video tube) of 1/2″. 1:2 will be 1/2 size, 1:3 will be 1/3 size and so on. In film, the 35mm academy frame is 16mm high and 22mm wide. In 1:1 reproduction a 22mm object will fill the entire frame. Most lenses of ordinary design can focus no closer than a ratio of 1:8 or 1:10.

EXPOSURE COMPENSATION IN MACROPHOTOGRAPHY

When a small image is being "spread" over a large piece of film, it naturally produces less exposure. With reproduction ratio's of greater than 1:10, exposure compensation is necessary. The formula is:

$$\text{Shooting f/stop} = \frac{\text{f/stop determined by meter}}{1 + \text{magnification ratio}}$$

Example: meter reading is f/8. Your reproduction ratio is 1:2 or 1/2 size. The calculation is $8/(1+.5) = 5.3$

DEPTH-OF-FIELD IN CLOSE-UP WORK

There are many misconceptions associated with macrophotography; perhaps the most basic is that "wide angle lenses have more depth-of-field." Depth-of-field is a function of image size, not focal length. While it is true that wide angle lenses have more depth-of-field, the problem is that once you have put a wider lens on, you still want the same image you had before and in order to accomplish that, you must move the camera closer to the subject. Once you have done this, the depth-of-field is exactly the same as it was before, since focus distance is also an important determinant of depth-of-field. The important aspects are:

- Depth-of-field decreases as magnification increases.
- Depth-of-field decreases as focus distance decreases.
- Depth-of-field is doubled by closing down the lens two stops.

Calculating Depth-Of-Field In Extreme Close-up Work

Calculation of depth-of-field in extreme close-up work methods in different from normal. At magnifications greater than 1:10, the depth-of-field is extremely small and it is easier to calculate the total depth-of-field rather than a near and far limit of the zone of focus. Total depth-of-field is calculated by the following formula:

$$Dt = \frac{2C \times N\,(1+M)}{m^2}$$

Dt = total depth-of-field
C = circle of confusion
N = f/number
m = magnification

Where magnification is calculated by the formula:

$$\text{magnification} = \frac{\text{image size}}{\text{object size}}$$

LENS DISPLACEMENT WHEN FOCUSED CLOSER THAN INFINITY

When focused closer than infinity front elements of the lens (or all the elements) are moved away from the focal plane. This is important in calculating exposure loss in extreme close-up work.

$$d = \frac{f^2}{a - f}$$

d = lens displacement from infinity position
f = focal length of lens in inches
a = distance focus in inches

CLOSE-UP TOOLS

Extreme close-up photography can be accomplished with a variety of tools; as with all optics, the basics are the same whether you are shooting film, digital, regular video or High Def.

DIOPTERS

Diopters are simple meniscus lenses which are placed in front of the camera lens and reduce the minimum focusing distance of the lens. The lenses are measured in diopters, which is the reciprocal of the focal length as measured in meters. A plus 1 diopter has a focal length of 1 meter, a plus 2 is 1/2 meter, etc. Minimum focusing distance with the lens set at infinity is determined by dividing the diopter number into 100cm. For example, a +2 diopter is 100/2 = 50 cm. This equals 19.68 inches. You will actually be able to focus a bit closer by changing the focus of the lens itself.

A diopter is defined as the reciprocal of the focus of this accessory lens in meters, that is, one divided by the focal length. Thus a plus one is a magnifying lens of one meter's focus; a plus 1/2 is a milder magnifier that focuses at two meters. A plus two focuses at one-half meter, 500mm. A plus three at 333mm.

This spec shows you the farthest working distance you can work; put a plus one-half on your normal camera lens, set it on infinity, the farthest, and objects two meters away are in focus. Nothing farther could be shot sharp. Put on a plus one and the max working distance is one meter. Put on a plus two and stuff has to be 500mm, or half a meter, or about 19″ away (from the front of the diopter, not the film plane) to achieve sharpness. All those cases are with the main lens (prime or zoom) "set at infinity." Of course you can go closer, depending on the closer focus of the main lens.

A split diopter is one of these magnifiers split in half, like a half-moon. It covers half your field, and the stuff seen through the glass is focused closer, and the other half, which is missing (just air) will be focused where the main lens is set. Put a plus one-half split on your camera. Focus the main lens at infinity. One half of the field, through the diopter, is sharp at 2 meters. The rest of the field is focused at infinity. If you set the main lens at 15 feet, the clear half is focused at fifteen feet and the diopter-covered half might focus at 1-1/3 meters.

The point is to fake deep-focus effects. There's a fuzzy line at the edge of the split diopter in the middle of your picture, and this has to be hidden artfully in the composition. Most of these shots are lock-offs, that is, static camera. As a rule, all diopter shots should be done stopped down to protect image quality, as diopters are not heavily corrected for color fringing and other aberrations.

Split diopters have a lens on one half and clear glass or nothing on the other side, which enables a shot to be in focus close-up on one side and at a distance on another side. This gives the appearance of a very deep focus shot. Since the line between the two will be slightly perceptible it is usually necessary to hide the line in some way. It is often possible to frame up the shot so that a door frame, lamp, tree or some other object falls along the line of the split diopter and thus disguises it. Diopter recommendations include:

- Use the lowest power diopter you can, combined with a longer focal length lens, if necessary.
- Stop down as much as possible.
- There is no need for exposure compensation with diopters.
- When using two diopters together, add the diopter factors and always place the highest power closest to the lens.

EXTENSION TUBES OR BELLOWS

The advantage of extension tubes or bellows is that they do not alter the optics at all, thus there is no degradation of the image. Extension tubes are rings which hold the lens farther away from the film plane than it normally sits, thus reducing the minimum focus distance.

Table 11.1. Focus with diopters.

Diopter - Focus Conversion Chart
(can be used with any focal length - any format)

Diopter power	Focus distance of lens	Actual distance from diopter to subject
+1/2	Infinity	78-3/4"
	25'	62-1/2"
	15'	54-3/4"
	10'	47-1/2"
	6'	37-3/4"
	4'	29-3/4"
+1	Infinity	39-1/2"
	25'	34-3/4"
	15'	32-1/2"
	10'	29-3/4"
	6'	25-1/4"
	4'	21-3/4"
+2	Infinity	19-3/4"
	25'	18-1/2"
	15'	17-3/4"
	10'	16-3/4"
	6'	15-1/2"
	4'	14"
+3	Infinity	13-1/4"
	25'	12-1/2"
	15'	12-1/4"
	10'	11-3/4"
	6'	11-1/4"
	4'	10-1/2"

A bellows unit is the same idea but is continuously variable with a rack and pinion. Either will give good results down to about 1:2. Extension tubes are generally incompatible with wide angle or zoom lenses. Lenses with larger minimum apertures generally give better results than high speed lenses. Optically, the best results at very high magnifications are obtained by reversing the lens (so that the back of the lens faces the subject) and mounting on a bellows unit. The simple rule is: to achieve 1:1 reproduction, the extension must equal the focal length of the lens. For 1:1 with a 50mm, for example, you would need a 50mm extension.

A variation of this is the swing-and-tilt mount, which gives the lens mount the same kind of controls used in a view camera. The lens cannot only be extended for macro work, but the plane of focus can also be tilted. This permits part of the image to be in focus and part of the image on the same plane to be out of focus. This had its vogue as a popular look in commercials and music videos.

MACRO LENSES
Macro lenses are actually specially designed optics, optimized for close-up work. They are good in the 1:2 to 1:1 range. Some macros have barrel markings for magnification ratio as well as focus distance; this facilitates calculating the exposure compensation.

CLOSE FOCUS LENSES
Close focus lenses differ from macros in that they are no different in design from ordinary prime lenses. For the most part, close focus lenses are primes that have had the "stop" pins removed so that the focus barrel can rotate more than a full rotation and thus focus closer than normal.

SNORKLES AND INNOVISION
Several types of "snorkle" lenses are available which are like periscopes. They generally allow for extremely close focus and for getting the lens into incredibly small spaces. Century Precision Optics, Cine Photo Tech and other companies make some excellent units. Some units require exposure compensation and some have the compensation built in; be sure to check which type you are using. Some of the units are immersible in water.

Innovision is a snorkle type lens which can be fitted on both video and motion picture cameras for extreme close-up work. It has the advantage of an extremely narrow barrel which can reach inside

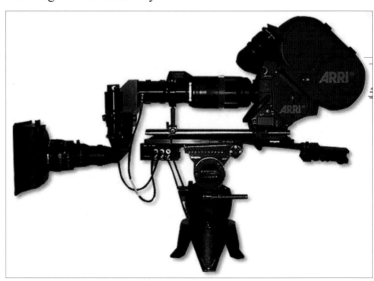

11.13. The Revolution lens system. (Photo courtesy of Keslow Camera.)

very small areas, even inside flowers. The f/stop is fixed and is very high, around f/32 to f/45, depending on the application, however, a high f/stop is generally needed for extreme close-up work in any case. Innovision has its own light source which is a small ring around the front element of the lens. It is a fibre optics rig and is remotely lit from a separate unit. It is approximately daylight balance and can be gelled inside the power unit for special effects or to match other sources in the shot.

FRAZIER LENS AND REVOLUTION
Specialized applications of the snorkle are the Frazier lens and the Revolution system (Figure 11.13). These have remarkable depth-of-field which seems to defy physics (it doesn't really) and also allows for the lens itself to rotate, pan and tilt. It is possible to have objects which are actually touching the lens in focus and still maintain usable depth in the distance. They can be used in conjunction with perspective control lenses such as the tilt focus lens shown in Figure 11.15. The Frazier has a maximum stop of T/7; as a bonus it also minimizes the distortion normally associated with very wide angle lenses. The Kenworth snorkle is similar to these.

LENS EXTENDERS AND FILTER FACTORS
Optical devices which increase the focal length of the lens have a corresponding effect on t/stop. To find the filter factor, square the extension factor. For example a 2X optic will have a filter factor of 4 and a 3X extender will have a filter factor of 9. A factor of 4 translates to 2 stops and 9 translates to approximately 3 stops, thus a 2X extender will turn a 200mm f/4 lens into a 400mm f/8 lens. When combining extenders, the factors must be multiplied. For example a 2X and 3X extender together would have a factor 36 (five stop increase in exposure). For best results, extenders need to be stopped down.

TILT FOCUS
Lenses which can tilt the plane of focus at the image plane were originally developed for perspective control such as reducing the "keystoning" when photographing architecture. They are based on the same principle as a view camera. Understanding view camera photography is essential in order to get the maximum benefit from this type of rig.

In the last few years they have gained popularity in commercials and music videos for their ability to render objects at the same image distance in and out of focus at the same time. As with many visual innovations, the trend was started by fashion photographers. Tilt focus can be accomplished with a tilt focus lens, such as Figure 11.15 but for maximum movement, a special adapter (Figure 11.16) allows the lens to be moved in all axes.

LENS CARE
- Never clean a lens with dry lens tissue.
- Never put lens fluid on a lens; put it on the lens tissue.
- Brush or blow off loose grit before wiping with lens tissue.
- Never use eyeglass cleaning cloth; it may contain silicon.
- In dusty or sandy conditions, try to keep a filter on the lens.
- Never use rubber cement or nail polish to attach a filter to the rear of the lens, use 1/2" ATG (Scotch ATG-924) otherwise known as transfer tape or "snot tape."
- Always close at least one latch on a lens case.
- Protect all lenses from shock.

11.14. A snorkle system in use. (Photo courtesy of Mark Weingartner.)

11.15. (below) Tilt focus. (Photo courtesy of Century Precision Optics.)

11.16. (bottom) A full swing and tilt system. (Photo courtesy of Century Precision Optics.)

11.17. Various types of lens tests. See text for a description of each.

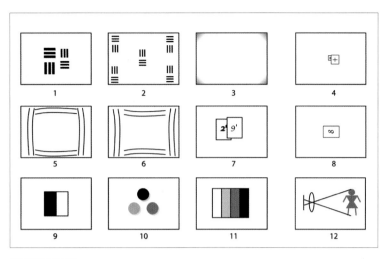

LENS TESTS

On the checkout day, the camera assistants will perform certain basic tests to ensure that the lenses you are renting are in good shape and properly matched so that there will not be severe changes in image quality or coloration when you change lenses on the set.

Some tests are more involved and are performed by the maintenance technicians. The technicians will also test flange focal depth, which is the seating depth of the lens in its mount. Some camera assistants carry the equipment to perform this test in the field. As shown in Figure 11.17, the basic lens tests are:

1. Resolution
2. Corner resolution
3. Vignetting
4. Optical shift during focus
5. Barrel distortion
6. Pincushion distortion
7. Collimation
8. Infinity focus
9. No veiling glare
10. Consistent color rendition
11. Contrast
12. Depth-of-field

video and high def

BASICS OF VIDEO

Even if you are purely a film person, it is essential to know the basics of video. There is hardly a set anywhere today that does not have a video tap monitor and often directors and producers make judgments from that monitor even when is badly out of specs and in no way represents what is actually being recorded on film or tape.

Today, nearly all editing and a great deal of postproduction is on video and we can envision a time in the near future when virtually 100% of it will be. Moreover, as the High Def age approaches, even film people must think ahead to the changeover.

No matter how well designed and "goof proof" a piece of video equipment is, it is still not a matter of "point and shoot." Even if certain systems are automated, this automation may have unwanted consequences down the line. To understand video, it is necessary to have an overview of the basic video signal. Black-and-white television broadcasts began in 1936 in Britain and in 1939 in the U.S. Standard television had a 4:3 aspect ratio. This matched the standard film projection frame of the time — a format going back to the time of Edison and Dickson. Over 60 years later this aspect ratio is still in use today, even though film has undergone many changes. Only now is there a move toward a wider 16 x 9 format.

THE VIDEO SIGNAL

NTSC is the name for the method used to transmit television signals in North America. It is named for the name of the group that sets the broadcast television standards in North America — the National Television Standards Committee, originally formed to standardize the method for color television broadcasting. The method chosen (augmenting the existing black-and-white composite video signal) was standardized in 1953 and is still the standard for North America and Japan.

The NTSC was given the mandate to introduce color to the television system without affecting the black-and-white system then in use. It was considered essential that people who owned black-and-white televisions not have to replace them and that color signals be viewable on these black-and-white monitors. While a laudable goal (and one that probably accelerated the acceptance of color) it caused the committee to impose certain engineering standards which still cause trouble today. Because the color signal had to be more or less "crowbarred" into the black-and-white signal, some very odd things had to be done which make the color signal variable and difficult to control.

Certainly if you have ever been in a TV store and seen how nearly every set is a different color (even similar sets from the same manufacturer) you know how deeply ingrained this problem is. Many people refer to NTSC as "Never Twice The Same Color."

Originally, black-and-white television had a frame rate of 30fps, which was half of the standard 60 hertz of the national power grid. When color was introduced, this was found to be a problem; as a result, the frame rate of NTSC video is 29.97 frames per second. It is 0.1% slower than the original 30 frames per second, to avoid interference with the color subcarrier part of the signal.

The scanning electron beam starts at the top left of the picture tube and scans one horizontal line. When it reaches the right hand side of the picture, the beam drops down and writes the next line. In the early television systems, this process of writing 525 lines created a very noticeable flickering because it takes 1/30th of a second for the whole frame to be scanned. 1/30th of a second is below the threshold level of persistence of vision.

12.1. (previous page) SMPTE 75% color bars — one of the most basic references in video.

You must be thinking: "But film is 1/24th of a second and we don't notice flicker there." Almost true. Film is shot at 24 frames per second. (With a 180° shutter this makes an exposure time of 1/50th of a second.) However, it is not *shown* at 1/24th of a second. If it was, there would be a noticeable flicker.

Projectors have a blade which passes across each frame as it is shown. This breaks each projected frame into two frames as seen by the eye: thus the film is being projected at 48fps. To reduce this flicker in video, engineers developed a system of "interlaced scanning." Interlacing means that as the beam scans down the screen it does not write the whole picture; instead, it writes every other line skipping every other line. This is called a field. A field is one half of the visual information of each frame. The two fields portray the same image but as alternate lines. The two of them together compose one video frame which is 1/30th of a second. Field one consists of all of the odd-numbered lines #1, #3, etc. Field two contains the even numbered fields #2, #4, etc. (Figure 12.2).

After field one is scanned for all the odd-numbered lines, a vertical sync pulse returns the scanning beam to the top of the picture tube and then scans all of the even-numbered lines. The persistence of the CRT phosphor is long enough that the first field remains displayed while the second is being written.

In NTSC, each frame is made up of 481 horizontal lines (240.5 lines per field) that are visible (sometimes called "active") plus another 44 lines (22 per field) that are blanked. These lines are blanked because they occur while the scanner beam is traveling back up to the starting point at the top left of the screen. If the beam was not blanked, there would be a smearing effect. This makes a total of 525 lines per frame. There are types of electronic information that come together to form a complete video image. Together they are called the television composite waveform, more commonly referred to as composite video (Figure 12.3).

12.2. Horizontal scanning on a video monitor.

THE COMPOSITE VIDEO SIGNAL

Early on the Institute of Radio Engineers divided this signal into units, called IRE units. It is now the IEEE — Institute of Electrical and Electronic Engineers, but most people in the field still call them IRE units. (IEEE is just too many syllables.) The basic signal 1 Volt Peak to Peak Video is divided up into 140 IRE units. This is done

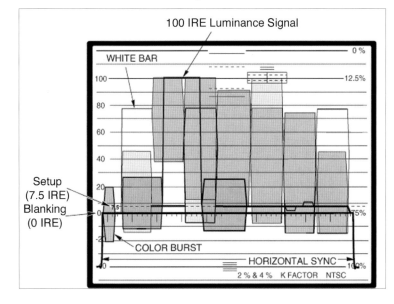

12.3. Components of the NTSC video signal. For more information on interpreting this diagram, see the following illustrations of the waveform monitor signal.

to make numbers for luminance levels easier to communicate. The amplitude of the video signal from blanking (zero volts) to peak white is 0.714286 volts or 100 IRE units. Synchronization signals extend from blanking to -1.285714 volts or -40 IRE units. The eight elements of the composite video signal include:

- Horizontal line sync pulse
- Color reference burst
- Reference black level
- Picture luminance information
- Color saturation information
- Color hue information
- Vertical sync pulse
- Horizontal blanking

Horizontal Sync Pulse
Before each line is scanned a horizontal sync pulse sets the electron beam to a locked position so that each scan line starts at the same position during scanning. The horizontal sync pulse tells each scan line where on the screen to start, so they don't wander around from field to field (Figure 12.4).

Color Reference Burst
To insure standard hue and color saturation, a 3.58 megahertz color reference burst is added before the picture information on each scan line. It is a sine wave with eight to nine cycles. Its phase is set at zero.

Reference Black Level
Black level is also called "setup" or "pedestal." Setup is one of the most basic adjustments we make to the video signal. It is variously called setup, pedestal or "picture" on a television set: but it's all the same thing — the lowest level of the video signal: basic black. Setup is 7.5 IRE units (Figure 12.5). For technical reasons it is not set at 0.0 units as one might expect. One critical difference between analog and digital video is that there is no setup in digital video; it is not necessary. All forms of digital video start at zero. This is because there is less chance for random variation, which the setup level is designed to protect against. Digital signals, at least at the processing level, are more controllable than analog signals. Once it gets to the display there is still variation.

Luminance
Luminance is the black to white range of the signal. It is the gray scale of the picture, without regard to color. Picture luminance ranges from 7.5 IRE units for black to 100 IRE units for peak white. This is what is called "legal video." Legal means that it is video signal that will work well on most monitors and television sets. It is important to understand that the video signal can go below 7.5 IRE and can go above 100, but this is liable to cause trouble in broadcasting or viewing.

But these limits are often exceeded, especially at the low end. "True black" that is 0 IRE units (0 volts on the signal) is a blacker black and gives a better picture. Cinematographers will often ask the telecine operator to "crush the blacks," meaning let the black end of the signal drop to near 0. This gives more contrast and a richer picture. (See the section on *Transferring Film to Video* later in this chapter for more on shooting gray scales and color bars in order to control your image in telecine.)

12.4. (below) The sync pulse on the waveform monitor. (Photo courtesy of Tektronix.)

12.5. (bottom) The black reference level on the waveform. (Photo courtesy of Tektronix.)

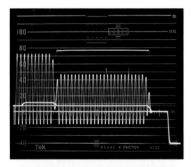

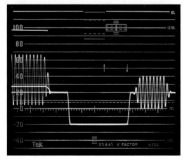

Color Saturation

Color information is interwoven with the black-and-white signal in the form of a 3.58 megahertz subcarrier. The saturation of the colors is determined by the amplitude of the subcarrier. The hue of the color is determined by comparing the phase of the subcarrier with the phase of the Color Reference Burst (see above).

Color Hue

As we recall from the chapter on color, hue is the spectral wavelength. It is what, in everyday language, we call "color." (See the chapter on *Color Theory*.) Color hue is also present in the 3.58 megahertz subcarrier. The accuracy of colors in the picture is determined by the phase or rotation of the color hue information.

Vertical Sync Pulse

When the scanning beam reaches the end of the bottom line, it must return to the top to start the next field. If it was visible while it swung back, there would be ghosting; this was a problem in early TV. The vertical sync pulse controls the length of time of the vertical blanking interval. The vertical blanking interval is sometimes used for inserting timecode, automatic color tuning and captioning information in the video signal. Since it doesn't have to carry video information it is a good place to place other types of data.

Horizontal Blanking Interval

There is also a horizontal blanking interval which occurs between the end of one scan line and the beginning of the next. This blanking interval is controlled by the horizontal sync pulse. As with the vertical interval, the scanning gun is turned off while the beam swings back to the left of the screen so there is no ghosting. Contained in this interval are the horizontal sync pulse and color reference burst.

THE WAVEFORM MONITOR AND VECTORSCOPE

To see the various elements of the composite video signal two special test oscilloscopes are used — the waveform monitor and the vectorscope (Figure 12.6). On a video shoot, the waveform monitor is your light meter and the vectorscope is your color meter. Color monitors, even very sophisticated ones, can be notoriously unreliable, but information for the waveform and vectorscope can almost always be trusted. Lighting "to the monitor" can lead to disaster, even in High Def.

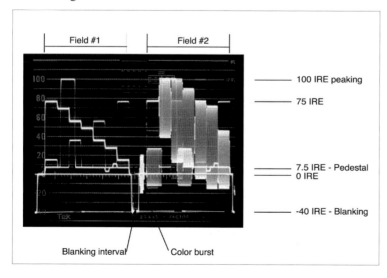

12.6. Video signal of SMPTE color bars on a waveform monitor. (Photo courtesy of Tektronix.)

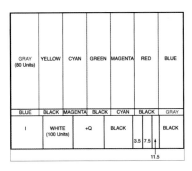

GRAY (80 Units)	YELLOW	CYAN	GREEN	MAGENTA	RED		BLUE

BLUE	BLACK	MAGENTA	BLACK	CYAN	BLACK		GRAY
I	WHITE (100 Units)	+Q		BLACK			BLACK

3.5 7.5
11.5

12.7. (above) SMPTE 75% color bars in diagram form. See 12.1 for a full color representation of the color bars.

12.8. (right) These color bars on a waveform show both fields. They include both luminance and chrominance information, which is why they are "filled in." (Photo courtesy of Tektronix.)

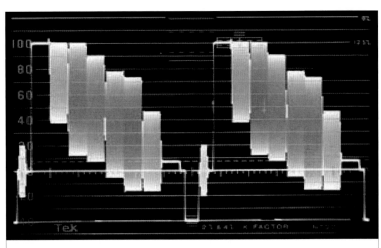

This 75% color bar signal also includes a 100% white reference.

The waveform monitor displays the black-and-white video signal information. It allows you to analyze the information from an entire frame or from just one line of video. The waveform monitor displays the signal on a scale seen in Figure 12.6.

Signals that are below 7.5 units (pedestal) lose detail and those above 100 units (maximum white) are washed out and without detail. Peaking above this signal can cause other problems in the system as well. If there is skin tone in the picture and it is in the +50 to +80 range it should appear properly exposed.

SMPTE COLOR BARS
Standard reference color bars are shown in Figure 12.1. On the waveform monitor they appear as in Figure 12.8. Remember, the waveform monitor measures luminance or brightness only, not color. What is represented here is the luminance value of each section of the color bar plus chrominance (saturation).

On the set you might wonder why you couldn't just look at a standard video monitor to see if your picture is what you want. The problem is that an ordinary picture monitor is not a reliable guide to the signal you are recording or to how that picture will look in the finished videotape; for that matter, even a very expensive monitor (and high end video monitors can cost $20,000 and more) will not be a true representation if it is not set up properly.

Monitors can be manipulated in terms of brightness, contrast, color balance, even sharpness. There is just no guarantee that they represent a true image of what you are shooting or of what is on tap. (See section below on Setting Up a Color Monitor.) When used with a video camera, the waveform monitor is a reliable guide to exposure and contrast range. If the average value of important information in the picture is over 100 or under 7.5 IRE units, the exposure is off. (Note the phrase important information. Clearly deep shadows may fall near or below 7.5 and some highlights may exceed 100). This exposure can be adjusted by changing the camera's aperture and/or by adjusting the lighting or the composition of the frame (if, for example, a "hot" window is in the shot). In telecine, the waveform monitor gives an accurate picture of the signal that is going to tape.

In post production the waveform monitor works the same way only this time it measures the values of images from videotape or other online devices like character generators or special effects generators.

At this point the video signal can still be manipulated in a number of ways: we'll look at those in another section.

THE VECTORSCOPE

Used in conjunction with the waveform monitor, the vectorscope measures the chrominance (color) of the video signal (Figure 12.9). The scale of the vectorscope is a circle overlaid with the color amplitude and phase relationship of the three primary colors (red, green and blue). In the center of this circle graph is the luminance (black-and-white) value of the signal. Through this center point, three axes represent the primary colors.

The vectorscope screen for setup shows a display of a SMPTE color bars test signal with all of the dots in their boxes and the color burst correctly placed on the horizontal axis. Chroma phase error translates as "the color is off" as shown in Figure 12.10. Notice how color is conceptualized as a circle and we rotate the circle around its center to adjust the hue. This relates to the original Newton color wheel. Also, notice how not all of the target boxes are equidistant from the center reference. This is a reflection of the same principle we saw in the Munsell color system: some colors reach full saturation (full chroma) at different levels. Now you see why we had to go through all that technical color theory stuff.

All vectorscope graticules are designed to work with a color bars signal. Remember, the color bars signal consists of brightness information (luminance) and high-frequency color information (chrominance or chroma). Each bar of the color bars signal creates a dot on the vectorscope's display. The position of these dots relative to the boxes, or targets, on the graticule and the phase of the burst vector are the major indicators of the chrominance (color) signal's health.

Proper white balance of a video camera is indicated by a fuzzy spot centered on the vectorscope display when the target or signal being displayed is a white object (Figure 12.16).

Chroma Gain

With the SMPTE color bars displayed the dots represent the peaks of chrominance. How far they are from the center indicates how much chroma gain there is; if they extend beyond the boxes, the chroma is too hot and can cause problems.

In post production, be it telecine transfer, off-line editing, on-line editing or tape duplication, the standard procedure is to record 60 seconds of color bars at the beginning of every tape. This insures that when processed and manipulated down the line, the colors will be the same from tape to tape.

LUMINANCE AND COLOR

The NTSC luminance component is very much like the signal for monochrome video — containing information about the amount of light in each element of the picture. This is one of the key reasons the NTSC system is "compatible" with older monochrome equipment — monochrome sets simply ignore the color information and display using luminance only.

Luminance is derived from RGB color signals. While the tristimulus theory requires three different colored lights, it assumes that each color contributes the same amount to our perception of brightness of an area in the image. In fact, for the particular colors chosen (a certain green, a certain blue, and a certain red), green contributes about 59% of our perception of brightness in a white part of the image.

The red light contributes about 30%, and blue only about 11% of

12.9. (top) The vectorscope. Think of it in terms of the color wheel. (Photo courtesy of Tektronix.)

12.10. (second from top) Hue error; notice how the color is shifted clockwise — the dots indicating the key hues are not in their proper boxes. (Photo courtesy of Tektronix.)

12.11. (third from top) Vectorscope showing correct chroma. The dots are in their boxes and also are not too far from or too near the center, indicating correct levels of chroma. (Photo courtesy of Tektronix.)

the brightness of white. As we recall from the discussion of the eye/ brain perception of color — the eye is most sensitive to color in the yellow/green range, and much less sensitive in the blue range. These numbers are called the luminance coefficients of the primary colors. The luminance signal is produced by combining (adding) the video signals from each primary color channel, taking into account the luminance coefficients of each primary, i.e., $Y = 0.59G + 0.30R + 0.11B$.

Color Difference Signals: B-Y And R-Y

To process all information as R, G and B is inefficient because each separate channel contains both color information and gray scale (luminance) information — this is redundant. As we recall from the chapter on color theory, black-and-white (gray scale) actually conveys the great majority of information about an image. For this reason, most video systems distill the chroma information into color difference signals. Luminance is notated as "Y," since "B" already stands for blue.

There are many systems in use, but basically, color difference is derived by taking the blue component and subtracting the luminance (gray scale) information: B-Y (blue minus luminance). Similarly, luminance is subtracted from red: R-Y. This process is fairly easy to accomplish with electronic circuits. (Sometimes, another set of color difference signals are used — I and Q. We'll discuss I and Q a little later.) With the color information now in the form of luminance (Y) and color difference components (B-Y and R-Y) we still have three signals and the associated bandwidth and interconnect problems. A bit more processing is needed to get it all into the "one-wire" NTSC signal format.

ENCODED COLOR

Another characteristic of human vision is we can't see fine detail nearly as well for changes in coloring as we can for changes in luminance. In other words, the picture won't suffer very much if we reduce the bandwidth of the coloring components, provided we can maintain essentially full bandwidth of the luminance signal. In fact, this is a good reason for developing color difference components in the first place.

Even a full bandwidth luminance signal doesn't have very much energy in the upper end of its spectrum — the higher frequency signals are quite a bit lower amplitude almost all the time. These two facts (less bandwidth required for the color information and some "room" available in the luminance spectrum) allow the NTSC system to place the color components in only the upper portion of the luminance spectrum.

THE PROCESSING AMPLIFIER

In addition to the waveform monitor and the vectorscope, the two most fundamental video tools, there is another — the processing amplifier. Commonly called a proc amp, this device can modify both the chroma and luminance values of the video signal. The proc amp should be used with both a waveform monitor and vectorscope to insure that the changes you are making are what you think you are making. As with most stages in the video system, it is just as easy to screw things up as it is to make them better.

This is similar to how you operate an ordinary household television. By adjusting color, contrast and the other controls, you can change the appearance of the picture. But you are not changing the actual signal of that picture — you are only changing the display of that signal. The proc amp lets you change the actual signal rather than just the display. This makes it in some ways more valuable and in some ways more dangerous. The proc amp can be an invaluable tool for correcting the color and luminance elements of a video signal. However, it must be used in conjunction with a waveform monitor and vectorscope for predictable results.

SETTING UP A COLOR MONITOR

The most important thing you can learn about video is how to properly set up a color monitor. Even with other equipment such as a waveform monitor and vectorscope on hand, the monitor is still a crucial part of previewing and judging the picture. As we saw in the chapter on color theory, there is not an exact correlation between the mathematical representation of color and the human perception of it.

Color bars are an artificial electronic pattern produced by a signal generator which may be in a video camera (most professional video cameras have a "bars" setting) or a separate piece of equipment on the set or as a standard piece of equipment in any video post-production facility, be it telecine, editing or duplication. Color bars are recorded at the head of every videotape to provide a consistent reference in post production. They are also used for matching the output of two cameras in a multi-camera shoot and to set up a video monitor. On top on the left is a gray bar: it is 80 IRE units.

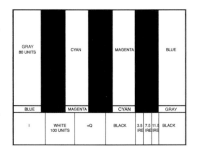

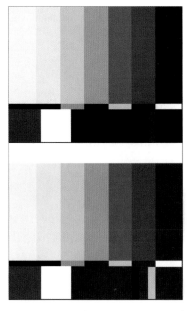

MONITOR SETUP PROCEDURE

To set up a monitor, start with the following steps:

- Allow the monitor to warm up.
- Shield the monitor from extraneous light.
- Display color bars on the monitor: either from the camera or a separate generator.
- Set the contrast (also called "picture") to its midpoint.
- Turn the chroma (also called "color") all the way down until the color bars are shades of black-and-white.

The PLUGE

Notice the three narrow bars labeled 3.5, 7.5 and 11.5 on the bottom right (Figures 12.12 and 12.14). These are the PLUGE, which stands for Picture Lineup Generating Equipment.

The PLUGE was developed at the BBC. It was generated at a central location in their facility and sent by wire to each studio. This way all of the equipment could be calibrated conveniently. This was the PLUGE alone, not combined with the color bars.

The middle black is set at 7.5 IRE black, (or in the digital realm, 16,16,16). The first chip, superblack, is set at about 2.5 IRE below black, and the third chip, dark gray is set at about 3.5 IRE above black. None of these really work to adjust a monitor to properly display 0 IRE black, so the following procedure is standard.

- Adjust the brightness control until the middle (7.5 units) PLUGE bar is not quite visible. The lightest bar on the right (11.5 units) should be barely visible. If it's not visible, turn the brightness up until it becomes visible.
- Since 7.5 units is as dark as video gets, you should not see any difference between the left bar (3.5 units) and the middle bar (7.5 units). There should be no dividing line between these two bars. The only division you should see is between 11.5 and 7.5. This same technique is used in setting the black-and-white viewfinder on a video camera.

12.12. (second from top) Diagram of blue only signal.

12.13. (third from top) Correct monitor setup, shown here in black-and-white.

12.14. (bottom) Incorrect luminance; notice how all three of the PLUGE bars in the lower right are visible.

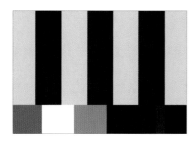

12.15. Blue-only color bars shown in black-and-white for clarity. Notice that the bands are of equal intensity and in the upper portion the large and small bars are equally gray or black.

- The next step is to set the contrast control for a proper white level. To do so, turn the contrast all the way up. The white (100 unit) bar will bloom and flare. Now turn the contrast down until this white bar just begins to respond. The image below shows what it should look like at this point.

Adjusting Color

It is possible to "eyeball" the yellow and magenta. This is the "down and dirty" method and should only be used if other methods are not practical. The yellow should be a lemon yellow without orange or green. And the magenta should not be red or purple. This quickie method is not recommended except in emergencies; it is much better to do it the professional way.

Blue-Only Adjustment

Most professional monitors have a blue-only switch (Figure 12.15). This turns off the red and green guns, leaving only the blue. If your monitor does not have a blue-only switch, you can use a piece of blue gel (full CTB) or a Kodak Wratten #47 — the purest blue in the wratten series. View the monitor through the gel. If you see any of the red, green or yellow colors, double the blue gel over to increase the blue effect.

By using the blue-only switch or a piece of blue gel, you have removed the red and green elements of the picture. Only the blue remains. If the hue is correct, you should see alternating bars of equal intensity.

- With the blue switch on (or your blue gel in front of your eye) turn the chroma or color until the gray bar at the far left and the blue bar at the far right are of equal brightness. You can also match either the gray or blue bars with their sub-bars.
- Adjust the hue control until the cyan and magenta bars are also of equal brightness. You can also match either of them with their sub-bars. Now the four bars — gray, blue, cyan and magenta should be of equal intensity. The yellow, green and red (which are black in the diagram below) should be completely black. Here's a diagram (Figure 12.15) and in color (Figure 12.16.)

Once you have set up your monitor, leave it alone. Unless you have a waveform and vectorscope, it's the only instrument you have to see how accurate your video is. This is true of your camera viewfinder, your field monitor and your studio monitor.

CAMERA WHITE BALANCE

Just as we use film stocks of different color balance and camera filtration to adjust, in video, the white balance function compensates for variations in the color range of the source lighting. White balance is accomplished by aiming the camera at a pure white surface (usually a white card) and selecting the white balance function on the camera. The internal electronics then compensate for variations in color. Naturally, it is essential that the light illuminating the white card be the same as is in the scene, just as the light on a gray reference card in film must be the same as is on the scene.

Also, as in film, if you are using filters to alter the color, this must be removed for white balance or their effect will be erased by the white balance. The white balance function can also be used to "fool" the camera. If, for example, you want the overall color balance to be warm, you can put a cooling filter (blue) over the lens while doing color balance. The circuitry will then compensate and when you remove the filter over the lens, the image will then be warm. This

12.16. (bottom) White balance on a vectorscope — no chroma. (Photo courtesy of Tektronix.)

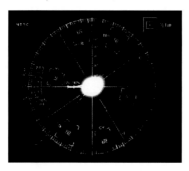

EFFECT DESIRED	USE FOR WHITE BALANCE
85	Harrison Blue #5
81EF	Tiffen Cyan #2
Tiffen Coral #2	Harrison Blue #5
Harrison Coral #2	Tiffen Cyan #1 or Harrison Blue #2
Harrison Coral #3	Harrison Blue #5
Tiffen Straw .3	Tiffen 80C
Tiffen Straw .6	Tiffen 80B+80D
Fries Tobacco #1	Tiffen 82B
Fries Tobacco #2	Tiffen 82C
Fries Tobacco #3	Tiffen 80C
Fries Tobacco #4	Tiffen 80C + 82B
Fries Tobacco #5	Tiffen 80B + Cyan #1
Tiffen Sepia #1	Tiffen 82B
Tiffen Sepia #3	Tiffen 80C
Tiffen Chocolate #2	Tiffen 82C + Tiffen Cyan #1

Table 12.1. Using color gels to "fool" the white balance for desired effect. (Data courtesy of Fotokem Film and Video.)

works for any color tone you want to add and can be accomplished by placing a filter over the light illuminating the card just as well as over the lens.

The same technique can be used in film when shooting the gray card. Table 12.1 indicates filters which will produce a specific effect in white balance or shooting the gray card.

ANALOG AND DIGITAL COLOR SPACE - RGB, YUV, YCbCr

There are many different colorspace systems and notations used to derive and define color video, especially digital video. Color cameras analyze the image to create video signals for the three primary colors: Red, Green and Blue. Since each of these RGB signals carries part of the information in the image, and all are required to recreate a complete image, they are referred to as "components" of the color video.

ANALOG/DIGITAL CONVERSION

Conversion of the video signal from analog to digital occurs in three parts; signal preparation, sampling and quantization (digitizing). There are two types of component signals; Red, Green and Blue (RGB), and Y, R-Y, B-Y but it is the latter which is by far the most widely used in digital video. R-Y and B-Y, the color difference signals, carry the color information while Y represents the luminance. Cameras, telecine, etc., generally produce RGB signals.

Y'CBCR, YCBCR

Y'CbCr is the color space used for all digital component video formats. Y' is the luma component and the Cb and Cr components are color difference signals. Cb is B-Y and Cr is R-Y. The technically-correct notation is Y'Cb'Cr' since all three components are derived from R'G'B'. Many people use the YCbCr notation rather than Y'CbCr or Y'Cb'Cr'.

Y'IQ, YIQ

Y'IQ is a color space optionally used by the NTSC video system. The Y' component is the black-and-white portion of the image. The I and Q parts are the color difference components; these are effectively nothing more than color placed over the black-and-white, or luminance, component. Many people use the YIQ notation rather than Y'IQ or Y'I'Q'.

Y'UV, YUV

Y'UV is the colorspace used by the NTSC and PAL video systems. Y' is the luminance component while the U and V are the color difference components. In the YCbCr (or YUV) representation, Y (luminance) information occurs only once, and the color is determined by the chrominance data in Cb (U) and Cr (V). Cb and Cr are difference values, derived by subtracting the luminance value from the blue component and from the red-luminance component. When the picture is displayed, the green component is reconstructed using the Cb and Cr values to reconstruct the RGB information.

DIGITAL VIDEO ENCODING

Digital video is fundamentally different from NTSC and PAL video in the way it is encoded and processed. Various types of processing equipment manage the digital video information in different ways. These are classified by the way in which they encode the information:

4:2:2

This is a set of frequencies in the ratio 4:2:2, used to digitize the luminance and color difference components (Y, R-Y, B-Y) of a video signal. For every four luminance digital samples, there are two digital samples of each color difference channel. The human eye is not as sensitive to color as to luminance detail enabling this form of compression. RGB video is usually represented with an equal number of bits for each of the three color component channels but RGB is not normally transmitted and bandwidth is not as big a factor when dealing with a connection between the computer and display device.

The four represents 13.5 MHz, the sampling frequency of the Y channel, and the twos each 6.75 MHz for both the R-Y, B-Y channels. D-1, D-5, Digital Betacam, and most digital disk recorders use 4:2:2 digitizing. 4:2:2 is the most common format used in the United States today.

4:1:1

This is a set of frequencies in the ratio 4:1:1, used to digitize the luminance and color difference components (Y, R-Y, B-Y) of a video signal. The four represents 13.5 MHz, the sampling frequency of the Y channel and the ones each 3.75 MHz for both the R-Y, B-Y channels. When U and V are sampled at a lower rate, the color information from the last pixel is simply replicated for the next pixel (or next three pixels for 4:1:1).

4:2:0

This is a set of frequencies in the ratio 4:2:0, used to digitize the luminance and color difference components (Y, R-Y, B-Y) of a video signal. The four represents 13.5 MHz, the sampling frequency of the Y channel, while both the R-Y and B-Y are sampled at 6.75 MHz

4:4:4

YUV = four 8-bit Y samples, four 8-bit U samples, and four 8-bit V samples per unit of time. Some very high end equipment uses this encoding scheme.

IS IT BROADCAST QUALITY?

"Broadcast quality" is a term that frequently gets misused. It does not mean, as many people think, a "good quality" picture or merely a certain level of resolution. Broadcast quality is actually a complex and arcane set of standards for the timing, synchronization and levels of the video signal. It is something that can only be measured with expensive and arcane test equipment. It is purely the province of video engineers. However, even some manufacturers misuse the term to mean a "high quality" video signal or tape format.

TIMECODE AND EDGECODE

Film has long had an identifying edgecode to identify each frame (or nearly each frame) in the post production process. To provide a similar identifier for video, the Society of Motion Picture and Television Engineers (SMPTE) formalized Timecode as a method of giving each frame a unique address. This code is an eight digit number, based on the 24 hour clock and the video frame rate. Timecode measures time in Hours:Minutes:Seconds:Frames. Since most tapes are one hour or less, the first segment is often used to designate the "roll number" of the tape. This is important in post production as it prevents duplication of timecodes when using more than one tape, important since all but the shortest of productions involve multiple tapes.

The values range from 00:00:00:00, to the largest number supported by this format; 23:59:59:29, or, no more than 23 hours, no minutes or seconds greater than 59, and no frames above the highest allowed by the rate being used (29 in this case for 30 frames/sec). This format represents actual clock time — the duration of scene or program material, and makes time calculations easy and direct.

There are two ways to do timecode in the course of shooting. In the first method, each tape is cued up to the beginning and the timecode is set to start at all zeros, except for the hours, which designate tape number. In the second method, the timecode is left to run free, based on clock time. This gives each tape unique numbers, unless you shoot past midnight, in which case there is some chance of duplication.

VIDEO FRAME RATE

The frame is the smallest unit of measure within SMPTE Timecode and is a direct reference to the individual "picture" of film or video. Some timecode readers display a small blip or other symbol at the end to indicate odd or even field, but there is no number designation for it.

The rate is the number of times per second pictures are displayed to provide motion. There are four standard frame rates (frames/sec) that apply to SMPTE: 24, 25, 30, and 30 "Drop Frame."

- 24fps Frame rate based on U.S. standard motion picture film
- 25fps Frame rate based on European motion picture film and video, also known as SMPTE EBU (PAL/SECAM color and b&w)
- 30fps Frame (also called "30 frame Non-drop")
- 30fps Drop Frame

The frames figure advances one count for every frame of film or video, allowing the user to time events down to 1/24th, 1/25th, or 1/30th of a second. Unless you have an application that specifically calls out one of the above frame rates, it doesn't matter which timecode is used as long it is consistent. Most SMPTE applications outside of broadcast video use the 30 frame non-drop rate because it matches real time.

12.17. A timecode slate in use on a film set. As shown here, it can be setup to display the date for a couple of frames after slating.

DROP-FRAME AND NON DROP-FRAME

29.97 video can be written in either drop-frame or non-drop-frame format. The difference between the two is that with drop-frame format the frame address is periodically adjusted (once every minute) so that it exactly matches real time (at the 10 minute mark), while with non-drop-frame format the frame address is never adjusted and gets progressively further away from real time. See below for an explanation of drop-frame numbering.

29.97 VIDEO

Frame rate is the rate at which video records and plays back frames. As with film, it is expressed as frames per second. Before the introduction of color, video ran at a true 30 frames per second (fps). When the color portion of the signal was added, video engineers were forced to slow the rate down to 29.97fps. The reason for this is to prevent interference with the color subcarrier. This slight slowdown of video playback leads to disagreement in the measurement of video vs. real time; one second is not evenly divisible by 29.97.

A frame rate of 29.97fps is 99.9% as fast as 30fps. It is 0.1% (or one-thousandth) slower: 29.97fps / 30fps = .999 (or 99.9%). This means that a frame rate of 30fps is 0.1% (or one-thousandth) faster than 29.97: 30fps / 29.97fps = 1.001 (or 100.1%).

If it were running at precisely 30fps, one hour of video would contain exactly 108,000 frames. 30 frames x 3600 seconds = 108,000 frames total. However, since video does not actually run at 30fps, playing back 108,000 frames of video will take longer than one hour to play because: (108,000 frames) / (29.97 frames/sec) = 3,603.6 seconds = 1 hour and 3.6 seconds. In timecode this is written as 01:00:03:18. All this means that after an hour, the playback is 108 frames too long. Once again, we see the relationship of 108 frames out of 108,000, or 1/1000th. Sixty seconds of 30fps video contains 1800 frames. One-thousandth of that is 1.8. Therefore, by the end of one minute you are off by 1.8 frames. You cannot adjust by 1.8 frames per minute, because you cannot adjust by a fraction of a frame, but you can adjust by 18 full frames per 10 minutes. Two frames in 2000 accumulates 18 frames in 18,000, and there are 18,000 frames in 10 minutes.

HOW DROP FRAME SOLVES THE PROBLEM

Because 10 minutes is not evenly divisible by 18 frames, we use drop-frame timecode and drop two frame numbers every minute; by the ninth minute, you have dropped all 18 frame numbers. No frames need to be dropped the tenth minute because actual frames and timecode frames are once again in agreement.

Thus the formula for the correcting scheme is: drop frame numbers 00:00 and 00:01 at the start of every minute except the tenth. (This also translates to dropping two frame numbers every 66 2/3 seconds.) This sequence repeats after exactly ten minutes. This is a consequence of the ratios of the numbers: Two frames in 2000 accumulates 18 frames in 18,000, and there are 18,000 frames in 10 minutes (30 frames, times 60 seconds, times 10 minutes. In Table 12.2 — 00:10:00:00 in drop-frame is the same as 00:10:00:00 in real time. Also, 10 minutes of NTSC video contains an exact number of frames (17,982 frames), so every tenth minute ends on an exact frame boundary. This is how drop-frame timecode manages to get exactly one hour of video to read as exactly one hour of timecode.

TO DROP OR NOT TO DROP?

It is not necessary to use drop-frame timecode in all instances. Drop-frame is most important in applications where exact time is critical,

Minute	Start Position	Frames Lost	Drop Frame	Adjusted Position
1		1.8 lost this minute	drop 2 to correct	0.2 ahead
2	0.2 ahead	1.8 lost this minute	drop 2 to correct	0.4 ahead
3	0.4 ahead	1.8 lost this minute	drop 2 to correct	0.6 ahead
4	0.6 ahead	1.8 lost this minute	drop 2 to correct	0.8 ahead
5	0.8 ahead	1.8 lost this minute	drop 2 to correct	1.0 ahead
6	1.0 ahead	1.8 lost this minute	drop 2 to correct	1.2 ahead
7	1.2 ahead	1.8 lost this minute	drop 2 to correct	1.4 ahead
8	1.4 ahead	1.8 lost this minute	drop 2 to correct	1.6 ahead
9	1.6 ahead	1.8 lost this minute	drop 2 to correct	1.8 ahead
10	1.8 ahead	1.8 lost this minute	drop 0	

Table 12.2. How drop-frame timecode works to correct errors.

such as broadcast television. For short pieces that are not going to be broadcast, standard timecode is acceptable, the slight mismatch will be of no consequence. In 25 Hz video (all countries that don't use NTSC), such as in 625/50 video systems, and in 24 Hz film, there is an exact number of frames in each second. As a result, drop-frame is not necessary. There is no drop frame in 24p High Def video.

TIMECODE SLATING TIPS
When slating with timecode, always pre-roll audio and timecode for at least five seconds. This is critical for syncing up the dailies in telecine. Timecode driven equipment (which includes the telecine and audio syncing decks, as well as playback and edit decks) takes at least five seconds to come up to speed and lock. Not having good pre-roll can definitely cause problems. Pre-roll is handled by the sound recordist. Where in the old days, the AD would call "roll sound" and the mixer would only call "speed" when the old tape decks finally lumbered up to the correct speed, the mixer now waits the appropriate time for pre-roll to lay down before calling "speed."

In telecine there is an "offset" that occurs. Sometimes the smart slate numbers and the sound don't line up. This must be dealt with at some point down the line. There is a valuable additional feature with the Denecke timecode slate. As the clap stick is help open, the timecode rolls freely so that it can be checked. As the clapper is brought down, the timecode freezes momentarily, which makes it easier for post-production people to read it without searching for the exact frame that matches the clap. But after that, the date appears momentarily. This additional feature insures that there will be no duplication of timecode and adds another identification that simplifies keeping things in order.

TIMECODE ON VIDEOTAPE
Timecode is recorded onto analog videotape in two different ways: Longitudinal Timecode (LTC) and Vertical Interval Timecode (VITC). Digital video is an entirely different matter — it is just part of the digital signal.

Longitudinal Timecode
Timecode is recorded on studio videotape and audiotape recorders in the same way as audio is recorded. LTC is interfaced in the studio as an audio signal. At normal play speed, LTC can be decoded from tape as long as the playback system. To recover timecode at the shuttle rates of a high-quality studio VTR — about 60 times play speed — requires an audio bandwidth about 60 times higher. Due to

the limitations of stationary head magnetic recording, longitudinal timecode from a VTR (or ATR) cannot be read at very slow speeds or with the tape stopped.

Vertical Interval Timecode
Vertical Interval Timecode (VITC) has a key advantage over LTC: it can be read even when the tape is not running at normal speed. In the vertical interval system, scan lines in the vertical interval of the video signal contain timecode data. This can be done because during the vertical interval, when the scan is returning to the top left of the screen, information is not needed to create video — it can be used for other purposes.

SHOOTING HIGH DEF VIDEO
High definition video is similar to shooting ordinary video in some ways, but quite different in other ways. High Def cameras offer considerably more control than other types of video cameras. These controls are either accessed through menus on the camera or through remote "paint box" units which come in a variety of configurations from fairly simple ones which can be used by a trained videographer or cinematographer on the set to very complex ones which are the province of engineers. The 16x9 format is shown in Figure 12.19.

Any paintbox should be used only by people who know what they are doing as it is permanently affecting the image on tape — many effects cannot be undone in post and there is always a possibility you may be making your choices based on an improperly set up monitor or viewfinder.

High Def cameras, including the Panasonic 27V (Figure 12.21), the Sony 900 series (Figures 12.18 and 12.20) and the Panavision 24p camera based on it, use 2/3" CCD video receptors. This gives them a depth-of-field similar to 16mm. As we discussed in the chapter on *Optics*, the smaller the format, the greater the depth-of-field. This poses a problem when trying to shoot with a shallow focus or attempting a dramatic rack, especially when trying to throw the background out of focus to lessen the effect of distracting colors and objects behind the talent. You will want to avoid using regular video zooms on HD cameras — they just don't have the resolution. This doesn't appear on normal video or digital video but is very apparent in High Def. Lenses designed for HD, or better yet, film lenses, are

12.18. (right) The Sony F900 Cinealta — a High Def camera that can shoot 24p and other HD formats.

12.19. (below) Comparison of standard television format and High Def standard.

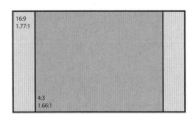

Table 12.3. High Def formats.

VERTICAL SIZE	HORIZONTAL (Pixel width)	INTERLACE or PROGRESSIVE	ASPECT RATIO	FRAME RATES
480	640	i	4:3	30
480	640	P	4:3	24, 30, 60
480	704	i	16:9	30
720	1280	P	16:9	24, 30, 60
1080	1920	i	16:9	30
1080	1920	P	16:9	24, 30
1080	1920	P	16:9	24, 30

the best choice to get maximum performance from these cameras.

There are a number of High Def formats; each one is appropriate to specific types of shooting, as shown as Tables 12.3 and 12.4. Not all High Def cameras can shoot all formats. Twenty-four frame progressive, or 24p is the format most often used for theatrical features. Progressive means that the scan lines are not interlaced as they are in normal video. This is especially important if the High Def video is going to be transferred to film for projection. There are several companies that handle this conversion to film and it is important to adhere to their varying requirements for shooting the original HD video in order to optimize the transfer to film.

Partly because the High Def cameras so closely resemble a normal video camera such as might be used for BetaSP production, it is often assumed that it is something of a "point and shoot" technology. This is definitely not the case, particularly if you are trying to get the most that the format can offer. A good deal of technical knowledge and experience are necessary to maximize the results, especially if you are trying to get a "film look."

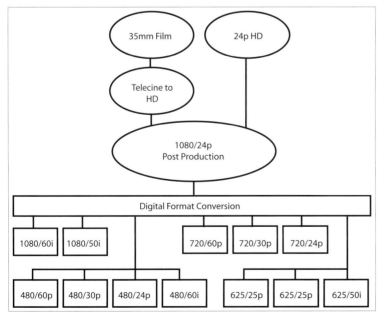

Table 12.4. (left) Typical interchanges between film and HD video formats.

12.20. (below) The Viper Filmstream camera from Thompson. Filmstream refers to its ability to record uncompressed RGB High Def data directly to a hard drive in the field. (Photo courtesy of Thompson Broadcast Solutions.)

12.21. The Panasonic AJ-HDC27V High Def camera set up for film style production. (Photo courtesy of Panasonic.)

Another myth is that you can choose to just "shoot it straight" and everything else can be done in post. This is not true; although there is more manipulation that can be done in post than might be possible in film, there are definitely some things you can do on the set that cannot be done in post and there are things you can screw up badly.

10 THINGS TO REMEMBER WHEN SHOOTING HIGH DEF

Here are some tips specific to working with High Definition cameras for narrative filming in general and particularly for digital projection or for transfer to film for standard projection:

- Control highlights: HD has trouble with them. This is similar to other types of video although not as bad.
- Don't crush the blacks. This sort of manipulation is perfectly valid, but is most likely something best left until post-production as it is irreversible.
- Nail exposure when you can, but if not, err on the side of underexposure, not overexposure (i.e., like reversal film).
- Don't turn up the detail if you are transferring to film.
- 1080 is a better choice for narrative storytelling. 720 is good for sports.
- Interlace always looks like video.
- Very wide lenses are not now available, although that may change.
- Biggest problem is too much depth of field — remember, focus is an important storytelling tool.
- Second biggest problem is seeing too much detail in things like makeup, sets and wardrobe.
- Shoot at 23.98 or 29.97, not 24 or 30. This will reduce artifacts later in the process.

LIGHTING FOR HIGH DEF VIDEO

High Def is much closer to film than non-High Def video but there are still differences. It tends to "see into the shadows" much more than film and it sees detail much more than film. This means that shadows you would expect to go black or nearly black in film are still visible in HD. This can have the effect of ruining the illusion; the same is true of HD's tendency to see more fine detail. The makeup and wardrobe departments must be especially on their toes. Tiny imperfections of sets and props can suddenly become obtrusive where on film they were more than acceptable. This is a big part of the "video look," which, while far less apparent on High Def can still be a problem if not dealt with properly. This problem is more complex than just detail resolution: it can be partially dealt with using diffusion filters but by no means entirely. Also, dealing with it in this way may mean using diffusion filters where you do not want to.

The idea that HD requires less lighting is quite simply a myth. HD cameras have a speed equivalent to around ISO 320 — not really that fast in relation to film. People who claim that HD video needs less lighting are probably just willing to settle for bad lighting.

This is much the same as happened with the advent of high speed lenses and high speed film (ISO 320, which is now more of a medium speed film, with ISO 500 and 800 being the real high speed stocks). Overenthusiastic supporters claimed that fewer people would be needed on the crew and fewer lights. None of this is true, of course. At best, you need a smaller generator and lighter gauge distribution cable and slightly smaller lights.

Think of it this way — say you light a scene beautifully with four lights: a 12K through the window, a 10K raking down the hallway, a 2K bounce for a key on the scene and a baby-junior for a backlight. Let's now assume that the speed of your video camera (or motion picture film) doubles (a very big jump in speed). Does this mean you need fewer lights? Not unless you want to do less lighting — that is, give up something important. You still need four lights — the only difference is that instead of a 12K you need a 6K, instead of a 10K you can use a 5K, and so on. Doubling the speed is a giant leap technologically, but in terms of exposure and lighting it is only one stop. Can you "get an exposure" using fewer lights? Of course you can. But as a cinematographer or director, if you are willing to say that just "getting an exposure" is your goal in lighting, then you don't need to be reading books like this one.

"Video lighting" has a bad reputation. This is not really the fault of video or of the people who shoot video. It is really a result of production circumstances: video is for the most part employed where producers don't have the money for film. Since video is perceived as not being capable of delivering the image quality of film, the producers also usually make the decision to spend less on lighting. How often have you seen a normal video production with five electricians and five grips and a 10-ton truck of lighting and grip?

The result is that video has a reputation as something you "don't light as much" as film. The great danger of High Def is not that it will replace film but that the expectations and values of the decision makers and the audience will decline and that this lower level of production value will become the accepted norm. This is not to be confused with the idea that simpler lighting can be more beautiful — it often is. Indeed, most DPs find that as they learn more about lighting and have the benefit of years of experience and experimentation that they tend to use fewer lights to get the same effect.

This is a function of a greater knowledge of what you can do with few units and the wisdom of years of doing it. This is a different issue, however. The key words are "the same effect," not "settling for less" just because it's video. Of course, there are times when you can light an entire scene with nothing but a china ball, (and it can be a thrilling experience when it really works), but there are many more times when you cannot. In terms of people and equipment you need what you need to light adequately — not to mention artistically and expressively in the service of the storytelling. Convincing a reluctant producer of this is an important skill to learn as a DP.

SHOOTING DIGITAL VIDEO
Digital video exists in many forms — DigiBeta, DV, DVCam, DVCPro and MiniDV. These differ in methods of compression, recording formats, tape speed and tape cassette size but all are similar in that they take an analog signal and convert it to digital — see the previous section on *Analog/Digital Conversion* for more on the various formats.

As with all things digital, the equipment available changes almost on a daily basis; as you decide what to use for your project side-by-side comparisons will be most helpful. Naturally the producer will be most concerned about the cost/benefit ratio of the various formats. Although video is generally much cheaper than film, shooting on video may have very serious implications for your post-productions costs and for the sales value of the finished product. These are the producer's concerns but it is your job as the cinematographer or director to make sure that the cost concerns are balanced with both the visual quality the system can produce and what its other capabilities are. For example, at the present time, no video camera, not even a top-of-the-line High Def camera can shoot true high speed. This has implications especially if you are shooting action sequences or anything else that requires a true slo-mo effect.

Certainly if you are attempting to bring to bear the entire arsenal of methods and techniques of cinematography, the lens systems will be of primary importance to you. Some cameras do offer interchange-able lenses and the quality of video lenses is improving. The size and quality of the CCD (the video receptor) is also important, not only for image quality but for focus — the smaller the CDD the greater the depth-of-field. At first glance this might seem like a good thing, but remember that depth-of-field is an important storytelling tool; too much depth-of-field restricts or even eliminates the possibility of using this important tool. This has implications beyond just the camera; for example, some cinematographers shooting projects on digital video that were formerly shot on film are finding that without the ability to restrict focus to the main subject, that distracting background set dressing or props are more obtrusive. Since the possibility of throwing them out of focus is restricted, redressing the set or changing the background is a last resort stopgap. This calls for co-operation from other departments and from the director.

Beyond this, the day-to-day operation of a digital video camera is much the same no matter what the recording format: white balancing, setting up the monitor, setting exposure and so on are essentially the same. Although much less than in the past, lighting ratios much be accommodating to the particular camera; although as we have pointed out, it is not always simply a matter of "adding more fill," indeed in some cases, negative fill may be required as you are seeing too much into the shadows.

TRANSFERRING FILM TO VIDEO

NTSC AND 3:2 PULLDOWN
When transferring American system film (24fps) to NTSC video (29.97fps), there is a mismatch of speed which must be corrected. NTSC has 60 fields/second (2 fields per frame), thus five fields take 5/60 second = 1/12 second time, which is exactly the amount it takes for a film to show two frames. The solution to the problem is that each frame of film is not transferred to a corresponding frame of video.

The first film frame is transferred to 3 NTSC fields. Next the second film frame is transferred to 2 NTSC fields. The total time for the original film should be 2/24s = 1/12s, which is exactly the same it took for NTSC to transfer the same frames (3/30s+2/60s = 5/60s = 1/12s). This process alternates for successive frames. This is called 3-to-2 pulldown, usually written as 3:2 pulldown. The problem with this is that every other film frame is shown for 1/20 of a second, while every other is shown for 1/30 of a second. This makes pans look less smooth than what they did in the movie theater or in PAL video, which does not require this process (Figure 12.22).

PREPPING FOR TELECINE
A great deal of film that is shot now goes from the processing lab to a telecine house where it is transferred directly to video (Figure 12.23). Even features intended for theatrical release are telecined for non-linear editing and for video dailies. It is important to follow the correct steps to prepare for telecine. Failure to do so will cost the producer considerably extra, which is not good for job security.

- If you are doing anything at all out of the ordinary: green-screen, unusual color balances, off speed shooting, etc., it is best to confer with the telecine house before you start.

12.22. How 3-to-2 pulldown works.

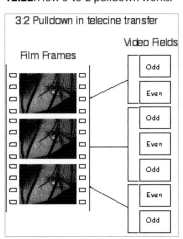

3:2 Pulldown in telecine transfer

Video Fields

Film Frames

Odd
Even
Odd
Even
Odd
Even
Odd

- Film will be transferred at 24 frames per second with standard SMPTE framing unless specifically requested otherwise. Transfer rates other than 16-30fps may not be available at all telecine houses — check before you shoot.
- Shoot a properly exposed and color balanced Gray Scale. It's a good place for the colorist to start.
- Communicate with the telecine operator. A phone call, a memo or notes on the camera reports are important. Some DPs also send audio recording with comments and also Polaroids of the scene; even pictures from a magazine that you are using as a reference or similar material.
- Full and accurate camera reports. This is especially important if you are shooting at an off-speed frame rate AND want the footage transferred at that rate.
- Write it on the slate. All slates have spaces to record if the shot is day or night, interior or exterior and frame rate. Some also have places for filtration and other key data.
- Make sure the slate is in focus and lit to be readable.
- Mark the camera reports as "Prep for telecine." When this is requested, the lab cleans the negative and joins the camera rolls into lab rolls no larger than 1200 feet with 6 feet of leader on each end. In some cases, editors may request hole punches at head and tail of each camera roll and a KeyKode log. KeyKode is a written log recording the first and last KeyKode number for each camera roll within a lab roll. It is prepared by the lab during negative assembly and used by the Editor to check the accuracy of the flex file (a computer file database).
- Use correct slating procedures (see chapter on Set Operations). This is especially important if you are doing MOS takes or tail slating. If an MOS take is not properly slated, the transfer technician can spend considerable time looking for audio that does not exist.
- Shoot a framing chart and communicate to the colorist what framing you are shooting. This is especially important with formats such as Super 35. Be sure that the framing chart agrees with your ground glass and also that all the ground glasses on your shoot agree.

AUDIO FOR TELECINE
Most transfer houses require that sync audio for telecine be recorded at 30fps not using Drop Frame timecode. Audio should never be

recorded at 29.97fps. When shooting sync sound, a timecode slate can save considerable amounts of time and money. See the section on Timecode for information on timecode slates. Don't forget that the slate has a brightness adjustment — be sure it is set properly for your shooting conditions and if it's too bright, use a gel to take it down — unreadable slates are expensive! See the chapter on *Set Operations* for proper use.

PRE-ROLL

Always pre-roll audio for 5 seconds or more. This is done by rolling audio (which is recording timecode) before syncing with the slate (either a timecode slate or an ordinary slate).

The audio and smart slate timecodes must be in sync. It is important to re-jam the slate frequently to make sure it is in sync with the audio recorder. The slate is "jammed" by connecting it to the timecode output of the audio recorder. The timecode from audio is loaded into the slate where it runs on its own crystal clock. This is usually accurate for several hours, but it MUST be rejammed periodically. Some slates will say "Feed Me" when they sense they need rejamming.

The AC and operator should also look at the slate as the 2nd AC holds it up before the take; sometimes the timecode will not be running. Stop and correct the problem before you shoot. To help check for sync between audio and timecode, before the first take of the day roll 10 seconds with the slate open and sound running at speed, and then clap the sticks and run 5 more seconds. The sound recordist should make note of the timecode of any wild tracks.

EDITORIAL NEEDS

Because of the needs of non-linear, computer based editing, editors often request additional services during the dailies transfer to assist them in editing and finishing the project. Preparing elements for non-linear editing can be considerably more involved than for old-style one light film prints.

The editor may require KeyKode, a simo audio DAT with address track timecode, 2 or more simo 3/4″ SP or Beta cassettes, (with or without burned in windows), digital flex files with floppy discs or print outs, KeyKode logs, etc. A simo DAT is a first generation digital clone DAT of the audio made during the dailies transfer with timecode that matches the video dailies tapes. It is used by the editor for auto conforming sound during the final transfer and mix. A simo may also be a 3/4″ Umatic tape or BetaSP tapes.

A flex file is a computer file created at the time of the telecine transfer. It is a relational database that logs all timecode, keykode, audio code in and out points for every telecine edit. It also has scene, take, camera roll, lab roll, audio roll and tape numbers. The flex file is used by the editor to digitize dailies into a non-linear edit system and to create a negative cutter's list from the timecode EDL. It may be a KeyKode log disk, Evertz log, etc. It is important to check with the editor to make sure what is needed before the time of telecine transfer. Doing it later can be much more expensive.

SHOOTING A GRAY CARD REFERENCE

Using a gray card applies to both film finish and to film transferred to video. It is discussed here in relation to telecine and adjusting on the waveform monitor but lighting and shooting are the same for both situations. In video, a gray card may be used but the real standard is color bars, which are discussed in the chapter on video.

GRAY CARD PLUS

Kodak makes a simple tool which can be very helpful in telecine transfer. It is the Gray Card Plus, which consists of a large 18% neutral gray area bordered by 3% and 90% reflectance black-and-white patches to provide further reference for grading. The surface is specially treated to minimize glare. The Gray Card Plus (Figure 12.24) can be used to determine telecine transfer points, provide exposure information and help the telecine colorist or film timer create the effect the cinematographer is looking for.

THE GRAY CARD PLUS AS A REFERENCE IN TELECINE

In the telecine transfer room, the colorist shuttles to a frame showing the gray card and stops the film. She then adjusts the controls of the telecine and watches the results on the waveform monitor. Kodak recommends waveform monitor settings of 80 IRE units for the 90% reflectance patch, 45 IRE for the 18% gray card and 20 IRE to correspond to the 3% reflectance black patch. Some people feel these values result in initial grading that's too flat.

Many cinematographers prefer that they be placed at something more along the lines of white, 85 IRE, gray, 50 IRE and black, 15 IRE. The settings you suggest will produce snappier looking dailies, with more contrast and "blacker blacks" — sometimes called "stretch and crush." The recommended IRE values of 80 - 45 - 20 IRE were chosen partly with tape-to-tape transfers in mind; the intent being to preserve a wider range of contrast for final grading options. This goes along with the philosophy of many telecine facilities. If they are producing video dailies which will then be used for the final edit in a "tape-to-tape" transfer, they will always keep the initial transfer fairly neutral and without much manipulation.

This can be very frustrating for the cinematographer who is trying to achieve a certain look with off-color lighting or other than normal exposures. The dailies will come back looking very bland and neutral and uninitiated directors and producers will think you are not doing your job correctly. It is painful and embarrassing but in the end, it does provide a product with greater range of manipulation in the final result.

You should always insist on being present for the tape-to-tape transfer. This is where the real grading decisions will be made; just as they used to be made by sitting in a screening room with the film timer. Kodak says in the instructions, "Make corrections, if needed, to improve overall color and contrast." The dark patches reflect 3%; the light patches 90%. Why 20 IRE instead of 7.5 for the dark patches and 80 IRE instead of 100 for the light patches?

The values that are used were chosen to be slightly above the toe and just below the shoulder of the contrast curve. This makes them less susceptible to variations in the film stock. Emulsions tend to differ more in the toe and shoulder areas than they do in the straight line portion of the characteristic curve.

Also, a solid black and a pure white would narrow the threshold of adjustment on a wave-form monitor. It is difficult to set a pure black-and-white reference precisely at 7.5 and 100 IRE (0 and 700mv) respectively when you're operating low on the toe and high on the shoulder. There's also the effect of lens flair to consider with only a solid black bottom reference. Even though the finish of the card (as is true of most high quality gray cards) is as matte as possible, there is always going to be the possibility of some slight glare. Some people also put an absolute black (nonreflective) reference such as fuzzy Velcro or good quality velvet on the chart and then ask the colorist to place that chip at absolute black of the color system. If

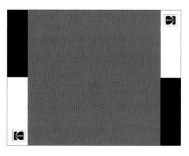

12.24. The Kodak Gray Card Plus.

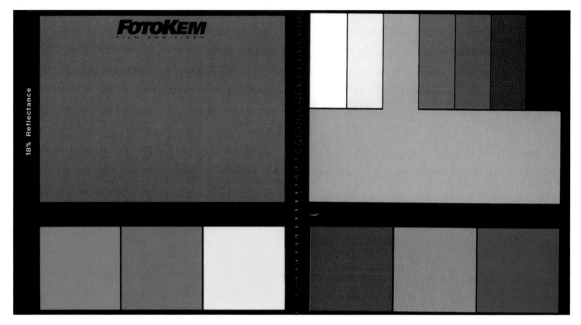

12.25. A color chart and gray scale. (Photo courtesy of FotoKem Film and Video.)

you set a black velvet patch at 7.5 IRE (0 mv), the 3% dark patches on the GC+ should read around 15 IRE (100 mv).

The biggest problem with any gray card reference is the way it's shot. With uneven lighting on the card or a hasty shot in the scene with little relevance to the lighting, there's no way a gray card can serve as an accurate reference. A gray card should be shot out of the scene and lit specifically as a grading reference or as an exposure reference to determine transfer points. For example, suppose you are lighting a scene with the key as moonlight blue — which you intend to be very dark and shadowy (Figure 12.25).

If you then place the gray card in this moonlight blue and shoot it, the colorist or film timer (absent other instructions) would have no choice but to make the gray card "neutral gray" as it is supposed to be. This would be done by taking out all of the blue and raising the exposure to lighten it up. Thus everything you have tried to do with the lighting would be erased. The proper way to shoot a gray card reference is this:

For a tungsten lit scene: position the gray card so it fills all or most of the frame. Have your gaffer light it with a unit that is as near to pure 3200° Kelvin as possible. Make sure there are no filters on the light and it is not on a dimmer. The light should cover the card as evenly as possible, without shadows. No other colors of light should be leaking onto the card from elsewhere in the scene. Make sure that the camera filtration is neutral also: remove any effects filters you have on. Meter the gray card without regard to your metering of the scene. For real precision it is best to take both an incident reading right at the card and also a reflected reading with the spot meter. They should agree. Shoot the card at that stop. Shoot several seconds, but there is no need to get carried away. The telecine operator will freeze the frame on the card and make adjustments. Similarly, the film timer can stop the film on the Hazeltine machine. They don't try to do it "on the fly."

If you are shooting daylight balance follow all of the above instructions but make sure your gray scale light is 5500° Kelvin. The ideal situation is to light the gray card (or gray scale or color chart) so that the exposure on it is exactly the same as the stop at which you

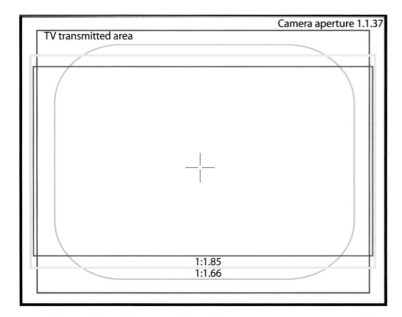

12.26. Framing chart for video, film 1.85 and High Def. (Photo courtesy of Mako Kowai.)

are going to shoot the scene. Then it becomes a two step procedure. Shoot the gray card as outlined above. Move the gray card and shoot a few seconds of the scene as you have it lit — color gels, camera filters back in, etc. This gives the colorist not only a neutral reference, but also shows the scene in relation to that neutral reference. It is mostly psychological — it is way of showing the timer; "Yes, I really meant for it to look that way."

The exception to all of the above is when the card is to serve as a guide for color correction, e.g., fluorescent lighting without camera filter correction, no 85 filter outdoors, etc. For example, if you are shooting under fluorescents and you want the lab or the telecine operator to *remove* the green and make the lighting neutral, then by all means make sure that the "contaminated" source is what is lighting the gray card. This is much more exact and under your control than just writing "correct for fluorescent" on the camera report, although you must always note it on the report as well.

Use of a gray card or gray scale in this way applies equally to both NTSC and PAL video transfers, analog or digital. Gray scales are just as helpful as gray cards and should be lit and shot in the same way. Color charts are also useful but not nearly as much as a neutral gray reference, the reason being that a gray reference can be quantified on the waveform and vectorscope.

Even though charts such as the Macbeth color chart are produced under rigorous conditions, and extremely accurate, they have one flaw: the timer or colorist has no direct reference. Unless he or she has the same color chart in the room, there is no way to know how it is supposed to look. Even in this case, the lighting in the telecine room would not match what is on the set — remember metamerism. Other ways of communicating with the colorist or timer include Polaroids, references to photographs from magazines (which you send over), notes on the slate or camera report, phone calls and even audio tapes with commentary.

FRAMING CHARTS

Another part of your vision that you need to protect with references is the framing. Without a reference on the film, the telecine colorist has no way of knowing for certain what your exact framing is. Remember that he can move the frame up/down, left/right

12.27. Frame options in telecine: X, Y and Z axes. Not all telecines have the Z or zoom axis.

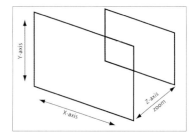

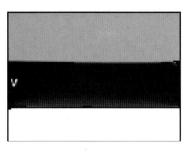

12.28. Kodak TEC test frame.

and zoom in or out over the entire area of the negative or positive frame. A framing chart is something he can copy to the frame store and quickly call it up to transfer all scenes exactly as you intended. Figure 12.26 is a typical framing chart. Figure 12.27 shows the framing options in telecine.

If you don't have a pre-made framing chart like this, you have other options. One is to set a white card on a stand in front of the camera. You can then direct an assistant to make marks on the card to outline a frame. If you have long arms you can put the extension viewfinder on, flip it over and do the drawing yourself. Both of these methods are awkward and inexact.

A better option is to shine a small light (a tweenie or a pepper) down through the viewfinder and it will be projected onto the card, thus easily traced. This will need to be done in a darkened area. Use at least a 50mm (in 35mm) or 25mm (in 16mm film). Shorter lenses may introduce some distortion. Naturally in any of these methods it is important that the card be perfectly perpendicular to the optical axis, otherwise some "keystoning" distortions will occur.

TELECINE

When color negative is transferred directly to videotape the image is electronically changed to a color positive image. During this operation the telecine operator, called the colorist, must calibrate the equipment to produce optimum results.

This is often done with an Eastman Kodak product, Telecine Analysis Film (TAF), which is a standardized negative, produced under very controlled conditions, that the colorist can put in the machine to calibrate the entire system. The Gamma and Density company makes a similar product which, together with their patented gray test charts, affords a great deal of control over your dailies.

The TAF is an objective tool for initial setup and centering of the color-grade controls on a telecine before transfer of images from motion picture film to video. Kodak provides TAF as a benchmark and tool for achieving optimum color-timing control.

TAF provides a test target with known characteristics. After using TAF for setup, the operator is able to transfer many scenes without major equipment adjustment. A frame of TAF contains an 8-color bar test pattern, a neutral-density gray scale, and a neutral-density gray area on the outside edge. The grayscale chart is eight steps. The colorist then uses the waveform monitor to set the values as follows:

TAF Gray Scale	Voltage	IRE UNITS
Step 1 (film black)	50mv	7.5
Step 8 (film white)	56mv	80
Gray patches	320 - 350mv	45 - 50

The colors represent typical saturated colors that are encountered in motion picture production. TAF color bars will not match electronically generated color bars but phase relationships should be about the same.

TELECINE EXPOSURE CALIBRATION FILM

Kodak makes a test film which can be used to calibrate the telecine system to act as a (very expensive) densitometer which can provide the cinematographer with quantifiable evaluation of the exposure for individual scenes. This restores to video finish the direct numerical feedback that is available in film finish in the form of printer lights (Figure 12.28).

image control

COLOR PRINTING

Negative is printed either on a continuous contact printer or on a step printer. The step printer works somewhat like a projector in that the movement is intermittent. Registration is achieved through register pins which allows several passes to be made, as may be the case with black-and-white separation negatives.

ADDITIVE AND SUBTRACTIVE PRINTING

A printer must control the red, green, and blue components of the white-light source to achieve correct density and color balance. Two methods of control are commonly used: additive and subtractive printing. In a subtractive printer, color balance is achieved by inserting color correcting filters in the light path between the light source and the printing aperture.

Overall light density changes are made either by a variable aperture or a neutral density filter. Subtractive print involves using filter packs and neutral density filters to make corrections. As a result, it is difficult to make changes in setup. Subtractive printing is sometimes used for release prints, because there are no scene-to-scene color changes. Printing requiring any scene-to-scene color corrections is not practical on a subtractive printer. The most common printing method is additive printing. In additive printing, there are three light sources. These can then be combined in various percentages to control both the density and color balance. The red, green, and blue components are controlled with a set of dichroic mirrors.

PRINTER LIGHTS

The variations in each color channel are quantified on a scale from 1 to 50. These are called printer "points" or printer "lights." The addition of a printer point adds 0.025 Log Exposure, so adding 12 printer points adds a stop (0.30 Log Exposure) of exposure. The standard printer setup for a laboratory is usually 25-25-25 for the red, green, and blue color channels.

In theory an 18% gray card perfectly exposed and processed will print at 25-25-25. In actual practice this turns out to be only a general guideline. Some labs use 30-30-30 as their aim density. Beyond this, there are other minor variations due to differences in printer optics and chemistry. This can be disconcerting, but in practice it is not important. Lab numbers are self-referential — they are used within the same system at the same lab. Difference in one light causes difference in .07-.1 density which is 1/6 — 1/7 of an f/stop; a 3 light it is 1/2 stop. Any deviations beyond this are of concern. If a lab cannot print the same negative twice without half stop deviation, then there is clearly a problem.

This standard can really only apply to answer prints and release prints, not to the dailies. The same level of quality control for dailies would be economically prohibitive in most cases. Essentially printer points are a closed system within each lab. Generally, most labs are within a couple of numbers of each other. However, there are other reasons why a lab may choose to set its reference point a little higher or lower than another one. Printing machines have an overall line-up or offset known as the trim setting which is used to even out lamp, stock, filter, process and other differences between machines so that they produce the desired result.

So prints from different labs can still look identical, even if they have different lights, because all the other factors are different as well: its only the total combination of settings that matters. If you judge your exposures by the rushes lights, you should ask the lab what the "normal" lights are for the specific stock you're shooting

13.1. (previous page) CCE, a bleach-bypass process, is a critical factor in this image from *City of Lost Children*.

on. Since many productions now get dailies only on video, the cinematographer no longer gets the benefit of these printer numbers to check on the quality of the negative. Video dailies are without a doubt the worst thing to happen to cinematographers in recent times. The only thing that comes close to replacing the printer numbers is the Kodak Telecine Exposure Calibration system (TEC), which is discussed in the chapter on *Video and High Def.*

ONE LIGHT DAILIES

At most labs, you can request that your dailies be printed at a "standard" light — or a fixed light selected during camera tests. That way the DP doesn't need to juggle with lights on lab reports, but can use his/her eyes to judge the exposures each day.

These are called "one-light" dailies. For producers, one-light means the cheap deal, but for DPs it can be a useful test and feedback. If the dailies are printed at a constant setting, the DP can judge by looking at the dailies if they are too dense, too thin or if color balance is off. The downside is that the lab does nothing to correct for mistakes or variations. This means that the producer and director see the scenes exactly as shot — they may tend to panic if they don't understand what can be done in the remaining steps of post production.

In the days of black-and-white, the increments on the old printers were twice as much (i.e., 0.05 logE). One stop in camera neg exposure then resulted in a grading change of about 4 b/w lights. In terms of CC (color correction) filters, a change of one printer light can be judged by laying a 10CC filter of the appropriate color over the print.

ADDITIVE COLOR CONTROL

Printer timing values are normally in the sequence red - green - blue (RGB). These numbers represent the color of light in the printer, not the effect on the print. In color negative, each color controls the amount of the complementary color in the final print. For example: increasing blue will make the print more yellow. Because of this reverse effect, some labs list printer values in the complementary colors: yellow-magenta-cyan (YMC). For timing color prints from color negatives the changes in value are shown in Table 13.1.

With color timing there is considerable room for altering color balance and density. There is room for correction of minor problems or exposure errors. In the long run, however, nothing can substitute for a properly exposed negative with the color balance shot as planned by the cinematographer.

CONTROLLING COLOR AND CONTRAST

There are many other methods of controlling the image at various stages of production.

HOW FLASHING WORKS

Flashing has been around for some time. Originally it was accomplished by pre-exposing the film to a controlled amount of light. This has the effect of raising the inertia point of the film. As we recall from the discussion of exposure, the inertia point is the exposure level at which the film starts to react photochemically to light. Needless to say, taking your unexposed camera negative out of the film cans and exposing them to light is not recommended for the faint of heart — it is a nerveracking experience. Let's look at it in terms of the Zone system. Exposure in this chart is in units. To help visualize the effect think of them as foot-candles.

Clearly, the effect is much greater at the lower end. In Zone I, for instance, the total exposure is tripled, in Zone II it is doubled. In

PRINTER	PRINT VALUE
+B	more yellow
-B	less yellow
+G	more magenta
-G	less magenta
+R	more cyan
-R	less cyan
+BG	more red
+GR	more blue
+RB	more green

Table 13.1. Effect of color controls in printer timing.

Zone IX, however, the increase is from 256 to 258. This increase in exposure would not likely be detectable even with laboratory equipment. The end result is that the shadow areas are increased considerably in exposure but the highlight areas are hardly affected at all. This reduces overall contrast. Panavision's Panaflasher flashes the film in the camera.

VARICON

There is an alternative to pre-exposing which does the same job but safer, more predictably and in a more controlled manner. Devices are available which work by flashing the image, rather than the film, either before or after exposure.

Varicon is a device which places optical glass in front of the lens (partially silvered mirror in one case and clear in the other) and introduces a limited and controlled amount of veiling glare on the glass. This has the same effect as flashing the film. Simple devices which mount on the matte box rods, these units are reasonably compact and simple to use. In design, an on-camera flasher is clear glass plate which sits in front of the lens; around the edge of the glass are eight 6 volt halogen bulbs. The bulbs inject light into the optical flat (which is called the emitter plate) and it glows evenly. It adds light to the image in amounts small enough that they affect only the low exposure areas. It works in exactly the same way as pre- or post-flashing, except that it flashes the film at the same time that the image is being recorded.

Adjustment of the degree of contrast reduction is by means of a simple mechanical handle on top of the unit. The dimming is mechanical so that there is no color change. The effect is visible in the viewfinder. Using the Varicon has two distinct advantages over using low contrast filters. The first is that it decreases contrast without degrading the image. It does not produce halations and double images that are common around bright sources when seen through LC filters. The second advantage is that the Varicon affects only the low exposure areas of the image in normal use.

These systems can be used, as can flashing, to introduce an overall tone to the image, which is more visible in the shadows and therefore perhaps more subtle than an overall tone from a color filter. In color work, it is possible to selectively color the shadow areas without affecting the highlights. For example, the shadow areas can be warmed while a blue sky would remain unaffected. Using a warming filter would, of course, affect the entire image.

Varicon has advantages over flashing as well. Flashing can be somewhat unpredictable and cannot be viewed at the time of shooting. No cameraman in the world can rest easy as his exposed footage, representing days of work and hundreds of thousands of dollars; is taken out of the can and purposely exposed to light. With Varicon, the effect can be viewed through the lens and can be adjusted from shot to shot and even during the shot. Other filters can be used at the same time as the Varicon.

Degree of flashing is controlled mechanically, but the Varicon has a meter which registers the amount of light reaching the emitter plate. The meter is marked in f/stops from f/1.4 to f/11. With the unit are cards for various film ASAs. The cards are calibrated in terms of equivalence to low contrast filters, which are effects which should

ZONES	I	II	III	IV	V	VI	VII	VIII	IX
Basic exposure in units	1	2	4	8	16	32	64	128	256
Added units from flashing	2	2	2	2	2	2	2	2	2
TOTAL UNITS	3	4	6	10	18	34	66	130	258

Table 13.2. How flashing affects shadow areas more than highlights.

be familiar to most camera people. To use the charts you first select the one for the ASA you are using, for example ASA 100. You then read the f/stop at the lens (example: f/2.8). You then find the row corresponding to the low contrast effect that you want, say LC 1. Read across to the column for the lens f/stop. Immediately underneath is the correct setting for the Varicon. In our example the result would be f/4. You then adjust the handle until the meter on the flasher reads f/4 and you have a contrast reduction of LC 1. For low light situations you can put neutral density material in the gel holders and for very bright situations you can use two emitter plates (the second one is standard with the rig).

13.2. The Arriflex Varicon. (Photo courtesy of Arri Group.)

Ansel Adams notes that in the days before coated lenses, a slight controlled flare could be used to reduce contrast. This principle was used on the film *Saving Private Ryan* as explained later in the chapter. Overdoing flashing, either in the camera or in the darkroom, can lead to a veiling effect or a false tonality. The mere suggestion of exposing valuable, undeveloped footage to light is enough to give some producers and directors apoplexy and may be useful in getting them to approve an additional lighting order as an alternative.

If you plan to pre-flash or post-flash a film, extensive discussion with the lab and testing beforehand is essential. The most common method of specifying the degree of flashing is to specify a density above base density plus fog (the basic density of unexposed, processed film).

Like light-scattering filters or smoke, flashing lowers color saturation by adding a wash of white light over the image, also lowering the contrast. The advantage of flashing over filters is that it doesn't soften definition or produce artifacts like halos around light sources. Some labs will post-flash the negative before development but most do not like to get into this because of the chance of damaging the negative through over-handling; there are also liability issues. Prints can also be flashed, which lowers contrast by darkening the bright highlights — it also slightly softens colors but not as much as negative flashing.

OTHER METHODS OF DESATURATING COLOR
Many techniques can be used to control the amount of color saturation and contrast in a film.

- Filters such as ProMist, Fog, Double Fog, Low Cons, Ultra-Cons, etc., cause highlights to bleed or wash into the shadows which lowers contrast and softens color saturation. (See the section later in this chapter for more on contrast control with filters.)

- Smoke or fog (or even smog) has a similar effect to filters in that contrast and color are lowered because light is scattered more or less uniformly. Smoke has the advantage of affecting objects in the background more than in the foreground. This is more three dimensional than a filter which reduces the contrast uniformly for the entire scene. Artificial smoke on a closed set is somewhat controllable. A talented effects person can control whether the smoke is concentrated in the foreground or background.

- Softer lighting desaturates; harder lighting emphasizes contrast and color saturation. Specific color lighting can also be used in conjunction with post-production to remove some color. On the film *Heart* — a remake of a black-and-white film, burgundy (magenta) gels were added to all lights. Then in printing, the magenta was pulled out of the image thus desaturating the color by removing red and blue evenly.

LATENSIFICATION

Latensification is similar to flashing in that it "pre-exposes" the film uniformly, however, it is done with chemicals instead of light. It is accomplished by exposing the film to the vapors of various solutions. Latensification is also used to drastically increase film speed.

IN THE LAB:

There are a number of processes which can be performed in the lab to affect the characteristics of the film.

- Pull-process developing can lower saturation a little, but is mostly used to lower contrast, especially when combined with silver-retention printing. Conversely, push processing tends to increase contrast. Of course, pull processing has the effect of lowering the effective speed of the film and push processing increases the speed — however at the cost of increased grain.

- Double printing. Starting with the original color negative a color I.P. is struck. At the same time a black-and-white positive is made. These elements are then printed together. The black-and-white positive acts as a mask to control highlights and color saturation. This is a highly controllable process since the exact density of the black-and-white positive can be varied with great subtly. This is similar to a technique used by still photographers to control prints. The final result is a desaturated dupe negative. How desaturated the image is depends on what percentage of the total exposure came from the b&w or the color I.P. This technique was used in some scenes of *The Natural*, photographed by Caleb Deschanel. There was a variation in this case. Normally the black-and-white print is slightly out of focus so that hard edges are not noticeable. In *The Natural*, the reprinted color image was printed out-of-focus over the sharp black-and-white image, which creates a diffusion effect.

- Video post. Color is easily manipulated in telecine transfers or using digital techniques. In the movie *Breaking the Waves* the film was transferred to videotape; the video image was manipulated to taste, then scanned back to film.

- Art direction. The simplest and sometimes the most effective way to control color can be achieved by selection of colors for the set, the costumes and makeup. A good art department makes a huge difference in controlling the look of the film.

- Locations. Selection of locations is critical to the look of the film. Once locations are chosen, the choice of what time of day to shoot can also make a significant difference. The painting and dressing of locations, to whatever extent possible, are also important.

- Film stock selection. Kodak Vision 5277 (320T) and Fuji 8582 (F-400T) have a lower overall contrast and a subdued color rendering. Agfa for many years made a film that was lower in contrast. It was used very effectively on the film *Out of Africa*, where the hard African sunlight would have otherwise been a problem for DP David Watkin. There is generally a correlation between lower saturation and lower contrast / softer blacks, since the black density can affect how saturated we perceive a color to be. The general term for less saturated color is pastel. Painters make a color pastel by mixing white into it — similar to letting highlights bleed into the shadow.

- Bleach-bypass and other silver retention processes are discussed separately later in this chapter.

PUTTING IT ALL TOGETHER: THE COLOR PALETTE

All of these techniques can be used in various combinations for a wide range of control. It is usually best to begin with selection of locations, art direction and costuming. After that comes selection of time of day to shoot and lighting and grip control.

It is always best to use the simplest means to achieve a goal. Primary colors tend to desaturate less noticeably than pastel colors when using some sort of desaturation technique. Skintones are generally pastel; they will lose their color much faster than a primary color in the frame.

Some DPs use a contrast/desaturating technique such as flashing, and then use a silver retention printing technique to restore the blacks in the prints. Two of the earliest films to use some of these techniques to moderate contrast and desaturate color were *McCabe and Mrs. Miller* shot by Vilmos Zsigmond and *Heaven's Gate* photographed by Nestor Almendros. (Conrad Hall took over for some scenes at the end when Almendros had to leave for another picture.)

The primary technique used in *Heaven's Gate* was the simplest one of all: many of the exterior scenes were shot during morning or evening "magic hour" when the light is soft and even. This is a simple method but a very expensive one. Few productions can afford to restrict exterior filming to a few hours a day. Also the farm location in Alberta naturally had a lot of dust in the air which acts like smoke to soften the light. Almendros also used negative flashing and print flashing together to soften the colors and contrast.

McCabe and Mrs. Miller (Figure 13.3) was one of the first films to use pre-flashing of the negative. Underexposure and push-processing were also used. Double Fog filters were also part of the package. The result is a stunning film with beautiful subtlety of color rendition.

On *Saving Private Ryan*, DP Janus Kaminski had the anti-reflection coating stripped off some of the lenses to make them reproduce some of the internal flares that were characteristic of lenses of the war period. These internal reflections also lower contrast. He also used a combination of on-camera flashing (the Panaflasher) and the ENR process. Combining the flashing compensates for the negative getting very "heavy" from the bleach-bypass.

Darius Khondji's stunning work on *Seven* combined flashing with Deluxe's CCE printing — a silver retention process. For contrast control on the film *The Thin Red Line*, black smoke was used to create artificial clouds. Staging of scenes within the sunlit and shadow areas was also done with great care. *City of Lost Children* (Figures 13.1 and 13.5) employed the CCE process in addition to set design and a carefully controlled palette, all of which was facilitated by the fact that it was entirely a studio film. *Payback* used the CCE printing process, combined with shooting without the 85 filter outdoors on tungsten stock, and using a blue filter indoors — the blue-bias on the negative ensured that skintones would be consistently desaturated. The print was timed to the blue side to keep any reds from becoming more saturated.

BLEACH-BYPASS AND OTHER PROCESSES

Silver retention as a means of controlling the image has gained popularity in the last few years. It offers several new techniques for the cinematographer to alter the look of the film. All silver retention processes are based on the same phenomenon. When color film is processed, the dark areas are where the most silver is developed. The highlight areas don't have many silver halide crystals that have been

13.3. A frame from *McCabe and Mrs. Miller* (Warner Bros., 1971), shot by Vilmos Zsigmond using preflashing, underexposure, push-processing and filtration.

affected photochemically. When color stock is developed the silver halide crystals are replaced with color dyes. Normally, the silver itself is removed by a bleaching process. By either altering the chemistry or skipping this bleaching process (either partially or entirely) some or all of the silver is left in. Leaving the silver in is somewhat like leaving a black-and-white photo on top of the color image. It reduces contrast and color saturation.

Since most of the silver is now concentrated in the darkest areas, these parts of the image will be affected differently from the mid-tones and highlights. This has the effect of making the blacks denser and also desaturating the color rendition. Silver retention is usually done on the print. The effect on the print is much greater than when done on the negative. On the print, silver retention affects the blacks most; on the negative it does the reverse; it affects the whites most — it makes them very white, which results in a blown out background. The effect is the greatest where there is the most silver to begin with. In the print, these are the black areas. On the negative these are the white areas — the highlights. When done on the print, silver retention doesn't add much grain because the effect is concentrated in the blacks. On the negative, where the highlights are most affected, it adds grain and noise.

ENR

ENR is a proprietary Technicolor process. It was invented by Ernesto Novelli Rimo (hence its name) of Technicolor Rome and first used by Vittorio Storaro on the 1981 film *Reds*. Since then, Storaro has also used it on films such as *Dick Tracy*, *The Last Emperor* and *Little Buddha*. It has also been used on films such as *Jade*, *The Game* and *Saving Private Ryan*.

ENR is a color-positive developing technique which utilizes an additional black-and-white developing bath in order to retain some of the silver. After the film has been bleached, but prior to the silver being fixed out of the film, this extra bath allows for a controlled amount of silver to be redeveloped, adding density blacks. ENR is used on the release prints. As a result, each print roll must have the same amount of ENR applied. As a general rule, however, ENR is applied to the entire film.

Not only does it make the blacks blacker, but by increasing contrast in the shadows, there is a slight increase of the shadow detail and an increase in apparent sharpness due to a small edge effect around the image. Note that this is apparent sharpness, not actual sharpness. Many people refer to ENR as a bleach-bypass process, but it is not. Bleach-bypass does have a similar effect, but chemically it is different. In the ENR process, the intensity of the effect can be varied controllably by varying the concentration of the chemistry. This makes it possible to add just a small amount of ENR which has the effect of making the blacks richer but without noticeable effect on color saturation. The ENR process which is variable in effect must be quantifiable so that the DP and lab can confer on how much is to be done. In the ENR process a densitometer is used to measure the level. In this case, it is an infrared densitometer. As a result ENR is classified in density levels, not percentages. For example, a certain print might be 50 IR. This means a .50 density, not 50%.

CCE

Deluxe, another film lab with a long history in Hollywood uses a process called Color Contrast Enhancement or CCE. CCE raises the contrast, deepens the blacks and adds grain but still preserves some shadow detail. As with ENR, the amount of silver retained is read with a densitometer centered on 1000nm. According to Deluxe, a pure bleach-bypass which retains 100% of the silver might yield an IR density reading of as much as 240, which translates to four times the amount of silver that would be found in a normal print. With CCE normally processed negative (no special processes) a nominal reading at 1000nm might be around 60. With CCE, a typical reading of D-max might be around 180 to 190 IR. This translates to about 75% silver left in the print; where retention of 100% of the silver will not only increase the density of the blacks but of the mid-tones as well. This can result in some unpleasant effects on skintone. By keeping the amount of silver retention in this range, there will be some desaturation of the color rendition, an increase in grain and denser blacks, but there will still be some detail in the blacks, unlike in 100% silver retention where the blacks might "plug up." CCE was used on the film *Seven* (Figure 13.4) and also on *Ronin* (Figure 13.8) and many others.

ACE
Also a Deluxe process, ACE stands for Adjustable Contrast Enhancement. ACE is variable in effect. With ACE it is possible to enhance the blacks without significant effect on color saturation. ACE is measured in percentages.

NEC
LTC Laboratories of Paris utilizes the NEC process, which stands for *noir en couler* — French for "black in color." NEC allows for silver retention in the interpositive stage. The advantage of this is that each individual release print does not have to undergo special processing. NEC produces denser blacks but has less effect on the overall contrast and tonal rendition.

BLEACH-BYPASS
Bleach-bypass is the oldest of the special processing techniques of this type. It involves simply skipping all or most of the bleach step of processing. Bleach-bypass was first used on the film *1984*, photographed by Roger Deakins. In the US, FotoKem, CFI and many other labs have variations on the bleach-bypass technique. Fotokem can perform bleach-bypass on prints, original camera negative and intermediate prints (interpositives and internegatives). CFI's process is called Silver Tint. It comes in two different levels: Standard and Enhanced. It can be used at different stages of print production.

In Silver Tint Enhanced, 100% of the silver is left in the print. In Silver Tint Standard, less silver is retained, resulting in an IR densitometer value of around 165 to 175. This produces increased contrast, deeper blacks and desaturated colors. In Enhanced Silver Tint, the effect is even greater — it is a very high-contrast, hard look. Enhanced Silver Tint was used on the film *Kansas City*.

Skip Bleach

Skip-Bleach is FotoKem's silver retention process. Bleach-bypass is essentially incomplete processing. The advantage of this is that it is reversible. Fotokem recommends a slight underexposure for negative intended for bleach-bypass. This is because leaving the silver in has the effect of increasing the density of the negative. Density is basically silver affected by photochemical reaction — if there is more silver there is more density. It is the same as if there was additional exposure. This is the case because you are skipping the bleach at the negative stage. Bleach-bypass on the negative not only makes the blacks blacker, it also makes the whites whiter — overall density increases.

This creates a look that is more radical than ENR or a bleach-bypass on the intermediates or the release print. In this way it is very similar to flashing the film. Flashing film is sometimes used by still photographers to increase the ASA of the film. Fotokem offers skip-bleach on the negative, the interpositive and the internegative. They can also combine flashing with skip-bleach on the interpositive and internegative.

All silver retention processes cost more than normal processing. This is true of any process in which the lab must alter its normal procedures — such as push or pull processing. In skip-bleach or similar process, there is an additional cost. Normally the silver that is taken out of the emulsion is recycled and sold. When it is left in, the lab can no longer resell it and they must pass this cost along to the production.

EXPOSURE COMPENSATION IN BLEACH-BYPASS

When shooting film intended for a silver retention process, some change in your exposure will usually be necessary. You are leaving silver in, which is essentially the same as adding exposure. Generally, you will want to underexpose by 1/2 to a full stop as the skip-bleach process may add as much as 1-1/2 stops. Instead of changing exposure, many DPs combine silver retention with flashing or the use of Varicon or Panaflasher. It is out of the question to use any type of silver retention, bleach-bypass or flashing without prior testing.

The catch is that bleach-bypass in the print stages is very expensive — for a large scale release, it can come to hundreds of thousands of dollars. As a result, few, if any, films have bleach-bypass done for all of the prints. This means that if you underexpose it will be compensated with extra silver in only some of the prints. Some prints will thus be underexposed. This is a judgment call and another reason for extensive testing before using any of these processes.

As a result of the cost of doing bleach-bypass in the release print, many DPs have experimented with doing the bleach-bypass in the original negative or in the internegative and interpositive. The results vary widely and also depend on the color palette of the sets and wardrobe, the lighting, exposure, filtration and lenses.

You must test before shooting with any of these methods.

OTHER TECHNIQUES

CROSS PROCESSING

Cross processing was first developed by still photographers. In cross processing, the original camera film is a reversal stock, such as Ektachrome. This reversal stock is then put through negative processing chemistry. The result is negative image on a clear based film. In other words it does not have the distinctive orange mask that all color negatives have.

13.5. Another frame from *City of Lost Children*. It is critical to remember that processes such as bleach-bypass are not a "magic button" that will automatically make your film look as good as these examples — it has to be used in conjunction with great lighting, set design, the color palette of wardrobe and props, filtration, effects and all the other tools at the disposal of the DP and production designer.

The effect of cross processing is increased contrast and more grain. Depending on exposure handling and processing variables, the effect can range from subtle to radical. Since there is no orange mask, a similar colored filter must be used in printing. As a result, normal or even slightly underexposed original camera film produces the best results.

Cross processing results can vary substantially. Some labs will not do cross processing as it involves the use of fomaldehyde to stabilize the magenta dyes and may also result in contamination of the lab's processing tanks. Without the formaldehyde or a similar stabilizer, the film will fade quickly. If the images are going straight to video transfer, this may not be a concern.

Cross processing was used extensively on the film *Three Kings* and bleach-bypass was used on some scenes (Figure 13.6) — the difference between the two looks was used to underscore the dramatic difference between the American Army camp and the Iraqi village. Perhaps the most noticeable effect in cross processed scenes was that the sky goes almost completely white in some shots. This is in stark contrast to other exterior scenes that were not cross processed. These scenes had a more normal blue tone.

PRINTING NEGATIVE AS INTERPOSITVE
An alternative to cross processing is to print camera negative as an interpositive onto standard print film. Film stock normally used for interpositives is lower in contrast than normal print stock. The reason for this is that successive print stages in post production usually result in a build-up of contrast; to counter this intermediate print stocks generally have a lower contrast. Printing an interpositive onto a print stock such as Kodak 5244 will increase contrast and grain and also result in color shifts. Both cross processing and interpositive printing result in stronger more saturated colors, which makes them very different from bleach-bypass techniques.

TRANSFER FROM PRINT
Another method which affects color and contrast is to transfer to video from a print instead of a negative. This can only be done where no print is needed for projection. Print stocks tend to be contrastier than negative stocks. This is because negative stocks will usually have to go through internegative, interpositive and final print stages. Each print stage adds contrast, so the original negative is designed to be lower in contrast to counteract this.

13.6. (below) *Three Kings* used two different techniques — in this frame cross-processing. (Warner Bros., 1999.)

13.7. (bottom) Bleach-bypass was used for some sections of the film.

13.8. Bleach bypass transforms this otherwise straight shot from *Ronin* into something that might well pass for a Cezanne.

DIGITAL INTERMEDIATE

For projects finished on video there is an enormous range of image control available, from simple adjustments of the gamma to complex Paintbox, Harry and DaVinci image manipulations. For adjusting gamma and enlarging the image, it is generally best to do so at the time of transfer. One practice that is increasingly common is to transfer the film negative to High Def tape master, perform digital manipulations and then transfer the HD master back to film. This is called a digital intermediate. If you plan to do a digital intermediate, it is critical that you coordinate in advance with the company that will be doing the transfers to and from the negative and whatever post-production people will be handling the digital stages. There are many different options and all of them affect the look of your images. Doing a test all the way from camera negative through the High Def stages and then back to negative (or print) is critical. Not testing with the conditions relevant to your project can have serious consequences.

TECHNICOLOR

As a final note, Technicolor is bringing back the original color imbition printing which helped make the Technicolor "look" so famous. This is the printing stage only; it does not involve shooting three separate rolls of film in the enormous Technicolor three-strip cameras.

This process involves a matrix which transfers the dyes to the receiving stock; it is completely different from a process which uses dye "clouds" to form the image. The method is the same as dye transfer in still photography, which is considered the highest quality color printing technique.

13.9. Various grades of diffusion — the Schneider Black Frost series. (Photo courtesy of Schneider Optics.)

FILTER TYPES

There are a few basic types of filters:

- Diffusion
- Exposure (Neutral density)
- Focus (diopters and split-diopters)
- Color balance
- Color alteration
- Effects

DIFFUSION AND EFFECTS FILTERS

There are many types of diffusion filters but they all have one common purpose — they slightly alter the image to make it "softer" or more diffuse or to reduce the contrast. They do it in a number of ways and with a variety of effects (Figures 13.9 through 13.12).

Diffusion filters are a very personal and subjective subject. Besides glass or resin filters which are placed in front of the lens (or in some cases behind the lens or even in a slot the middle of it), other methods can be used. Many cinematographers use silk or nylon stocking

13.10. (above left) No filter.

13.11. (middle) Black Promist 3. (Photo courtesy of Tiffen.)

13.12. (above, right) Warm Black Promist 3. (Photo courtesy of Tiffen.)

material which can have a very subtle and beautiful effect. One of the most favored of these is a difficult to obtain brand of French stocking which can cost $75 for a pair. Designations for filters are not standardized but they generally come in sets ranging from 1 to five or 1/8, 1/4, 1/2, 1, 2, and so on. An older type of filter that dates back to the early days of the studio system but which is still popular today are the Mitchell diffusions, which come in "A", "B" and "C." Others are known only by a name such as "star" or "dawn."

Other types of loose open material can be used as can as grease or petroleum jelly on a piece of glass. Ordinary cellophane or plastic wrap have also been employed in emergencies. Star filters, which create a pattern of streaks around a highlight, are basically clear glass with diagonal scratches.

The use of diffusion goes back a long way in film history. In the early twenties it became a common practice to use a heavy diffusion filter on close-ups of the female star. This made her appear more glamorous, sensuous and beautiful and also concealed any imperfections in her appearance. This effect was often used to such an extent that there was a jarring mismatch between the close-up of the female star, the close-up of the male star and the master shot. It didn't seem to bother anybody back then, but today it would hardly seem acceptable. The same applied to a glamorous highlight which appeared out of nowhere for a close-up of the female star.

NETS

Another form of diffusion is nets or voiles (mesh). Nets vary in their diffusion effect according to how fine their weave is. Nets can come in filter form sandwiched between two pieces of optical glass or they can be attached to the front or rear of the lens.

Attaching a net to the rear of the lens has several advantages. A net on the front of the lens can come slightly into focus with wider lenses that are stopped down. A net on the rear of this lens will not do this. Also, the diffusion effect will not change as the lens is stopped down or the focal length changes on a zoom. Attaching a net to the rear of the lens must be done with great caution as there is danger of damaging the exposed rear element of the lens or of interfering with the spinning reflex mirror. Putting a net on the rear should be done with easily removable material such as "snot tape"

or rubber cement.

CONTRAST FILTERS

Various filters are used to reduce or soften the degree of contrast in a scene. These generally work by taking some of the highlights and making them "flare" into the shadows. Traditionally these were called "lo-cons." There are a number of newer, more sophisticated varieties. Two types are shown in Figures 13.13 through 13.15.

EFFECTS FILTERS

There are many kinds of very special effects filters, ranging from the most obvious, a "disco" splash, to the more subtle — creating a faint rainbow effect. These are rarely used in film and video photography. "Sunset" filters give the scene an overall orange glow. Other filters can give the scene a color tone of almost any sort imaginable: from moonlight blue to antique sepia or chocolate reminiscent faded daguerreotypes. Besides the hundreds of varieties available, filters can be special made to suit a particular need. Also commonly used are sunset grads and blue or magenta grads to give some color to what would otherwise be a colorless or "blown out" sky (Figures 13.16 and 13.17).

In addition to filters which affect the entire scene, almost any type of filter is also available as a grad. A grad is a filter which starts with a color on one side and gradually fades out to clear or another color (Figures 13.18 through 13.21). Grads can be either "hard edge" or "soft edge" denoting how gradual the transition is. The most commonly used types of grads are neutral density filters which are often used to balance the exposure between a normal foreground scene and a much hotter sky above the horizon. ND grads come in grades of .3 (one stop at the darkest), .6 (two stops), .9 (three stops) and more rarely .12 (four stops). Be sure to specify whether you want a hard or soft cut as there is a considerable difference in application.

13.13. (left) No filter. (Photo courtesy of Tiffen.)

13.14. (middle) Ultracon 5, a low contrast filter. (Photo courtesy of Tiffen.)

13.15. (right) Softcon 5, a different type of contrast filter. (Photo courtesy of Tiffen.)

13.16. (left) Sunset shot with no filter. (Photo courtesy of Tiffen.)

13.17. (far left) With a sunset grad. (Photo courtesy of Tiffen.)

13.18. (opposite, top left) The scene with no filter. (Photo courtesy of Tiffen.)

13.19. (top right) A grape grad. (Photo courtesy of Tiffen.)

13.20. (bottom left) A plum grad. (Photo courtesy of Tiffen.)

13.21. (bottom right) A sunrise grad. (Photo courtesy of Tiffen.)

Whether you need a hard or a soft cut will also be affected by what focal length you are planning to shoot with.

COLOR TEMPERATURE AND FILTRATION

As we discussed in *Color Control*, the most common system used in describing the color of light is color temperature. This scale is derived from the color of a theoretical "black body" (a metal object having no inherent color of its own, technically known as a Planckian radiator). When heated to incandescence, the black body glows at varying colors depending on the temperature. Color temperature is a quantification of the terms "red hot," "white hot," etc.

There is another measure of light color that is important as well: the magenta-green content. Since many sources in lighting tend to have a component of green, it is important to measure and correct it; otherwise the film will be heavily tinted, usually in a very disturbing and unattractive way. Sources which produce disproportionate include fluorescents, HMIs and other bulbs with discontinuous spectrums.

HOW MIRED VALUES ARE USED

Another problem with color temperature is that equal changes in color "temperature" are not necessarily perceived by the eye as equal changes in color. A change of 50K from 2000K to 2050K will be a noticeable difference in color. For an equivalent change in color perception at 5500K, the color temperature would need to shift 150K and about 500K at 10,000K.

Because these changes are so unequal, the mired system has been devised. Mired stands for micro-reciprocal degrees. Mireds are derived by dividing 1,000,000 by the Kelvin value. For example, 3200K equals 1,000,000/3200 = 312 mireds. When calculating the degree of color correction needed for a particular combination, the mired system can be used. If you have a source at 5500K and wish to convert it to 3200K, subtract the mired value of the desired color from that of the source. 5000K = 200 mireds. 3200K = 312 mireds. 312-200 = 112 mireds. 85 orange has a mired value of +112. In practice these calculations are done by the color meter or by using a simple get chart. On the mired scale, a plus shift value means the filter is yellowish, a minus value means the filter will give a blue shift. When combining filters, add the mired values.

WHAT "COLOR BALANCE" MEANS IN FILM STOCK:

Unlike the human eye, which is assisted by the brain in compensating and adapting, no color film can accurately reproduce color under all kinds of lighting conditions. In manufacture, the film is adjusted to render color accurately under a particular condition, the two most common being average daylight (type D film), which is set for 5500K and average tungsten illumination (type B film) designed for 3200K. There is a third, which is based on the now disused "photo" bulbs, which were 3400K (type A film), rather than 3200K, but very few films are available in this balance.

Given the fact that providing tungsten light is costly, while sunlight is usually far more abundant, most motion picture films are type B, balanced for tungsten. The idea is that we put a correcting filter on when we can most afford to lose light to a filter factor — in the sunlight. Kodak does have several excellent daylight balance films available for which no correcting filter is need in daylight or HMI situations. They come in ASAs up to 250 which can be extremely useful on dark, cloudy days or when the sun is near the horizon — at the end of the day it gets dark surprisingly fast.

There are four basic reasons to change the color of light at the source: to correct the color of the lights to match the film type (instead of using a camera filter), to match different types of lighting sources and for effect or mood. Finally there are specialized situations like greenscreen or bluescreen.

To shoot with type B film under "blue" light (in the 5500° degree area) an 85 orange filter is used (Figure 13.22). The 80A or 80B blue filters for shooting daylight film with warm light are rarely used, and in most cases should be combined with a UV filter because tungsten film cannot tolerate the high proportion of UV in daylight and HMIs. There is some light loss when using a correction filter and the filter factor must be used to adjust the T/stop. For convenience, most manufacturers list an adjusted Exposure Index (or ASA) which allows for the filter loss.

Another form of filter that is sometimes used is a UV or haze filter. Skylight contains a great deal of ultraviolet radiation which can cause the image to go slightly blue. This is especially true at high altitudes where there is little atmosphere to filter out the UV. It is also called a haze filter because it will have the effect of slightly

13.22. (top) An 85B.

13.23. (middle) An 80B blue filter.

13.24. (bottom) 81A for slight warming effect.

reducing the effect of haze in the atmosphere.

Two different ASAs will be listed on cans of black-and-white film. This is not related to correction filters, since none are needed. It is because black-and-white films vary in their sensitivity to colors. In most cases the ASA for tungsten light will be 1/3 stop lower. Very important: when using this adjusted EI, do not also use the filter factor. Smaller color mismatches can also be corrected with color filters, as well. If the scene lighting is 2800K, for example (too warm), then an 82C filter will correct the light reaching the film to 3200K. Types of color filters generally used in film and video production are discussed in the next section. Filter families are shown in Table 13.3.

CONVERSION FILTERS
Conversion filters work with the blue and orange ranges of the spectrum and deal with fundamental color balance in relation to the color sensitivity of the emulsion. Conversion filters affect all parts of the spectrum for smooth color rendition. (LB) Light Balancing filters are warming and cooling filters; they work on the entire SED as with the conversion filters, but they are used to make smaller shifts in the Blue-Orange axis.

CAMERA LENS FILTERS FOR COLOR CORRECTION
Color compensating filters are manufactured in the primary and secondary colors. They are used to make corrections in a specific area of the spectrum or for special effects. They affect only their own narrow band of the SED. Don't make the mistake of trying to correct color balance with CC filters. Primary filters work in a limited band of the spectrum and correct only one wavelength.

However, since CC filters are not confined to the Blue-Orange axis, they can be used to correct imbalances in the Magenta-Green axis, such as occur with fluorescent lamps and most types of industrial lamps. A CC-30M is often a part of the basic filter package for standard tubes. 30M is a good starting point for most uncorrected fluorescent sources (Table 13.4).

COOLING FILTERS
The 80 series, which are blue conversion filters, are used to convert warm sources such as tungsten lights so that they are suitable for use with daylight film (Table 13.5).

WARMING AND COOLING FILTERS
The 81 series of warming filters (81, 81A, 81B, 81C) increase the "warmth" of the light by lowering the color temperature in 200K increments (Figure 13.24). The 81 shifts the color temp by the minimum amount required for the eye to perceive any change: -200K. For cooling, the 82 series works in the same fashion, starting with the 82 which shifts the overall color temperature by +200K. As with most color temperature correction filters, excess magenta or green are not dealt with and must be handled separately. Table 13.6 shows the Wratten 81 and 82 filters for warming and cooling. Wratten is a system of filter classification owned by Eastman Kodak. Corals are also a popular type of filter for degrees of warming.

85:	Conversion	Correcting daylight to tungsten light
80:	Conversion	Correcting tungsten to daylight
82:	Light balancing	Cooling filters
81:	Light balancing	Warming filters
CC's	Color	Primary and secondary colors

Table 13.3. The basic filter families: 85, 80, 82, 81 and Color Correction.

CONTRAST CONTROL IN BLACK-AND-WHITE

This characteristic of transmitting some colors and absorbing others makes color filters valuable in controlling black-and-white images. Most scenes contain a variety of colors, and to a certain extent scenes are "color coded" according to image content. In other words, the sky may be the only blue area in an image, a field of grass may be the only largely green element in a scene.

The basic principle of contrast control filtration in black-and-white cinematography is that a filter lightens colors in its own area of the spectrum and darkens the complementary colors. How strong an effect it has is the result of two factors: how strong the color differences of the original subject are and how strong the filter is. The scene we are shooting is the result of the colors of the objects themselves and the colors of the light that falls on them.

Color filters only increase or decrease contrast on black-and-white film when there is color difference in the scene. In a scene composed of only black, white and gray objects a color filter would only reduce exposure: it would not alter the contrast. When a filter is used to absorb certain colors we are reducing the total amount of light reaching the film. We must compensate by allowing more overall exposure. The exposure compensation necessary for each filter is expressed as the filter factor.

With warm colors (red, orange, yellow), the daylight filter factors are greater than the tungsten filter factors. In the violet and blue range, the daylight factors are less than the tungsten, but for the cyan/green range of the spectrum the daylight and tungsten filter factors are nearly all equal. The same is true for magenta, which is equally red and blue. The simple rule for black-and-white filters is: expose for the darkest subject in the scene that is substantially the same color as the filter, and let the filter take care of the highlights.

USING FILTERS IN BLACK-AND-WHITE PHOTOGRAPHY

These filters for black-and-white have alternate designations:

    #8 = K-2
    #15 = G-15
    #11 = X-1

Combining contrast filters for black-and-white does not have the cumulative effect that we might expect. For example, combining a #8 and #15 filter gives the same visual effect as a #15 filter alone (although the filter factor is changed by the combination of the two). Combining two filters of different groups is seldom necessary, since there is usually a single filter which will do the same job.

POLARIZERS

Natural light "vibrates" in all directions around its path of travel. A polarizer transmits the light that is vibrating in one direction only. Polarizers are extremely versatile filters and serve a variety of functions. Glare on a polished surface or on a glass window is, to a certain extent, polarized as it is reflected. By rotating a polarizer to eliminate that particular direction of polarization, we can reduce or eliminate the glare and surface reflection. Brewster's angle, 56° from normal, or 34° from the surface, is the zone of maximum polarization (Figures 13.25 and 13.26).

When working with glare on water and on windows it is seldom desirable to eliminate all reflections because this creates an unnatural effect. The polarizer can be used with color film to darken the sky. Maximum polarization occurs at about 90° from the sun. This works well for static shots, but care must be taken if a pan or tilt is called for as the degree of polarization may change as the camera

YELLOW (Absorbs Blue)	CC.025Y	-
	CC05Y	-
	CC10Y	1/3
	CC20Y	1/3
	CC30Y	1/3
	CC40Y	1/3
	CC50Y	2/3
MAGENTA (Red-blue)	CC.025M	-
	CC05M	1/3
	CC10M	1/3
	CC20M	1/3
	CC30M	2/3
	CC40M	2/3
	CC50M	2/3
CYAN (Blue-green)	CC.025 C	-
	CC05C	1/3
	CC10C	1/3
	CC20C	1/3
	CC30C	2/3
	CC40C	2/3
	CC50C	1
RED	CC.025R	-
	CC05R	1/3
	CC10R	1/3
	CC20R	1/3
	CC30R	2/3
	CC40R	2/3
	CC50R	1
GREEN (Absorbs Blue and Red)	CC.025G	-
	CC05G	1/3
	CC10G	1/3
	CC20G	1/3
	CC30G	2/3
	CC40G	2/3
	CC50G	1
BLUE (Absorbs Green and Red)	CC.025B	-
	CC05B	1/3
	CC10B	1/3
	CC20B	2/3
	CC30B	2/3
	CC40B	1
	CC50B	1 1/3

FILTER	CONVERSION		EXP. LOSS
80A	3200 > 5500	-131	2 stops
80B	3400 > 5500	-112	1 2/3 stops
80C	3800 > 5500	-81	1 stop
80D	4200 > 5500	-56	1/3 stop

	Filter #	Exp. Factor	Mired	To Get 3200K From:
COOLING	82C + 82C	1 1/3	-89	2490K
	82C + 82B	1 1/3	-77	2570K
	82C+82A	1	-65	2650K
	82C+82	1	-55	2720K
	82C	2/3	-45	2800K
	82B	2/3	-32	2900K
	82A	1/3	-21	3000K
	82	1/3	-10	3100K
WARMING	81	1/3	+9	3300K
	81A	1/3	+18	3400K
	81B	1/3	+27	3500K
	81C	1/3	+35	3600K
	81D	2/3	+42	3700K
	81EF	2/3	+52	3850K

Table 13.4. (bottom) Color Correction camera filters. (Data courtesy of Eastman Kodak.)

Table 13.5. (top) The 80 series.

Table 13.6. (middle) Wratten series 81 and 82 filters. (Data courtesy of Eastman Kodak.)

Table 13.7. Effects of filters in black-and-white photography.

WRATTEN #	COLOR	EXPOSURE FACTOR	INCREASE EXPOSURE	DEGREE	EFFECT IN DAYLIGHT
3	Light Yellow	1.5	1/2	Slight	Penetrates haze
8	Medium Yellow	2	1	Moderate	Corrects panchromatic color balance
11	Green 1	4	2	Light	Lightens green foliage
12	Yellow	2	1	Strong	Increases contrast
15	Deep Yellow	2.5	1 1/4	Heavy	Darkens sky, lightens faces
21	Light Orange	3	1 1/2	Slight	Heavy correction
23A	Deep Orange	5	2 1/4	Moderate	Penetrates heavy haze
25	Red	8	3	Heavy	Dark sky, white faces
29	Deep Red	16	4	Extreme	Strong contrast, black sky

moves. If the sky is overcast, the polarizer won't help much. Polarizers reduce transmission of light, generally at least 1 2/3 to 2 stops as a filter factor, which does not change as you rotate the polarizer.

DENSITY FILTERS
Neutral density filters are used to reduce overall exposure without affecting color rendition. They can be used in extremely high illumination situations (such as a sunlit snow scene or a beach scene) where the exposure would be too great or where reduced exposure is desired to crush depth of field. Neutral density filters combined with 85 correction filters (85N3, 85N6 and 85N9) are a standard order with any camera package for exterior work (Figures 13.27 and 13.28).

Also known as Wratten #96, the opacity of ND filters is given in density units so that .3 equals one stop, .6 equals two stops and .9 equals three stops. In gelatin filters, ND's are available in .1 increments (1/3 of a stop). If you combine ND filters, the density values are added. If you are using the arithmetic exposure factors, don't forget to multiply the exposure factor.

FILTERS AND BRIGHT POINT SOURCES
When shooting a bright point source such as the sun, filters will almost certainly show double or triple images. This is caused by the image of the source reflecting off the front surface of the lens back onto the filter. When shooting the sun especially, it is best to go with no filters if possible. However, some sort of ND filter is almost always necessary.

Some sophisticated matte boxes permit the filters to be set at a slight angle, which prevents this problem. If all else fails, slightly loosen the swingaway matte box and give it a bit of an angle. Be careful, though, too much angle and you are creating an opening which will cause other types of flares and reflections. Your 1st AC should always be checking for light leaks of this sort, especially in situations where the sun or other strong light is hitting the camera. As an added precaution, the grips should always provide a camera umbrella or "courtesy flag" to keep light off the camera as well as the operator and focus puller.

This applies to lit bulbs in the frame, candles or other hot spots. Candles are a particular problem since the rest of the scene is usually very dark. Another source of trouble is car or truck headlights. When they hit the lens they are surprisingly strong and flare out totally. The best trick is to have the grips cut a piece of Rosco scrim and place it over the headlights. Rosco scrim is an opaque material with lots of small holes. It is very effective in controlling the light, which still flares enough to disguise the scrim.

If that is not available, a heavy dose of black dulling spray or Streaks N' Tips will help. If Streaks N' Tips is not available, the

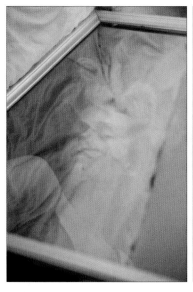 

13.25. A scene shot through glass-with no polarizer. (Photo courtesy of Tiffen).

13.26. With a polarizer; in this case the Tiffen UltraPol. (Photo courtesy of Tiffen).

hair sprays for men with thinning hair are available in lots of colors and they work just fine. Like Streaks N' Tips and dulling spray they wash off easily.

BEAM SPLITTER VIEWFINDERS AND POLARIZERS

When using cameras with video assist and modern beam splitters, it is necessary to use special polarizing filters called "circular pola filters." The term circular refers to technology used to make them, not their shape.

If these circular pola filters aren't used, there will be problems with either image in the finder or on the video assist. The image on the film is not affected. The reason for this is that modern beam splitters use a dielectric coating that has polarizing tendencies and since two polarizing filters can not be used together, there will be problems. The circular pola filter has a front and back. The front must point towards the subject or it won't be effective.

Some camera viewfinders exhibit a magenta appearance with ordinary pola filters. On other cameras, the video goes very dark. This does not happen with circular polas. If you own an auto-focus still camera or an auto-focus video camera, it also needs circular pola filters to work properly. Three chip video cameras also need circular polarizers.

CONTROLLING THE LOOK OF YOUR PROJECT

The "look" of a film or video production is a complex, interactive combination of dozens of different variables. In films where the look is very apparent, such as *Days of Heaven*, *Seven Samurai* or *Seven*, there are a few prominent devices which can be readily identified; in these cases, shooting primarily at magic hour, use of very long lenses or bleach-bypass.

As with most issues in art, it is, of course, not nearly that simple. You can make a film at magic hour, or use long lenses or bleach-bypass and there is a good chance that your project will look nothing like those films. These are just examples; this applies to all techniques and methods of visual production, and post-production as well.

The reason is that these simple techniques are not "magic bullets." Nor are they a special button you can push in post-production. Obviously, there are many variables within each technique that have to

Table 13.8. Filter factors and exposure compensation for neutral density filters.

FILTER	PERCENTAGE OF TRANSMISSION	FILTER FACTOR	EXPOSURE INCREASE IN STOPS
0.1	80	1-1/4	1/3
0.2	63	1 1/2	2/3
0.3	50	2	1
0.4	40	2 1/2	1 1/3
0.5	32	3	1 2/3
0.6	25	4	2
0.7	20	5	2 1/3
0.8	16	6	2 2/3
0.9	13	8	3
1.0	10	10	3 1/3
2.0	1	100	6 2/3
3.0	0.1	1000	10 1/3
4.0	0.01	10000	13
85 N3	32	3	1 2/3
85N6	16	6	2 2/3
86N9	9	11	3 2/3

be juggled and fine-tuned to achieve the desired look. Sometimes it is a question of budget, equipment, time, crew, weather or other factors, but this is not the point — if you educate yourself in the techniques, test and experiment and bring all the forces to bear, you can get them right. The real issue is that these methods must be used in co-ordination with all the other visual elements of the production. These include:

- Lighting style
- Color control in lighting
- Use of lenses
- Choice of locations
- Choice of camera angles
- Set design and color scheme
- Set dressing
- Wardrobe
- Makeup
- Casting
- Choice of film or video format

The point is that you have to think globally when you consider the visual style of your production — every choice, every happenstance, every decision becomes part of the mix that determines the overall look, and that look is itself a key element in the overall storytelling, emotional impact and final success of your project.

13.27. (top) Scene with no filter. (Photo courtesy of Tiffen.)

13.28. (above) With a neutral density filter for the sky. Although a polarizer might have achieved most of the same effect there are two important differences: the effect of the polarizer would depend on the angle relative to the sun and it would have also have eliminated the reflections on the water, which are an important part of the image. (Photo courtesy of Tiffen.)

13.29. (above, right) For this music video shot, we used a combination of techniques. A very light net on the lens and double printing over a defocused black-and-white dupe to desaturate and soften without getting mushy. (Photo by author.)

set operations

14.1. (previous page) Steadicam in use on the set.

14.2. (above) Orson Welles thought so much of the contribution of his cameraman Gregg Toland that he shared his title card with him on *Citizen Kane*.

The director, the cinematographer and the production designer are the three people directly responsible for all creative aspects of the film: how it looks, how it works, the "style" and the continuity.

The working relationship between the director and cinematographer is the key to getting a film made. Let's look at the responsibilities of everyone involved, first of all in a typical feature film. These procedures are general to most types of production including commercials and music videos and on small productions such as industrials and documentaries; many of these are omitted; but the essential functions are always the same.

In relation to the camera work, the director has a number of duties. It is the director who makes the decision as to what shots will be needed to complete a particular scene. She must specify where the camera will be placed and what the field of view needs to be. Some directors prefer to specify a specific lens, but most just indicate to the DP how much they want to see and then the cameraman calls for the lens to be used, or in the case of a zoom, at what focal length it will be set.

The director must also specify what camera movement, zooms or other effects will be needed. Most directors do all of this in consultation with the DP and ask for ideas and input. Problems most commonly arise when the director feels he must make every decision by himself without discussing it. Certainly it is their right to do so, but less experienced directors will sometimes call for specific lighting or camera moves that are time-consuming and ineffective when there are more efficient ways of doing the same thing more quickly and effectively (Figure 14.2).

One of the most common problems is when directors ask for long complex dolly or Steadicam moves. It can be very effective and dramatic to shoot an entire scene in one shot, with the camera moving constantly with the characters even as they go from room to room or make other types of moves. However, these types of shots are generally difficult to set up, difficult to light (since you are so often forced to hide the lights) and usually very demanding for the focus puller.

They also require many rehearsals and many takes to get all the elements to work together: the timing of actors' moves, the timing of camera moves, changes in focus and in some cases changes in

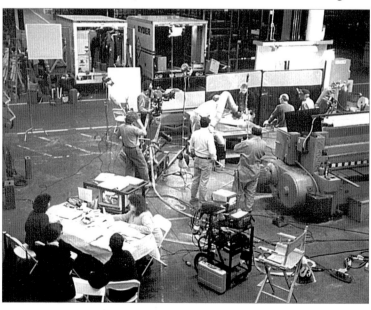

14.3. A working set: video village is at lower left, soundman's rig to the right of that and the trucks are at top of frame. (Photo courtesy of Jim Furrer.)

cinematography

T-stop. Lighting is much more complex because it is like lighting for multiple cameras with very different positions: it is very difficult to make the lighting work well for both cameras and hide all the equipment. As a result the lighting often has to be compromised and simply isn't as good as it might have been.

Long, complex shots are exciting to conceptualize and great fun when they are completed successfully. Also it sounds so quick and convenient to just "go ahead and get the whole thing in one shot." The problem is that almost inevitably, the shot gets cut up into pieces anyway, with inserts, close-up or other coverage. This means that time and effort spent to accomplish it were largely wasted.

Unless you absolutely know that the continuous take will be used, it is usually better to break it up into logical pieces. The director might also ask for special effects such as higher or lower shutter speeds, certain filtration effects and so on. Ideally, the director should arrive on the set with a complete shot list. This is a list of every shot and every piece of coverage needed for the scenes on that day's shooting. Some directors are extremely well prepared with this and others let it slide after the first few days, which is a mistake. It is true that shot lists are often deviated from, but they still provide a starting point so that everyone in all departments is headed in the same direction.

THE SHOT LIST
The shot list serves a number of functions. It lets the DP and the assistant director better plan the day, including possibly sending off some electricians and grips to pre-rig another location. It also helps the DP in determining what film stock should be used, what additional equipment should be prepped and how much time is reasonably allowable to light and set the shot within the constraints of what needs to be done that day. Even if the shot list doesn't get followed step by step, it will often at the very least provide a clue as to what style of shooting the director wants to employ — is it a few simple shots for each scene or detailed and elaborate coverage or perhaps a few "bravura" shots that emphasize style and movement and unusual camera positions?

In addition, it is very helpful in serving as a reminder for the director, the DP, the assistant director and the continuity person so that no shots or special coverage are missed. One of the gravest production errors a director can make is to wrap a set or location without getting everything needed. Reshoots are very expensive and there is always the possibility that the location or the actors will not be available to correct this mistake. Although all these people assist in this, it is the director's fundamental responsibility to "get the shots." This is far more important than being stylish, doing fancy moves, etc. None of these matter if scenes are not completed and usable.

Even if not a formal shot list, some directors will charge the script supervisor with keeping a list of "must haves." This is especially useful for cutaways or inserts that might easily be forgotten. It is also helpful for "owed" shots. "We owe a POV shot from the window," is a way of saying that there is a shot that is part of this scene that we are not shooting now but we have to pick it up sometime while at this location.

THE DIRECTOR OF PHOTOGRAPHY

The DP is primarily responsible for giving the director what she wants and also accomplishing the photographic style they have agreed on. Every director has a different style of working: some will be very specific about a certain look they want and exact framing while others want to focus on working closely with the actors and staging the scenes and leave it to the DP to decide on exact framing, camera moves and the lighting style, filtration, etc.

Ultimately the director is the boss; he or she may work in whatever fashion they wish. A truly professional DP should have the flexibility to work with a director in whatever manner they choose. It is important to discuss this before shooting starts and if the DP isn't comfortable with how a director wants to work, the time to bow out is as early as possible. Ultimately it is up to the DP to deliver for the director the kind of look and visual texture he or she is looking for and ensure that the director and editor have all the footage they need and that it is all editorially usable.

The DP's responsibilities are numerous. They include:
- The look and feel of the lighting.
- Communicating to the gaffer and key grip how the scene is to be lit: specific units to be used, gels, cuts with flags, silks, overheads, diffusion, etc. Directing and supervising the lighting process.
- Coordinating with the production designer, wardrobe, makeup and effects people concerning the overall look of the film.
- Filtration on the camera.
- Lenses: including whether to use a zoom or a prime lens (though this may sometimes be the director's call).
- If HMIs are used, insuring that there are no flicker problems (see the chapter on lighting).
- Being constantly aware of and consulting on issues of continuity: crossing the line, screen direction, etc. (see the chapter on continuity).
- Being a backstop on insuring that the director hasn't forgotten specific shots needed for good coverage of the scene.
- Supervising his team: the camera assistants, the electricians and the grips.
- Watching out for mistakes in physical continuity: clothing, props, scenery, etc. This is primarily the job of continuity and the department heads, but the eye looking through the lens is often the best way to spot these things.
- Specifying the film stock to be used and any special processing.
- Determining the exposure and informing the first AC what T-stop to use.
- Ensuring that all technical requirements are in order: correct film speed, shutter angle, etc.

Typically, when starting to light and set up a new scene, the assistant director will ask for an estimate of how long it will take to be ready to shoot. This is not an idle question and it is very important to give an accurate estimate. The AD is not just asking this to determine if the company is on schedule, there is another important consideration. She has to know when to start putting the actors "through the works." This means sending them through make-up, wardrobe and any special effects such as blood squibs.

Many actors do not appreciate being called to the set a long time before the crew is ready to shoot and in addition, if they have to wait, their makeup might need to be redone, the wardrobe might need attending to, etc. It may also affect the timing of rigging special effects, the arrival of special equipment such as water trucks and so on.

THE TEAM
The DP has three groups of technicians they are directly responsible for: the camera crew, the electricians and the grips.

CAMERA CREW
Typically on a feature or commercial the camera crew will consist of the camera operator, the First AC (assistant camera), the second AC, and the third AC or loader. If multiple cameras are used there will be more required and on very small productions or industrials the crew might be as small as a first and a second. Producers often question the need for a loader, but it is always your responsibility to remind them that if the camera crew is not sufficiently staffed, the production will be slowed down as the second has to frequently leave the set to load magazines (Figures 14.3 and 14.4).

Operator
The operator is the person who actually handles the camera: pans and tilts, zooms, coordinating with the dolly grip on moves. As she operates, she must always frame the shot as the director has called for, make the moves "smooth" and also be looking for any problem that might ruin the shot. Typical problems include the microphone dipping into the frame, lens flares, a piece of equipment visible in the frame, reflections in windows or mirrors of the crew or equipment, missed focus, a bump in the dolly track, and so on. Almost everyone uses a video tap these days, but the image on the monitor is never good enough to see everything. In addition, the director will probably be so focused on the actor's performance that small problems will not be seen. The person actually looking through the lens has the ultimate responsibility for this.

It is essential that the operator immediately report any problems. For example, if the sound boom gets into the shot, the operator should immediately call out "boom" loudly enough for both the boom operator and the director to hear. It is up to the director to decide whether to cut the shot or continue filming knowing that most of the shot is still usable or there will be coverage. This practice will vary from set to set; some directors, especially on larger budget projects may want it reported only after the shot.

On smaller projects, there will be no operator and the DP will operate the camera. Although many DPs prefer to operate, it does take time and concentration away from the other duties. On union projects it is absolutely forbidden for the DP to operate. Under the English system (also used in a number of other countries) the distinction is even more dramatic. In this way of working the DP is only responsible for lighting the scene (they are occasionally listed in the credits as "lighting cameraman"). It is often the operator who receives orders from the director about camera moves, dolly moves, focal length, etc. This applies to features only, of course.

First AC

The first AC is also known as the focus puller. The first is the crew member who directly works with the camera. Duties include:

- Loading magazines on the camera.
- Ensuring that the camera operates properly.
- Checking for hairs in the gate before any scene is wrapped.
- Guarding against flares, light leaks and any other problems.
- Setting the T-stop; also, frame rate and shutter angle.
- Measuring the focus distances.
- Controlling focus so that the proper parts of the scene are sharp.
- In some cases operating the zoom control (this is often done by the operator using a zoom control mounted on the handle).
- Moving the camera to the next setup, with the help of the other AC's and sometimes the grips.
- Guarding the camera against damage or malfunction.
- Making sure the proper film stock is loaded.
- Calling out the footage so that the second AC can note it on the camera report.

Focus may be determined by measuring or by eye. Measuring is generally done in two ways. Most cameras have a mark on the side that identifies the exact position of the film plane. Positioned precisely above that is a stud that the AC can hook a cloth measuring tape onto and measure the exact distance to all the objects that will be focused on. Most AC's also carry a carpenter's metal measuring tape, either 1" or 3/4" wide. This is useful for quick checks before close in shots. The metal tape extends out quickly and the AC can make last minute measurements in case something has moved.

The third method is eye focus. This can be done with either the operator and the AC's or by the first AC himself. Someone, either the actor, a stand in or the second AC goes to each of the key positions. The operator looks through the viewfinder and focuses. The first AC then marks it on the dial of the focus mechanism.

For critical focus it may be necessary for the second to take the top off a small flash light (Maglight). The exposed bulb provides an accurate and fast focus point that can be used even in low light situations. For complex dolly shots, the first may make tape marks alongside the dolly track, thus knowing that at a specific point he is x number of feet and inches away from the subject. The last component can only be described as "zen." Good AC's are uncanny in their ability to visually judge distance and make adjustments on the fly. The first AC is also the one who goes to the check-out. Check-out is usually the day before shooting starts. At checkout the first:

- Checks that all equipment ordered is there.
- Checks every piece of equipment for proper operation.
- Tests the magazines for jamming or scratching.
- Tests the camera for jamming or scratching.
- Makes sure the proper ground glass is in the camera and that it is properly seated.
- Cleans anything that needs it: lenses, groundglass, the mirror shutter, etc.
- Checks that all batteries are fully charged.
- If there are multiple cameras, labels each case appropriately (e.g., "A camera," "B camera," etc.) Usually, different colors of camera tape are used for this.

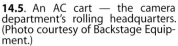

14.5. An AC cart — the camera department's rolling headquarters. (Photo courtesy of Backstage Equipment.)

Good ACs will always go through a mental ritual before every shot: is the T-stop properly set, is the focus prepared, is the camera set at the right speed and are their any flares? It is best to do it in the same order every time for consistency. In previous times this checklist was remembered as FAST: focus, aperture, speed and tachometer. Most cameras no longer have tachometers, but they do have frame rate controls which must be checked regularly. It takes no more than the errant flip of a switch to change the speed from 24fps to 23 or 25fps.

The first should also keep track of how much footage is used on the first take and then check to make sure there is enough stock left to get all the way through another take of the same shot. It can be very frustrating for the director and the actors to roll out in the middle of the take.

As soon as the director announces she is through with the scene, the first AC immediately checks the gate. This is to ensure that a hair or other piece of junk has not crept into the film gate and thus ruined the shot. Anything like this would not be visible through the eyepiece and if something is in there, everyone must know immediately so that it can be reshot. There are three ways of doing it. One is to look into the lens from the front. This can be difficult with zooms because there is so much glass between your eye and the gate. The second is to open the camera and gently lift the film up and examine the gate. Many ACs don't like this method because there is a possibility that something was there, but lifting the film moved it. The most reliable method is to pull the lens and look at the gate.

Second AC

When the DP call for a lens change, filter or any other piece of equipment, it is the second who will bring it from the cart (Figure 14.5) or the truck. The second assistant camera is also sometimes referred to as the clapper or the clapper/loader, especially in the UK. This is because on of her main duties is to operate the slate or clapper as it is sometimes called. The slate serves several functions. First, it allows the editor or video transfer person to coordinate the visual image of the stick coming down with the audio of the "clap," thus achieving sound sync.

The slate also identifies the scene number, the take number and the roll number. It will also identify a scene as day - interior, night - exterior, etc. The reason for this is that the timer at the lab or the video transfer person needs to know the general type of look the scene should have. It should also indicate whether a shot is sync sound or MOS.

The slate will also indicate any effects such as different frame rates. In the case of multiple cameras, each one may be slated separately or one slate might serve them all, which is called "'common marker." A variation on this is to "head slate" each camera with their individual roll number, frame rate and other information and then use a simple clapper or timecode slate to clap all cameras together. This insures the proper data for each camera but saves film by providing a single marker for all. The head slate need not be continuous; just roll off a few frames and then turn off the camera. This is called "bumping" a slate.

Slating Technique

At the time the AD calls "roll camera" and the AC announces "speed" (that the camera is up to sync speed), the second holds the slate where it is in focus and readable and announces the scene and take number so that it will be recorded on the audio tape. She then slaps the top stick down sharply so that the clap is clearly audible on the audio. She then quickly gets out of the way. In case adjustments are necessary, such as changing focus from the slate to the scene, the operator will call out "set" and the director can then call for "action."

Older slates could be written on with chalk. Most slates today are white plastic and an erasable marker is used. ACs tape a makeup powder puff to the end of the erasable marker; that way they will be conveniently together in one piece for both marking and erasing. This is referred to as the "mouse."

In some cases, it is not desirable to slate before the shot. This might include filming with an infant where the clapper might frighten them. In such instances a tail slate can be used. A tail slate comes at the end of the shot and must be done before the camera is switched off or it can't be used for synchronization. For tail slates, the slate must be held upside down. The clapper is still used.

Tail slates should be avoided at all costs. It is time consuming and expensive for the telecine operator or editor to roll all the way to the end of the take, sync up and then roll back to the beginning to lay the scene in. Another reason is that it is very easy to forget at the end of the take and switch off the camera before the slate comes in. It is also important to note the tail slate on the camera report. In the case of shooting without sync sound, everything is the same except that the clapper is not used. It may be necessary to open the clapper slightly on a timecode slate for the numbers to be visible and running but it is important not to clap it. If you do, the editor may spend time looking for an audio track that does not exist.

Timecode slates

Timecode slates include the usual information but also have a digital readout of the timecode which will match the timecode being recorded on the audio tape; they are also called "smart slates." Timecode slates make syncing up much quicker and cheaper and particular shots are more readily identified. The reason it is faster and cheaper in telecine is that the colorist rolls the film up to the frame which has the clapper sync on it. She then reads the timecode numbers that are displayed and types them in. The computer controlled audio playback deck then automatically rolls up to the correct point to lay in sync. Having the deck find it automatically is significantly faster than manually searching — and telecine time is very expensive. If there is not sufficient pre-roll for the timecode on the audio tape or if the slate is unreadable, then this automation fails and sync must be set up manually.

The clapper is still used on timecode slates. When the clap stick is up, the timecode will be displayed as it is running. When the clapper is brought down, the timecode freezes, thus indicating the exact timecode at the time of slating. An additional feature of Denecke timecode slates is that after the sync timecode freezes for a moment, today's date displays briefly. This helps keep things organized in post. The date can be set up to read in a variety of ways.

The timecode is generated by the audio recorder and the slate must be "jammed" at the beginning of every day and periodically throughout the day. Jamming is done by connecting the slate to the recorder, which then transfers the timecode it is generating. Since there is a tendency for the code to drift, this must be redone throughout the day. Some slates will also display a message when they determine that jamming is necessary. Usually it says, "feed me."

The second must be aware of the focal length of the lens and then estimate the proper distance at which to hold the slate. The slate must be readable and in focus; otherwise it will cause problems in syncing and for the editor who is trying to identify the shot.

Ideally, the slate must be as close to the focus distance as possible, thus eliminating the need to refocus after slating, however, this is not always possible. Another subtlety is that if the slate is held right in front of the actor's face, the clap should be as gentle as possible in order not to throw the performer's concentration off.

One variation of this is used when multiple cameras are continuously shooting a big event such as a concert. In this case it is often wise to position a continuously running timecode slate (preferably hardwired to the recorder) where every camera can pan over and see it. Then, when a camera has to stop to reload, as soon as it starts up again, the operator pans over, shoots a few seconds of running timecode and then pans back to the action.

Camera Reports

In addition to slating, the second will also maintain the camera reports (Figure 14.6). The camera report will include some general information:

- Name of production company.
- Title of the project.
- In some cases the production number.
- Name of director.
- Name of DP.
- In some cases the purchase order number.
- Sometimes, as a courtesy, the film lab will pre-print this information on a batch of camera reports.

Then, the information gets more specific to this roll of film:

- Camera number or letter (A camera, B camera, etc.)
- The magazine number (very important if you are later trying to identify which of the mags is scratching or jamming).
- Roll number of the film stock loaded.
- Date exposed.
- Raw stock type used.
- Scene number.
- Take number.
- Footage used for each take, usually referred to as the "dial."
- Whether a shot was with sound or "MOS."
- Circle takes: the take number of shots the director wants to be printed are circled.
- Remarks.
- Inventory: the total amount good footage (G), no good (NG) and waste (W).
- The total amount shot when the mag is downloaded. For example, "Out at 970."

A simpler type of camera report is used when a camera crew is working alone, such as in industrials, documentaries, etc. It is called a caption sheet. Camera reports are always three sheets and writing on the top sheet is transferred to the second two. The top sheet is white. This copy is folded and securely taped to the film can when the roll is finished. The second sheet is usually yellow. It is given to the production manager or first AD who then passes it on to the editor. The third sheet is retained by production for reference in case there are any problems. In some cases there may be additional sheets for other departments such as the production coordinator.

Standard procedure is for the loader to fill in as much of the infor-

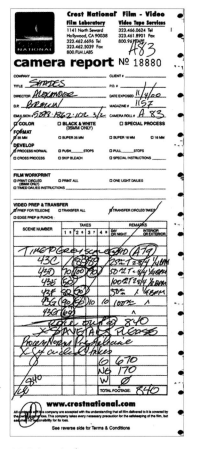

14.6. A typical camera report.

mation as possible and then tape the camera report to the mag before it is delivered to the set. When the mag is loaded onto the camera, the second will usually then tape the report to the back of the slate for convenience. After each take the second will then ask the first for the "dial": the cumulative footage shot as displayed on the counter. This is always rounded off to the nearest ten and only the first two numbers are given: e.g., "97" rather than "970."

The second is also responsible for providing the first with whatever he needs, most importantly the lens that is called for, fresh magazines, lens shades, charged batteries and different tripods or other mounting equipment. The equipment, especially the lenses, are under his care and he must safeguard them at all times. Once the camera is set up on the dolly, sticks or high-hat, the first AC or one of the other camera crew members should never be more than "two arms lengths away" from the camera.

Often the first AC and the DP are in places they can't easily leave, such as the top of a ladder, or more importantly on a crane. As was discussed in the chapter on *Camera Dynamics*, it is absolutely critical that no one step off the crane until the grips have rebalanced it. Doing so can result in serious injury and damage. Generally, the second will have some sort of camera cart that he will roll as close to the set as possible so that all equipment is readily available.

If there is one, the third AC or loader assists the second in maintaining the equipment, making sure it is available. She will also generally be the person running mags, batteries and other equipment back and forth from the camera truck or central camera location.

The second also handles all marking of actors. Once the actors' exact positions are determined by the director in the blocking rehearsal, the second quickly and quietly moves in and makes marks. Most often marks are made with camera tape or 1″ paper tape, either with a "T" indicating where the actors' toes must end up or with an open ended box for each foot. If there are several actors in the scene, colored tape is used to identify each one (Figures 14.7 and 14.8).

The most difficult situation is where the floor or ground is visible in the shot. In this case, ingenuity is called for. Outdoors a natural object such as a twig can be used. Indoors sometimes a small piece of black tape won't be obtrusive. In other cases, the actor must take a visual cue such as: "You end up exactly opposite the end of the pool table." The simplest form of emergency mark is the "spit mark" which needs no explanation.

As the old saw goes the only two things an actor has to do is know their lines and hit their marks (or as Spencer Tracy put it, "not bump into the furniture"). Especially when focus is critical or a dolly move or crane move has to be coordinated, it is extremely important that the actor hit the marks. If she doesn't, there's a good chance that the shot will be out of focus or the camera move won't work. A good AC can sometimes compensate by making a mental judgment of how far back or forward they are and adjust the focus, but this isn't always possible. As soon as the shot is over and the first AC has checked the gate and announced it clean, the second should remove all the marks so they don't confuse anyone later or accidentally appear in another shot.

Loader

The loader may be the low man on the totem pole, but her responsibility is a critical one: she must safeguard and properly handle the film stock. Not only is film stock very expensive but if it is accidentally exposed to light and the loader doesn't report it, the company might end up shooting several scenes which will then be unusable.

14.7. (below) Types of toemarks.

14.8. (bottom) Each place where an actor must stop is marked. Giving each actor their own color helps avoid confusion.

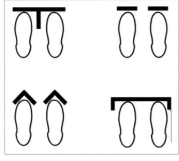

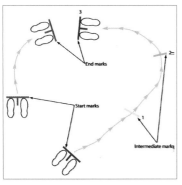

One prime rule applies to not only the loader, but the entire camera crew: if you make a mistake, report it to the DP immediately. The DP must then inform the director that the scene might need to be re-shot. If something happens, don't try to hide it and don't hesitate, even if it will make you look really stupid. You must report it. Mistakes happen and being honest counts for far more with most DP's than the occasional error.

The exact procedures for loading are beyond the scope of this book, but are available in books dealing with being a camera assistant. The loader also keeps extensive paperwork on the film stock inventory. These reports are beyond the scope of this book, but there are several excellent books on camera assisting which describe them in detail.

ELECTRICIANS

The electric crew carries out the DP's instructions on lighting. The crew consists of the gaffer (the head of the crew), the second electric and at least one other electrician. As the job gets larger the number of electricians must increase. An inadequate crew slows the entire production down. The gaffer is also sometimes referred to in the credits as Chief Lighting Technician. In England, electricians are called "sparks." The DP gives his orders to the gaffer who then instructs the electricians what to do. It is important that the gaffer always be nearby the camera. The DP should never have to spend time looking for him. This, of course, applies to the key grip or dolly grip as well.

The gaffer's chief assistant is the second electric, also called the best boy electric or assistant lighting technician. The second has three main duties: maintaining and overseeing all the equipment, supervising everything to do with electricity and directly supervising the crew. On location the second will spend a lot of time on the truck organizing and maintaining the equipment so that it will always be ready for use.

The second designs the layout of the distribution: the location of the generator, the size of the cables to suit the total load, where runs will break off, where distribution boxes will be placed, etc. Important duties include checking that the power supply, cables and distribution equipment are not overloaded, that the generator is running properly and supplying the correct voltage. With HMIs it is also critical to check that the generator is running at the proper frequency (see *Technical Issues*). In the United States it is 60 hertz and 50 hertz in many other countries. The second also supervises the crew to ensure they are being put to best use and working efficiently. The electricians do most of the actual work of bringing lights to the set, putting them in position, getting them to the height required by the DP, adjusting the barn doors, adding scrims if needed and plugging them in after checking with the second to make sure they don't overload a circuit. Adding gels or diffusion is split between the electrics and grips. If the gel is attached to the light or the barndoors, the electricians do it. If it is in a frame and set separate from the light, the grips do it.

GRIPS

The grip crew is headed by the key grip. His assistant is the best boy grip or second grip. Then there is the third grip and whatever additional grips are needed. As with electricians, a three man crew is the minimum for all except the smallest jobs. There may be a dolly grip whose sole responsibility is to push the dolly. It sounds simple but a good dolly grip is a real artist: timing the move exactly, hitting the marks and keeping everything smooth.

The grips have a wide range of duties:
- The grips handle all C-stands, high rollers, etc., and whatever goes on them: nets, flags, frames, etc. This includes any form of lighting control or shadow making which is not attached to the light itself (Figure 14.9).
- They also handle all types of mounting hardware, specialized clamps of all types which might be used to attach lights or almost anything else anywhere the DP needs them.
- They handle all "bagging." Once a light is set, the grips bring as many sand bags as are necessary to secure and stabilize it. They may also have to tie it off or secure it in another way in windy or unstable conditions.
- They deal with all issues of leveling, whether it be lights, ladders or the camera. Their tools for this are apple boxes, cribbing, step blocks and wedges.
- They handle all dollies, lay all dolly track and level it. Also any cranes are theirs to set up and operate. This is especially critical when a crane is the type that the DP and first AC ride on. Once they are seated, the crane grip then balances the crane by adding weights in the back so that the whole rig can be easily moved in any direction. Once this has been done, it is absolutely critical that no one step off the crane until the grips readjust the balance. Stepping off would make the front too light and the crane would shoot up, possibly injuring someone or damaging the camera. Deaths from crane accidents are not uncommon; everyone must be on their toes and very focused when working with a crane.
- The grips are also in charge of rigging the camera if it's in an unusual spot, such as attached to the front of a roller coaster, up in a tree, etc.
- The grips build any scaffolding, platforms or other rigs necessary for camera rigs or other purposes. They may assist the stunt men in building platforms for the air bags or mounts for stunt equipment. Any other small construction project that doesn't call for set builders is in their purview as well.
- The grip crew and the key grip in particular are in charge of safety on the set, outside of anything electrical.

This is the U.S. system; in other countries it is handled differently, the primary difference being that the electricians handle all lighting related issues such as nets and flags, etc.

OTHER UNITS

Three other types of teams will also be under the DP's control: second unit, additional cameras and rigging crews. Second unit is an important function. Usually it is used for shots that do not include the principal actors. Typical second unit work includes establishing shots, crowd shots, stunts or special effects and insert shots. Shots that include significant lighting are not generally considered for second unit, except in the case of special effects (Figure 14.10).

Second unit may be supervised by a second unit director, but often the team consists only of a second unit DP, one or two camera assistants and possibly a grip. It is the duty of the second unit DP to deliver the shots the director asks for in accordance with the instructions and guidance of the director of photography. The shots must be in a style that is consistent with the principal photography. It will often be up to the DP to specify what lenses are used, film stock and camera filtration. It is the DP's name that is listed on the credits as the person responsible for the photography of the film; the audience

14.9. A grip cart; sometimes called a taco cart. Mobility is the name of the game and keeping the essentials nearby is critical — the last thing a DP wants to hear is "it's on the truck." (Photo courtesy of Backstage Equipment.)

and the executives will not know that a bad shot or a mistake is due to the second unit. In light of this responsibility it is standard practice for the DP to have a say in who the second unit cameraperson is.

In the case where additional cameras are used in principal photography, they are designated "B" camera, "C" camera and so on. On a big stunt which cannot be repeated such as blowing up a building, it is not uncommon for a dozen or more cameras to be used. Some are used as a back-up to the main camera in case of malfunction, some are just to get different angles, some run at different speeds and some are "crash cams," small expendable cameras that can be placed in dangerous positions.

In slating with multiple cameras, there may be a separate slate for each camera, clearly marked as "A" or "B" slate. The slating AC then calls out "A marker" or "B marker" and claps the slate for that camera. Naturally, separate camera reports are kept for each camera. An alternative is to use a common marker. This is possible where all cameras are aimed at approximately the same part of the scene or where one camera can quickly pan over to catch the slate, then pan back to the opening frame. If this is the case, then the director must wait for all operators to call "set" before calling "action." Calling out "set" should be standard procedure in any case where the slating can't be right where the camera is ready for the opening frame, if the 1st AC has to refocus or another adjustment needs to be made. In the case of additional cameras, there is only one DP and the rest of the cameras are run by additional operators. Ideally, each additional camera should have its own AC and perhaps its own second AC.

In some cases, cameras are "locked off," usually because it is simply too dangerous to have an operator in that position. In these cases the camera is mounted securely, the frame is set and the focus and T-stop are set. They are then either operated by remote switch or as roll is called, an AC switches on the camera and runs to safety. Protective metal housings, called "crash boxes," may be used if their is danger to the camera. Protective Plexiglas or pieces of plywood with a small hole for the lens might also be used.

Motion picture and video production can be a dangerous business and safety must be taken extremely seriously. We are often under pressure to push the edge because a shot is important or time is of the essence. In such cases, stay cool and remind everyone: "It's only a movie." Traditionally the key grip is the general safety officer on a set and the gaffer is in charge of safety concerning electricity and fire. Either of these have the duty and the obligation to assess a situation as too dangerous and say, "Sorry, we're not doing this." The DP has the same obligation especially as regard cranes, camera cars, helicopter shots, etc.

COORDINATING WITH OTHER DEPARTMENTS

Besides his own crew, the DP must also coordinate with other crew members. The first is the production designer. If sets are being built or extensively dressed, it is essential that the DP look at them while they are still in plans or sketches, not after they are built. The DP will discuss with the designer what lighting opportunity will be part of the set. These include windows, skylights, doors and other types of places to hide lights or bring light into the set.

Also to be discussed are the practicals, that is, working lights that are part of the set, whether they are hanging lamps, wall sconces or table lamps. A good set dresser will usually have a couple of spare table lamps or hanging lights on the truck. These can be invaluable either as a lighting source themselves or as a "motivator" of light.

14.10. A second unit shot on the film *Event Horizon*. (Photo courtesy of Mark Weingartner.)

The situation may call for "wild walls," which are walls or other pieces of the set which can be easily removed to make room for the camera, dolly track and other equipment. Finally, it is important to consider not only the set, but how it will be positioned on the stage. There might be a window or glass wall that would be a great lighting opportunity, but if it is only a few feet away from the wall of the stage, it may be difficult or impossible to use it. On the set, the DP is in constant communication with the assistant director concerning the schedule, how much time is left before the actors go into overtime, what scenes are left to do, etc. Being the first AD is one of the most stressful jobs in the industry; a good one a real treasure.

Before the shooting begins the AD makes the schedule indicating what scenes will be shot on what days and a one liner, which is a one line description of each scene. The schedule also indicates whether scenes are day or night, interior or exterior whether the day scenes are to be shot during the day or night and vice-versa. This is essential for the DP in planning what equipment and supplies will be needed.

At the beginning of each day, a production assistant or second AD will hand out "sides." These are copies of the script pages to be shot that day which have been reduced to a quarter of a page, so that they can be easily slipped into a pocket. The sides are the "bible" for the day. Of all the principles of filmmaking perhaps the most important of all is that everyone must know what is going on and is working, as they say, "on the same page." Communication is the key — nothing can derail a production quicker than poor communication.

During shooting, the DP is under great stress and is thinking about a dozen things at the same time; complete focus and concentration are essential. One of the unwritten rules of filmmaking is that only certain people talk to the DP: the director, of course, the first AD, the first AC, the gaffer and the grip. A working set is no place for idle chit-chat, or as a great AD used to say, "Tell your stories walking."

SET PROCEDURES

Generally the lighting for the scene will be "roughed in" based on a general understanding of the scene as described by the director. This may range from everything fully rigged and hot for a night exterior to only having the power run for a small interior.

Once the DP is ready to begin lighting seriously, the steps of production are reasonably formalized. They are as follows.

- The director describes to the DP what shot is wanted first. At this stage it is important to have at least a rough idea of all of the shots needed so there are no surprises later.
- The director blocks the scene and there is a rehearsal.
- Marks are set; focus is measured.
- The AD asks the DP for a time estimate.
- The AD announces that the DP "has the set."
- The DP huddles with the gaffer and key grip and tells them what he wants.
- The electrics and grips carry out the DP's orders.
- The DP supervises the placement of the camera, the lens, etc.
- When all is set, the DP informs the AD that he is ready.
- The director takes over and stages final rehearsal with the actors in makeup and wardrobe.
- If necessary, the DP may have to make a few minor adjustments (especially if the blocking or actions have changed), called "tweaking." Of course, the less the better, but ulti-

mately it is the DP's responsibility to get it right, even if there is some grumbling.

- The DP meters the scene and determines the lens aperture. When ready, he informs the AD.
- The director may have a final word for the actors or camera operator, then announce that he or she is ready for a take.
- The AD calls for "last looks" and the makeup, hair and wardrobe people swarm in to make sure the actors are ready in every detail.
- The AC rechecks every detail of camera operation.
- If there is smoke, rain, or fire effects, they are set in motion.
- When they are finished, the AD calls to "lock it up," this is repeated by second second ADs and production assistants to make sure that everyone around knows to stop working and be quiet for a take.
- The AD calls "roll sound."
- The sound recordist calls "speed" (after having allowed for pre-roll.)
- The AD calls "roll camera."
- The first AC switches on and calls "speed." (If there are multiple cameras it is "A speed," "B speed," etc.)
- The first AC or operator calls "mark it" and the second AC slates, calling out the scene and take number.
- When the camera is in position and in focus the operator calls "set."
- When applicable the AD may call "background action," meaning the extras and atmosphere people begin their activity.
- The director calls "action" and the scene begins.
- When the scene is over the director calls "cut."
- If there are any, the operator mentions problems she saw in the shot and any reasons why another take may be necessary or any adjustments which may make the physical action of the shot work more smoothly.
- If there is another take the AD tells the actors and the operator tells the dolly grip "back to one," meaning everyone resets to position one.
- The second AC calls for "dial" (amount of film shot on that take) and makes his notes on the camera report.
- If there is a need for adjustments, they are made and the process starts over.

Some directors prefer that they be the only ones to call cut. Others ask that if something is terribly wrong and the shot is becoming a waste of film, the DP or the operator may call cut and switch off the camera. As mentioned above, the operator will usually call out problems as they occur, such as a boom in the shot, a bump in the dolly track, etc. It is then up to the director to cut or to continue with the shot. If you as the operator are in a mode where you call out problems as they occur, you certainly want to do it between dialog, so that if the director does decide to live with the problems, the sound editor can cut out your comments.

Most directors prefer that no one talk to the principal actors except themselves. For purely technical adjustments about marks or timing, most directors don't mind if you just quickly mention it to the actor directly — but only if it will not disturb their concentration or affect performance.

14.11. A good crew has to be prepared for anything that might come up on a set; the ability to improvise and solve problems is the mark of true professionalism. It comes from a combination of intelligence, creativity and most of all — experience. (Photo courtesy of Mark Weingartner.)

CONCLUSION

When everybody is in sync and everything is working right, a film crew at work is a pleasure to behold: a well oiled machine — efficient, creative and full of energy. Just be sure to remember how much fun it can be the next time you're having one of "those" days.

A MATTER OF STYLE

On the question of attire on the set, this from the *Steadicam Operator's Manual* by the legendary Ted Churchill. It applies primarily to Steadicam operators, but there is a lesson for anyone who works on the set. (Used by permission of Jack Churchill.)

"And more often than not the sole determining factor is nothing more than a matter of appearances — a matter of style.

First impressions, it is said, are the most important. One is often judged on looks alone. So what should one wear? Practically speaking, your attire should not be competitive with the executive producer, yet it need not inspire others to demand you plug in the coffee machine either. Leisure suits don't imply artistry, or designer jeans hard work.

Dress for the job: high concentration, worry, and enormous physical exertion. Be comfortable. Avoid clothing which easily shows perspiration, wrinkles easily or on which the colors are liable to run when in constant contact with moisture. Remember that if you arrive on the set really pressed out you're going to look like garbage at the end of the third take. On the other hand if you dress like garbage you will look approximately the same at the end of the day. So always opt for less apparent disintegration in your apparel. Always avoid wearing loud color combinations. If noticed you may be asked to shoot everything."

technical issues

SUN LOCATION WITH A COMPASS

For shots involving the sun or the moon three things are necessary: (1) The correct position of the celestial object at the time you want to shoot (2) a good compass and (3) geomagnetic declination information for the shooting locations.

First a word about compasses. You need a good one. Any compass will point to magnetic north, but you need one that is calibrated to at least 2° and which can be aligned precisely — this will usually mean either a compass with an optical sight or a military style lensatic compass. Particularly for shooting sunrises, great precision is necessary. Perhaps the least known fact about compasses is that they do not necessarily work equally well in all parts of the world. Compasses are manufactured with a certain amount of counter weighting and the proper amount of magnetizing to match certain locations, specifically north and south latitudes.

A compass designed for the U.S., as it nears the pole region, will increasingly begin to point into the earth (Figure 15.2). You'll have to hold the compass housing unevenly to get any kind of reading at all. All the needle wants to do is point into the ground, not to the horizon. So if you are going to locations significantly different in latitude from where you bought your compass, be sure to get a unit made for that area. Most compass manufacturers offer solutions to this problem. Silva, a Swedish manufacture of compasses, offers five varieties:

MN	Magnetic North.
NME	North Magnetic Equatorial.
ME	Magnetic Equatorial.
SME	South Magnetic Equatorial.
MS	Magnetic South.

Suunto makes the World Compass which can be used anywhere in the world. It works by having the needle and the magnet pivot independently. Other manufacturers also make compasses which can be used anywhere except for a large zone surrounding the magnetic North Pole and the Geographic North Pole where no magnetic compasses will work.

DECLINATION

There is one more problem to be dealt with in using a compass. Only at 2 North/South lines in the northern hemisphere does the compass needle point to True North. One is through Russia and the other is along a line which goes through Wisconsin to Alabama and south. These are called the agonic lines. At all other places on the globe, the compass will either point slightly East or West of the actual geographical True North.

The angle by which it is off is called "Magnetic Variation" or "Declination." Magnetic North is located about 1,000 miles South of Geographic North, near Bathurst Island, off the Northern coast of Canada above Hudson Bay. In the continental United States, this angle of error varies from 25° East, to about 23° West of True North. Alaska's declination ranges from 15° East to 36° East. If you are West of the agonic line, you subtract the declination. If you are East of the agonic line you add the declination. The following chart shows magnetic declination for various locations (Figure 15.3).

For even more accurate and localized information, you can always call the local airport's flight control center, 24 hours a day. On remote locations, it may be necessary to obtain good quality maps for the area and to use a GPS locator to determine exact latitude and longitude. Once you have done all this you now need the informa-

15.1. (previous page) A complex setup for a timeslicing shot. (Photo courtesy of PAWS, Inc.)

15.2. (below) World zones for compasses; a compass won't be accurate unless it is for the correct zone. (Map courtesy of Silva.)

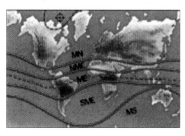

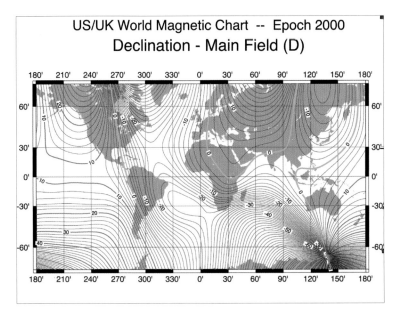

US/UK World Magnetic Chart -- Epoch 2000
Declination - Main Field (D)

tion for the celestial body itself. You need to know its azimuth (compass direction) and altitude (angle above the horizon) at any particular point in time. This can be obtained from nautical charts (see the *Filmmaker's Pocket Reference* for these charts) or from other information sources such as the U.S. Geological Survey. For convenience however, the best way is to use software that will tell you this information. The example in Figure 15.4 was obtained using SunPATH®, made by Widescreen Software.

This type of software can also be used to determine the length of shadows for nearby objects or as a guide in building a set or placing a window so that a particular sunlight effect will occur on a certain date (if it's not cloudy, of course). To determine shadows, it is necessary to also have a clinometer, which is a device that will tell you how many degrees above your level an object is.

The clinometer is especially important if you are attempting to fix an exact sunrise or sunset time and your horizon line is not the true horizon. In other words, if there are any hills or buildings between you and where the sun or moon rises/sets, the time listed in the local newspaper will not be accurate. Once you determine how many degrees above true horizon your visible horizon is, the software makes it simple to determine an exact rise/set time. All of this is especially critical if you are attempting a sunrise shot with a long lens. In this case, your camera must be setup and aimed with great precision literally "in the dark." One word of caution: many people will attempt to set up for a sunrise by watching the horizon and seeing where the most intense glow is, then aim the camera at that pre-sunrise glow. It does not work! The pre-rise glow will be several degrees off because the sun is moving south (or north, in the southern hemisphere) as it is rising — assuming you are not directly on the equator.

Use the software, have a good compass, then have faith. These methods can also be used to determine camera placement so that a sunrise or sunset occurs directly in line with a building, an aircraft takeoff or landing, a hill or anything else for which you can fix a location. Don't forget to set your watches to an accurate time source and have everyone on the production team synchronize them.

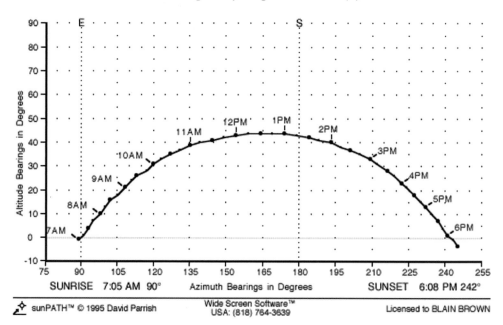

Los Angeles, California

Latitude	34° 03' N	Time Zone: 8 Pacific
Longitude	118° 14' W	Daylight Savings Time
Magnetic Declination 14° E		(4/ 1/01 to 10/28/01)

N

Azimuth Bearings are given for MAGNETIC NORTH. DO NOT make a correction with your compass.
The Magnetic Declination has been used in the calculations.

	Date	Dawn	SUNRISE	Azimuth	Day Length	SUNSET	Azimuth	Dusk
Wed	10/24/01	6:48 AM	7:05 AM	90°	11:03	6:08 PM	242°	6:25 PM

— **Wednesday, October 24, 2001** —

15 minute intervals

AZ°- Azimuth ALT°- Altitude

	AZ°	ALT°	Sf*		AZ°	ALT°	Sf*		AZ°	ALT°	Sf*		AZ°	ALT°	Sf*		AZ°	ALT°	Sf*
7AM	89	-1	---		113	26	2.05	12PM	154	43	1.07		201	37	1.33	5PM	232	13	4.33
	91	1	57.3		117	28	1.88		159	44	1.04		205	35	1.43		234	10	5.67
	93	4	14.3	10AM	120	31	1.66		164	44	1.04	3PM	209	33	1.54		237	7	8.14
	95	7	8.14		123	33	1.54		169	44	1.04		212	31	1.66		239	4	14.3
8AM	98	10	5.67		127	35	1.43	1PM	174	44	1.04		216	28	1.88	6PM	241	1	57.3
	100	13	4.33		131	37	1.33		179	43	1.07		219	26	2.05		243	-1	---
	102	16	3.49	11AM	135	39	1.23		184	42	1.11	4PM	222	23	2.36		245	-4	---
	105	18	3.08		139	40	1.19		188	41	1.15		224	21	2.60				
9AM	108	21	2.60		144	41	1.15	2PM	193	40	1.19		227	18	3.08				
	111	24	2.25		149	42	1.11		197	38	1.28		230	15	3.73				

* Shadow Length = Object Height x Shadow Factor (Sf)

SUNRISE 7:05 AM 90°   Azimuth Bearings in Degrees   SUNSET 6:08 PM 242°

sunPATH™ © 1995 David Parrish   Wide Screen Software™ USA: (818) 764-3639   Licensed to BLAIN BROWN

15.4. A sunchart produced by Sun-PATH® software.

FLICKER

As discussed in the chapter on *The Tools of Lighting*: there are two basic kinds of light sources. One is a filament (usually tungsten) that is heated by electrical current until it glows and emits light. The other type is a discharge source. These include fluorescents, HMIs, Xenons, mercury vapor, sodium vapor and many others. In all of these, instead of a filament, an arc is established between a cathode and an anode. This arc then excites gases or a plasma cloud, inducing them to glow. All discharge sources run on alternating current.

Any arc based bulb powered by alternating current has an output that rises and fall as the waveform of the AC varies. Alternating current rises and falls as it heats a tungsten filament as well, but the filament stays hot enough that the light it emits does not vary a great deal. There is some loss of output, but it is minimal, usually only about 10 to 15%, not enough to affect exposure. With discharge sources, the light output does rise and fall significantly throughout the AC cycle.

Although rarely perceptible to the eye, flicker appears on film as an uneven variation in exposure. This effect is a result of variations in exposure from frame to frame as a result of a mismatch in the output wave form of the light and the framing rate of the camera. Flicker can be bad enough to completely ruin the footage. The output of an AC power source is a sine wave. When the current flow is at the maximum (top of the wave) or minimum (bottom of the wave) the output of the light will be maximum: the light doesn't care whether the flow is positive or negative.

When the sine wave crosses the axis the current flow drops to zero. When that happens, the bulb produces less output. Since the light is "on" for both the positive and negative side of the sine wave, it reaches its maximum at twice the rate of the AC: 120 cycles per second for 60 hertz current and 100 cycles per second for 50 hertz current. For an HMI with a magnetic ballast (a copper coil wound around a core), the output at the crossover point may be as low as 17% of total output.

With film there is another complication: the shutter is opening and closing at a rate which may be different than the rate at which the light output is varying. When the relationship of the shutter and the light output varies in relation to each other, each film frame is exposed to different amounts of the cycle. The result is exposure that varies enough to be noticeable.

There are two possibilities: the frame rate of the camera can be unsteady or the frequency of the electrical supply can fluctuate or the frame rate of the shutter creates a mismatch in the synchronization of the shutter and the light output. The first two are obvious: if either the shutter rate or the light output are random, it is clear that there will be different amounts of exposure for each frame. The third is a bit more complex. Only certain combinations of shutter speed and power supply frequency can be considered acceptably safe. Deviations from these combinations always risk noticeable flicker. Four conditions are essential to prevent HMI or fluorescent flicker:

- Constant frequency in the AC power supply.
- Constant framing rate in the camera.
- Compatible shutter angle.
- Compatible frame rate.

The first two conditions are satisfied with either crystal controls on the generator and camera or by running one or both of them from the local AC mains, which in most countries are usually reliable in frequency.

The shutter angle and frame rate are determined by consulting the appropriate charts. A fifth condition: relationship of AC frequency to shutter is generally only crucial in high speed cinematography and is usually not a factor in most filming situations.

At 24fps camera speed, if the power supply is stable, shutter angle can vary from 90° to 200° with little risk. The ideal shutter angle is 144° since this results in an exposure time of 1/60th of a second and so it matches the frequency of the mains power supply. In actual practice, there is little risk in using a 180° shutter if the camera is

24 FPS	25 FPS
120	100
60	50
40	25
30	20
24	10
20	5
15	4
12	2
10	1
8	
6	
5	
4	
2	
1	

24FPS/50HZ POWER - SAFE FRAME RATES AT ANY SPEED				
1.000	4.000	6.315	10.000	**24.000**
1.500	4.800	6.666	10.909	30.000
1.875	5.000	7.058	12.000	40.000
2.000	5.217	7.500	13.333	60.000
2.500	5.454	8.000	15.000	120.00
3.000	5.714	8.571	17.143	
3.750	6.000	9.231	20.000	

25FPS/50HZ POWER - SAFE FRAME RATES AT ANY SPEED				
1.000	4.166	6.250	11.111	50.000
1.250	4.347	6.666	12.500	33.333
2.000	4.545	7.142	14.285	100.00
2.500	4.761	7.692	16.666	
3.125	5.000	8.333	20.000	
3.333	5.263	9.090	**25.000**	
4.00	5.882	10.00	33.333	

Table 15.1. (above) Simplified safe frame rates with 24 Hz power supply and 25 hz power supply.

Table 15.2. (right, above) Safe frame rates for any shutter speed with 24 hz power supply.

Table 15.3. (right, below) Safe frame rates for any shutter speed with 25 hz power supply.

crystal controlled and the power supply is from the mains or a crystal controlled generator (Tables 15.1 through 15.3).

With a 144° shutter opening, the camera is exposing 2-1/2 pulses per frame (rather than the exactly 2 pulses per frame as you would get with 144°) and so exposure can theoretically vary by as much as 9%. In other countries (especially in Europe) with a 50 cycle per second power supply, and shooting at 24fps, the ideal shutter angle is 172.8°. The above charts list the acceptably safe frame rates for shooting at any shutter angle (with either 50 or 60 hertz electrical supplies) and the acceptably safe frame rates for specific shutter speeds.

A simple way to think about it is to divide 120 by a whole number, e.g., 120/4 = 30, 120/8 = 15. For 50 hertz (Hz) power systems, divide 100 by a whole number. This results in a simplified series as shown in Table 15.1. Any variation in the frequency (which may occur with a generator) of the power supply will result in an exposure fluctuation of approximately .4 f/stop. The time for one cycle of fluctuation will depend on how far off the power supply is.

Any generator used must be a crystal controlled. Governor controls are never sufficient for the accuracy demanded. A frequency meter should be used to periodically monitor the generator. Most generators have a frequency readout, but it is often not precise enough for this purpose. For most purposes, plus or minus one-quarter of a cycle is considered acceptable. Flicker-free ballasts are available which minimize the possibility of flicker even under high-speed conditions. Flicker-free units use electronic ballasts instead of iron-core, wire-wound reactance ballasts. They utilize two basic principles: square-wave output and high frequency. Flicker-free ballasts modify the wave form of the power supply by squaring it so that instead of the normal rounded sine wave, the output is angular. This means that the rising and falling sections of the wave are a much smaller portion of the total. As a result the light output is off for less time.

Flicker-free ballasts also use increased frequency. The idea is that with 200 or 250 cycles per second it is less likely that there will be a mis-match from frame to frame. Since there is an increase in the noise from a ballast in flicker-free mode, some flicker-free units can be switched from normal to flicker-free operation. Flicker-free units are now available in every size of HMI, including the largest units;

also most HMI sunguns are flicker-free. With high speed shooting, flicker can also sometimes be a problem with small tungsten bulbs, especially if they are on camera because the smaller filaments don't have the mass to stay heated through the cycle as do larger bulbs. Although not nearly as noticeable as with HMIs it may still be distracting. At higher than normal speeds ordinary fluorescents will certainly flicker.

FILMING PRACTICAL MONITORS
Because a monitor is a scanned image, most reflectance meters (spot meters) don't accurately read the exposure off of video monitors. They usually underestimate the exposure, often by a stop or more. Use tests and check with a Polaroid (preferably a color Polaroid). You can use the brightness control on the monitor to turn it down to more closely match the scene. Also, most monitors run very blue; you can either adjust the color towards orange or put some CTO over the screen to match your scene lighting. It will need to be flat and smooth enough so that wrinkles don't show.

If you are running your own source material through the monitor and you have the luxury of setting up to color bars, you can read the green band, (which correlates reasonably well to 18% gray) with a spot meter and open 2/3rd to 1 stop. Alternate method: read white and expose the picture Zoned between VI & VII. You will be surprised how dim you need to set the TV so it won't look washed out on the film later. The monitor will generally end up being set much dimmer than you would have it for normal viewing. You can't trust your eye or the meter; trust the Polaroids, they do not lie. Because NTSC video runs at 29.97 frames per second, televisions and monitors in a scene will exhibit a roll bar unless precautions are taken to prevent it. This includes computer monitors, radar screens and many other types of CRT (cathode ray tube) displays. The solution will depend on the nature of the monitor and the requirements of the scene being filmed.

NTSC video (the American broadcast standard for all television and video recording) is based on a 3.58 Mhz (megahertz) subcarrier which results in a frame rate of 29.97. Thus each video field is "on" for approximately 1/60th of a second (actually 1/59.94). The frame rate of a motion picture camera with a 180° shutter is 1/48th of a second. It is the discrepancy between these two frame rates which results in the "roll bar" effect.

CRTs will be one of three types:
- NTSC, PAL or SECAM video from broadcast television, cable or prerecorded videotape on the set.
- A computer monitor, graphics workstation, radar screen, video game or other type CRT display.
- Specially prepared video to match a 24fps or 25fps frame rate on the camera.

There are four kinds of final results you will be aiming for:
- Film shot for theatrical projection with sync sound.
- Film shot for theatrical projection at 24fps without sync sound.
- Film shot to be transferred directly to videotape, either with sync sound or without.
- Film which will be edited as film work print, then transferred to video. While film editors and video transfer houses can accommodate film shot at non-standard frame rates (even with lip-sync dialog) the inconvenience may be undesirable.

Unfortunately, it is impossible to lock a roll bar off the screen at the standard 24fps camera speed. There are several methods available to achieve the desired result. The simplest case is film transferred directly to video. A crystal control is used to run the camera at 29.97fps with a 180° shutter. This works only with a shutter angle of 180° or more. This method works for both MOS and sync sound filming.

For theatrical projection (24fps) which must be shot at sound sync speed (24fps): use a 144° shutter and crystal controlled camera at 23.976fps. This works because a 144° shutter equals 1/60th of a second exposure which approximates the video exposure time. A roll bar will still be visible but can be minimized and can be locked in place on the screen. There is a 1/3rd stop loss in closing down to 144° shutter angle.

This method can only be used with cameras that have adjustable shutters. Always discuss it with the rental house when you are going to be dealing with practical monitors so that they can insure that all equipment is compatible.

MONITORS AND MOS SHOOTING

When the filming is MOS and is intended for projection at 24fps: shooting can be at 29.97fps with 180° shutter or at 23.976 with 144° shutter. At 29.97, there will be a noticeable slowing of the action when projected at 24fps; if this is not acceptable, the 23.976fps method should be used. If the film is to be transferred to video, either method may be used, but be sure to slate the film clearly and log the variation onto the camera reports so that the video transfer house will know how to deal with it. Without appropriate slating to alert them to this, all of the video dailies will be out of sync.

There is an alternate method which makes filming monitors very simple. Specialty video houses can transform the video source material to 24fps video, which may then be filmed at normal camera speeds without a roll bar. This must be used in conjunction with a camera capable of supplying a framing pulse as output.

CRTs such as computer screens, radar screens, medical monitors or video games have a wide variety of frame rates. In some cases they are raster scans (like a normal TV) or vector scans (where each line is traced separately). In many cases it is necessary to either determine the frame rate from manufacturer's specifications with a frequency checker or by observing the image through the viewfinder or gate while varying the frame rate of the camera with a crystal speed control. Several very accurate meters are available which will tell you what the frame rate of a particular CRT is. The simplest and most reliable method is to take a portion of the video signal and use it to drive the camera. This is accomplished with a synchronizer unit as described below.

Although shooting NTSC videotape of an NTSC monitor will present no problems with a roll bar, shooting videotape of computer monitors can be just as difficult as filming them. Because computer monitor frame rates usually differ from standard NTSC video the screen will seem to flicker, which may be unacceptable for some applications. It is often necessary to alter the scan rate of the computer monitor to conform to video standard. Some video cameras have a facility to alter the frame rate of the video camera to match different monitors. In Sony Betacams, it is called Clearscan.

Synchronizers are available which will alter the scan rate of some monitors. For computers, software patches can be used to adjust the scan rates. As a last resort, it is possible to replace the video tube in the monitor with a similar tube which has long persistence phosphors. If the decay rate of the phosphor is longer than the scan rate, the flicker will be eliminated, but some "smearing" of the image may result. When shooting computer monitors, two pieces of information are essential: the filming scan rate of the monitor and the shutter ratio of the camera.

SHOOTING PROCESS PHOTOGRAPHY

CHROMA KEY

Chroma key, also known as bluescreen, greenscreen or process photography, is a method of producing mattes for compositing. The basic principle is the same for all processes and for both film and video: by including an area of a "pure" color in the scene, that color can then be made transparent and another image can be substituted for it. It is accomplished by different methods in film and in video but the idea is the same.

15.5. Redscreen is often preferred for shooting models. (Photo courtesy of Kino Flo.)

Green and blue are the most common colors used, but in theory any color can be used. There is one fundamental principle that must be remembered. Whatever color you are using to become transparent will be replaced for the entire scene. Thus, if the background is green and the actor has bright green eyes, his eyes will become transparent. The color chosen for the process background should be one that does not occur in the foreground.

Red screens are often used for shooting motion control passes of miniatures particularly in television sci-fi work (Figure 15.5). The theory is that first you shoot a "beauty pass" — a motion control pass against a black backdrop, with the subject model lit for beauty. Then you shoot the same model with no subject lights against a red screen, so what you get is the black silhouette of the model against a solid red background. The red screen produces an excellent matte, which is then used to composite the beauty pass. Some people also shoot magenta screen. Redscreen is almost never used in shooting people. As with all types of color process photography, the choice of background color is dependent on the color of foreground subjects — it's the difference between them that matters most.

CHROMA KEY AND ULTIMATTE

Ultimatte is a sophisticated form of chroma key video developed by Peter Vlahos. According to *Ultimatte Technical Bulletin #3,* "There are several reason why it may be advantageous to shoot Ultimatte foregrounds on film rather than video. The most obvious advantage is the possibility of non-real-time photography. Film currently offers greater flexibility than video for high speed slow motion photography or stop motion, animation and motion control photography." It is important to always discuss any matte shots with the post house that will be doing the keying. Each house has its own preferences for exposures and balances.

If there is any camera movement in a matte shot, the post house will most likely request that you include motion tracking reference marks. These can be as simple as little black "x" marks made of black tape. They might be placed on the green screen itself as a clue to the movement that will be required of the background element that is to be laid in. In other cases, the marks might be needed on the subject itself. The marks can easily be removed in post with a simple "garbage matte."

Another important safety is to shoot a reference frame. This is a shot of the same green or bluescreen background without the foreground element. This is useful in case there is any problem with the matte. The post people can use pieces of the reference shot to fill in "holes" in the matte shot with the foreground elements. Other recommendations include:

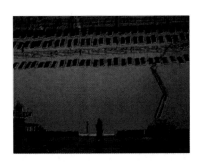

20' X 20'
USING
4ft 4BANKS

FRONT

20' X 20' BLUE SCREEN

45°

10'-0"

6'-0"

45°

SIDE

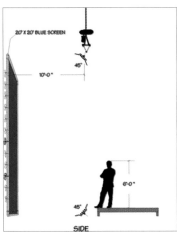

15.6. (top) A large bluescreen setup lit with Kino Flos. (Photo courtesy of Kino Flo.)

15.7. Typical lighting setup with Kino Flos. (Photo courtesy of Kino Flo.)

15.8. Spacing is important for even illumination of the cyc, which is critical for a good process shot. (Photo courtesy of Kino Flo.)

- Use a pin-registered camera such as a Panaflex, Arri BL or 535, Arri III, 435 or similar.
- Use the lowest grain film possible. Grain introduces noise into the image. 35mm is much preferred over 16mm.
- Do not use diffusion over the lens. Do not use heavy smoke effects. Keying software can deal with some smoke effects, but there are limits.
- Always shoot a gray scale lit with neutral light (3200K or 5500K) at the beginning of each roll. Shoot the gray scale (or chip chart for video) in a place where they will not be contaminated by splash back from the background or floor.
- Whenever possible use a polarizing filter to eliminate specular glare, especially off the floor.
- Especially with a video camera, but also with film cameras, avoid shooting with the lens wide open. The reason for this is that many camera lenses vignette very slightly when wide open which can create problems with the matte.
- In video, never compensate for low light levels by boosting the gain. Never push film.
- The video camera should be color balanced for the foreground subject.
- To match the depth of focus of the foreground, shoot the background plate with the focus set at where it would be if the foreground object was actually there.
- Carefully plan the screen direction and perspective of the background plates; it is essential that they match the foreground. If you are shooting video, note that there is a slight difference in perspective between a 1/2" video tube and a 2/3" camera.
- Either before or after shooting the scene, it is a good practice to remove the foreground subject and shoot a clean plate of the colored background as you have it lit. This can later be used as a reference in post-production and can save marginal shots.

LIGHTING FOR BLUESCREEN/GREENSCREEN
Optimum exposure levels depend on the nature of the subject and the setup. Ultimatte needs at lease 30 IRE units of separation between the background color (blue or green) and the higher of the other two colors (Figures 15.6 through 15.9).

In general, you want the exposure of the background to be about the same as the foreground. There is no general agreement on this. Some people set them to be exactly the same, some people underexpose the background by up to one stop and some people light the background by as much as one stop hotter than the foreground. The bottom line is simple: ask the person who will be doing the final composite. Different special effects houses will have varying preferences which may be based on the hardware/software combination they use. Always consult with your effects people before shooting. According to *Ultimatte Bulletin #3*: "A 1:1 lighting ratio between the foreground subject and the backing is a safe choice, even it is not the ideal one."

When a green background can be lit separately from the foreground, it is advisable to reduce the light on the background to one stop below the foreground. Ultimatte does not advise using blue light on a blue background, which they have found can produce certain transition anomalies. Set pieces (such as tables, boxes to sit on, etc.) which are painted to give the actor something to walk behind or interact with present problems. The top of the piece will almost always be hotter than the shadow side. This will definitely cause problems with the composite. Lighting can help but it may create problems of its own. One trick is to use paints of different reflectances on the top and side surfaces. Ultimatte recommends Gothic Ultra Blue on the top surface and Ultimatte Blue on the shadowed surfaces. The Gothic Ultra has less luminance than the Ultimatte Blue.

Nothing will undermine the believability of a composite more than a mismatch of lighting in the foreground and background. Careful attention must be made to recreating the look, direction and quality of the lighting in the background plate. Some of the following information is courtesy of Ultimatte and Kino Flo:

- Guard against backsplash.
- Block off whatever blue/greenscreen not in use.
- Do not use a complementary color as a back light.
- Ask if they need to see the floor — seeing the floor means dealing with shadows.
- Don't use diffusion.
- Don't use smoke.
- Don't include the matte color in the scene.
- Try not to have anybody lying on the floor or on a table if it is at all possible. Sometimes a mirror on the floor will help fill in the background color in tight spaces.
- Use black-and-white Polaroid and a blue filter (47B) to check the uniformity of the background lighting and meter with spot meter and incident.
- Always shoot a film test to determine the true ASA of the film stock, the Exposure Value (EV) and color density.
- Spot meters vary widely when measuring blue light; some brands are as much as three f-stops from other brands. Always use the same meter for testing as for principal photography.
- Kino Flo lit bluescreens are typically best illuminated at 1/2 an f-stop to 1-1/2 f-stops EV below nominal key, depending on the meter.
- Kino Flo lit greenscreens are usually best illuminated at key to a full f-stop below key, depending on the meter.
- Film stocks react differently to reflected green light than to blue light. The green layer of Kodak 5248, 5279, 5293, and 5298, for example, creates an ersatz matte line photochemically on highlight edges that must be fixed in post production. However, with pure blue light, the anomaly barely shows up. Note: Kodak has developed a "hybrid" color negative film stock specifically for visual effects lighting called SFX 200T. The new stock does not register the type of edging seen in film types mentioned above.
- Illumination contrast — the difference between foreground lighting and background lighting — can assist in the matte extraction process. However, too much contrast can devalue the matte.
- Many DPs prefer a blue background when foreground plates include warm colors, such as lighter skin tones. When the foreground subject is biased in the cooler range, the DP and the post-production supervisor and effects house may prefer a green background.

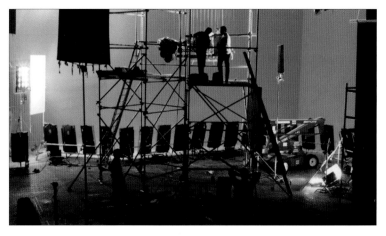

15.9. A greenscreen setup. Keeping backsplash off the foreground subject is important to limit contamination. (Photo courtesy of Mark Weingartner).

LUMINANCE KEY

Luminance key is the same concept as chroma key except that the difference between light and dark objects is used as the key for producing a difference matte. If the subject is primarily light colored then the background and all parts of the scene that you want to become "transparent" so that the composited background plate will show through should be black. The opposite is true if the subject is predominantly dark.

Luminance key is fairly simple to create but the inherent problem is that any shadow areas in the foreground subject will become transparent to the background matte: this creates severe limitations on lighting. For a good key, the foreground objects should be about 20 to 25 IRE units above black.

DIMMERS

There are a number of ways we control the intensity of light output at the unit itself:

- Flood-spot
- Wire scrims
- Grip nets
- Diffusion
- Neutral density filters
- Aim (spilling the beam)
- Switching off bulbs in multi-bulb units (soft lights)

The alternative is to control the power input into the light with dimmers. There are advantages and disadvantages. The advantages are:

- Fine degree of control
- Ability to control inaccessible units
- Ability to quickly look at different combinations
- Ability to do cues
- Ability to preset scene combinations
- Ability to save energy and heat buildup by cooling down between take

The disadvantages are:

- Lights change color as they dim; see Table 15.4
- Some lights cannot be dimmed: particularly HMIs
- Necessity of additional cabling
- Cost

The first dimmers invented were resistance units. They operate by placing a variable resistance in the power line. The excess energy

TYPE	LAMP COLOR SHIFT	DIRECTION	SHIFT
Incandescent / Tungsten Halogen	Orange-red	Lower	Marked
Fluorescent	Not discernible	Negligible	Negligible
Metal Halide	Blue	Higher	Drastic
Mercury	Not discernible	Negligible	Negligible

Table 15.4. Most light sources shift in color when dimmed.

is burned off as heat. Resistance dimmers are still available up to 10K; they are heavy and clumsy but cheap. The major problem with resistance dimmers is that they must be loaded to at least 80% of their capacity in order to operate. If you put a 5K on a 10K dimmer; for example, the dimmer will only reduce the output a small amount; you won't be able to dim all the way down. This sometimes necessitates the use of a dummy load to operate.

The next generation of dimmers were autotransformers. They operate as variable transformers and alter the voltage. They do not have to be loaded to capacity and they don't generate excessive heat but they do operate only on AC. Known as variacs (for variable AC) they are still standard equipment, particularly in the 1K and 2K sizes.

For larger applications, silicon controlled rectifiers are used. Known as SCRs, these are electronic devices which are small in size, quiet and relatively low cost. They can be controlled remotely by dimmer boards, which means that the dimmer packs themselves can be near the lights, which saves cabling; only a small control cable needs to run from the board to the dimmer packs. The remote cable carries a control voltage of 0 to 10 volts and can be run up to 200 feet. The signal is multiplex and can run up to 192 dimmers.

SCR dimmers do not alter the voltage, they work by "clipping" the waveform so that the voltage is heating the filament for a shorter period of time. The result of this is that the output of this type of dimmer cannot be read with an ordinary voltage meter, only a VOM (volt-ohm meter) which reads root mean square voltage (RMS) such as the high end Fluke meters will work.

There must be a load on the circuit to read the output. The shorter rise time can sometimes cause filament sing and create RF (radio frequency) and AF (audio frequency) noise. The RF interference can be transmitted back along the power line and can cause problems, particularly for unbalanced high impedance type sound systems. In most cases, with properly grounded audio systems, there should be no problem, but a portable radio can be used to test and find the source of any trouble.

When using an SCR dimmer with a generator, the gennie must be frequency controlled, the loss of sync will cause flicker; also, since most dimmers are voltage regulated, raising the voltage of the generator will not increase the output. An anomaly of these systems is that the neutral load can, in some cases, be higher than the hot line.

SCR dimmers are basically theatrical equipment so their connectors will often not be compatible with the rest of your equipment. As a rule the outputs will be theatrical three pin connectors, either 60 amp or 100 amp. It is important to order adapters to whatever plugging system your are using.

The input side of most dimmer packs are Camlock connectors. Frequently the neutral is reversed (male instead of female); the easiest way to run into trouble with dimmer orders is to forget to order feeder cable with the neutral reversed or "turnarounds": female to female connectors.

Control panels vary in sophistication. Some are simply sets of

15.10. The Unilux system, a high power strobe system capable of frame rates up to 500fps with strobe durations as short as 1/100,000th of a second. (Photo courtesy of Unilux.)

slider switches: one for each circuit, others include masters and sub-masters and may have separate banks for X and Y scenes, making it possible to do a cue from one preset to another. The next level is "soft patching" which allows for electronic routing of each line to a dimming circuit. The most advanced feature computer control, timed cues and other sophisticated control features. Most control panels will run any set of dimmers. The effect of dimming on color temperature varies with the source is shown in Table 15.4.

WORKING WITH STROBES

There are several types of strobe lighting for cinematography, the most widely known being Unilux (Figure 15.10). The Unilux package consists of a power supply and from one to three strobe heads. Several units can be controlled together for a greater number of heads. Frame rates of up to 500fps are possible. The strobes are fired by a pulse from the camera which signals when the shutter is open. Any camera which provides such a pulse is compatible with the system. In some cases a pulse contact is added to a moving part of the camera and this provides the sync signal.

Strobe lighting in film has three basic uses:

- To light cooler (strobes produce substantially less heat than tungsten heads), which can be a tremendous advantage when shooting ice cream, for example.
- To produce sharper images. The exposure duration for each flash can be as short as 1/100,000th of a second, as a result, the image is "frozen" and appears sharper than if photographed on moving film at standard exposures.
- To provide sufficient exposure for high speed photography with a small power input.

It is often used in "spray" shots of soft drink cans being opened: the strobe effect captures each droplet of spray crisply. In fact, it can be too sharp for some people. In shower scenes for shampoo commercials it can appear that the shower is a series of razor sharp drops rather than a soft spray. As a result, for beauty applications, it is common practice to combine Unilux with tungsten lighting. In most cases, the Unilux light is balanced with an equal amount of tungsten within a range of plus or minus one stop. This presents an interesting exposure problem.

Like most strobes, Unilux is blue, about 6000° Kelvin; appropriate filtration is required. When mixing with tungsten use an 85 to obtain 3400K and an 85B to reach 3200K. To maximize the Unilux, use 80A or CTB or the tungsten lights. Most people prefer to light only the moving object with strobe and the rest of the scene with tungsten. Strobes are fan cooled and noisy and so are not useful for sync sound shooting.

STROBE EXPOSURE

Consider this situation: you are shooting at 96 frames per second and the desired effect is equal amounts of tungsten and strobe lights. Every time you increase the frame rate of motion picture camera you are decreasing the amount of time the shutter stays open: you are decreasing exposure. 96fps is four times faster than normal, the shutter speed is 1/200th of a second instead of the normal 1/50th (assuming a 180 shutter). This is an exposure loss of two stops. This is simple enough to deal with; to achieve a f/5.6 for example, you light to an f/11.

But the same is not true of the strobe lighting. The strobe is instantaneous: it fires for only a few thousandths of a second at some time while the shutter is open, as a result, it is completely independent of the frame rate. It doesn't matter whether the film is moving at six frames a second or 600, the exposure will be the same.

Here's the problem. We read the tungsten and have to compensate, we then read the Unilux with a strobe meter and we don't have to compensate. Clearly we can't read them at the same time. How do we arrive at a setting for the lens? The answer is intuitively obvious, but mathematically a bit complex: we read them separately and then add the two exposures. As it turns out, adding f/stops is not especially simple. Let's take the simplest case first. We read the Unilux by itself (and it is very important to turn off all tungsten lights when we do this) and find that they are an f/5.6. We have to balance the tungsten to that. As we know, at 96fps, we have to set the tungsten lights for f/11, which will be f/5.6 at 96fps. The temptation might be to average them; that would result in a very incorrect exposure: we must add them.

What is f/5.6 plus f/5.6? (No, it's not 11.2.) In effect we are doubling the amount of light: the tungsten is providing f/5.6 and the Unilux is supplying an entirely different illumination which is also f/5.6. Twice as much light as f/5.6 is f/8. Recall that each f/stop represents a doubling of the amount of light. Now it gets a bit stickier. Let's say that the Unilux is f/8 and the tungsten is f/5.6. Think of it this way: if f/8 is a base of 100%, then the tungsten light is 50% (one stop less equals 1/2 the amount of light). We then have 150% of the base light. 150% of f/8 is 1/2 stop hotter than f/8 — f/8 and a half. If the one of the sources is f/8 and the other is f/4, the correct exposure is f/8 and 1/4. F/4 is only 25% the amount of light of f/8: 125%. Although a flashmeter is the preferred method many ordinary electronic light meters can read high speed strobes. The reason is that at 60 flashes per second, it is perceived as continuous by many meters.

TYPICAL EXPOSURES

Unilux is switchable for four intensity levels, the Unilux H3000 System is switchable to 16 speed ranges, which gives 1/4 stop level control. The levels are determined by the speeds at which the lights are flashing. Remember that the flash rate is twice the camera speed because there is one flash for the shutter and one for the viewfinder. The lights only come up to full intensity when the camera goes to speed. If you want to take a reading, the lights must be running at speed. Other considerations:

- Shutter angle should be opened to the maximum.
- Check the synchronization frequently. This is done by removing the lens and looking at the shutter with camera running and strobes operating. The shutter will be "frozen" and it should appear open.
- For reflex viewing, the strobes can be run in "split sync" mode. In this case there are two flashes for each rotation of the shutter: one for the exposure and one for the viewfinder.
- Unilux always comes with a technician; don't forget to budget for him. Some types of strobe units are rented without operator, but be sure to check.
- Unilux requires 208v-240v 3-phase and a ground. It cannot be run thorough a stage box because there is no ground. Standard Unilux consumes 5 amps per light. The Unilux H3000 system requires 220 volt single-phase and 10 amps per light.
- Some cameras (such as the Photo-Sonics Actionmaster 16) must be fitted with an additional pickup for synchronization.

15.11. The Photo-Sonics 4B, capable of frame rates up to 3250 fps, 100 to 1000 fps in phase lock. (Photo courtesy of Photo-Sonics.)

HIGH SPEED PHOTOGRAPHY

High speed photography (Figure 15.11) differs mainly in the amount of light needed and in the calculation of exposure. Variations in frame rate are covered in the chapter on exposure. A few other formulae are also useful. (Thanks to Photo-Sonics, Inc., for the following calculations.)

- 1/Exposure Time = 360° ÷ shutter angle x frame rate.
  Example: 360° ÷ 120° x 360fps = 1/1080 exposure time. Don't forget to compensate if there is a beamsplitter in the camera — usually 1/2 stop.
- Times Normal Speed = Frame Rate ÷ Transfer Rate (e.g.: 24 or 30fps).
  Example: 360 ÷ 24 = 15 Times Normal Speed.
- Frames Exposed = Frame Rate x Event Duration.
  Example: 360 x .5 second = 180 Frames Exposed (for an event that lasts 1/2 second).
- Screentime = Frame Rate x Event Duration ÷ Transfer Rate.
  Example: 360 x .5 ÷ 24 = 7.5 Seconds Screen Time.
- Frame Rate Required = Screen Time ÷ Event Duration x Transfer Rate.
  Example: 7.5 Seconds ÷ .5 x24 = 360fps required.
- Run Time = Frames Per Foot x Footage ÷ Frame Rate.
  Example: 16 x 1000' ÷ 360 = 44.4 Seconds Run Time.
- Screentime for moving objects = Field of View ÷ Object Velocity x Frame Rate ÷ Transfer Rate. (Note: Field of view and object velocity must use the same units of measurement.)
  Example: 2' Field of View ÷ 20' per second x 360fps ÷ 24 = 1.5 Seconds Screentime.

LIGHTING FOR EXTREME CLOSE-UP

There are two basic considerations in lighting for extreme close-up. The first is that due to extremely small depth of field (which is inherent in close focusing) and the need to stop down for improved optical performance, very high light levels are needed. Particularly with high-speed photography, an uncorrected stop of f/64 and higher is often called for. Since the area being lit is usually small there is generally no problem with this, although in dealing with large units it can be quite a job just to get them close together and all focused on a small subject (Table 15.5).

The other problem is caused by the lens being so close to the subject. In some cases the front of the lens may be no more than an inch away from the subject. This makes it difficult to achieve any kind of front lighting or fill: the lens and the camera are in the way. It is more difficult when the subject is reflective. In this case no matter how much light is poured on the subject what you will see in the reflective surface is a mirror image of the lens itself, which will appear as a large black circle.

There are two solutions: one is to cut a hole in a reflector card just large enough for the lens. Sometimes it is not even necessary for the hole to cover the entire front optic; with experimentation you will find that the actual working area is smaller and that the hole can be smaller without interfering with the image. A number of subtleties are possible with a little imagination.

The other solution is a half silver mirror. The mirror is placed between the lens and the object and angled slightly to reflect the image of the light source onto the subject in axis with the lens. Don't

Table 15.5. Magnification requires an increase in exposure.

Magnification ratio	Exposure increase in stops
1:10	1/3
1:6	1/2
1:4	2/3
1:3	1
1:2	1 1/3
1:1.4	1 1/2
1:1.2	1 2/3
1:1	2

FILM TYPE	FORMAT	RESULT	ASA
667	professional pack	coaterless positive print	3000
107C	pack	coaterless positive print	3000
107	pack	positive print (requires coating)	3000
084	professional pack	positive print (requires coating)	3000
87	square picture pack	coaterless positive print	3000
57	4x5 film packet	positive print (requires coating)	3000
47	roll	positive print (requires coating)	3000
FINE GRAIN PRINT			
53	4x5 film packet	positive print (requires coating)	400
42	roll	positive print (requires coating)	200
POSITIVE/NEGATIVE			
665	professional pack	positive print and negative	75
55	4x5 film packet	positive print and negative	50
SPECIAL PURPOSE			
410	roll	positive print for oscilloscope	10000
51	4x5 film packet	high con positive print	320
146L	roll	high con positive transparency	200
46L	roll	positive transparency	800
611	professional pack	low contrast positive print	n/a
COLOR PRINT			
669	pack	color print	
668	pack	color print	

forget that the mirror has an exposure factor which you can measure with a spot or incident meter. Ring lights, which are any type of unit which fits around the lens, may be useful in lighting for extreme close-up, if they are made small enough.

Table 15.6. Types of Polaroid film for lighting tests and scene preview.

POLAROID PREVIEW
Polaroid has become a popular way of checking exposure and balances on sets. Used in conjunction with metering, it can be a useful "confidence restorer." There are several Polaroid emulsions commonly used and it is important to select the film which best suits the circumstances in which you will be shooting (Table 15.15). Polaroid doesn't keep long even in the fridge; never freeze it.

No Polaroid emulsion matches film or video in contrast ratio or spectral response; as a result Polaroids are similar to the video monitor in that they require considerable interpretation. They should never be used as anything other than a rough guide. Over-reliance on the video monitor or a preview Polaroid can lead to problems, don't use them as crutches or as a substitute for a searching eye and a properly used light meter or waveform monitor.

100 series films (e.g., 107) are amateur films. The 600 series (667, etc) are professional emulsions and generally exhibit greater stability and consistency from batch to batch. Since the rated speed of the Polaroid seldom matches the rated speed of the film stock or video camera, it is usually necessary to make some exposure compensation. There are several methods for doing this: relabeling the lens, neutral density filters and altering shutter speed.

UNDERWATER FILMING
Most professional cameras have underwater housings specially designed for them and they are widely available for rental. Water, even fresh water, acts as a filter, absorbing the red wavelengths first, then on down the spectrum, until all frequencies are absorbed. This is why there is no light at all below a certain depth, which varies

according to the clarity of the water. There are several underwater lighting units available, most of them smaller "sungun," battery operated units. Observe the manufacturer's rated maximum depth carefully; exceeding it may lead to an implosion and short circuit.

SEAPARS

The SeaPar® by HydroImage is built around a 1200 watt Sylvania HMI PAR bulb, encased in a watertight container which can withstand depths of up to 220' in salt water (110 lbs/inch^2). The fresnel is permanently bonded to the front of the bulb to reduce the amount of glass, so instead of changing lenses, it is necessary to change lights. This is made easier by the inclusion of an underwater pluggable connector which can be detached underwater. It includes an aluminum retainer ring for gels and accessories and a bonded ground return line back to the ballast which operates above water and is equipped with a 20 amp ground fault interrupter. A flicker-free ballast is also available. LTM makes the AQUAPAR which is similar.

Tungsten-halogen PAR 64s (1000 watt) and PAR 36s (650 watt) are also available in watertight housings. The PAR 36 can be configured for use with an underwater battery pack which can run two lights for an hour. In the tungsten units, the bulbs can be changed to alter the beam from wide-flood to narrow-spot and for daylight or tungsten balance.

MEASURES OF IMAGE QUALITY

No matter what medium we are dealing with: video, film, still photos, computer monitors, we need ways to describe their ability to reproduce an image accurately. What we subjectively call "sharpness," whether in lenses, emulsions, or video tubes, is actually a combination of factors.

MODULATION-TRANSFER FUNCTION

The modulation transfer function is a measure of an imaging system's ability to reproduce fine detail. Physically, the measurement evaluates the effect of the image of light diffusion within the emulsion. It is sometimes called the contrast transfer function. Modulation is an expression of the difference between lightest and darkest areas of a test pattern.

The film is exposed to a test pattern which consists of alternating black-and-white lines which become smaller and closer together.

15.12. Smoke adds a great deal to this shot, especially when you realize it is a studio set. (*City of Lost Children*.)

After development, the image is read with a micro-densitometer. Where the lines are large and far apart, the image system will have no trouble reproducing them as completely black or white, which is a modulation factor of one (the modulation of the reproduced image exactly matches the modulation of the test target), but where the lines get smaller and closer together, the image system will begin to blur them together until they eventually are reproduced as a uniform gray. The graph of the modulation transfer function shows the system's ability to accurately reproduce at all spatial frequencies (line pairs or cycles per millimeter).

The measurement shows the degree of loss in image contrast as the detail becomes finer (i.e., a higher frequency of modulation). The rate of modulation is defined by the formula; where M is modulation and E is exposure:

$$M = \frac{E\ max - E\ min}{E\ max + E\ min}$$

The result is the ratio of modulation of the developed image to the modulation of the exposing pattern.

$$\frac{Mi}{Mo}$$

The ratio is plotted on the vertical axis as a percentage of response. The spatial frequency of the patterns is plotted on the horizontal axis as cycles per millimeter. When the detail is large, the film reproduces it accurately, as in the left hand part of the curve. As the detail is finer and the lines closer together (the right hand part of the curve) the film is less able to reproduce it accurately.

For most of us modulation-transfer functions are only useful in comparison to each other, but they can be useful in judging films, lens, imaging systems, etc. The MTF of each component of a system (lens, emulsion, print stock or lens, video tube, tape, monitor) can be multiplied to arrive at an MTF for the entire system. When judged in a comprehensive manner such as this, film still has a clear superiority as a total imaging system over even high definition video.

EFFECTS

SMOKE
Many types of smoke are available for use on sets: incense in bee-smokers, smoke cookies, smoke power and others. They have all been found to be hazardous to health except for cracker smoke. Cracker smoke is atomized oil: baby oil, cooking oil and other types of lightweight oil are used. The oil is atomized by forcing compressed air or nitrogen through extremely small holes. Cracker smoke is very white, and fills an area with thick billowing smoke very quickly. The smoke has the added advantage of hanging for an extremely long time which can be a tremendous time-saver in production. Other types of smoke required "smoking it up" before every take, followed by wafting it around, then waiting for it to settle: a laborious, boring process. Smoke crackers are available in all sizes, from small hand carry units up to big industrial size crackers with compressors that are moved on dollies (Figures 15.12 and 15.13).

FIRE
Real fire almost always needs help. It may deliver enough exposure itself but if it is in the frame or even near the frame, it will flare the image badly and destroy the shot. The secret of fire shots is to use several sources on dimmers or flicker boxes — fire jumps around, it doesn't just go up and down (Figure 15.14). One light or even

15.13.Without smoke and water, this shot from *Nine and 1/2 Weeks* would be nowhere near as powerful.

two lights on dimmers that just get brighter and darker won't be convincing because the shadows don't flicker and jump like real flame. Fire is established by a low key orange flickering effect. CTO can be used to warm the light and the flicker can be accomplished in a variety of ways. Silver foil, waving hands and rotating mirror drums are used, but the simplest and most convincing effect is usually to place the source light on a dimmer and have an electrician with an "eye" operate it.

A more high-tech method is the use of a flicker generator. Two kinds are available. One is a random generator which can be programmed for various rates of random flicker. The other uses an optical sensor to "read" the light of a candle or fire and drives a dimmer in sync with it. This is particularly effective for scenes where the dimmer or fire is the primary source and is visible in the scene. McIntire Enterprises makes several "magic boxes" which can drive up to 10K dimmers and a smaller unit which directly controls up to a 2K (Figure 15.15).

Small handheld candles or oil lamps can be executed with an Inky socket and a small bulb. They can be AC powered with a wire running up the actor's sleeve or DC powered with a battery hidden on the actors body. Flame bars, which are pipes with holes spaced along them through which gas is pumped, are far more reliable and controllable than real fire.

15.14. For this beer commercial, the director asked for a "Caravaggio" look. There is motivation from a nearby fireplace, candles and lanterns. A fire-light rig with multiple flicker units was built by my gaffer. This was operated by an electrician who could give us just the right amount of fire flicker and level. The director's only other request was to keep the scene very dark and moody.

TV AND PROJECTOR EFFECTS

Like fire effects, the look of a flickering TV is best accomplished with dimmers. The source, which might be a fresnel or practical bulbs in porcelain sockets with some diffusion, are usually placed in a snoot box to confine the light in a realistic pattern. In general 1/2 or full CTB cools the light to simulate the blue look of black-and-white television. This is a convention even though most people watch color TV, which projects a variety of colors. Here again, it is important that the person operating the effect have some sensitivity to the mood of the scene and keep it random. Actual television flickers considerably less than is usually portrayed, but the activity helps sell the effect.

Projection effects can be accomplished the same way with the addition of sometimes bouncing the light for a softer look: film projection is bounced off a large screen, while television is a smaller direct source. Projection can also be simulated by running actual film through a projector and aiming it at the audience. Obviously it is necessary to defocus the projector or remove the lens so the image won't appear on the faces. The drawback of this method is that the projection is likely to make too much noise.

15.15. A multifunction flicker box. (Photo courtesy of McIntire Enterprises.)

DAY-FOR-NIGHT

With the advent of high speed film and electronic gain for video cameras, high-speed lenses, high efficiency HMIs and sunguns, day-for-night is not done as often. In black-and-white infrared film can be used for night effects, generally in conjunction with a filter such as a Wratten #25 (Figure 15.16).

Traditionally, day-for-night is done at mid-day since long shadows will give away the fact that it is day. Of course, showing the sky is strictly forbidden. In color (both film and video), it is possible to achieve a reasonably convincing effect by underexposing from 1-1/2 to 2-1/2 stops. Moonlight blue can be simulated by removing the 85 filter with tungsten balance film or white balancing the video camera for tungsten. Subtleties of color balance can be achieved with color correcting filters depending on the feel that is desired.

Harrison and Harrison make a series of day-for-night filters. The #1 is blue-red, the blue gives the night effect while the red component helps hold the skin tones in balance. The #2 is the same color but also lowers the contrast, which can help maintain the night illusion; the #3 filter offers a greater degree of contrast control. They have an exposure factor of 2 stops. In other parts of the world, day-for-night is often named for the place where it was presumably invented and is known as "American night." In fact, the original title of Francois Truffaut's film known in the United States as *Day For Night* is *La Nuit Américaine*.

15.16. Day for night, such as this shot from *Yojimbo* (Toho, 1961), is much easier to achieve realistically in black-and-white.

15.17. Rain can never be effective unless it is backlit as in this shot from *Nine and 1/2 Weeks*.

MOONLIGHT EFFECT

As you recall from our discussion of the Purkinje effect, it is a widely accepted convention that moonlight is blue. The use of blue for moonlight is controversial and many purists insist on using no more than 1/2 CTB for the effect. More common is full CTB or double blue. Of course, these are all in addition to whatever blue is used to establish basic color balance. Some people also add just a touch of lavender for a romantic look that is slightly more pleasing to the skintone of the actors.

WATER EFX

The dapple of light reflected on water can be a beautiful and subtle effect. It can be achieved in a number of ways. Some people use broken mirrors or crumpled aluminum foil to reflect a strong directional light (usually a fresnel or a PAR). These tend to be somewhat stilted and artificial. The best effect is always achieved by using actual water. In a shallow pan with a black backing water itself can be highly reflective if you use a strong enough unit.

RAIN

Rain is the province of the prop department, but it does have implications for lighting. To be visible, rain must be backlit (Figure 15.17). Front lighting will not work with anything but the most intense downpours, and even then the result will be anemic. Even with the most carefully controlled rain effect, water gets everywhere. Several precautions are necessary:

15.18. The Thundervoltz from Lightning Strikes provides portable power for 70K lightning effects. Undersizing your lightning effects units can be a serious mistake. (Photo courtesy of Lightning Strikes.)

- Raise all connectors, especially distribution connectors, off the ground on apple boxes. Wrap them in plastic and seal with tape. Use electrical tape as gaffers tape won't withstand water.
- Ground everything you can.
- Put rain hats on all lights. Protect the lenses of all large lights; water on a hot lens will shatter it with the possibility of glass flying out.
- Cover equipment racks and other spare equipment with heavy plastic.
- Crew members should wear insulating shoes and stand on rubber mats whenever working with electrical equipment.
- Observe all electrical safety rules religiously.

Most rain conditions (which includes real rain as well as rain towers) call for a camera umbrella, which is a large sturdy beach or patio type umbrella and perhaps an aluminized space blanket or rain cover for the camera. Be sure that the filters are protected as well — rain drops on the filter or lens are very noticeable.

For heavier water conditions a rain deflector may be necessary. Based on an idea used for the bridges of boats, a rain deflector is a spinning round glass in front of the mirror. It rotates fast enough to spin the water off and keep the lens area clear. One caution: when tried with a Steadicam, the spinning glass acts as a gyro and tends to pull the camera off course strongly enough for the Steadicam operator to be unable to control it. There is another device which blows compressed air or nitrogen toward a clear filter to keep water off. This system can also be used to keep dust away from the filter in shots which stir up a lot of debris such as explosions.

LIGHTNING

Because lightning must be extremely powerful to be effective, it generally calls for a specially built rig. Nearly universal now is the use of machines from Lightning Strikes (Figure 15.18), which are basically incredibly powerful strobes. Included with them are a controller which can vary the timing and intensity of strikes to very accurately reproduce actual lightning. For further realism, several units should be used. Except when a storm is far away, actually lightning comes from several different angles. If a storm is approaching in the scene, a skilled operator will increase the intensity and frequency as the storm nears.

Most older lightning rigs are based on carbon arc technology. They consist of an arc ballast and a set of carbons which can be pushed together then rapidly withdrawn with a levered handle. The resulting arc produces a powerful and momentary blast of light which is very convincing. A brute arc itself can be used by reversing the polarity of the DC so that it is "wrong" and then throwing the striking lever. The carbons will produce a brief, powerful arc but won't strike because the polarity is wrong.

Understandably, these effects can be very hard on a generator, so be sure you have plenty of headroom before attempting these effects. Sometimes flashbulb rigs are used for the effect. Small flashbulb effects may be appropriate where lightning is only needed for one shot and rental of a dedicated unit would be impractical. M type flashbulbs, which have a long burn time, are most effective for this purpose. Regular flashbulbs fire very quickly and they might burn while the shutter is closed, resulting in no exposure.

GUN SHOTS

Gun shots are flashes of short enough duration that they might occur while the shutter is closed. The standard procedure is for the operator to watch for the flashes. If the operator sees them, then they did not get recorded on film. If the operator saw them, it means the flashes occurred while the mirror was reflecting the image to the viewfinder. Depending on how critical they are, another take may be necessary.

Several things can be done to alleviate this problem. There are prop guns that do not use gunpowder but instead use an electrical pulse coupled with a chemical charge to produce a flash. This has the added bonus of being much safer. More safety in itself is good, but it also means much less need for safety rigging, which can be a time consuming process. Also, a licensed pyrotechnician/armorer and fire safety officer are not needed. These electronic guns also produce a longer duration flash which means fewer retakes.

There are also some systems which time the gunfire to the shutter, thus assuring a good take nearly every time. The Rolls-Royce of such systems is AatonTCGun, which has a timecode generator on each gun, jam-synced to the camera. In addition to locking the firing of each gun to the shutter it can be rigged with a timecode controlled limiter which automatically drops the record level of a digital audio recorder for the duration of the gunshot. This is important for two reasons: first, gunshots can be very hard on the hearing of the sound recordist and the boom operator, both of whom are hearing them through the headphones. Secondly, very loud sudden noises such as gunshots actually drop out on most recorders: the mic is so overloaded that it actually produces a momentary blank spot on the tape instead of a very loud noise.

SAFETY WITH GUNS
Guns should only be handled by a licensed pyrotechnician/armorer — in most places this is a legal requirement. The same applies to bullet hits planted on people, props or the set. Bullet hits are small black powder charges and can be dangerous. If the gun is not firing in the shot, the armorer should open each gun, verify that it is empty, then show it to the actors and camera crew with the action open.

If firing of blanks is anywhere near towards the camera a shield should be set by the grips to cover the camera, the operator and the focus puller. This is usually done with Lexan: a clear polycarbonate that is optically smooth enough to shoot through but strong enough to protect the people, the lens and the camera. This shield needs to be secured and bagged so that it won't get knocked over by an errant diving stunt man or a chair that gets kicked in the action. Great care must be taken by the grips as the disadvantage of Lexan is that it scratches very easily. Always get more Lexan than you think you need because after a few gun fights, many areas will be too scratched to shoot through. Anytime anyone is testing the gun they should shout "fire in the hole" before shooting.

EXPLOSIONS
The same type of shield is necessary for small explosions, rockets, shattering glass, etc. For small explosions, the camera crew also need to be protected from objects that get blown into the air. Often a furny pad (called a sound blanket on the East coast) over the heads of the crew is enough.

For larger explosions, the camera should be either locked down and switched on remotely, or operated with a remote control head and video assist. In this case, either very heavy duty crash boxes are needed or expendable cameras. Explosions are usually filmed with multiple cameras at various frame rates; at least one or more of the cameras will be run a high frame rate; often up to 120fps or more. HMI PARs are available in explosion proof housings. This does not mean that they are impervious to explosions, it means that they are sealed so that no electrical spark will cause a problem in an explosive environment.

TIME LAPSE PHOTOGRAPHY
Time lapse is usually done with an intervalometer — an electronic device which controls the timing and duration of each exposure. The Norris Intervalometer starts at an exposure of 1/16 of a second and gets longer from there. The interval between exposures can be anywhere from a fraction of a second up to several hours or even days apart. With longer exposure you get not only a time lapse effect but may also get blurring of the subject. This can be strongly visual with subjects such as car lights or moving clouds. For moving clouds, a 10 to 15 second interval is a good starting point.

One issue with time lapse shots is that the exposure may change radically during the shot: especially if it is night-into-day or day-

THE STEELE CHART
TIME COMPRESSION/INTERVALOMETER

SCREEN TIMES	1S	2S	5S	10S	15S	20S	30S	1M	2M	5M	10M	20M
FRAMES	24	48	120	240	360	480	720	1440	2880	7200	14400	28800
INTERVAL	EVENT DURATION											
12Frm/Sec	2S	4S	10S	20S	30S	40S	1M	2M	4M	10M	20M	40M
8Frm/Sec	3S	6S	15S	30S	45S	1M	90S	3M	6M	15M	30M	1H
6Frm/Sec	4S	8S	20S	40S	1M	80S	2M	4M	8M	20M	40M	80M
4Frm/Sec	6S	12S	30S	1M	90S	2M	3M	6M	12M	30M	1H	2H
3Frm/Sec	8S	16S	40S	80S	2M	2M 40S	4M	8M	16M	40M	80M	2H 40M
2Frm/Sec	12S	24S	1M	2M	3M	4M	6M	12M	24M	1H	2H	4M
1Frm/Sec	24S	48S	2M	4M	6M	8M	12M	24M	48M	2H	4H	8H
2Sec/Frm	48S	96S	4M	8M	12M	16M	24M	48M	96M	4H	8H	16H
3Sec/Frm	72S	2M 24S	6M	12M	18M	24M	36M	72M	2H 24M	6H	12H	24H
4Sec/Frm	96S	3M 12S	8M	16M	24M	32M	48M	96M	3H 12M	8H	16H	32H
5Sec/Frm	2M	4M	10M	20M	30M	40M	1H	2H	4H	10H	20H	40H
8Sec/Frm	3M 125	6M 24S	16M	32M	48M	64M	96M	3H 12M	6H 24M	16H	32H	2D 16H
10Sec/Frm	4M	8M	20M	40M	1H	80M	2H	4H	8H	20H	40H	3D 8H
15Sec/Frm	6M	12M	30M	1H	90M	2H	3H	6H	12H	30H	2D 12H	5D
20Sec/Frm	8M	16M	40M	80M	2H	2H 40M	4H	8H	16H	40H	3D 8H	6D 16H
30Sec/Frm	12M	24M	1H	2H	3H	4H	6H	12H	24H	2D 12H	5D	10D
1Min/Frm	24M	48M	2H	4H	6H	8H	12H	24H	2D	5D	10D	20D
2Min/Frm	48M	96M	4H	8H	12H	16H	24H	2D	4D	10D	20D	40D
5Min/Frm	2H	4H	10H	20H	30H	40H	2D 12H	5D	10D	25D	50D	100D

STEP 1: Decide how long you want the event to last on screen
STEP 2: Decide how long you want to film the event in real time.
STEP 3: Set interval according to data in the far left column.

NOTE: This chart is a guideline only. If the specific numbers you're looking for are not on the chart, you can use the chart to "guess-timate" by finding the closest corresponding numbers.

© The Steel Chart, Lance Steele Rieck, 1997

EXAMPLE: The DP wants 15 seconds time-lapse footage of clouds passing. You have six hours to film. First, look under SCREEN TIME for "15S". Follow column down till you find "6H" or six hours. Follow row to the far left INTERVAL column where you will find the interval: 1Min/Frm.
FORMULA: Event duration in seconds divided by screen time in frames equals the interval.

into-night, also if heavy clouds move in during the shot. This can be controlled with a timing device or it may be necessary to stand by and do exposure changes manually. If you don't want the depth-of-field to change during the shot, you may want to add or subtract ND filters or alter the shutter setting. Also, with long intervals between exposures it is possible for enough light to leak around the normal camera shutter to fog frames. An additional shutter, known as a capping shutter, is added to prevent this. Capping shutters are available from the same places that supply intervalometers. Table 15.7 shows screen time vs. event duration for time lapse photography.

Table 15.7. The Steele chart for calculating time lapse shots. (Courtesy of Lance Steele Rieck.)

TIME SLICING

This is the effect that was popularized in a series of Gap ads and most famously in the film *The Matrix*. This is the effect where a character is suddenly "frozen" but the camera dollies around the figure or the object. This effect is accomplished with an array of 35mm still cameras arranged around the subject. A regular film camera is

15.19. Time slicing shots require extensive setup. The PAWS system uses miniature motion picture cameras instead of still cameras, but the principle is the same. (Photo courtesy of PAWS & Co.)

part of the array. At the moment of freezing the action, the entire circle of still cameras is fired. These still photos are then scanned and blended together to form a film shot (Figure 15.19).

Visualize it this way: imagine a film camera on a mount that can be dollied around the subject instantaneously, let's say 90°, with the film running at very high speed. Since the dolly is instant, it "sees" the subject from all points around that arc before the subject can move. This is what the still cameras do: they see the subject from as many points of view as you wish — all at the same time. In practice, the subject is often placed on greenscreen and then the green background is replaced with live action footage of the original scene, usually matching the dolly action simulated by the still array. The result is a dolly around a live action scene with a frozen subject in the middle. The still cameras can be arranged in any type of move imaginable; the effect is not restricted to a dolly around.

professional formats

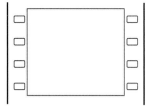

16.1. (previous page) A VistaVision frame from Hitchcock's *Vertigo* (Paramount Pictures, 1958).

16.2. (above) Full aperture
Aspect ratio: 1.319:1
.980" x 735"
.72 sq. in
25mm x 18.7mm
464.5 sq. mm

16.3. Academy aperture
Aspect ratio: 1.37:1
.864" x .63"
.544 sq. in
21.95mm x 18.6mm
351.2 sq. mm

16.4. Aspect ratio: 1:66:1
.864" x .63"
.544 sq. in.
21.95mm x 16mm
31.2 sq. mm

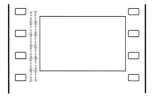

16.5. (above) Aspect ratio: 1:85:1
.864" x .469"
.405 sq. in.
21.95mm x 16mm
351.2 sq. mm

FULL APERTURE

Before the introduction of sound, the entire width of the film was exposed. This is called full aperture or silent aperture. It is still used today for formats such as Super35 (see below). The format is essentially what was developed in the Edison labs at the very invention of motion picture film (Figure 16.2).

ACADEMY APERTURE

With the introduction of sync sound, the Academy aperture was created in 1932 to allow space for the optical soundtrack. With the introduction of sound, room had to be made for the optical track. To do this, the size of the aperture was reduced. This was called the Academy aperture (Figure 16.3).

1.66:1 AND 1.85:1

The next step in the evolution was the wider 1.66 frame. After the wide screen craze of the fifties, there was a need for a wider format that did not call for special cameras or wide screen projection equipment. The response to this was the introduction of the 1.85:1 aspect ratio. In the United States this is still considered the "standard" format for anything going to theatrical projection. Anything wider is considered widescreen (Figure 16.4). When shot for television and standard video release, the 1.33 aspect ratio is used.

TRUE WIDE SCREEN

For true widescreen, anamorphic lenses "squeeze" the image onto 35mm film. In projection, the image is then "unsqueezed" to provide an image wider than standard 1.85. On the camera negative, the aspect ratio is 1.18:1. When unsqueezed, the aspect ratio in projection is generally 2.35:1.

ANAMORPHIC

Anamorphic photography was invented in France in 1927. A special lens was suspended in front of the prime lens which compressed the image horizontally to one-half its width, then unsqueezed it again when projected. The horizontal compression was eventually engineered into the prime lens itself so an additional optic in front of the lens was no longer necessary. Several versions of this system are in use today, and most major lens manufacturers also make high quality anamorphic lens sets (Figure 16.6).

VISTAVISION

VistaVision runs standard 35mm film horizontally. Each frame spans 8 perforations, twice the area of a regular frame. It is still in common use especially for any kind of special effects or plate work. The reason it is used for this type of work is that something that is shot for a background plate or as part of a special effects piece will likely go through several stages of optical printing or perhaps digitizing. The larger format prevents the build up of excessive grain and loss of resolution. 70mm is also used for plate work on films for which the production format is 35mm.

IMAX

Currently the largest projection format is Imax, which is 70mm film run through the camera and projector sideways, in a manner similar to VistaVision. This results in a negative roughly the size of that produced by a 2-1/4 still camera. This extremely large negative allows for a very large projection screen up to five stories high. Omnimax is a variation which employs a curved screen and anamorphic lens.

ALTERNATIVES TO ANAMORPHIC

There are many problems with anamorphic photography. First, anamorphic lenses are never as fast as standard spherical lenses. Secondly, because of the squeeze, the depth-of-field is 1/2 of that for the same image size. Both of these conditions mean that substantially more lighting is required for anamorphic photography which can be a problem in terms of time and budget.

16.6. Anamorphic
Aspect ratio: 1.18:1
.864" x .732"
.633 sq. in.
21.95mm x 18.6 mm
408.27 sq. mm

SUPER35

One method developed to answer these problems is Super35. The basic concept of Super35 is to use the entire width of the negative: the same full aperture originally used in silent films.

From this full width negative, a widescreen image is extracted. This is done with an optical print. This optical step is necessary to slightly reduce the image to leave room for the sound track and to squeeze it for anamorphic projection. Although the resulting image is not the full aperture, the original negative uses more of the available space. This is necessary because there is still a need for a sound track. Even though several alternatives have been developed to substitute for the sound track on film, including digital audio, because these systems are not universal, it is usually necessary to give back that audio track space on the side. The Univision format, discussed later, also relies on eliminating audio track.

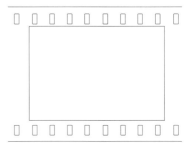

16.7. Vistavision frame
Aspect ratio: 1.5:1
1.485" x .991"
1.472 sq. in.
37.72mm x 25.17mm
949.7 sq. mm

COMMON TOPLINE

For the DP, the director and especially for the operator, one of the greatest advantages of Super35 is that a common topline can be used. Because 4:3 video is more square, the top of video is always higher than the top of the widescreen format. As a result, it is necessary to frame for two formats at the same time. This is difficult at best and it is always a compromise. Since the Super35 format is extracted from the film in an optical process, there is the freedom to extract any part of the negative you like. Thus the top of the video frame can be the same as top of the widescreen frame, thereby reducing the need to compromise the format.

Having a common top is most important, as the information in the upper part of the frame is nearly always more important than the lower part of the frame. Cutting a character off at the belt instead of across the chest usually makes no difference, whereas cutting off the top of the head can be very awkward. The fact that the sides of the frame are different is still inescapable and will remain so until widescreen TV becomes a standard.

The drawbacks of Super35 are the additional cost of the optical print and the slight increase in grain and contrast due to this extra step. However, with the recent improvements in film stock, these are now quite acceptable. Many major films have been shot in Super35. Nearly all cameras in use today have their optical axis centered on the Academy aperture. As a result they are not centered on the full negative. For Super35, the lens mount must be repositioned by 1mm to re-center it on the full aperture. Only lenses which cover the full area of the negative can be used. The ability to use standard spherical lenses and the lessened requirement for lighting and schedule may offset the cost of the optical print.

Once the Super35 full aperture is shot, any number of formats can be extracted from it. Except in very unusual cases, a hard matte would never be used to mask the negative to these aspect ratios. These illustrations demonstrate what would happen in the post-production process, not what happens in the camera. This is one of the beauties of this process: a single negative can be used for many dif-

16.8. The Imax negative is a 15 perf image on 70mm film stock.
Aspect ratio: 1.43:1
2.740" x 1.910"
5.24 sq. in.
70mm x 48.5mm
3430 sq. mm

16.9. 65mm 5 Perf
Aspect ratio: 2.28:1
2.066" x .906" - 1.872 sq. in.
54.48mm x 23.01mm -
1207.58 sq. mm

ferent formats. See the ground glass chart for some of the combinations of Super35 and other formats.

If the film is going directly to video, there is no reason to waste film for an optical sound track that will never be added. In this case, it is possible to use Super35 "as is." This is sometimes called Super TV.

3 PERF

All of the above methods are adaptations which deal with one basic built-in drawback of 35mm film; one that goes back to it's very invention. Since its inception, 35mm has been advanced by 4 perforations for each frame. Unlike the aperture gate, this is not something that is easily changed. Worldwide, there are tens of thousands of cameras, optical printers, lab equipment, telecines and theater projectors that are based on this system (Figure 16.20). Some systems advance the film by three perforations for each frame. Specially modified cameras must be used for this process.

Since it would be impossible to change the entire world system to suit this, the 3 perf negative is converted at some stage to 4 perf. The original advantages in shooting remain. If the project is going directly to video, then it is not a problem, except that the telecine must be suited to this process. Arriflex can now make any of their cameras available in 3-perf formats. 3 perf systems also have the advantage of using less film stock and longer running times out of each mag. Most television shows shot on film use 3-perf.

UNIVISION

Another variation of 3 perf was developed by Vittorrio Storaro. It is called Univision (sometimes spelled Univisium). Storaro's conclusion was that too much film is being wasted between frames; also, many soundtracks are not optical anymore. In his articles and interviews, Storaro makes a convincing argument for this format. Univision has an aspect ratio of 2:1.

The following are some of Storaro's observations on this format: In normal widescreen film, filmed in 1:1.85, there is a lot of wastage in camera negative. With Univision 1: 2 aspect ratio and digital sound (the sound track not on the film itself), using only three perforations for frame on a 35mm negative and positive, it is possible to have:

- 25% saved on camera negative, with absolutely no compromise in the quality of the image. It actually increases the average quality of any panoramic and anamorphic picture.
- 25% more shooting time in the camera magazine; less frequent mag changes.
- Quieter running cameras because less film is moved through them.
- No need for anamorphic lenses on cameras and projectors.
- No distortion of horizontal and vertical lines due to the use of anamorphic lenses.
- Greater depth-of-field due to not using anamorphic lenses.
- Less lighting required because of spherical lenses.
- No use of anamorphic lenses.

16MM

16mm is considerably simpler; there are two basic formats — regular 16 and Super 16. Super 16 currently enjoys enormous popularity. It can be easily blown up to a 35mm projection print and it transfers with little or no compromise to widescreen video such as High Def.

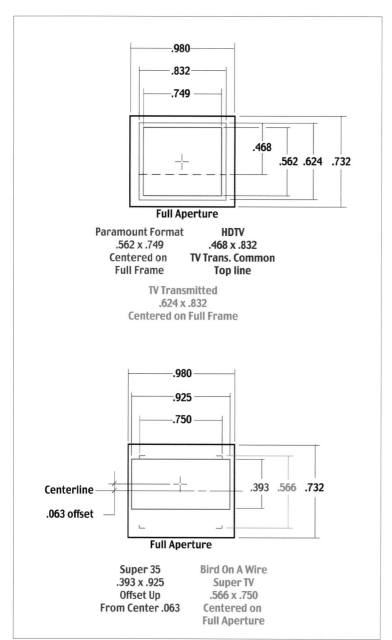

Full Aperture

Paramount Format	HDTV
.562 x .749	.468 x .832
Centered on	TV Trans. Common
Full Frame	Top line

TV Transmitted
.624 x .832
Centered on Full Frame

Centerline

.063 offset

Full Aperture

Super 35	Bird On A Wire
.393 x .925	Super TV
Offset Up	.566 x .750
From Center .063	Centered on
	Full Aperture

16.10. Super TV
Aspect ratio: 1.33:1
.945" x .709"
.67 sq. in.
24mm x18 mm
432 Sq. mm

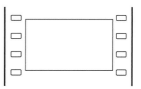

16.11. Super35 for 16x9 (High Def).
Aspect ratio: 1.78:1
.945" x .561"
.502 sq. in.
24mm x 13.5mm
324 sq. mm

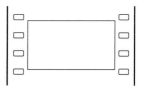

16.12. (above) Super35 for 1.85.
Aspect ratio: 1.85:1
.945" x .511"
.483 sq. in.
24mm x 12.98mm
311.52 sq. mm

16.13. (left) Dimensions of various formats in Super35.

Many companies are using Super 16mm as a way of protecting for future release of their production in widescreen HDTV.

Standard 16 transfers easily to 4:3 video. With the improved film stocks and digital post-production, the quality of a film originated on 16mm can be surprisingly good.

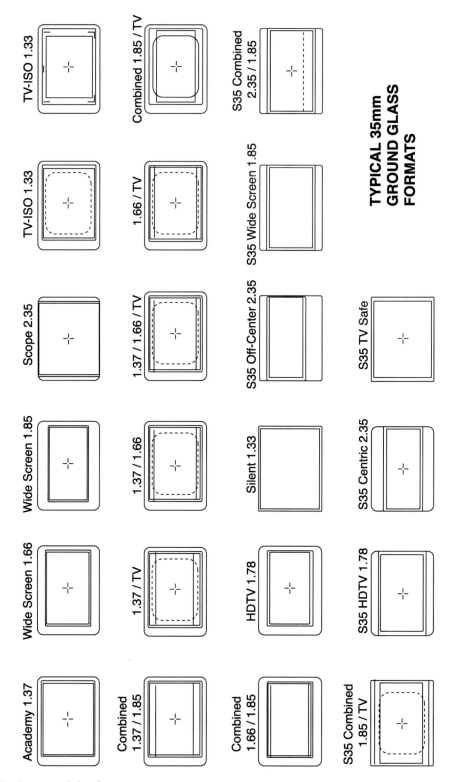

TYPICAL 35mm GROUND GLASS FORMATS

TV-ISO 1.33

Combined 1.85 / TV

S35 Combined 2.35 / 1.85

TV-ISO 1.33

1.66 / TV

S35 Wide Screen 1.85

Scope 2.35

1.37 / 1.66 / TV

S35 Off-Center 2.35

S35 TV Safe

Wide Screen 1.85

1.37 / 1.66

Silent 1.33

S35 Centric 2.35

Wide Screen 1.66

1.37 / TV

HDTV 1.78

S35 HDTV 1.78

Academy 1.37

Combined 1.37 / 1.85

Combined 1.66 / 1.85

S35 Combined 1.85 / TV

16.14. Combination groundglass formats for 35mm.

THE AUTHOR
Blain Brown is a cinematographer based in Los Angeles. He has been the director of photography on features, commercials, documentaries and music videos on all types of formats from 35mm and 16mm film to digital and High Def 24P video. He can be reached at www.BlainBrown.com.

ACKNOWLEDGMENTS
This book is dedicated to my wife, Ada Pullini Brown. Special thanks to the many people who have helped me in the writing of this volume.

Aaton, s.a.
Adobe, Inc.
Airstar Lighting, Inc.
Arri Group
Backstage Equipment, Inc.
Bill Burke
Birns and Sawyer, Inc.
Camtek, Inc.
Canon, USA
Century Precision Optics, Inc.
Chapman/Leonard Studio Equipment
Chimera Lighting
Color TheoryDV/Toolfarm
Consolidated Film Industries
David Mullen
Derry Museum, Derry, England
Eastman Kodak, Inc.
Fisher Light, Inc.
Flying Cam, Inc.
FotoKem Film and Video
Fuji Film, Ltd.
Gamma and Density Co., Inc.
Geoff Boyle and everyone at CML
Great American Market (GAM)
Hollywood Camera
Ilford Film
Ira Tiffen and The Tiffen Company
J.L. Fisher, Inc.

Keslow Camera
Kino-Flo, Inc.
Lance Steele Rieck
Lee Filters
Lightning Strikes, Inc.
Lowell-Light Manufacturing, Inc.
Mark Weingartner
Mark Wood
Matthews Studio Equipment Corp.
McIntire, Inc.
Mole Richardson Co., Inc.
Panasonic, Inc.
Panavision, Inc.
PAWS, Inc.
Photo-Sonics, Inc.
Rosco Laboratories, Inc.
San Luigi dei Francesi, Rome.
Schneider Optical, Inc.
Softlights
Sony Corp.
Sunray, Inc.
Tektronix, Inc.
Ultravision, Inc.
Ultimatte, Inc.
Wade Ramsey
WideScreen Software, Inc.
and all the cinematographers, videographers and others who read the manuscript and contributed.

Illustrations, page design and layout by the author. Photos and frame enlargements not credited are from projects photographed by the author, except where noted.

bibliography

Adams, Ansel. *The Negative*. Little, Brown & Co. 1983

Arnheim, Rudolf. *Art and Visual Perception*. University of California Press. 1954
  Film as Art. University of California Press. 1957
  Visual Thinking. University of California Press. 1969
  The Power of the Center. University of California Press. 1982

Barclay, Steven. *The Motion Picture Image: From Film to Digital*. Focal Press. 2000

Bordwell, David and Kristen Thompson. *Film Art: An Introductio*n. McGraw-Hill. 1997

Brown, Ada Pullini. *Basic Color Theory*. Unpublished ms. 2000

Brown, Blain. *Filmmaker's Pocket Reference*. Focal Press. 1995
  Motion Picture and Video Lighting. Focal Press. 1995

Campbell, Russell. *Photograhic Theory for the Motion Picture Cameraman*. A.S. Barnes & Co. 1974
  Practical Motion Picture Photography. A.S. Barnes & Co. 1979

Carlson, Verne and Sylvia. *Professional Lighting Handbook*. Focal Press. 1985

Case, Dominic. *Film Technology In Post Production*. Focal Press. 1997
  Motion Picture Film Processing. Focal Press. 1990

Cook, David. *A History of Narrative Film*. W.W. Norton & Co. 1982

Davis, Phil. *Beyond The Zone System*. Van Nostrand Reinhold Co. 1981

Dmytryk, Edward. *Cinema: Concept and Practice*. Focal Press. 1998
  On Screen Directing. Focal Press. 1984

Eastman Kodak. *Professional Motion Picture Films (*H-1). Eastman Kodak Co. 1982
  Kodak *Filters For Scientific and Technical Uses* (B-3). Eastman Kodak Co. 1981

Ettedgui, Peter. *Cinematography: Screencraft*. Focal Press. 2000

Fauer, John. *The Arri 35 Book*. Arriflex Corp. 1989

Feldman, Edmund Burke. *Thinking About Art*. Prentice Hall. 1996

Fielding, Raymond. *Special Effects Cinematography*. 4th Edition. Focal Press. 1990

G.E. Lighting. *Stage and Studio Lamp Catalog*. General Electric. 1989

Grob, Bernard. *Basic Television and Video Systems*. McGraw-Hill. 1984

Happe, L. Bernard. *Your Film and the Lab*. Focal Press. 1989

Harrison, H.K. *The Mystery of Filters*. Harrison and Harrison. 1981

Harwig, Robert. *Basic TV Technology*. Focal Press. 1990

Hershey, Fritz Lynn. *Optics and Focus For Camera Assistants*. Focal Press. 1996

Higham, Charles . *Hollywood Cameramen: Sources of Light*. Garland Publishing. 1986

Hirschfeld, Gerald. *Image Control*. Focal Press. 1993

Hyypia, Jorma. *The Complete Tiffen Filter Manual*. Amphoto. 1981

Jacobs, Lewis. *The Emergence of Film Art*. Hopkinson and Blake. 1969

Janson, H.W. *The History of Art*. 6th Edition. Harry Abrams. 2001

Jones, et. al. *Film Into Video*. Focal Press. 2000

Kawin, Bruce. *Mindscreen: Bergman, Godard and First Person Film*. Princeton University Press. 1978

Maltin, Leonard. *The Art of The Cinematographer*. Dover Publications. 1978

Mascelli, Joseph. *The Five C's Of Cinematography*. Cine/Grafic Publications. 1956

McClain, Jerry. *The Influence of Stage Lighting on Early Cinema*. International Photographer. 1986

Millerson, Gerald. *Lighting For Television and Motion Pictures*. Focal Press. 1983

Nelson, Thomas. *Kubrick: Inside A Film Artist's Maze*. Indiana University Press . 1982

Perisic, Zoran. *Visual Effects Cinematography*. Focal Press. 2000

Rabiger, Michael. *Directing - Film Techniques and Aesthetics*. 2nd Edition. Focal Press. 1997

Ray, Sidney. *Applied Photographic Optic*s. Focal Press. 1988
  The Lens In Action. Focal Press. 1976

Reisz, Karel and Gavin Millar. *The Technique of Film Editing*. 2nd Edition. Focal Press. 1983

Rogers, Pauline. *More Contemporary Cinematographers On Their Art*. Focal Press. 2000

Samuelson, David. *Motion Picture Camera Data*. Focal Press. 1979

        Panaflex User's Manual. Focal Press. 1990

Sharff, Stephen. *The Elements of Cinema.* Columbia University Press. 1982

Shipman, David. *The Story of Cinema.* St. Martin's Press. 1984

St. John Marner, Terrence. *Directing Motion Pictures*. A.S. Barnes. 1972

Sterling, Anna Kate. *Cinematographers on the Art and Craft of Cinematography*. Scarecrow Press. 198t

Stroebel, Leslie. *Photographic Filters.* Morgan & Morgan. 1974

Sylvania. *Lighting Handbook,* 8th Edition. GTE Products. 1989

Thompson, Roy. *Grammar Of The Shot.* Focal Press. 1998

Truffaut, Francois. *Hitchcock/Truffaut*. Simon and Shuster. 1983

Ultimatte Corp. Ultimatte Technical Bulletin #3 *"Shooting Film For Ultimatte."* Ultimatte Corp. 1992

        Ultimatte Technical Bulletin #4 *"Lighting For Ultimatte."* Ultimatte Corp. 1992

Walker, Alexander. *Stanley Kubrick Directs.* Harcourt Brace. 1969

Wilson, Anton. *Cinema Workshop*. ASC. 1983

filmography

TITLE	DIRECTOR	DP	COMPANY	YEAR
Angel Heart	Alan Parker	Michael Seresin	Carolco/Tristar	1987
Barry Lyndon	Stanley Kubrick	John Alcot	Warner Bros.	1975
Big Combo	Joseph H. Lewis	John Alton	Allied Artists	1955
Big Sleep	Howard Hawks	Sidney Hickox	Warner Bros.	1946
Black Stallion	Carroll Ballard	Caleb Deschanel	United Artists	1979
Carl Lewis Promo	Tim Alexander	Blain Brown	ASAP	2001
Citizen Kane	Orson Welles	Gregg Toland	RKO Radio Pictures, Inc	1941
City of Lost Children	Caro/Jeunet	Darius Khondji	Studio Canal+	1995
Crystal Spring Water	Blain Brown	Blain Brown	Leap Frog Prod.	1997
Days of Heaven	Terrence Malick	Nestor Almendros	Paramount Pictures	1978
Dr. Strangelove	Stanley Kubrick	Gilbert Taylor	Columbia Tristar	1964
Event Horizon	Paul Anderson	Adrian Biddle	Paramount	1997
Fargo	Joel Cohen	Roger Deakins	Grammercy/PolyGram	1996
High Noon	Fred Zinnemann	Floyd Crosby	Republic/United Artists	1952
Il Conformista	Bernardo Bertolucci	Vittorio Storaro	Mars Film/Paramount	1970
Jacob's Ladder	Adrian Lyne	Jeffrey L. Kimball	Carolco/Tristar	1990
JFK	Oliver Stone	Robert Richardson	Warner Bros.	1991
Jules and Jim	Francois Truffaut	Raoul Coutard	Carrosse/Janus	1961
Killer's Kiss	Stanley Kubrick	Stanley Kubrick	MGM/UA	1955
Lady In The Lake	Robert Montgomery	Paul Vogel	MGM	1947
Lawrence of Arabia	David Lean	Freddie Young	Columbia Pictures	1962
Macy's Fashion	Blain Brown	Blain Brown	Studio Ten	1989
McCabe and Mrs. Miller	Robert Altman	Vilmos Zsigmond	Warner Bros.	1971
Mildred Pierce	Michael Curtiz	Ernest Haller	Warner Bros.	1945
Monsoon	Jag Mundrha	Blain Brown	Everest Pictures	1998
New Amsterdam Beer	Mark Sitley	Blain Brown	Chelsea Pictures	1998
Nine 1/2 Weeks	Adrian Lyne	Peter Biziou	MGM/Warner Bros.	1986
No Goodbyes	Jeno Hodi	Blain Brown	Film Ventures	1996
Paths of Glory	Stanley Kubrick	Georg Krause	United Artists	1957
Perfect Duo	Jeno Hodi	Blain Brown	Vidmark Ent.	1993
Rain Man	Barry Levinson	John Seale	United Artists	1988
Ronin	John Frankenheimer	Robert Fraisse	MGM/UA	1998
Seven	David Fincher	Darius Khondji	New Line Cinema	1995
Seven Samurai	Akira Kurosawa	Asakazu Nakai	Toho/Columbia	1954
The Blind Cellist	Lawrence Hunger	Blain Brown	Cameo Films, Inc.	1999
Shades of Gray	Jag Mundrha	Blain Brown	Everest Pictures	1997
Shanghai Express	Josef Von Sternberg	Lee Garmes	Paramount Publix Corp.	1932
Spartacus	Stanley Kubrick	Russell Metty	Universal Pictures	1960
Stage Coach	John Ford	Bert Glennon	United Artists	1939
Strong City	Jeno Hodi	Blain Brown	SCP, Inc	1996
Surrender	Kelley Cauthen	Blain Brown	Cameo Films, Inc.	1999
The Draughtsman's Contract	Peter Greenaway	Curtis Clark	BFI/UA Classics	1982
The Great Train Robbery	Edwin S. Porter	Blair Smith	Edison Man. Co.	1903
The Lady From Shanghai	Orson Welles	Charles Lawton Jr.	Columbia Pictures	1948
The Lost Boys	Joel Schumacher	Michael Chapman	Warner Bros.	1987
The Natural	Barry Levinson	Caleb Deschnael	Tristar/Columbia	1984
The Third Man	Carol Reed	Robert Krasker	London Film Prod.	1949
Three Kings	David O. Russell	Newton Thomas Sigel	Warner Bros.	1999
Touch of Evil	Orson Welles	Russell Metty	Universal Pictures	1958
Vertigo	Alfred Hitchcock	Robert Burks	Paramount Pictures	1958
Woman To Die For	Kyle Lewis	Blain Brown	8th Avenue Prod.	2000
Yellow Taxi Woman	Blain Brown	Blain Brown	Chamisa Prod.	2000
Yojimbo	Akira Kurosawa	Kazuo Miyagawa	Toho Company Ltd.	1962
Woman On Fire	William Hames	Blain Brown	Factory Films	1998

index